Behind Closed Doors

Behind Closed Doors

Conflicts in Today's Church

Francis Anthony Quinn

Library of Congress Control Number: 2014921573
ISBN: Hardcover   978-1-5035-2327-2
                 Softcover   978-1-5035-2328-9
                 eBook   978-1-5035-2329-6

Rev. date: 12/08/2014

To order additional copies of this book, contact:
Xlibris
1-888-795-4274
www.Xlibris.com
Orders@Xlibris.com
671764

Dedicated to my Families- families by blood and by faith and to Mary

ACKNOWLEDGEMENTS

I would like to express my deepest gratitude to the following people: Jean Tamaki, who transcribed the manuscript and offered suggestions and encouragement throughout the writing; Anita Martin, Andrew Martin who did the editing, Kathryn Clark, Donnnel Quinn, Ernest Barbeau, Rev. John Chendo, Lou Persano, Joseph Franzella, Don and Michael DeHaven, Margaret Cervelli, James O'Malley, Gerard Murphy, John Lyons and Armando Garzon-Blanco; all of whom I would also like to thank the many individuals whose statements I have quoted in the text: Luigi Barzini, The Italians; Hilaire Belloc; Robert Bly; Gabrielle Brown, The New Celibacy; Michael Buckley, S.J.; Walter Burghardt, S.J.; Ann Caron; Ralph Chaplin; Daniel Levenson, Seasons of a Man's Life; Michael Medved; Madeline Bartlow Ontis; George Thorne; Judy Wargs, Twas the Year '62; Sean Mary O'Connaill; Gary Wills; America's Music: The Growth of Jazz; A Reflection Guide on Human Sexuality and the Ordained Priesthood, Copyright 1983 United States Catholic Conference, Washington, D.C, used with permission.

Several sections of this story have come from thoughts I have gathered and passages I have read over the years. Try as I might, I have not been able to identify all the authors, but I express my indebtedness to these sources now.

The characters in this story, with exceptions in minor references, are fictional. Some events and place names are fictitious and some are real.

AN IMPORTANT NOTE
TO THE READER

Although Behind Closed Doors is written as a novel, this book might be seen as a new and different genre of writing, namely "creative memoirs". The narrative of the relationship between the characters Ladd Franklin and Willow Caprice, the charge of the sexual molestation by Tyler Stone and the court trial that follows, the account of the accidental tape recording which leads to hectic pursuit to recover the tape through Argentina and Brazil as well as the selection of David Carmichael as archbishop are all fictional events, as are several other passages. However, all other incidents are real memoirs of real priests, bishops, lay men and lay women.

PROLOGUE

Saint Peter's Basilica was particularly quiet in the early moments of dusk. The streams of sunshine that showered upon the grand baldiccino had now faded. Save for a few tourists milling about, this magnificent house of God was eerily empty.

Whatever sunlight came through the large windows was now shining upon the likeness of Saint Peter. The statute, which might have seemed massive and immoveable to the thousands of tourists who flocked to see it, seemed less majestic to the priest sitting just a few feet away in an empty pew.

To anyone else, the man, slightly balding with wisps of remaining auburn hair around the edges, might have been any ordinary priest, one of the hundreds who walk about the Vatican and throughout the streets of the Eternal City each day. He dressed as many do, in a simple black cassock and the large round black hat that resembles an Italian version of a sombrero more than the signature feature that bespeaks a man of God.

The man sat in silence, not even bothering to open the pages of his small prayer book, or the breviary, a collection of prayers each priest uses to express his love for Christ and Holy Mother Church. For the moment, he attached his eyes to the statue of Peter, garbed in the uniform of the church, complete with the tiara atop his head. The blackish grey figure commanded authority over the church he helped to build

This man was no simple priest. He was David Carmichael, an archbishop, one of a few hundred who gathered in Rome to talk with the pope about the status of the church. It would be his last day in Rome – his plane would depart for a red-eye flight that night, bound for the United States and to his flock in San Tomas in southern California.

But for a few minutes he sat quietly - not in prayer – but deep in introspect over the events that shook the Vatican. So many thoughts were going through his head; had the church fathers really talked about changing its views toward homosexuality, same-sex marriages, or even the idea of allowing divorced Catholics to receive communion?

His head, it seemed, was split; on the one hand he knew such conversations would bring about hope for those who, for decades, felt disconnected. But the same words would bring angst to those who felt the church had slipped away – not the same church with which they grew up, married into, or raised their daughters and sons.

As he looked intently at each of the statue's features, he wondered what Peter himself might have to say about all of this. And then he thought about his own journey to this moment. After all he spent much of his life as a parish priest, serving the archdiocese in almost every aspect of daily life that keep the wheels of the church connected to their spoke.

David closed his eyes and attached his thoughts to his first days at Seminary more than five decades ago. It would be a world of new ideas for the young man who spent much of his life among the vineyards of Napa Valley. He remembered the sweet lush smell of honeysuckle bushes that covered the grounds. And the stoic oak trees, which stood the test of time having witnessed many a young man, transform into priesthood – and some who had not.

And he would remember the bonds of friendship he would form with his two closest friends, Tyler and Ladd, two other men who, with some trepidation, had also chosen to become priests.

David wished to go back to those days where he spent countless hours with Tyler and Ladd. It wasn't so much the conversation – neither student felt the impact of theologic reasoning – at least not during their first few years of seminary. Instead they remained in the secular world, sharing thoughts about the war in Europe, the latest box scores from the previous day's ball games, or even the inward emotions they still had for the one or two girls that passed through each man's life at one time or another.

He wished those days had never ended. Not because he did not want to become a priest. For David, these were the years he felt most free, amongst his two closest friends. It would be a freedom from the rules and rigidity of the church that would come along soon enough.

He wished Tyler and Ladd could have been there in Rome with him that week. He was sure they too would be amazed at just how much their church had changed. He would want to share a plate of pasta with them, sip red wine from a chianti, and muse about the young men and women sharing kisses in the romantic background of Rome's embrace. He was sure they would all share the same thoughts and feelings about the church they had grown to love.

But he was alone now, deep in thought. It was a long journey from those days at seminary. It was thousands of miles away from the young man who hard first stepped into a vocation that he never envisioned would bring him to this moment in his life. It was light years away from the two men he most admired, even loved. It was too distant for him to remember everything save for the memories that meant most to David.

Andrew Martin

PART I

CHAPTER 1

David Carmichael jumped aboard the Soscol Avenue streetcar out of Napa Valley. It was a Saturday. He was making his way to Holy Cross Church in Vallejo, away from the seminary and his home parish, where the priest wouldn't recognize his voice.

He trembled. "Bless me, Father, for I have sinned. It has been three weeks since my last confession."

"I cursed under my breath several times.

I was envious of classmates five times.

I was angry, but I didn't let it show.

I told lies to make myself look better.

I cheated in an English test, so I could win an academic premium at school.

For these and all the other sins I cannot now remember, I ask pardon from God and penance and absolution from you, Father."

From the other side of the screen: "That was a good confession, son. It is obvious you are a sensitive young man."

That was the kind of thing David wanted to hear.

. . .

As a teenager David was told he resembled his father. He was pleased that he had at least some connection with the parent whom he had hardly known.

David was tall for his generation, nearly 6 feet 3, lanky, well knit. His features were strong, not handsome; his hair a shade darker than brown.

He was likeable, self-effacing, and cheerful. But secretly he was fearful-a worrier though his demeanor never revealed itself

This anxiety never showed on the surface. David was self-centered and protective. Something drove him to succeed, to be better than others. Unknowingly to others, he was hurt when no one looked to him.

. . .

David Carmichael and Ladd Franklin were college freshmen. They had entered Regina Cleri Seminary the same day five years earlier.

Ladd just wanted to become a good priest.

David wanted always to be the leader.

Both hoped only to survive the 12 seminary years. The number that persevered from the time of entrance into the high school seminary until ordination was one out of ten.

CHAPTER 2

The earliest memory David Carmichael had was from the age of four, climbing into bed between his mother and father in the middle of the night. It was the warmest and safest place on earth in the Highland Park neighborhood of Los Angeles.

David grew up with Irish parents off Anandale Boulevard, where Highland Park turns into Eagle Rock. He dreaded the first day of kindergarten at Anandale Boulevard School and feigned a stomach ache until his mother came to take him home.

Los Angeles days, for David, were filled with trips with his dad and older brother, Vincent, to Venice Beach; the scratchy wool full-body swim suits; the misunderstanding of the whole concept of the Dodge-Em bumper cars at Playland, complaining to his father that his brother was "banging" into him; riding with his father and mother in the 1926 Nash four-door sedan with isinglass windows.

The street the Carmichaels lived on ran west for five blocks up the hill to an undeveloped wooded area. To the east, Tipton Street went two flat blocks to Anandale Boulevard.

David wandered the neighborhood and explored the west wooded hill with playmates. The Mormons across the street had several sons and daughters. Mrs. Rankin, a widow lived next to them. And behind the Mormons and Mrs. Rankin, there was the tall house and the man who would scare the neighborhood children by protruding the top plate of his false teeth like a vampire.

These were feverish, active days, collecting sample cans of Chinese red paint, given away at Elwood Hardware store on Anandale, the rubber tire swing at the Kirgan's home near the end of the block, and the coffee grinding machine in Lawton's Grocery store around the corner. Sunday trips made to visit Aunt Ruth and Uncle Carl in their rambling fieldstone home in La Cresenta; the Satsuma plum tree in the Carmichael's yard; David's mother's relatives who visited from Northern California. Even Fred Twomly, who never came to the house without bringing candy,.

One early spring day when the first buds were peeking through the leaves of the Satsuma plum tree, David's father was rushed to Queen of Angels Hospital.

Only six, David could not comprehend illness but he knew something was terribly wrong. His mother spent most of her time at the hospital. David saw her crying for the first time.

The illness, Appendicitis, had not been diagnosed in time. The appendix burst. Peritonitis set in.

David and his brother were sent to a neighbor's house. It was the first time David could remember being away from his family overnight, the first time he didn't sleep straight through till morning.

Near dawn, he heard his mother speaking to neighbors in the kitchen. He could make out only bits and pieces of the conversation, but he would remember the words, "Death rattle."

Robert Carmichael died at the age of 44.

David barely remembered him. He knew that his father worked in a leather glove factory. His father seemed always to be smiling; he often picked David up and held him high in the air. He knew his father loved his mother. David never heard his parents raise their voices to each other - although they must have now and then, out of earshot of the children.

Troubled, incomprehensible days followed his father's death. The family, smaller now, would move to Northern California where his mother would feel at home with her brothers and sisters.

. . .

Four months later, an uncle came to Los Angeles and drove Elizabeth Carmichael and her two sons over a highway called the Ridge Route, 400 miles north to the Wine Country.

Napa was a place David only vaguely remembered from earlier visits. He recalled staying at the home of Uncle Willard and Aunt

Agnes, which had a tank house and a windmill in the backyard. He remembered the Carbonettis next door and their house full of children.

Bing Carbonetti had made a model airplane for David -- the most treasured gift he had ever owned.

Now, on the way to Napa, somewhere near Saint Helena, David flew his airplane at arm's length outside the car window where it dropped out of his hands. He was too ashamed to ask his uncle to stop the car to retrieve it.

It would not be the last time he felt such embarrassment.

. . .

The Valley, as we all came to affectionately know it, was a necklace of vineyards strung north from Napa itself, through Yountville, to St. Helena and Calistoga, and then south again along the Silverado Trail. The historian Hillaire Belloc once called the valley one of the most captivating parcels of geography on earth.

The complications of uprooting a young family meant little to David. His life had simpler concerns.

Elizabeth moved Vincent and David into a two-story house on Adams Street. Six-year-old David was fascinated by the stairs inside the house and its hot water heater, too small to provide enough hot water for his bath.

On Saturday nights, he sat in a tub while his mother warmed water on the wood stove and poured full pots over his back. The water was really not that warm, but his mother contended the stove had "taken the chill out of it."

Uncle Rodney, Elizabeth's brother, came to live with them on Adams Street. He would provide a male model for the growing David and Vincent. Since Rodney was a bachelor, the arrangement would also give him less expensive lodging.

Rodney taught David how to box, how to lead with his left, keep his thumb outside, and not curl inside his fingers when he fought barefisted. He took David jack rabbit hunting with a 22 rifle in the field west of Napa Union High School. When David reached teenage, Uncle Rodney, without knowing it, provided David and David's friend Buddy with a Plymouth coupe for joy rides. They wanted to see if they could reach the speed of the saying of the day, "Going like 60", on the roads around Mount George. On several occasions they even exceeded that. Uncle Rodney's discovery of grease spots on the driver's side upholstery put an end to such covert excursions.

His mother made sure David and Vincent had plenty of Stornetta Dairy milk and scrambled eggs each morning. Meals were nourishing - and often predictable. School lunches consisted of peanut butter and jelly sandwiches on fluffy white bread. Butter. After school snacks - powdered sugar and brown sugar on toast. Evening meals followed an inevitable rotation: shoulder lamb chops, beef stew, pounded round steak (tough meat pounded tender), or meat loaf.

. . .

Catholic life was simple and uncomplicated. For David, these were the boyhood years of Fridays with creamed tuna on toast or macaroni and cheese, Novenas, 40 Hours' Devotions, the Latin Mass with the priest's, back turned toward the people.

David and his friends made dwarfed Signs of the Cross passing the parish church, St. Christopher's, but they were not allowed even to look into Protestant churches.

Every Mass ended with the same prayer: "Blessed Michael the Archangel, defend us in the day of battle, be our safeguard against the wickedness and snares of the devil."

Other staples of his religion - Monsignor Fulton Sheen on Sunday afternoon radio and the Baltimore Catechism (Why did God make you? God made me to know Him, to love Him, to serve Him in this life and to be happy with Him forever in the next) The bus driver who always put his hand over the fare box when a priest or Sister entered the bus;

brown scapulars as big as postage stamps on the boys' chests and backs at the public swimming pool; collections in school for Pagan Babies; "J.M.J." spontaneously scrawled at the top of homework papers.

Gary Wills drew the picture of those days vividly: "Firemen at a church fire, with poles and axes, genuflecting as they pass back and forth before the tabernacle. Girls without hats, hair-pinning Kleenex to their heads, fluttering as they strode to the Communion rail."

At the moment of the Mass when the priest consecrated the bread and wine, there was always that hush. Neither a cough nor a sniffle

– just silence. Only when the priest kneeled for the second time did those familiar sounds resume, all the coughs and sniffs inhibited during the consecration formed a firecracker series of soft percussions.

At communion, as one knelt on a hard marble step, the altar boy nicked each Adam's apple, sometimes accidently but often gleefully with his cold paten.

For David, Catholicism was a vast set of intermeshed childhood habits, prayers offered, heads ducked in unison, chants, christening, grace at meals, beads, incense, candles, nuns in the classroom - alternately sweet and severe, an annual cycle of liturgical symbols: the crib in winter, purple Februarys, lilies in the spring - all things going to a rhythm, old things always returning, eternal - per omnia saecula saeculorum, forever and ever.

CHAPTER 3

Napa was hot summer days and cold winter nights with the smell of wood burning in the kitchen stoves and fireplaces. Why was it that cold always seemed cozy until Christmas, and then after Christmas cold seemed damp and miserable?

The happiest hours were after school and on weekends and during the long summer days when David raced with his friends all over town, usually with his dog, Bonzo, struggling to keep up.

David's childhood memories would forever remain: the pillow fights with his brother Vincent in David's bedroom with the knotty pine walls, which Uncle Rodney had constructed as a gift for David; working at Grayson's Grocery store on Fuller Street where David learned to roll a cigarette with Bull Durham tobacco folded tightly at both ends, smoking in the back room as he waited for customers.

He pumped Flying A gasoline for 18 cents a gallon in front of the store. And he could do nothing about huge George Rample who broke the law by buying six bottles of Grace Brothers beer and drinking it on the premises.

David sold Popsicles and Fudgesicles to the neighborhood kids and occasionally helped himself to the same, looking for the word "FREE" printed at the end of the stick under the frozen treat.

The climax of the year was Christmas Eve, with the opening of presents at Uncle Willard and Aunt Agnes' house with all the family gathered around. The thrill of the parka jacket with the simulated fur collar, the most elegant clothing David had ever owned; his first bicycle, second-hand but freshly coated by his brother Vincent with the Chinese red paint brought up from Los Angeles. In more violent generations later, David would see his grandnephews receive for Christmas gifts - laser guns and power rangers.

. . .

Throughout David's growing years, America was admittedly the best country in the world, the strongest, the most honest, the most generous, the most prosperous, and the envy of every other nation. It did not enter his head to question this.

God must surely be on our side because He had blessed us so abundantly, and we, as a people, had always been dedicated to godly principles.

Later would come the first distant, hardly recognizable rumblings of doubt and dissension when the country would become engaged in disputed conflicts overseas. For the first time, these issues would leave America unsure of itself and begin to divide its people.

Still, David had that unshakable, abiding sureness that "God was in His heaven and all was right with the world."

David's heroes were Joe Louis, Max Baer, and Al Nicolini who played left half-back to the Galloping Gaels of St. Mary's College in Moraga.

When he was just twelve, David would meet Nicolini at New Year's Eve party at Cavagnaro's Restaurant on Third Street in Napa.

. . .

As the years went on, St. Christopher's School became the center of David's life.

Catholic school students always told horror stories of the brutal treatment exerted by the nuns. Decades later, bumper stickers would appear, "I Survived Catholic School".

But David would not know any of this. He and his friends often stayed after school to be with the Dominican Sisters, women not much older than them.

The Sisters were good company, down to earth and unthreatening. They were friends as well as teachers.

Each year at First Communion time, nuns would drill the students in the meaning of the Blessed Sacrament. Students were taught that

Napoleon Bonaparte, who lived in exile on the Island of Elba, always remembered his fondest day as the one in which he made his First Communion. This, from an emperor who led armies and conquered nations.

The Sisters rehearsed the students on proper conduct in church, the Sign of the Cross with holy water on entrance, the genuflection, the silence, the refraining from carving initials in the wooden pews.

The sacred gestures became such an embedded part of David's life that he once genuflected in the aisle at the Uptown Theater before entering the row of seats.

David's report cards showed mostly A's and B's in the three R's, in geography, history, and straight A's in courtesy, application, neatness, punctuality and obedience. But the sharp focus of the teaching at St. Christopher's was Christian Doctrine – the words that flowed from the gray covered Baltimore Catechism. It was a keepsake book that David would still have in his file fifty years later.

It was at St. Christopher's where David received his first mitt and played first base for the school's CYO team.

. . .

Apart from the church, David embraced other memories of childhood, like the songs of the day -- songs like "Blue Moon" and "Isle of Capri." –He knew every amorous lyric. "You give me your lips and your lips are so heavenly," without ever adverting to the meaning of the words. The melody was the thing.

A constant companion, the radio opened David's world to "The Gilmore Circus," "Bobbie Benson," and the "Blue Monday Jamboree."

On Saturday afternoons, David and his friends would venture to the Fox Theater to see movies like "Just Imagine," or the westerns with Hoot Gibson and Ken Maynard along with any movie starring Laurel and Hardy and Buster Keaton.

David's all-time favorite was "King Kong," starring Fay Wray, Robert Armstrong and Bruce Cabot.

David and Buddy would sit as long as they could for the second showing - in the dark theater so long that the late afternoon sun blinded them when they emerged through the side exit on Randolph Street.

If there was still time before dark, they headed for the Modern Dairy on Main Street for a 15 cent milkshake -- nectar of the gods.

Perhaps David's most memorable boyhood adventure was the mammoth water drain pipe that stretched from the A Street creek to Napa Union High School.

For 12 city blocks, David and his friends stooped over in total darkness and explored their way through the conduit of west Napa's street refuse.

For all they cared, that mysterious tunnel could have been the Carlsbad Caverns, King Solomon's Mines or the pestilence pit of Calcutta. Still, one seemed to be the worse for wear.

CHAPTER 4

At St. Christopher's on Saturday afternoons, young David stood in line at the confessional making up sins for Father Claudel. In later years, he would not have to fabricate sins.

The Gothic-styled church stood on the corner of Caymus and Main streets It was a second home to the Carmichaels. It was the church where his parents were married, his brother Vincent was baptized and where David would experience the steeled slap from Archbishop Jose Gutierrez during his confirmation, making David a "true soldier of Christ.

. . .

David was petrified the Sunday morning Father Claudel peeked out of the sacristy door and beckoned him to come to the altar.

"The altar boy hasn't shown up. I need a server."

Just a sixth grader, he'd only had one lesson in serving Mass. That would have to do.

In the boys' sacristy, David fumbled through the cassock robes. Even the shortest one was too long for him, but he knew the pastor was waiting.

He dressed as fast as he could, tucking the long cassock under the belt of his pants and searching desperately for the smallest surplice. Father Claudel, vested and carrying the covered chalice, was arriving at the foot of the altar when David joined him.

"Introibo ad altare Dei," the priest began. "I will go to the altar of God."

"Ad Deum qui laetificat juventutem meum." "To God who gives joy to my youth."

That was the first Latin response and David had memorized it well.

Things were uncomplicated enough until time came for changing the Mass book from the Epistle side to the Gospel side of the altar.

He's seen this done a hundred times, so he circled around to the right side of the altar, ascended the steps, lifted the brass missal stand with the Mass book on top. It was much heavier than he had expected.

He descended the steps to the middle then started up to the Gospel side. Navigating the steps with trepidation, he sensed something was wrong. Only then did David realize he was walking up the inside of his cassock.

Suddenly, the trampled-under front part of his cassock brought the robe's collar slamming against the back of his neck. Unable to stop himself, David hurled the heavy Mass book and the brass stand against the back of the startled pastor.

Without a second thought, he picked up the book and stand, and put them on the altar where they belonged.

The rest of the Mass was a blur.

After mass he moved to avoid the priests' sacristy and Father Claudel. He caught up with his mother outside the church.

"Well, that was quite a show, David. I was so embarrassed."

. . .

Regularly, David's fox terrier, Bonzo, followed David to Mass, came up the linoleum center aisle, jumped over the altar rail and sat down next to David as he served Mass before David would lead him to the sacristy for the remainder of Mass. However, on this day, David rushed out without Bonzo in tow, scurrying to take his cassock and surplice to be laundered that night at home. Bonzo was forgotten through the day and worried about overnight. Young David was devastated.

It was not until the next morning's Mass that David found the dog still in the sacristy. Paint and wood had been scratched and chewed away all around the walls and doors.

David fully expected an explosion from Father Claudel that never came. David concluded that maybe, just maybe, priests could be good friends.

The fox terrier was the love of David's life.

Bonzo followed a 3:15 p.m. daily ritual. Each day the dog waited at the corner of B Street and Adams. At the first sight of David. Bonzo would race to his master.

On summer nights, he would sleep at the foot of David's makeshift bed in the backyard pup tent. Bonzo followed David and his schoolmates all over Napa on their bikes, even miles out of town to Vichy's swimming pool, though the terrier's lungs must have been bursting.

One Saturday morning on Hayes Street, David turned on his bike at the moment he saw a car hit Bonzo. The fox terrier's back was clearly broken, his body twisted at right angle as he struggled to stay on his feet. The dog looked toward his master, still wagging his tail as if asking for help.

Without slowing its speed, the car drove on.

Wheeling his bike with one arm, David carried the lifeless body of his friend home. He thought of what Sister Hyacinth said in sixth grade religion class: "With the loyalty and love they have there must be a heaven for dogs."

. . .

Though Napa would eventually become a prestigious address, the town of Napa meant only one thing in the 1930s: it was the home of the state's insane asylum, Imola.

Father Doyle would take him and Buddy to the asylum to serve Mass for the inmates.

Mass was held in the large dining hall. Tables had been removed and folding chairs arranged for pews.

The boys and Father Doyle would prepare as long rows of residents began filing in.

"Are you scared?" Buddy asked.

"No, are you?"

"No."

The priest and his two acolytes entered the make-shift sanctuary on a raised platform at the south end of the cafeteria.

David and Buddy faced each other, kneeling at either side of the altar. Quiet and devout, the inmates made little noise save the shuffling and scraping of metal folding chairs. David noticed that male guards or attendants in white smocks moved along the aisles.

As David handed the priest the wine cruet at the Offertory, an inmate halfway back in the congregation flashed a pocket mirror in David's eyes.

In a few moments, he saw the same reflection flashing on Buddy's face and again on Father Doyle's chasuble. David caught Buddy's eye and the giggling began. They fought to stifle outbursts of laughter.

Something inside him told David he shouldn't be convulsing with giggles at the sadness of the scene, but there was something about the absurdity of the situation -- the incongruity of the solemn ritual and the pathetic child-like behavior of the mental patients.

Except for the moment of Communion when a guard suddenly restrained a young inmate in his twenties who had lunged at the priest, the Mass ended without incident.

. . .

David did not lack affection in his home. Because of his ready smile, he was easily accepted by adults.

Elizabeth Carmichael worked as a seamstress at the Rough Rider pants factory. She walked three miles to and from work each day. David attended quarterly union meetings with her.

Elizabeth was always conscious of the need to fill the role of father as well as mother. She exerted tight discipline and made it a point not to let her sons think too highly of themselves. Her philosophy was that if she put the boys down often enough, they would try harder and eventually excel.

This included frequent advice: "Always remember to listen to people who are smarter than you, David. And then she would add, "And it should be easy for you to find people who are smarter than you."

But David knew that he was loved by his mother. As a matter of fact, because he was cheerful and never made demands on others, he was really accepted by everyone. He got along well.

Imperceptibly and subconsciously, he came to think of himself as special. He liked this role, but it led gradually through his boyhood to an excessive fear of failure. He was not accustomed to criticism. He would hide his faults, like burning The Saturday Evening Post magazines, rather than letting his family know he had failed to deliver them.

David became secretive in insignificant ways. He was showing the first signs of compulsiveness. He would be an over-achiever.

. . .

David noticed particular girls in school. They were the ones that looked like movie stars.

Jean, in the class ahead, reminded him of Gloria Swanson.

Claire was Carol Lombard.

Barbara, in the seventh grade, was Clara Bow.

He couldn't help looking at them -- they were the ones he dreamed about.

Melissa was different. More friend than anything else, she shared David's sense of humor and she had wisdom beyond her years. It was to Melissa that David confided in February that he was going to study for the priesthood.

"Why do you want to do that?"

"I just think I'd like to be a priest."

"Did Father Corcoran talk you into it?"

"No, none of the priests has talked to me about it."

"I'll bet your mother is all for it."

"I think she'll be happy if I get to be a priest."

"Yes, she'll be happy because she will still have you."

"What do you mean? She won't still have me. I'll be going away to live at the seminary."

"Yes, but she'll have you. I know your Mom. She has no husband. She should have gotten married after your Dad died."

"She always says she doesn't remarry because she wants to be faithful to my Dad."

"Well, she has no one to hold on to but you. And I think she would rather have you be a priest than lose you to some girl. Besides, she'll lose Vincent when he gets married."

This all seemed strange to David -

the conversation made no sense to him.

CHAPTER 5

Ladd Franklin grew up in an Irish-Italian family in San Francisco.

As a toddler, he charmed grocery clerks out of free candy in the Mission District. His smile was innocent and disarming.

As a growing boy, Ladd Franklin was genuine. He was, above all, honest.

There was no dissimulation in Ladd - no hidden agenda; no inordinate ambitions. One felt comfortable to be with him.

His most vivid memory as a boy was the day he was pushed at breathtaking speed down the 16th Street hill in his red Irish Mail wagon by one of his brothers, ending in an overturned wagon and a broken collarbone.

Why were older brothers always causing misery to their young siblings?

. . .

Spiritual heroes and heroines were honored in the Franklin home: pictures of St. Patrick, the Madonna, the Sacred Heart; statues of St. Francis of Assisi and Anthony of Padua.

Ladd did not have much success in tracking down his ancestors.

"I've checked with a historian in Dublin and a librarian in upstate New York," Ladd said. "They have been helpful, but I have not been able to learn the family tree for sure beyond my father.

"My grandfather came to this country before the famine in Ireland in the mid-19th century, and not many records exist before that. Maybe they came from County Clare, Donegal, Tyrone – that's where our name often appears."

My father would tell us that his father lived in Pennsylvania for a while before marrying my grandmother, Margaret O'Neill, in Ovid, near Lake Cayuga and Cornell University in New York State

Liam came to San Francisco as a young man, where he met and married his own wife, Regina Rontini. Liam, a fervent Irishman, deferred to his wife's Italian side in raising his family.

Above all else, Italians loved family and his parents were no different. Nothing was too good for Ladd and his siblings.

Ladd's mother's life revolved around her children and her husband, almost to the point of excessive devotion. If it was, she never saw it that way.

Like any other family, Ladd's family members fought amongst themselves. He grew up in the loving surroundings of his mother's relatives. Rarely did a Sunday go by without a visit to the home of an aunt or uncle in North Beach.

No holiday would be the same without a get-together of all the relatives. It was as natural as San Francisco's chilling fog.

During most holidays the smaller children would sit at a separate table, their glasses filled half with wine, half with water.

The young ones, bored and slack-jawed, pushed aside their vegetables and formed castles out of their mashed potatoes. Their parents would often linger at the adults' table for three or four hours at a time.

Ladd fully understood the root ingredients found in Italian life; a warm kitchen, the aroma of pasta and sauce that simmered for hours and the appearance of an immaculate living room, where shades were drawn and the mother of the house kept everything dusted – the "living" room where no one was ever allowed to live.

But there were other flavors; the importance of education, the joys of baptism, the raucous weddings, and the tearful funerals.

It was as the journalist Luigi Barsini's accurately described Ladd's heritage.

"In the heart of every man, wherever he is born, whatever his education and tastes, there is one small corner which is Italian . . . that part which finds regimentation irksome, the dangers of war frightening, mindless morality stifling and dreams of . . . a liberation from the structures of a tidy existence."

In the Mission District of San Francisco, gang wars were common between the Irish kids and the Italian kids.

Since Ladd and his brothers were a mixture of both, they could jump in on either side - depending on who was winning.

"In these fights," Ladd told his parents, "the Italian kids would throw firecrackers at the Irish kids. The Irish kids would light them and throw them back."

Ladd's father thought that was hilarious - and so did his mother.

Ladd enjoys jokes about his heritage. At least subliminally he is not hyper-sensitive or defensive. However, he often experienced disparaging remarks regarding his Italian background. He made it a point to read Italian history and learn about his Italian heroes and recite them to his non Italian friends.

As a national group, they do not suffer insecurity because of their unparalleled historical heritage – the good and the bad: the artists - Raphael, Michelangelo, Leonardo Da Vinci; political leaders – Machiavelli, Lorenzo de Medici; military geniuses - Napoleon, Garibaldi; musicians - Verdi, Puccini; discoverers and scientists - Columbus, Marconi, Galileo; literary giants - Dante, Boccaccio; giants in the church - Catherine of Siena, Francis of Assisi, Thomas Aquinas. Robert Browning wrote, "Open my heart and you will see graven inside – Italy."

Tuition at parochial schools was a dollar a month. Even this was difficult for a low-income family, but the Franklins saw to it that their children attended Divine Savior School.

Ladd was not particularly devout, but he was fascinated with the lives of the saints and other stories in religion class.

Father Rock instructed Ladd's second grade First Communion class. "If your family is like my family," the priest began. "when all our relatives get together for a big dinner at Thanksgiving or Christmas or Easter, the adults sit at the big table to eat, and the little children sit at their own table on the side. Then when you get to be older, you take your place at the big table with your parents and your aunts and uncles.

"When you receive First Communion, you will be graduating to the big table in the church - joining the adults at the Communion table. He said that heaven is a place we all want to go. We should think of heaven often, because there, after we die, we will be happier than we have ever been in our life. In order to get to heaven we have to be good."

At the end of First Communion class, Father Rock gave a quiz:

"Where do you want to go?" he asked the second graders.

All together, the class responded, "Heaven!"

"And what do you have to be to get to heaven?"

"Dead!" they shouted.

Father Rock decided they had enough theology for the day and dismissed the class.

. . .

Fifth grade was a turning point in Ladd's life.

He was becoming a young man and the Immaculate Heart Sisters had set up structures to deal with their charges who had entered upon boyhood.

Ladd and Dennis Fogarty partly because everyone sat alphabetically but also because of their behavior.

One particular Monday morning, Sister Mary Clarice began firing questions at her students.

"How many of you were at Mass yesterday? Raise your hands."

Most of the class raised their hands, including Ladd and Dennis.

Ladd fell into her trap.

"Yes, I know you were there, Ladd Franklin. I saw you laughing and talking during the Mass. What do you have to say for yourself?"

"Nothing Sister."

"Don't you know that's sinful?"

"Yes Sister."

"You know I've caught you before."

She then turned her sights on Dennis.

"You, too, were laughing and talking in church. Do you have any explanation for your behavior?"

"No Sister."

"Don't you know that playing in church is sinful?"

Averting eye contact with Sister, he simply nodded his head, hoping to escape punishment.

"You two come up here to my desk and stand facing the class."

The nun took a 12-inch ruler, gave it to Dennis who was forced to slap his friend's hand, slamming the wood onto Ladd's palms.

"Five more times and harder, Dennis," Sister said.

Then it was Ladd's turn and he made sure that he matched the velocity of Dennis' strokes, to Sister Clarice haunted words "As you measure out, so will it be measured unto you."

The two laughed the pain away as they made their way home from school that afternoon.

Sister Clarice would also enjoy laughter as she told the story to the other sisters at dinner that night.

But she made her point, reinforcing the atmosphere of discipline at Divine Savior School.

Not wanting to tell their parents, Ladd and Dennis smartly knew that calling attention to the incident incited further punishment, not sympathy as they would have hoped.

. . .

Ladd and his friends were mischievous in other ways, hanging on to the retracted "cow-catchers" on the back of the city streetcars - out of sight of the conductor.

More often than not, both boys used their rollerskates to navigate the streets of the mission and their bikes to journey to other parts of the City.

Skates, wheels, or bikes, one thing was for sure, they knew San Francisco from almost every point; the Cliff House to Hunter's Point; North Beach to the Zoo.

They were more fortunate in their mobility than boys their age living in the lower rent districts. There were 10-year-old African American children in the western addition that had never seen Golden Gate Park.

Not many Negroes, as they were then known, lived in the Mission. But Melvin Barker, close in age to Ladd and Dennis, lived nearby with his family and the three were friends.

Ladd attended Divine Savior School, Melvin went to Castro Public.

Ladd and Melvin were inseparable during grammar school years, an oddity given racial tensions at the time

The Barkers were well accepted in the neighborhood, possibly because they were the only family of Blacks. The small family posed no threat and they were personable.

Though he was instructed that it was not appropriate for Catholics to enter Gethsemane Baptist Church on the next block or any Protestant church for that matter, Ladd was taught nothing but love for Blacks, other races and people of other faiths.

· · ·

Ladd had a mischief streak.

He, Dennis and Melvin's days were filled with laughter and pranks. Before the days of "Trick or Treat," it was not uncommon for "law-abiding" boys at Halloween to soap car windows, overturn garbage cans, and break windows in deserted warehouses.

On one occasion, Ladd, shot out three street-lights with a BB gun just to see the cascading shower of phosphorescent light. It was innocent mischief back then today it was almost criminal.

· · ·

Students at Divine Savior School were required to attend the 9 a.m. children's Mass on Sundays – with attendance duly noted on their report cards.

The girls sat to the right side of the center aisles, the boys to the left with nuns sitting right next to them.

The fence that separated the school from Diamond Street was a chain-link fence. Every morning, the eighth grade girls were teased by boys going six blocks east to James Denman Junior High. The chain-link fence was part of their taunts.

Daily class work was repetitious, especially the Palmer Method of Handwriting. Ladd still makes ovals and push-pulls when he doodles.

Friday afternoons were fun-filled days of music, art, reciting memorized poems ("Old Ironsides" and "Abou Ben Adhem") and spelling bees.

CHAPTER 6

Ladd lived in surroundings considered by many as one of the most beautiful cities in the world. Like most kids, he took for granted the Twin Peaks which looked down upon the Franklin home; the Bay, which half-circled the tip of the San Francisco Peninsula; the constant wail of the foghorns which city dwellers often no longer heard that engulfed the "seven" hills; the cable cars which climbed them and the spectacular sunsets out in the Avenues, Ocean Beach and the Cliff House.

Ladd delivered one of the City's many newspapers, The Call Bulletin to the Victorian homes for which San Francisco had become so famous.

On those rare occasions when the Franklin family could go out for dinner, it was to Clinton's Cafeteria, Bernstein's Fish Grotto, the Pig 'n' Whistle or, in affluent times, to Schroeder's.

Ladd's followed the City's two baseball teams, the Seals and the Missions baseball teams at "Old Rec" on Valencia Street -- and later Seals Stadium. His heroes were Lefty Gomez, Paul Waner, Earl Averill, Gus Suhr, Willie Kamm and Frank "Lefty" O'Doul. His family would gather around the radio to listen to their favorite shows like "One Man's Family, keeping daily tabs on the show's main characters, Henry and Fannie Barber, daughters Claudia and Hazel and son Jack. They mused at the goings on of Amos and Andy in their Fresh Air Taxi Company with Madam Queen, Kingfish, Lightning and Sapphire. Ladd's favorites were "Inner Sanctum" and "Lights Out." All of these were interrupted by Ipana, Ovaltine, Lucky Strike and Doctor Straska's tooth paste commercials.

The City had no shortage of entertainment; the extravagant new Fox Theater was under construction on Market Street, and the San Francisco-Oakland and Golden Gate Bridges were rising on the Bay.

Ladd and his friends could not afford the 35-cent admission to Loew's Warfield or the Paramount to see Ginger Rogers and Fred Astaire in "Top Hat." They would have to wait until it came to the neighborhood's Castro or El Capitan in the Mission.

. . .

In the spring of the eighth grade, the girls at Divine Savior were very much aware of the boys. The one they most talked about was Ladd Franklin.

Ladd and his friends were thinking more and more about girls. The one Ladd thought most about was Jennifer Purcell.

Jennifer was slender, strawberry blonde and already maturing into womanhood. She was almost as tall as Ladd, and like her eighth grade girlfriends, months and months ahead of their classmate boys in physical development.

Jennifer liked sports. After school, she would often play basketball with the boys. One April morning during the Easter break, Jennifer came to the playground with a basketball looking for her friends. Ladd was the only one there and so the two began a one-on-one pickup game.

Jennifer was leading 10 to 6, in part because Ladd was "easy" on her when a dispute arose as to who touched the ball last before it went out of bounds.

Jennifer had possession of the ball. Ladd playfully tried to knock it from her hands. She held on. Ladd struggled with the girl to get the ball back. He let go with his right hand and dug his fingers into her ribs.

The tickling made her laugh even louder. She would not let go, so he circled her body with his arms, again clutching at the ball.

But then, a sudden feeling that he could not understand – came over him like waves and waves of warm pulsing around his loins. It was like reaching the peak of a mountain and being wondrously exulted. Then it was over. He wanted to let go of Jennifer, but if this is how it felt struggling with her, he didn't want it to end.

Ladd experienced his sexual awakening.

. . .

In his own fashion, Ladd was religious.

Early one Sunday morning he and Dennis filled an empty champagne bottle with Nehi orange drink, climbed down to Fort Point nearest to the newly laid foundation of the Golden Gate Bridge and "baptized" what was to be the new suspension bridge marvel of the world.

In their own way, Ladd and Dennis had become urban Tom Sawyers and Huck Finns.

Ladd's Italian mother, ever fearful, ever protective, and often unknowingly comical in her commands to her son, on more than one occasion, called him and his playmates down from precarious perches around the Mission District.

Ladd particularly remembered the day he was in the upper reaches of a eucalyptus tree in Mission Park, when his mother called out, "Ladd Franklin, you come down from there. If you fall out of that tree and break both your legs, don't come running to me!"

. . .

This first week of June of eighth grade was a milestone week for Ladd.

On Wednesday, the class of 1935 graduated from "grammar" school.

And, on Sunday, Archbishop McHenry came to Divine Savior Church to administer the Sacrament of Confirmation to Ladd and the parochial school and released-time public school graduates.

Monsignor Epperson and more than fifteen visiting priests in cassocks and surplices sat in a semi-circle in the sanctuary.

Ladd was fascinated with the Confirmation pomp and circumstance of the ritual; The Archbishop was asking questions about Confirmation, and Ladd wanted no part of the dialog. He had not studied consistently. Rather, he took refuge behind Chubby Locarini who sat in the next pew.

It was well known that the prelate gave virtually the same sermon at every Confirmation and asked the same questions.

Consequently, the Sisters did what most Sisters did. They had prepared the candidates with the answers in the usual order to the questions ahead of time. The Archbishop peppered the kids with a variety of questions; such as what were the parts of the vestments, what was a mitre, and what was that large staff he held while asking the questions?

Suddenly he realized the answers had been "coached", so he decided to change the subject all together. The next question would have been "What is the bishop's pectoral cross"? Instead he asked "What is a monsignor?"

Ladd had been building confidence all along. He hardly waited for the end of the question to wave his hand.

"Yes, son," the Archbishop said. "What is a Monsignor?"

"Your Excellency, a Monsignor is the cross a bishop wears around his neck."

The congregation, not accustomed to laughing in church, could not contain itself.

And the priests in the sanctuary were doubled over in laughter, pointing at a red faced Monsignor Epperson.

Ladd wondered what had gone wrong. But he knew he must have answered incorrectly.

Save for the impending slap on the face by the Archbishop, Ladd was too distracted to remember much else in the ceremony. If nothing else, he was overjoyed that he's taken the name of his best friend, Dennis, as his own confirmation name.

At dinner in the convent that night, even Sister Clarice was still laughing at Ladd's answer. "Imagine that boy wants to be a priest. He is the last one in the class I would think would want to go to the seminary."

. . .

Later that year, Ladd would spend his summer days at Fleishhacker's' salt water pool, one of the largest in the world, at the end of Sloat Boulevard.

The pool's overall 1000 feet length allowed a straightaway race of 220 yards. Six lanes spanned its 30-yard width. The six million gallons of water pumped from the Pacific were cold and summers in the Sunset District were perpetually fog bound; but kids only paid a nickel to swim.

As Ladd pulled himself out of the deep end under the diving tower, a man standing outside the chain link fence called to him.

"How's the swimming?"

"Fine," Ladd said.

"Do you know where Sutro Baths are?"

"Yes, it's just up the highway."

"I'd like to see it. Could you show me?"

"You mean now?"

"Yeah, it will take just a little while."

The man seemed all right. Ladd wanted to be helpful. "Okay, wait 'till I tell my friends and change."

"Don't bother changing. We will only be gone a few minutes."

Ladd got into the late model car in his swimming trunks and directed the stranger to head north on Ocean Highway, driving past the Shoot the Schutes at Playland at the Beach.

They pulled into the parking lot above Sutro's and Ladd began to get out of the car. He was interested in seeing the six hot and cold pools and the special diving pool he had heard his classmates talk about.

"We don't have to go in," the stranger said. "I just wanted to know where the place is, so I can come later."

The driver pulled out of the parking space and started south along Ocean Beach back toward Fleishhacker's.

He looked at Ladd beside him and said, "Do you run into many homosexuals around here?"

Ladd wasn't sure he knew what the stranger was getting at.

"No, not many," he answered.

"Would you like to do something like that - just for the experience?"

"No, I don't go in for that kind of stuff," Ladd said, with an overwhelming feeling of uncomfort. The stranger drove back to Fleishhacker's and let him out of the car.

Ladd told his friends about it at the pool. They wanted to hear details.

"How old was he?"

"I guess about 30."

"What happened? What did he do?"

"Nothing."

Dennis and some of the others laughed.

"Come on, let's go back in."

They headed for the diving boards at the fourteen foot water depth end of the pool.

. . .

Ladd made the most of his last summer before boarding school. He even inveigled permission out of his parents and hers to take Jennifer Purcell to a dance.

He then persuaded two high school friends to drive them to the Marin County car ferry, across the Bay and on to Larkspur to the Rose Bowl. There, he danced with Jennifer to the music of the Ernie Heckscher Band - "Shuffle Off to Buffalo" and "Stars Fell on Alabama."

CHAPTER 7

Tyler Stone would be the youngest looking and youngest in years of the freshmen in the class of 1935 at Regina Cleri Junior Seminary.

Born and raised in Arizona, which had no seminary of its own, Tyler would enter the minor seminary in the Archdiocese of San Francisco under the auspices of the Bishop of Tucson.

Tyler's parents had separated when he was an infant. (the father never really knew his son.) An only child, Tyler lived with his mother on 29th Street, near downtown Tucson.

Evelyn Stone and her son attended Santa Cruz Church. She was overjoyed when Tyler asked if he could study to be a priest. Actually, his mother had, in subtle ways, been guiding the boy in this direction for more than two years.

His mother shepherded most of Tyler's life in the tough neighborhood of south Tucson.

Tyler grew up obedient, respectful and sensitive, well-liked by his elementary school teachers.

. . .

Evelyn Stone's relationship with her son Tyler was a loving, caring relationship. It was more than that as she often reminded him.

"You know, Tyler, you are 'my sunshine.'"

Evelyn wanted the best for her son, and she gave insightful advice. In some respects, she was far ahead of her time.

"I don't want you smoking, Tyler. That dirty habit can't be good for you."

And when Tyler was at the Tucson City Pool continuously during summer vacation months, his mother would warn him: "I don't know why you want to be getting so brown. I think all that sun is bad for your skin."

. . .

In the Jordan's yard on Campbell Avenue, his friend and neighbor Teddy Jordan explained the workings of his BB air rifle to Tyler.

Teddy was the one rich kid Tyler knew, and the Jordan house was the "mansion" of the neighborhood.

The two boys shot BBs at a Morton's salt box and a Pennzoil can on the back fence.

"See if you can hit that bird at the edge of the lawn, Tyler."

Tyler saw the quail and pumped three or four shots at it, but missed on all of them. The bird didn't move.

Tyler crept closer and drew a bead again. Then, through the gunsight, he saw a small bubble of blood on the quail's breast. It had been hit, but the mother wasn't moving from the nearby nest of her young.

Tyler lowered the gun.

. . .

All the neighborhood boys looked forward to the first day of trout season. Artie, the Stone's neighbor, invited Tyler to join him on a fishing expedition to the Santa Cruz River. The two took their bamboo fishing poles and headed for a fishing hole near the old adobe, just off the Nogales highway.

Tyler caught the first one. As he tried to pull the hook loose from the mouth of his catch, he was conscious of the eyes of the fish, like two marble agates, looking at him.

He finished the day with Artie, but it would be last time he fished again.

. . .

On a warm September day, when Napa's D'Agan plum trees were heavy with their purple fruit, San Francisco's summer fog had withdrawn into the Pacific, and the southern Arizona sunsets were theatrical, David, Ladd and Tyler left their homes for the seminary.

CHAPTER 8

It was late during the first weeks of seminary; David would share his accounts with his mother.

"Dear Mom: I have finally found time to write. It is now 8:15 p.m. We are in study hall. During study is about the only time you have to write.

At eight-thirty, we go into night prayers, so I'll have to hurry if I want to finish tonight.

I am finally straightened out. I have all my books except a missal and Latin book. They haven't come in yet.

There are three teams that play sports here. They are called the 'Ramblers,' 'Trojans,' and the 'Bears.' Everyone is picked to be on one of these teams. When you are picked, you play for that team in every sport all during the years at this school. I am on the 'Ramblers.'

We go to bed at nine o'clock every night and get up at five to six. It has been swell. Tomorrow we go into the science laboratory. That ought to be fun.

We have two hours of Latin, one hour of science, one hour of English, and one hour of algebra every day. Every Monday we have speech class for fifty minutes."

As he was writing, he began to hear the now familiar sound of night.

"Oh! Oh! There goes the bell for night prayers . . .

Believe it or not, it is now study hour at eight-fifteen in the morning. I guess I'll be able to finish before we go into Latin. I sure did sleep well last night.

Every day, different boys wait on the tables for dinner. One of my friends, Ladd, says it will be my turn next Friday.

Tomorrow is Thursday, so we will have the day off. Some of the boys said that we will get out of school to see the football game between Stanford and Santa Clara at Palo Alto.

Say hello to Vincent and Oznob for me.

"Well, I'll have to stop now. I'll write again next week. I'll be seeing you Visitors' Sunday. Love.

David

"P.S. I am O.K."

It was his first letter home, expressed in his careful copperplate handwriting with an envelope bearing a purple George Washington three-cent stamp. David had just turned fourteen.

Though he had made a decision to give his life to serving God, there was no mention of religion in the letter - just sports, class subjects and waiting on tables at meals.

Regina Cleri was pretty much like any high school, except there were no co-eds and there was no going home after classes.

David was assigned to a room on the fourth floor - a single bed with swayback springs and a straw mattress, a desk, a wooden chair, a small closet, and a wash basin completed the room.

. . .

Ladd Franklin arrived at the high school seminary that same September day.

On the San Francisco Peninsula, it was still summer. The Golden State was blanketed with the usual sun-parched brown groundcover stretching over Regina Cleri's campus, east to Maryknoll and west to Mount Baldy. The summer smells of tarweed and eucalyptus were everywhere.

Ladd had a sinking feeling in his stomach as he entered through the seminary gates. It was the same feeling he would have each time he returned to the seminary following Christmas and summer vacations.

David met Ladd Franklin on the day of arrival as they were bringing in their luggage. Their assigned rooms were next to each other on the freshman corridor.

"Looks like we're neighbors," Ladd said to David.

My name's David Carmichael, as he extended his hand to Ladd. What's yours?"

"I'm Ladd Franklin. I'm from Divine Savior. Where are you from?"

"St. Christopher's."

Ladd thought everyone was from San Francisco. "Where's St. Christopher's?"

"In Napa."

"Oh."

Ladd thought of the mental institution, but he said nothing.

Ladd liked David from the start.

. . .

The first days at seminary were difficult ones.

Just finding their way around the cavernous corridors, the concrete metal-plated stairways and the expansive grounds required most of David and Ladd's attention for the first month.

It was not easy to be this far away from home overnight for the first time in their lives. Ladd possibly would not have stuck it out if it hadn't been for his new friend.

The shrill of the wake-up call each morning rang loudly throughout the corridors. Twenty minutes to wash, to get dressed and to get down to chapel for morning prayers – that was the drill. For most boys, those twenty minutes were cold and sleepy.

Morning Prayer was said on the knees in chapel, and then twenty minutes of sitting in the pews and listening to "Meditations." The Sulpician Fathers, who were in charge of the seminary, always emphasized in three points – in meditations, talks, sermons . . . in everything.

The 14-year-olds really didn't mind meditation, although they hardly understood it. They took it for granted that it must be good for them. And it probably was, though their minds wandered most of the time.

One of the necessary but prized possessions acquired earlier in seminary life was the chapel kneeling-pad made out of sponge rubber.

It seemed to be a concession to the weakness of human nature, and that was normally not allowed. Not having such a simple staple would have brought about "water on the knee" or other afflictions which, in the long run, might prove costly in medical expenses.

Not everything in the chapel was pious. Plenty of dozing-off went on and snickers of laughter. John Lewellyn, kneeling next to David, had the practice of improvising during the Litany of the Saints. His repetitive response to the names of the saints was not "Pray for us," but "Hurray for us."

Meditation was followed by daily morning Mass which, in turn, was followed by another Mass of Thanksgiving.

Breakfast mostly consisted of oatmeal or cream of wheat, toast or corn bread, and maple syrup. On Thursdays a cut of beef, less than prime, might be included. Fridays meant inscrutably baked beans and vinegar.

Materially, David improved his life by going to the seminary. Though his mother had always made sure that her sons had nutritional food, living conditions were a step above what he had at home. He never actually adverted to it, but David came from a poor family.

. . .

As though to make sure that her son reached his destination, Evelyn Stone, herself, drove Tyler to Regina Cleri Junior Seminary on that warm September morning, 1935.

Driving north and west from Tucson through the arid desert, lush green began to appear as they neared Parker, and suddenly met the Colorado River. Heading up 95, the blue Colorado accompanied them on the left, rugged mountains on the right, giving the first hint of what the Grand Canyon looks like where the river enters Nevada and then California.

From Las Vegas, they traveled further north and west through the Nevada desert to Lathrop Pass, then right-angled west into California's Death Valley Junction.

Then, they travelled out the other side of Towne Pass, down 5,000 feet to Panamint Springs. In less than an hour's traveling time, from over a hundred feet below sea level, they saw highest point in the contiguous 48 states, Mount Whitney at 14,500 feet. The Sierra Nevada

Range stretched on their west as they headed north to the Tioga Pass into Yosemite.

Soon enough they would see California as they pictured it, and headed through agricultural fields to Stockton.

From there they drove west to the San Francisco Peninsula and the beauty of the Bay area with the Golden Gate, positioned in a setting of hills, ocean and bay.

. . .

In the first days at Regina Cleri, Tyler Stone from Tucson noticed the friendship between David and Ladd, and admired them. Before the end of September, the two classmates took Tyler into their circle. He was a better than average athlete and shared many of the same interests as David and Ladd.

In the intra-mural league, Tyler was a "Bear" but, in the pick-up games, he joined with these two "Rambler" friends at the barn for basketball, on the campus field for soccer and football, and at the pool for water polo.

. . .

Regina Cleri was a six-year seminary, offering a basic liberal arts curriculum for freshmen high school through the sophomore year of college.

Classes were conducted Monday through Wednesday, and on Friday and Saturday. Thursdays were holidays to break up the week.

David, Ladd and Tyler joined a class of 40 students from a variety of western states.

After breakfast, the day followed a set routine: bed-making, study hall, classes, lunch, classes, recreation and sports for two and a half hours in the afternoon, dinner, study hall, night prayers, lights out at nine, bed, and up again at 5:55 a.m.

CHAPTER 9

It was visiting Sunday in October. Ladd invited David's family to join his for the picnic lunch. Ladd led the usual introductions:

"Dave, this is my Mom and Dad, and my sister and brother, Laura and Larry."

"It's nice to know you," said David. "This is my mother and my brother, Vincent."

Because his family had lived mostly in an Irish community and environment, David added in the direction of his mother, "Ladd's mother is Italian, Mom."

"That's all right," said Mrs. Carmichael.

David heard Ladd's mother smother a soft chuckle.

Ladd's mother and father, and his brother and sister, unfolded an oversize bedspread next to their 1934 Chevrolet. Opposite to the Franklin and Carmichael families, across the service road toward "the Barn," Gordon Caprice's family claimed a spot for their picnic.

On this first visiting Sunday, all the families were strangers. A half hour had passed before Mrs. Franklin called across the road: "We are Ladd's family. How are you?"

"Fine. We are visiting our boy, Gordon."

"Yes, Ladd was telling us about Gordon, Mrs. Franklin said"

Actually, Ladd was not thinking of Gordon at the moment. He had noticed Gordon's sister, who seemed about Gordon's age, 13 or 14. She was blond, athletic looking, and clearly the center of the Caprice family.

"Do you have everything you need, Ladd?"

"Yea, Mom."

Larry, his brother, asked "How is the food here?" But Ladd wasn't listening. His eyes kept roving back across the road to Willow Caprice.

This hadn't gone unnoticed on the other side of the road. Willow asked her brother, "What kind of boy is that Ladd Franklin?"

"He's O.K."

"He's nice looking."

"I guess so."

On visiting Sunday from then on, Ladd saw Willow growing from month to month.

. . .

Terry Braxton, a fourth year man, caught up with Tyler on the senior side cloister.

"Do you have a place to go for Thanksgiving? I know you're from Arizona."

"No, I'll probably stay here. They have a special Thanksgiving meal for the ones who stay."

"You're welcome to come home to our place in San Francisco," Braxton said.

"Thank you, but do you think your family will want that?"

"Sure, they'll be glad to have you."

Tyler was surprised a senior would invite him. But Terry had talked to him on several occasions before, so he felt he knew him.

"Well, O.K. That'll be fine, if your parents don't mind."

What was developing here was a tradition known at Regina Cleri as a "pop-kid" relationship. It was natural for an older student to befriend a younger student - probably the big brother instinct.

Two days later, Ladd invited both David and Tyler to join the Franklins for Thanksgiving in the City.

"Thanks, Ladd, that'll be great," David said.

The two of them turned to Tyler.

"I'd really like to, Ladd, but just the other day, I promised Terry Braxton I would go to his house."

"You mean the fourth high guy?"

"Yea"

"I think he's your pop, Tyler," Ladd said.

"Yes, he's been good to me - for one of the seniors."

"I think this pop-kid stuff is just because we don't have girls at the school," Ladd said.

. . .

The Braxtons had six children in all, and Terry was the second oldest.

Tyler was awed by the constant action at the Thanksgiving meal. The mother was up and down continually. The family banter was incessant. The young children were all over the table, stretching for more portions.

Dad shouted at 11-year old Willie, "You're reaching in front of our guest. Ask for things you want. Don't you have a tongue?"

"Yea, but my arm is longer."

Tyler enjoyed the give-and-take, the warm companionship throughout the evening. How different from the quiet meals at home with his mother in Tucson.

After an evening of animated sharing about life at the seminary and life at home, it was time for the family to get to sleep.

"You kids go off to bed," Ellen Braxton said. "I have to make some lunches; tomorrow's Friday so we'll have to save the turkey leftovers until Saturday."

"Tyler, all the bedrooms are full," the mother continued. "You'll have to sleep with Terry, but it's a double bed; you'll have plenty of room."

Terry and Tyler talked for a while about the family and then turned off the light and soon were sound asleep.

Tyler awoke around three in the morning, embarrassed by a wet dream, an experience which puzzled him.

"Of all the nights to have this happen," he thought.

He would have to guard that part of the bed, so Terry wouldn't notice. Tyler hoped it would dry out by morning. He slept fitfully the rest of the night.

. . .

At Christmas vacation time at home, his mother and brother and his pal Buddy noticed the change in David; a subtle sophistication in the country boy. He had been exposed to a wide variety of new acquaintances. He carried himself more confidently.

Even Oznob treated him with more respect.

Oznob was the new dog David had rescued from the City Pound to replace Bonzo. The name, Oznob, spelled Bonzo backwards, was meant to be a tribute to the dog's predecessor.

. . .

The return to Napa was a revelation to David. He could sleep for as long as he wanted, listen to Glen Miller's "Adios" and Ella Fitzgerald's "Three Little Fishes" and watch "Top Hat" with Fred Astaire and Ginger Rogers dancing "Cheek to Cheek."

But when he first walked in, it seemed to him the house had shrunk. It was as if the ceiling and walls were crowding in on him after three and a half months of institutional-size corridors and halls at Regina Cleri.

The town had also changed -- from the foliage of summer to the bare limbs of winter.

The very next morning, he and Buddy headed to Albert's and Carrither's Department Stores to see the Christmas toys' and men's clothing.

He felt like Oliver Twist travelling about town with his Rose. For the next two weeks, David and his friends were everywhere.

In eight years, David had covered so much geographical territory in his home town that, now every street and store had a story. Almost every home, had a memory.

It was to this house that he delivered The Saturday Evening Post, and to that house The Country Gentleman, and to three out of ten houses on another block The Napa Daily Register.

. . .

Gordon Caprice was the brightest student in the class. He was an avid reader, and the Caprice family was wealthy.

Gordon's father was a successful attorney for several San Francisco corporations. He had accumulated enough wealth to move his family to an exclusive neighborhood in suburban Los Altos, not far from Regina Cleri Seminary.

Gordon was the first one in David's class to own an electric shaver, the one who received regular packages of See's English toffee from home.

When December came, Gordon wore the newest fashion of the young generation - the wrap-around overcoat.

During the winter break, Ladd and half the class asked for wrap-around top coats for Christmas.

. . .

On the third day of Christmas vacation, Tyler had no idea on how to approach a doctor.

He entered the Cobre Building and finally summoned the courage to open the door of the reception room for Dr. Warren Biaggi. After paging through magazine articles and pictures, which he really didn't read or see at all, he was called in.

"What can I do for you, son?" The doctor seemed to be about forty years old.

"I think I have something wrong with my kidneys."

Tyler had heard radio commercials about Doane's Pills for backaches caused by kidney problems.

"What makes you think so?" the doctor asked.

Now came the hard part.

"Well . . . at night when I am sleeping, I have . . . uh . . . uh."

"You mean a wet dream?"

"A wet dream?, Tyler curiously replied"

"You don't know about wet dreams? Don't you and your friends talk about these things?"

"No, "Tyler stammered. "I guess we are not supposed to be talking about these things. I'm in the seminary studying to be a priest."

"Well, that's good," the doctor said, "but there is nothing wrong with wet dreams. That happens to everyone."

That was enough for Tyler. Relief flood all over him. There is no feeling more liberating than when a doctor tells you, you are not sick.

Tyler turned to leave. "Okay, thank you, Doctor . . . do I owe you some money?

"No, no charge. Just level honestly with your friends from now on."

CHAPTER 10

During the days together at Regina Cleri, the seminary community became the seminarians' family. They lived, studied, played together through the years. They virtually became blood brothers.

Their bonding would last a lifetime.

Though the drudgery of study and routine made the days drag for Ladd, the time raced for David.

David enjoyed seminary life. Perhaps it would be better if it were more difficult for him. His vocation was never really put to the test. Better to be tested now than in the priesthood later.

Minor seminary days raced by in a thousand vignettes:

parsing, conjugating and declining, exploring Caesar, Cicero, Virgil and Horace in Latin.

Gordon Caprice borrowed from Horace's Ode to Mount Soracte, when he was called on for an example of alliteration in English class. Gordon extemporized:

"I see Soracte stand in snow.

With boughs that bend beneath the pack."

Adventures in the Greek language through the Odyssey and Iliad.

Bunsen burners and the smell of sulphur in the chemistry lab.

David, read Lew Wallace's Ben Hur and Kenneth Robert's Northwest Passage, after lights-out, under the covers of his bed, with the use of an exposed light bulb and an extension cord. It was adventurous and sweaty.

Ladd rubbed soap in his eyes during the epidemic to simulate "pink-eye," earning himself a four day stay in the infirmary, away from classes and with access to a radio -- Orson Wells' War of the Worlds, Mae West on the Edgar Bergen/Charlie McCarthy Show, and Wee Bonnie Baker squeaking out O Johnny, O Johnny.

Nurse Lettie Shriver wasn't fooled by the malingering. She enjoyed having company in the infirmary.

David was elected president of the class, and Ladd, athletic director. Tyler was appointed "excitator." It was his duty to ring the house bells that regulated the daily schedule, including the wake-up bells at five to six each morning.

On his own floor, after ringing the general bell, Tyler was required to rush down the corridor, pounding on each door and shouting, "Benedicamus Domino!" (Let us bless the Lord). The called-for response from each room was, "Deo Gratias" (Thanks be to God!).

Half of the time no response came; more often than not, Tyler could hear expletives instead.

In the refectory, the faculty sat on a raised dais for the noonday meal and supper, as students waited on tables.

Waiting on tables was done in rotation by the various student tables of nine. Waiting on the professors' table was special. Two seminarians performed this duty at each meal. There was a reward attached to the task; all waiters enjoyed the food from the professors' table after the others had left the refectory. David, Ladd and Tyler became "house" waiters, the name given to students who volunteered to take the place of other seminarians whose turn it was to serve. They did this as often as they could, savoring the special fare from the professors' menu.

During the years in seminary, serious events were occurring overseas. The seminarians, by Sulpician rule, had no access to newspapers or radio. They gathered only bits and pieces of Hitler's war building in Europe.

In the cloister, on the way to the dining room, Father Horgan would whisper 1938 news flashes to David. "Austria has capitulated to the Blitzkrieg. Chancellor Schuschnigg is in prison."

Later, "Roosevelt has accused Mussolini: 'the hand that held the dagger has struck it into the back of its neighbor.'"

But world news was not the priority for teenagers.

David and Ladd, as upper classmen, leading the "Ramblers" to championships in baseball and football. The two were the battery in baseball with Ladd pitching. In football, David was the tailback who did the passing, and Ladd was his main receiver. These were the priorities that mattered most.

The stand-out events of Regina Cleri days were not in chapel or the classroom. Not even attending Mass at San Francisco's Holy Trinity Cathedral where they participated in the transfer of the body of leper Father Damien from Molokai to his native Belgium.

For Ladd, the outstanding memory would be the Monday starting Christmas vacation, in their freshman year, when Eric Callahan and Ladd hitch hiked rides to San Francisco up El Camino Real. The first ride dropped them off in Palo Alto.

Ladd remembered that the West team was practicing at Stanford stadium for the East-West game.

The two worked their way into the practice field and, incredibly, were able to shake hands with Coach Babe Hollingberry, several consensus All-Americans and unanimous All-American Paul Chrisman from the University of Missouri.

David's most impressive moment was at that same location on another date, when he and his classmates entered the Palo Alto stadium for the season opener between Stanford University of San Francisco game. It was the first college game David had ever witnessed, and he was overwhelmed by the sight of the crowd at the 80,000-seat stadium.

On the field that day, Clark Shaughnessy unveiled the T-formation with a backfield of Frankie Albert, Norm Standlee, Hugh Gallerneau and Pete Kemetovic. David would never be the same after witnessing his first college football game.

Back at seminary, a persistent myth or fact circulated among the student body that saltpeter was added to the dining food to deaden sexual urges. The seminarians perpetuated the allegation from generation to generation, though most of them didn't know what saltpeter was or whether it had the effect attributed to it.

It was also alleged that during the previous summer vacation, the bright white lights in the refectory were replaced by soft amber colored bulbs to make the white margarine on the tables look like butter.

Seminarians were carefully shielded from impure temptations and concupiscence of the eyes. Twice a year the student body saw a meticulously selected movie. This semester it was "David Copperfield." And all went well until Maureen O'Sullivan appeared on the screen drawing wolf whistles from the boys. Just as quickly as they began, Father Madigan, the rector, charged the projector and shut it off.

The house lights came up and the stern faced priest cautioned the audience. "That behavior is totally inappropriate for a seminarian. There will be no more movies until you can show some maturity."

The boys would have to read the book to see what happened.

The next movie shown was "Journey's End." It featured an all-male cast.

Lunch and supper were eaten in silence, except on holidays. Students rotated turns reading aloud from sacred scripture before meals and a roll call of saints and martyrs afterward.

During the freshman year, two novels were completed during meals: Death Comes for the Archbishop by Willa Cather, and Wild Bill of the Mounties.

For the first several weeks of the fall semester during supper, the "rhetoricians," or sophomores read papers they had prepared in philosophy and science during the preceding summer months.

When David's turn came his assigned topic was "The Mechanism of Descartes." Ladd's task was to explain the concept of motion in Einstein's theory of Relativity.

This is the way seminary was forming young men in the attributes which it was hoped they would possess as priests.

The regular religious devotions each day would help them develop habits of prayer: morning prayer, meditation, Mass, prayer before and after meals, the Angelus, prayer before and after class, the Rosary said privately along the cloisters or in the central courtyard, spiritual reading, weekly confession, evening exhortation from the rector, night prayers.

The rector's evening conference dwelt on generosity, being thoughtful of one's fellow students, unselfishness. The coat-of-arms motto of Regina Cleri could well have been "Fraternal Charity." Rector Madigan used the expression at least five times each night in his conference.

David, Ladd and Tyler took part in liturgies they never knew at their parish churches. On Sunday afternoons, they were introduced to Gregorian Chant at the Vesper services, all in Latin.

David served Tenebrae (Darkness) on three days of Holy Week. He was fascinated as candles in two sets of candelabra on the altar were extinguished one by one, while psalms were sung antiphonally by the students facing each other across the nave of the chapel in choir stalls.

And the climax of Tenebrae especially came as a surprise. As the last candle was put out by an acolyte holding the long-handled candle-snuffer, the chapel was enveloped in darkness and the entire congregation of seminarians pounded on the choir stalls with their heavy chant books, the Liber Usualis. The commotion brought the pews' termites to the surface.

It was, the freshmen had been forewarned, a dramatic representation of the earthquake and darkness that fell over Jerusalem at the hour of the crucifixion.

Ladd's favorite religious observance was the annual Corpus Christi procession when he was called on to swing the censer with the burning charcoal. The entire student body and the faculty, in cassocks and surplices, would circle the campus, followed by the rector, vested in an embroidered shoulder-to-ankle length cope.

The rector carried the "Corpus Christi," the white wafer of consecrated Bread in the gold sunburst-shaped vessel, the ostensorium. Ladd remembered cutting out a picture of an ostensorium and pasting it in his religion class composition book at Divine Savior School. As he remembered it, the Sisters at St. Christopher's called the vessel a monstrance.

The celebrant concluded the outdoor ceremony by blessing the assembly with the monstrance from the elaborate temporary altar the upperclassmen had constructed on the baseball diamond.

CHAPTER 11

Willow asked her brother, "Do you know Ladd Franklin very well?"

"Sure, I know him – he's in our class."

"What kind of guy is he?"

"Well, he's just like anyone else. He's a good athlete. He brings up a lot of questions in class."

"What kind of questions?"

"He likes to challenge the professors. I don't think they like his attitude."

"Why are you so interested?"

"Oh, no particular reason. I think he's sort of cute."

"Yes, I thought you'd probably like him. Mothers like good boys, but the chicks like the bad boys."

"Why? Is he bad?" Willow asked.

"No, he's not bad, but he likes to take chances and he has a mind of his own. If you're interested, why don't you drop by Lawton's Store out on Taylor Road and meet him? Most of the class is out there on the Walk every Thursday afternoon."

Willow said nothing, but she made a note of the time and place.

. . .

On the morning of the weekly holiday, Ladd reminded David, "Remember, we're leaving at one-thirty."

Lawton's Store was the all-purpose creamery, grocery store and a gathering place in Los Altos for the seminarians on Thursday afternoons - when they could get permission for "the walk."

David and Ladd reached Lawton's about two-fifteen. A couple of dozen students had already clustered at the counter with milkshakes and hot dogs.

Ladd ordered a chocolate milkshake, David a Royal Crown Cola.

"I always choose RC Cola," David said, "because RC really stands for Roman Catholic."

"Yeah, right," Ladd said. "You choose it because it's a bigger bottle for the same price."

On the counter radio, Erskine Hawkins' band was playing Green Grass but you could hardly hear it. Just as at meals in the refectory, when there was talking instead of reading, the conversation was bedlam -- everybody talking at once.

Suddenly, there was a lull. David looked toward the door. A blond girl in hiking shorts and a Los Altos High T-shirt had stepped in, Her eyes were circling the room, obviously searching for someone.

Gordon, at the table at the other end of the store, got up quickly and moved to the entrance.

Then David remembered. "That's Gordon's sister."

Ladd looked up. "Yeah, that's Willow Caprice."

Willow was tall for a girl, Coppertone-tanned.

She smiled when Gordon greeted her. "Hi, Willow, what's doing?"

"I just came by to say `hello.'"

"Do you want something to drink?"

"I'll have a Coke, but I have to hurry."

Gordon led her to the counter. He reached over next to David to ask the counter-girl for two Cokes.

"Hi, David," Gordon said. "This is my sister Willow."

"Hi."

"And this is Ladd Franklin."

"Hi. Yes, I've seen you on visiting Sundays," Willow said.

Ladd flushed a bit and stood up. He didn't need an introduction. He thought of Willow often.

"Why don't you sit with us?"

Gordon and his sister sat down between David and Ladd. Gordon knew Willow had come to meet Ladd, so he sat next to David and engaged him in conversation.

"You guys have the day off?" Willow started.

"We don't have classes on Thursdays," Ladd said, but he was sure Willow knew that from her brother.

"How come you're not in school?" Ladd asked.

"We just got out. I'm on the way to the stables with two girlfriends. We're going to do some riding."

"You own a horse?"

"Yes, I've had my horse, 'Excalibur' since I was a little girl. You like animals, Ladd?"

"Oh yes, we've always had dogs and cats at home. But there is no place for horses where we live in San Francisco — except maybe up on Red Rock Hill."

Ladd was making conversation, but his mind was on Willow. He was noticing especially her pastel blue eyes and her hair which, if he remembered correctly, was called a "page boy" cut.

"Maybe you could come over some day with Gordon and David for a horseback ride."

"Yea, that would be good."

"Well, I have these friends waiting for me outside. They were too bashful to come in. I'd better go."

Turning, she said, "David, it's nice to meet you. Gordon, I have to leave. I'll tell Mom and Dad I saw you. Is there anything you need?"

"No, everything's O.K. See you soon."

"Goodbye."

Gordon walked to the door with his sister. She gave him a quick kiss on the cheek and was gone.

The high decibel conversations resumed.

. . .

David and Gordon were the brightest students in the class -- Gordon had the highest I.Q. He came from a family of readers. David was a plodder. He worked hard at his studies, tried to be attentive in class, took copious notes, and crammed for examinations.

David felt the rivalry with Gordon. Gordon envied David's popularity and what he saw as leadership qualities in David. But he did not consider David a legitimate competitor in scholarship.

On the last Tuesday night of each semester, academic premiums were awarded as the student body gathered in the study hall.

Father Cummings, the Academic Dean, stood at the podium to announce the winners of the scholarly honors at each grade level.

David had been through this for three years now. But he was just as nervous tonight as he had been in the first year of high school.

He knew he had a good chance of taking first premium in Latin, Religion, English, and possibly Civics.

As he did every year, Father Cummings began with the Sixth Latiners, the youngest students. Then he moved on to the Fifth Latiners, announcing winners, subject by subject.

As each name was called, the winner would come forward to the platform and receive a book wrapped as a gift.

Then came the third high announcements. David's stomach tightened as the time drew near.

He would tell himself he didn't have much chance, but this was a way to prepare for the worst and to head off disappointment. Deep down, he had hope.

Now Father Cummings lifted the list of David's class from the desk and began to read:

"For the fourth year of high school, in the subject of Latin: first premium -- Gordon Caprice."

David's heart sank, but he smiled and looked over at Gordon as Gordon rose to approach the podium and receive his book.

The Academic Dean resumed his announcements: "Second premium in Latin - David Carmichael."

David felt his face flush as he walked forward to receive his prize.

"First premium in Religion - David Carmichael and Gordon Caprice - ex aequo." They would share the award.

The next subject was English. "First premium - Gordon Caprice; Second premium - Robert Garcetti."

"And for the subject of American Civics, first premium - Gordon Caprice. Second premium: David Carmichael."

The announcements droned on. David knew he was not in the competition for Chemistry, Math or French.

Gordon won one more first premium and two more second premiums.

When the session was over, David congratulated Gordon, who was, by this time, weighed down with volumes under both arms.

David thought, "Well, he really is smarter than I am."

. . .

Gordon began to suspect that his sister Willow was too serious about Ladd.

Willow had asked Gordon to invite Ladd over to their home on the next "eight to eight," those rare holidays when the seminarians were allowed to go home from eight in the morning until eight at night.

At the Thanksgiving Day break, Gordon turned to his sister during the family meal. "Willow, I think you are off on the wrong track with Ladd Franklin."

"What do you mean?"

"I think you are trying to get him interested in you."

"No, I'm not. I just like him."

"Well, remember, he has decided to be a priest and it's not right for you to be taking him away from that."

"Isn't he in the seminary to find out if he wants to be a priest? He can decide for himself, can't he?"

Willow confirmed his suspicions.

"He's in the seminary to keep him away from the temptation to go back into the world," Gordon said.

"Well, I just think he would make a good friend."

Between mouthfuls, Emily Caprice was taken aback by the conversation between her two children.

She thought this subject was too delicate for the family table.

"I think you should discuss this some other time," she said.

At the head of the table, the father had his own mind. "I think Gordon is right. You are a beautiful girl, Willow, and you can make it very difficult for that boy to persevere in his vocation."

When George Caprice spoke, it usually concluded the discussion. It had not concluded the matter in Willow's mind.

. . .

Two weeks later, Ladd asked David if he was doing anything after dinner.

"I want to talk to you about something."

That evening the two headed for the Walk to the far end of the campus. David could tell that something serious was on Ladd's mind, but he waited until Ladd took the initiative.

"You know, Dave, I sort of like Gordon's sister Willow."

"Yes, I gathered that."

"And I think she likes me."

"I think she's had her eye on you ever since Sixth Latin."

"It's made me wonder whether I really have a vocation to the priesthood. I've been thinking about her quite a bit."

This was one of those situations David didn't like. How was he going to give advice to Ladd? He really had no experience of this kind of thing himself. He didn't want Ladd to leave the seminary and he certainly didn't want to be the one who gave him advice to leave.

"I don't know what to tell you, Ladd. But I don't think you should make any decisions hastily. You've been in the seminary a long time now and you've always wanted to be a priest."

"I know, but I've never had thoughts like this before."

"Have you talked to your confessor about it?"

"No, you're the first one I've talked to."

"Well, I would give it some time. It's a decision for your whole life and you don't want to rush into it."

David knew he wasn't really giving Ladd much help. Ladd was going to make up his own mind any way; he just needed someone to talk to.

CHAPTER 12

At the start of summer vacation, David stayed overnight at Ladd's house on the way home to Napa. The two had just graduated from seminary high school and they would celebrate by exploring the San Francisco World Fair, the Golden Gate International Exposition which had opened three months earlier on Treasure Island.

David was thrilled to see the Fair's entertainment celebrities in person. Ladd was more interested in other attractions.

"Let's go over to the Gayway, Dave. Maybe we can get in to see Sally Rand." David knew Ladd was trying to get a rise out of him, so he called his bluff.

"Yeah, I've always wanted to see a fan dance." They climbed aboard a moving elephant train and headed for what is best described as the carnival of the Exposition.

Once inside the Gayway, they kept their eyes open for the Dude Ranch and jumped off the train when the flashing marquee of Sally behind her fans came into view.

What David suspected would happen, actually did.

Ladd led the way to the box office.

"Two tickets, please."

"How old are you, kid?"

"Eighteen." Ladd had lied.

"Have you any identification?"

Ladd thought of his "student body" card, drew it out of his wallet and handed it through the half circle window of the box office.

"Regina Cleri . . ." came the puzzled voice from the box office. "Isn't that the seminary?"

"Yes, sir," Ladd answered, halfway between embarrassment and bravado.

"What are you doing at a place like this? You ought to be ashamed of yourselves."

"Why did we have to run into a Catholic ticket seller?" Ladd thought to himself.

He wanted to say, "What are you doing selling tickets in a place like this?" but refrained - thinking it might jeopardize their chances for admittance.

"Besides," the voice behind the window lectured on, "this card says you won't be eighteen until November."

By this time David was pulling on Ladd's sleeve. "Come on, let's go, Ladd."

Ladd retrieved his student body card and heard the parting shot from the box office. "Be sure to tell your parish priest where you were this afternoon."

The seventeen-year-olds had to settle for two whipped cream topped Belgian scones.

On the occasion of the 50th anniversary of the Golden Gate Exhibition, David would write:

"Later world fairs may have been more sophisticated with exotic media shows, but for its time Treasure Island was dazzling.

"The joy of it then was in our youth. Sometimes today I can't understand how my grandnephews and nieces, when they go to places like Disneyland or Universal Studios, aren't interested in the more educational exhibits. They just want to take rides and listen to rock groups. But looking back on it, that's exactly what interested me when I was 17.

"The splendor of the buildings and of the scientific exhibits was dazzling. The Fair was like today's malls which are the gathering places of teenagers. It was the place to go."

. . .

America was listening to Frank Sinatra singing "I'll Never Smile Again" when David's class graduated from high school in June, 1939. But there had been no graduation ceremony. Regina Cleri was a six-year school, four years of high school and two years of junior college.

For their mortar board cap and gowns, David's class had to wait until 1941.

Two years later, in early June, the graduates rose alphabetically to receive their diplomas and to hear the level of honors each had achieved - in ascending order: No honors, Cum Laude, Magna cum Laude, Maxima cum Laude or Summa cum Laude.

They had reached the C's in the alphabet.

"Gordon Caprice, Summa cum Laude—the highest honor. There was a burst of applause from the families seated in the courtyard.

The procession to Father Madigan at the podium went on.

Two students later: "David Carmichael." (David's heart stopped.) "Maxima cum Laude."

Just a step behind Gordon Caprice, again.

CHAPTER 13

The step into the major seminary was a giant one. Now David and Ladd would be wearing the long black cassock and the white reverse collar every day.

This shoulder-to-ankle clerical robe, the cassock, was to be "the first garment put on in the morning and the last taken off at night."

St. John Vianney Major Seminary had been built out in the country in the early 1900's, but now Atherton and Menlo Park were encroaching upon it. Still, it was secluded from "the world," as a seminary must be, by 40 acres of uncultivated fields and eucalyptus, oak, and olive trees.

The red brick building had survived the 1906 San Francisco earthquake, though the top floor was destroyed by the temblor. That floor was eventually replaced with a residence floor, its exterior faced with gray shingles in mansard style.

Architecturally, St. John's was designed like all Sulpician seminaries -- a quadrangle with a central courtyard patterned after the mother seminary, San Sulpice in Paris.

Walkways circled the main buildings, but the rest of the sprawling property was undeveloped. An ancient water tower looked down on the northern end of St. John's and, next to the water tower, a wooden fence enclosed a swimming pool and, to the side, two paved tennis courts.

Normally, this would be home for the next six years, but it would be only five years for the class of 1946, because of what would occur in December, during David and Ladd's first year in the major seminary.

. . .

On December 7, 1941, at the after-lunch break, at the east steps of St. John's, Father Proctor announced to the students gathered to receive their mail:

"The Japanese have just bombed Pearl Harbor. Hundreds of men have been killed and a substantial part of the United States Fleet has been destroyed."

Reactions were varied; the seminarians knew this would mean war.

Colin Murphy, the class iconoclast, invariably against the government, wanted to know "what our fleet was doing in a foreign port anyway?"

Like most Americans on that December morning, Colin had no idea where Pearl Harbor was, let alone that it was a United States possession.

Father Walter Erskine, anxiety-prone under even the most tranquil circumstances, worried aloud to the students around him, "That is a devastating blow. We should swallow our pride and capitulate."

Raymond Goddard, a second philosopher and a romantic, commented, "I know I shouldn't say this, but in a way I hope the war is still on three weeks from now when we're home for Christmas. This will be an exciting time in San Francisco."

. . .

The weeks leading up to Christmas vacation were electrically charged.

Blackout curtains were installed on the seminary windows, buckets of sand were placed in the corridors to extinguish fires from enemy shells. Air raid sirens in Menlo Park and Palo Alto sounded on six different occasions during that three-week period, triggering a "lights out" in all the seminary rooms and corridors.

A paramedic from Redwood City Hospital was brought in to give a special course in First Aid. Faculty and students turned to the radios in the common room and out behind the gym to hear the latest reports. The seminarians were allowed to hear President Roosevelt's "Day of Infamy" address to the nation.

On the way home three days before Christmas, on the Greyhound bus, David saw air defense balloons tethered by heavy cable floating over the oil refineries near Pinole and the Carquinez Bridge and over Mare Island Shipyards in Vallejo.

Soon there would come the days of food rationing and gasoline windshield stickers, draft notices, a massive mobilization of America's resources by the Roosevelt administration, and a tightening of the belt throughout the home front.

David and his classmates were learning new words in English vocabulary class and in every day newspapers' parlance - words that would eventually become a natural part of daily conversation: fifth column, Quisling, Axis, Fuhrer, Nazi, Blitzkrieg, black-out, fellow-traveler, concentration camp, Flying Fortress, Jeep. New technology was introducing new language: fiberglass, plastic, air-conditioning, Polaroid, FM (frequency modulation), nylon. And words that we might have thought were always part of our language: hairdo, bobby pin, jalopy, Bronx cheer, station wagon.

. . .

The September that Ladd entered St. John's, Willow Caprice enrolled as a sophomore at Stanford University, on the other side of Palo Alto, across from the major seminary. Late afternoons and on weekends, Willow worked as a sales clerk at Peninsula Book & Gift Store in Menlo Park.

Ladd learned this from Gordon and made it a point to receive permission for a walk to purchase personal supplies the second Thursday of the new term. Actually, he had wanted to buy Roget's Thesaurus.

Willow saw Ladd the minute the door chime sounded as he entered. She had expected him to drop by eventually, but the sudden sight of him excited her. She moved quickly to the front of the shop to make sure she would be the one to wait on him.

"Hello, Ladd. I was hoping you would come by. How have you been?"

"Fine. How are things with you?"

"Busy. I'm carrying sixteen units at Stanford and working here six days a week. How's seminary treating you?"

"Things are going okay."

"Can I help you find something here, Ladd?"

"Yea, I need a Roget's Thesaurus. Do you have it?"

"Oh yes, lots of students ask for Roget's - hardback or paperback?"

"I'll take the paperback."

As Willow placed the book in a Peninsula Book and Gifts bag, she tried to think of other subjects to detain Ladd. Ladd also would have liked to stay a little longer, but both were tongue-tied in each other's presence.

"Why don't you come over to our home sometime when we're both free? My family would like to meet you. You know where we live in Los Altos, don't you?"

"Yeah, I'll talk to Gordon about it. See you around, Willow."

Why couldn't he carry on a normal conversation? Why was it that he felt guilty when he talked with Willow?

. . .

The summer of 1942 arrived and Ladd was nineteen. It was the last three-month summer vacation Ladd would have until the war was over.

He made the most of it, working as a ship fitter's helper at Moore shipyards in the East Bay. He helped build cargo ships and submarine tenders, but he wondered how any of them ever floated. The draft-exempt men he worked with didn't seem to know any more about shipbuilding than he did. Ladd's pay for this work was seventy dollars a week.

An episode that summer might end Ladd's training for the priesthood.

He had saved the last two weeks of August to drive to San Diego with Dave, Tyler and Gordon. The next 14 days followed a set routine. Ladd and David bunked in the same room at the Glorietta Bay Motel in Coronado Island; Tyler and Gordon also slept in twin beds in the adjacent room.

Each one woke up in the morning, showered, dressed and walked a block and a half to the Avenida Restaurant for breakfast. Usually, before the first one up had finished breakfast, the other three joined him in the booth. After breakfast, it was off to the Coronado City golf course for 18 holes. Then back to the motel by mid-afternoon and across Orange Avenue, through the historic Coronado Hotel grounds, for swimming and surfing on Coronado Beach.

The sands were white and the water temperature 75 degrees. The San Diego sun seemed perpetual.

Myth has it that the needles on the thermometers in downtown Coronado are painted on . . . fixed at 79 degrees.

After showers and dinner at one of the Coronado restaurants, usually Maria's Trattoria or the El Pueblo for Mexican cuisine near the old San Diego-Coronado ferry landing, it was off to an Abbot and Costello movie or a western, depending on who won the argument.

Then back to the motel, sometime before midnight. And up again between eight and ten the next morning, he ritual beginning all over again.

On the next to last weekend, it was David's idea to do something different.

"Let's go to Tijuana to see a bullfight." Tyler was against it but the majority prevailed.

The four drove along the Pacific shore through Imperial Beach, Chula Vista and San Ysidro, where they were waved across the border by the Mexican customs official. It was the first time any of them, except Gordon, had been in a foreign country. They passed the greyhound race-track in Agua Caliente, the Tijuana Golf course, finally located the bullring.

As Gordon pulled the car into a parking space on the shady side of the arena, Ladd said, "You guys go on in. I think I would rather just walk around and see Tijuana."

"Don't you want to see the bullfight?" David asked.

"No, I can do that some other time. I'll see you back here at the car when the bullfight's over."

The three turned to the stadium and Ladd headed toward the town.

. . .

Ashley was probably not her real name, but from her looks, Ladd thought it should be. Her darker than nut-brown hair fell naturally below her shoulders. She wore no makeup; she didn't need it.

Her skin was smooth and tan, soft and cool to the touch. Now he knew why beautiful eyes are set widely apart. They accented the prominent cheek bones and the slightly shadowed hollow of the cheeks themselves. But what fascinated him most were the extraordinary full lips. Without words they called to him, invited him. Ashley's soft shoulders framed two breasts that were best described as fresh, firm, still growing. Her body was long and lean with a firm flat stomach and slender limbs that could have been a teenager's - with sculptured feet.

Ashley led Ladd to a spacious room with a king-size tub.

He was directed to disrobe.

"Do you want a massage?"

"Okay."

She turned on the spigot in the tub and felt the water turn warm.

"Get into the tub," she motioned to Ladd.

She cupped handfuls of the warm water over Ladd's shoulders and back.

Though the water was at warm body temperature, Ladd shivered from sensations he had never felt before.

She held out her hand and led Ladd from the tub, still slathered in warm soap suds. What happened next seemed to come so naturally.

He later remembered thinking he did not feel like a novice. He just fell easily into embracing and kissing. He lost all track of time.

Then that was enough for Ladd. There was no intercourse. He found himself thinking, "Am I still a virgin?"

He showered and dressed, paid ten dollars, brushed Ashley's cheek with a kiss and left.

As he walked out into the sunlight, he really didn't feel guilty. He felt, "I can do it like anyone else."

Later, he would experience guilt -- or perhaps only fear that somehow the seminary faculty would find out about the escapade and he would immediately be expelled.

As Ladd came out of the brothel, he hurried past the Jai Lai Fronton Palace to get back to the car before the others returned from the bullfight.

Suddenly he saw Gordon on the other side of the street. Had he seen Ladd come out of the building? How could he have missed him?

Ladd turned his face away and slipped into a tourist curio and souvenir shop. Once inside, he looked through the window to see if Gordon was watching him. Gordon eventually moved on down the street.

Pretending he was interested in souvenirs, Ladd wandered around the shop for ten minutes and then left to join his companions.

Twenty minutes after him, all three, including Gordon, arrived.

"How was the bullfight?" Ladd asked. Gordon said nothing. "It was great, David said"

"I didn't think much of it," Tyler said. "I don't think the bull has a chance. I was pulling for the bull. They stick the bull and torment it in every way they can. I should have stayed with you, Ladd. What did you do?"

"I just wandered around the town to see what it looked like."

He tried to look casual as he eyes shifted around the group to see Gordon's reaction. Gordon looked at him steadily, but said nothing. Ladd was now sure Gordon had seen him coming out of the house.

They drove back to the customs check-point at the border and waited in line with seven other cars ahead of them.

Finally, at the gate, the U.S. official peered into the car and waved them on through into San Ysidro and the United States.

. . .

Peter Matsumoto was a third year man - a first theologian.

After the first of the year 1942, word came from Washington that all west coast residents of Japanese descent would be interned for the duration of the war.

The seminarians were angry when it was learned that Peter would have to leave St. John's. The student body officers organized a collection for Peter and the seminary faculty intervened with government officials.

The relocation office reversed the decision. Peter would not be interned at Tulelake on the California/Oregon border. He would transfer to St. Thomas Seminary in Denver here he continued his training for the priesthood.

. . .

As the war raged on, David sensed there was something different about America. It was the first time he understood the meaning of a word the spiritual directors were always emphasizing - community.

Suddenly, the entire United States seemed to be pulling in one direction. Young and old, poor and rich, opposing political parties, the churches, the ethnic groups - Japanese, German, Italian-Americans, all seemed to come together.

David had not noticed its absence when community was not present, but when it happened, it was almost palpable.

Often families experience community; sometimes a fraternity or a sorority; on occasion an entire city. But this was embracing a nation.

It seemed the only one positive by-product of the horrifying armed conflict.

Popular songs also helped glue the social fabric of the war years.

Young and old were singing the same songs:

"A Nightingale Sang in Barkley Square"
"The White Cliffs of Dover"
"My Sister and I"
"I'll be Seeing You"
"You'll Never Know"
"Sentimental Journey"
"Till the End of Time"

There was one Hit Parade for adults and youngsters.

When the war ended, the community would gradually move to separation, alienation and generational differences.

The young would edge toward Rhythm and Blues and on to Rock and Roll, which the older generation found hard to comprehend. The elderly stayed with the ballads.

. . .

Ladd rapped on David's door on the third floor, Theology side.

"Dave, can I see you after dinner tonight?"

"Sure, I'll see you outside the refectory."

Coming out of dinner, Ladd motioned Dave down the ramp to the outside walk.

"I've wanted to talk to you about this ever since we got back from the Coronado trip. You know, when you guys went to the bullfights and I walked around Tijuana? Well, I think I may have gotten myself into some trouble."

He went on to tell David the whole story.

David didn't know how to react.

"Uh . . . that is a problem. I don't know what to say."

Then David went on, "I guess the best thing to do is make sure you tell it in confession, and the put the whole thing behind you. We all make mistakes."

"But another thing, Dave. I think Gordon saw me coming out of that place. I thought he was with you and Tyler at the bullfights."

"No, Gordon decided not to go to the bullfights. He said he just wanted to wander around and see the sights."

"I'm sure he saw me and, if I know him, he's going to think it's his obligation to tell someone on the faculty about this. You know how he is. If the faculty finds out about this, I'll be thrown out of the seminary for sure."

CHAPTER 14

So that draft-exempted seminarians would be not so much in the public eye, the seminary authorities, with the approval of the archbishop, decided to cancel the three months summer vacation for the duration of the war thus deflecting criticism of young men in their early 20's who were still civilians.

On a Thursday morning in the Spring of 1943, David and Ladd came out of Woolworth's in Palo Alto, where they had made weekly purchases. As they headed east on University Avenue, Ladd noticed that they were being followed by four young men in Army uniforms.

The two seminarians turned the corner at Middlefield Road and headed west. The military still followed them.

In an aside, without turning his head, Ladd said, "I think we're being pursued."

"Just keep walking," David said.

Then a voice from the rear: "How come you guys aren't in the Service?"

"We're 4-E," said David.

"You mean 4-F; there's something wrong with you?"

"No, we're 4-E. We have an exemption because of our graduate studies." They kept walking.

From behind: "That sounds like a good deal. I wish we could have continued our studies."

"We're seminarians, studying for the priesthood," David said.

"I wish I had thought of that when the war started," said the shortest soldier of the four.

By this time, David and Ladd had stopped and were facing the soldiers.

"You can probably still apply for the seminary," said Ladd.

"No, we wouldn't study to be ministers just to avoid the draft."

"We entered the seminary and started to study for the priesthood in 1935, a long time before the war started," David said.

"Well, it's still a good way to avoid military service."

"You can still apply," said Ladd. "The seminary is right up ahead here on Middlefield Road. But it's for the Catholic priesthood. If you want to get out of the service and get into a 'soft life,' you have to promise to be celibate from now on."

The soldiers noticed the edge in Ladd's voice and so did David.

David pulled Ladd by the arm and said, "We had better get back to St. John's. There will be the usual discipline if we're late."

"That comment was probably lost on them, Ladd said wirily. I doubt if they know what the word 'celibate' means. It's three syllables."

. . .

It was the Sulpician tradition to keep seminarians sheltered from "the world." No radios in the seminarians' rooms, no newspapers, no magazines. For all intents and purposes, they were sequestered for twelve years.

The seminarians' link to the outside was a Philco console radio behind the gym. There, they gathered at the half-hour break following breakfast and supper to hear what was happening in a world at war.

They learned about the '40s through the voice of Gabriel Heater intoning, "Oh, there's good news tonight."

They cheered when they heard Eric Sevareid report the carpet bombings of Dresden and Jimmy Doolittle's thirty-second raid on Tokyo -- though years later some of them wondered if such cheering was immoral.

. . .

In the dogmatic theology class on the sacraments, the second theologians were studying the sacrament of penance. Father Reardon had reached the point of priests counseling penitents in the confessional.

"If you are hearing the confession of an adult, man or a woman, marriageable age, and they make no mention in their sins about birth control, it is advisable to put the question to them. This is a serious sin. A marriage couple that keeps contraceptives in their home is obviously committing a premeditated act. There is grave matter, serious reflection and full consent of the will."

"Should we advise a penitent who confesses birth control to study and use a natural form of birth control like the rhythm method?"

"The rhythm method is moral," the priest answered, "because it is a form of birth control which nature provides. However, it is best not voluntarily to introduce the subject of the rhythm method because it is not the ideal. It may cause a married couple gradually to take on a contraceptive mentality."

At this point, Ladd raised his hand. Father Reardon rightly guessed he was in for a challenge. "Yes, Mr. Franklin."

"It seems to me, Father, that we might be making it unnecessarily difficult for a married couple who have too many children -- or some good reason for not having a pregnancy -- if we don't inform them of the moral way they can have sexual intercourse without conception."

"If the penitent brings up the subject, it is certainly all right to let them know that the Church approves of natural birth control, but we must be very careful that we are not encouraging people towards contraception," the professor responded, hoping to end the conversation.

Ladd continued. "Also, why is it, Father, that we are specifically advised to question married people on the subject of birth control? Why is that singled out? If we are going to bring up specific possible sins, shouldn't we question them on other sins, like sins against justice or charity? I mean things like cheating people at work, fighting in the family, or running down a person's reputation in gossip -- those kinds of things."

"Yes, you are probably right. But we do have to move on to the rest of the subject for today."

It was just as well that the dialog ended there. David was about to kick the back of Ladd's chair, since he sensed that things were getting argumentative.

. . .

David and his classmates went through Regina Cleri and St. John's Seminary during what was probably the period of strictest discipline. The Sulpicians ran tight ships.

David could not remember during his six years at Regina Cleri seeing any of his schoolmates smoking on campus - although he suspected that some of this was going on down at the Permanente Creek, which ran south to north through the center of the campus.

At St. John's, smoking was permitted outside the seminary buildings. Only on two or three occasions did David surprise one of his schoolmates, finding them lighting up in their rooms.

It was true that magazines, milkshakes, and other delicacies were, from time to time, smuggled in. For the most part, the rules were effectively enforced.

One of the regulations forbade any seminarians from entering the room of another. This, too, was well observed. David and most of the seminarians surmised that this was a long-standing tradition in Sulpician seminaries to ensure that time was not wasted by social visiting and that good study habits would be maintained.

Particular friendships were strongly discouraged by the faculty. Seminarians were to be inclusive in their friendships, not limiting their relations to a circle of friends. They were all to be brothers to each other.

This rule made sense to David because of the requirements of thoughtfulness and consideration of others in the virtue of charity.

Ladd put an additional interpretation on the rules. He guessed that, because of the centuries of practical experience on the part of the Church generally and the Sulpicians particularly, the rules of not entering another student's room and of not forming special friendships were meant to be a safeguard against personal intimacy.

But homosexuality was a concept not spoken about and hardly even adverted to in their generation.

. . .

The seminarians were not allowed to date; they were not allowed to go to dances.

To be sure, there were relationships in their lives with women: cousins, aunts, sisters, casual friends. They never felt deprived.

Most of them accepted it as the normal condition for becoming a priest.

Just as he never adverted to the fact that he was from a poor family, David did not reflect that he was denied relationships which other young people were routinely enjoying.

. . .

Tyler enjoyed St. John's. He was liked by his classmates and was well thought of by his teachers. They noticed that he applied himself earnestly to everything he was called upon to do.

His efforts were reflected in his improved grades in every subject.

Father Conaty, Tyler's confessor, made a point of encouraging him.

"You are to be commended, Tyler," the priest said, "but you must be good to yourself, too. Remember, we all need relaxation. Do you think you might be a perfectionist, trying to do too much?"

"I take recreation, Father. I play most sports."

"Well, if you find yourself trying to be perfect in everything, stop and think what's driving you."

Tyler wasn't sure he understood what his confessor was trying to tell him, but he would think it over.

In the mild months, when the pool was open, he would relax there. He liked swimming and lying in the sun. That was the Arizonan in him. He wanted to keep his desert tan.

. . .

As the major seminary years passed, David's companions noticed that he was becoming more serious.

Nearly all college juniors and seniors believe they are seeing vistas that no one before them has seen. For David, it was more than that. He enjoyed engaging in philosophical discussions and he worked harder on preparing for class and writing term papers. He was more attentive at lectures and spent a good part of the Thursday holidays studying.

Though David still liked sports, he began to see many games as time-wasting. His focus turned to the priesthood ahead. He began to think of his "career." Without articulating it even to himself, or being conscious of it at all, he was strategizing for advancement. This was contrary to what spiritual directors had encouraged for the past eight years.

The classroom subjects were now more sharply focused on the priesthood.

Epistemology, metaphysics, English language, Church history, dogmatic and moral theology, Sacred Scriptures, elocution, canon law, liturgy and social justice. The courses in the major seminary extended over six years, two in philosophy to complete the bachelor's degree and four graduate years of theology. Tanquerey's three volumes on dogma, three volumes on moral, and one volume on ascetical theology were the basic textbooks. Biology in the fourth year of college completed the natural science cycle begun at Regina Cleri.

David particularly liked the biology classes, but Tyler had problems with some of the laboratory experiments. On the morning the class had to dissect a frog, he wanted to be absent. And in the session for studying the composition of blood under a microscope, Tyler fainted after he pricked his finger.

. . .

Ladd felt he could talk candidly to Father Carlisle. This was a priest who related well to the seminarians. He spoke their language. He joked with them.

"I can see why adultery is wrong, he would confide to the priest. It is a matter of injustice. It steals something from your wife and from the husband of the woman with whom you commit adultery. And I can see how it is sinful to force someone to have sex, even a single person who is an adult.

"But I think it is more difficult to argue against other sex acts just from pure reason. Apart from our Catholic faith, why is it wrong for two single consenting adults to have sex voluntarily?"

Father Carlisle wasn't used to getting questions like this from first theologians. Without having to think about it, his response was, "Fornication is wrong because it is against nature. It hurts human society. It causes habits in a person that later jeopardize a marriage . . . there are lots of reasons why it is wrong."

Ladd could see some validity in these points.

"How about masturbation?" Ladd persisted. "How is that a mortal sin? Mortal sin is supposed to be a deliberate turning away from God. But I can see a person masturbating and still loving God very much."

"Well, it is a terrible way to show God you love Him," Father answered.

That was no answer. In Logic class, they would call that begging the question.

The class discussion went on to other subjects, but Ladd's thought continued on its course. He wondered if he should enliven the class with the story he had heard the day before about the long line waiting for admission at the gate of heaven. They had been standing for hours. Suddenly, there was a loud uproar at the front of the line near the entrance. Shouting . . . clapping . . . hats thrown into the air.

Finally, word passed along from person-to-person to the end of the line.

"What was all the cheering about?" the one bringing up the rear asked the man ahead of him.

"They announced up at the gate that fornication doesn't count!"

Ladd was startled out of his reverie when Gordon raised his hand and the professor acknowledged it.

"There is no real point in this discussion. It is completely theoretical. The fact of the matter is that we have the teaching of the Church on human sexuality. It is based on Sacred Scriptures, the Gospels as well as St. Paul. It has been the constant tradition of the Church supported by Augustine and the Doctors of the Faith. We don't live in a theoretical world. We do not have a 'reason' existence separate from a Faith existence. The teachings on the sinfulness of these sexual acts that we are talking about have stood the test of time and universality."

It was a vintage Gordon Caprice statement and Ladd knew it was directed at him.

Ladd suspected that Gordon was carefully cataloging any inquiry Ladd made about orthodox Church teaching in class discussions.

He also wondered if Gordon was sharing his opinions about Ladd's "heretical leanings" with the faculty.

. . .

St. John's professors gathered for the monthly faculty meeting.

Agenda items ranged from better security on the outside doors of the seminary to consideration of a special eight to eight holiday because of the particularly severe winter just passed.

But the sensitive matter to be faced was the possible expulsion of one of the third theologians.

Father Rector opened the discussion.

"We have had several interventions about the conduct and the attitude of Ladd Franklin. It has been proposed by Father Tilton that Mr. Franklin be considered for expulsion. Would you lead off the discussion, Father Tilton?"

(By long Sulpician tradition, the Rector reserved his comments until last.)

"I think Ladd Franklin is a very gifted young man," Father Tilton began. "He is a good student and he is a good leader."

Then, pausing carefully for the right words on a delicate matter, he continued, "I do not know if you have had the same experience I had, but this seminarian asks questions and offers comments in class which make me wonder about his orthodoxy."

As though in a pre-arranged plan, Father Randall broke in to support Father Tilton's statement.

"I too, have the same concern. Even one of his classmates has come to me on two occasions to contend that he worries about Ladd's obedience to the Magisterium."

The youngest member of the faculty, Father Warner, was next. "It is all well and good to have an inquisitive mind and the courage to ask questions, but Ladd doesn't seem to accept, on faith, the Church's teachings."

Father Domenici reversed the tide somewhat. "Well, I suspect that the seminarian who complained is Gordon Caprice. He is probably the most gifted student we have, but he is rather over-anxious about heresy. Franklin has exceptional potential for leadership. He has a social conscience. Because of his youth, he sees or imagines injustice and hypocrisy quite easily; but I think he is loyal to the Faith."

Father Tilton, who introduced the problem, persisted.

"No, I think it is more than that. Ladd questions our teachings and our rules so often that I wonder why he wants to be a priest."

Father Wallace interrupted, "We must keep in mind that precisely because of his leadership qualities, he is influencing other students to think the way he does. We could have more trouble on our hands than just Ladd Franklin."

Father Compton spoke up for the first time. "Another thing, remember, is the report that we received from Regina Cleri on some incident in Mexico. Something about a house of ill reputed."

"I don't think that was ever substantiated," the Rector reminded his colleagues.

The discussion continued for another fifteen minutes in the same vein.

After a pause in the comments, Father Proctor said, "Well, I do not think we have enough information on this at the present time. We will put off a decision on the matter until a future meeting." The faculty turned to the remaining agenda.

. . .

At the end of the first Theology year, a student was traditionally selected to continue to complete his theological studies at the Casa Maria - the United States Bishops' Seminary in Rome. Because of the war, the archbishop and the faculty had determined that this would not be advisable. Rather, they would send the outstanding student in the first Theology class to Catholic University of America in Washington, D.C., the highest of academic honors for the seminarian who was chosen to attend Theology years at the Sulpician Theological College in Washington.

In the minds of most seminarians and probably the faculty, the choice had narrowed down to Gordon Caprice and David Carmichael.

On the first day of May in 1943, the announcement was made.

"The Basselin Scholarship for the fall semester at Theological College in Washington, D.C., has been awarded to Gordon Caprice. Mr. Caprice will begin studies at Theological College in the fall semester."

Though he was disappointed, David wasn't overly upset by the decision. He had come to recognize Gordon's exceptional talent. Besides, he had become attached to St. John Seminary and his friends there.

CHAPTER 15

Heading southeast from Tucson to Mountain View and Sonoita, Tyler drove through rolling mountains and hills covered with high desert scrub brush.

In Sonoita, he climbed to 5,000 feet. Wide horizons in all four directions were capped by massive roiling, boiling thunderstorm clouds. To the west, lightning crackled from white and gray cloud billows to the peaks of the Santa Rita mountains.

Southeast Arizona skies and landscapes that day were, at the same time, soothing, angry and violent. The jagged mountains were dramatic in their contours.

The measurement of the distance from lightning is the time span between the sight of the lightning and the sound of the thunder. That time span can be as much as ten seconds for lightning seen on the far horizon.

Just north of Harshaw, Tyler knew that he was in the immediate vicinity of lightning. The lightning flash and thunder exploded at the same instant, though he didn't know what it struck. That lightning bolt couldn't have been more than yards or even feet away.

And then came the Arizona monsoon.

The wind racing from east to west was sweeping the sand, undisturbed through the long dry spring and early summer months, across the highway on both sides of the road. The mesquite trees were fiercely agitated. Sage brush tumbled across the highway, the first drops of rain splattered on Tyler's windshield. To the south, lightning squeezed from the clouds in crazy patterns against the graying skies.

Here and there, a flying hawk struggled unsuccessfully against the wind.

Suddenly, the rains hit and the washes were running full as Tyler pulled into Kateri Tekakwitha end-of-summer camp.

Tyler had volunteered to serve as a camp counselor for two weeks.

His days consisted of organizing activities for the 10 to 15 year old campers - boys the first week, girls the second.

The hours were long supervising hikes in the Patagonia Mountains, swimming lessons at the camp lake, patrolling the bunk beds, and sleeping bag dormitories.

. . .

The first Friday night of the summer camp, a fight broke out in the girls' locker room.

Lauren Collins, a first year camper, was the one who told Tyler.

"There are three girls fighting in the showers - you'd better get in there and break it up."

Tyler moved fast, left the reports he was working on at his desk, looked briefly for one of the women counselors, and finding none, ran to the locker room with Lauren following.

Two of the campers were wrestling on the floor; a third was trying to pull the bigger girl off the smaller scuffler. Four or five other campers were standing around, some wrapped in towels, enjoying the fight.

Tyler pushed aside the apparent peace-maker and got a headlock on the older girl. When the battler recognized it was the camp counselor who had a hold on her, she loosened her grip on her opponent and the fighters were separated.

Tyler turned toward the crowd and said, "Finish up here, get dressed and return to your bunks."

He turned to the two girls standing in front of him and said, "What is this all about?"

Predictably both of them said, "She started it."

"Well, we're not going to settle this tonight. But I want to see both of you in the Camp Director's office tomorrow morning immediately after breakfast."

Tyler liked working with young people. He admired them. He felt himself even envying them. It occurred to him that he really didn't have adolescence like they seemed to be enjoying.

He got along well with young people, probably because the young people recognized that Tyler, unlike older people, had an unusual respect for them. As time passed, Tyler realized that he felt more at home with young women and young men than he did with adults. He enjoyed the company of young women.

Tyler seemed cemented in adolescence. He still had the tastes of a 14-year old.

He had been afraid to try the risks of boyhood for fear of upsetting his mother.

. . .

Because they had no other way to get there, Tyler agreed to drive two of the girls home at the end of camp. The first, Norma, was from Nogales, a city divided by the Mexican-Arizona border. Before she was taken in by a compassionate Mexican family, Norma had run with the "tunnel rats" - homeless youths who inhabit the underground passageways connecting Sonora, Mexico, with Arizona. These youngsters, separated from their families, frequently harassed tourists and Latin Americans illegally crossing the border into the United States.

Leaving Norma with her new family in Nogales, Tyler and Esther traveled Tombstone, the fabled town of Wyatt Earp, his brothers, and Doc Holliday.

From Bisbee and Douglas, Tyler angled northeast across the New Mexico state line to Lordsburg and Silver City.

The topography of Silver City, Clifton and Morenci is breathtaking. The two travelers had a sense of being on another planet in these mining towns, with their sheer cliffs, and jagged hills – all remnants of ice glaciers, earthquakes and other cataclysms in the passage of millions of years.

Tyler drove east to catch the Rio Grande River and the main highway through Truth or Consequences, where the fabled river widens into the Caballo Reservoir and Elephant Butte Lake; on to old Albuquerque with historic St. Philip of Neri Church facing the town square.

In Santa Fe, Tyler dropped Esther off across the street from the greater than life bronze statue of J.B. Lamy, first Archbishop of the Southwest, standing guard in front of his cathedral.

Though it took him far out of his way on the return trip to San Francisco, Tyler had welcomed the chance to travel to Nogales and Santa Fe with Norma and Esther.

Esther was a strikingly beautiful, personable young girl.

Tyler was young enough to have the same interests as the high school senior. Though he was not normally loquacious around adults, he and Esther carried on a lively conversation during the entire journey through the southwest desert from Nogales to Santa Fe.

Tyler continued on through pueblo-style dwellings on Route 68 to meet with friends at the Pueblo de Taos Indian Reservation in Kit Carson country.

On Highway 64, crossing the Rio Grande gorge, he headed due west through Jicarilla Apache territory to Farmington, past Shiprock which dominates the horizon near Four Corners, then down the Devil's Highway, 666, to Gallup.

Finally west through Navajo, Hopi and Zuni country to Tuba City and the south rim of the Grand Canyon, where the autumn colored strata on walls rising from 1300 feet at the bottom to 7400 feet at the rim, tell the story of 2 billion years.

. . .

At St. John's, the rector convened the first faculty meeting of the new semester, opening with a prayer and making several routine announcements. After attending to minor agenda items, Father Proctor one again brought up the issue of Ladd Franklin."

Father Wallace spoke first.

"I do not know if any member of the faculty spoke to Mr. Franklin, but I must say that I do not detect any change in his attitude. I am of the same mind that he is not a suitable candidate for the priesthood. I move for his expulsion." Father Randall seconded the motion.

"You have heard the motion," Father Proctor said. "The floor is open for discussion."

"Must we bring this to the point of expulsion? Father Clancy asked. Might it be better to give Franklin a strong lecture and clip him from the next minor orders that he is to receive?"

"Clipping" meant denying a seminarian from advancing in the ranks he must achieve on the way to priesthood. It was a serious sanction. Ladd would be denied ordination to Porter and Exorcist when his class received these minor ordinations.

Father Carlisle spoke.

"I think that would only delay the problem. Mr. Franklin has repeatedly questioned authority, and I think the longer that we let it go; the more it is going to give bad example to his classmates and jeopardize the morale of the community. I call for the question."

Father Proctor waited to hear if there would be other statements. Hearing none, he said, "I have my own reservations for taking the drastic step of expulsion in this case, but I will accede to the vote of the faculty."

"All those in favor of expulsion, signify by writing a 'yes' on a piece of paper from the pad in front of you. Those opposed to expulsion, write 'no'. If any of you wish to abstain from the vote, write 'abstain'.

"Father Domenici, would you and Father Kavitz act as tellers and collect and count the votes?"

The two youngest priests rose from the table, gathered the slips of paper, went to the far end of the room and began to make the tally.

There was silence in the room while the count was being taken.

Father Domenici came back to the table, stood beside the Rector and said, "The vote is six for expulsion, four against and one abstention."

The Rector said, "The vote is so noted and will be recorded in the minutes by the secretary. I will inform Mr. Franklin that he is to leave the seminary at the end of this semester."

There was uneasiness in the room as the faculty turned back to its agenda.

· · ·

A note came to the prefect on the third floor, Philosophy side. Father Rauch walked down the corridor and slipped the note under Ladd's door.

"Ladd Franklin: Be at my office this afternoon at the beginning of recreation." It was signed, "Father James Proctor, Rector."

The Rector! Seminarians did not get notes directly from the head of the seminary. Ladd knew this meant trouble.

At the break after lunch, he stopped David and told him about the summons.

"I'll bet, before he left for Washington, Gordon told somebody on the faculty about Tijuana. I am probably going to be expelled."

"It could be anything, Ladd. No use thinking the worst."

"You know Gordon – he's a stickler for the rules. "Gordon isn't a snitch," David said.

"No, but he thinks his conscience tells him it is his duty not to let unfit people get into the priesthood."

"Well, all you can do is wait till 3 o'clock and then see what it's all about. If it will do any good, I'll stand up for you, Ladd."

During that early afternoon, Ladd saw everything around the seminary differently; the olive trees in the courtyard, the water tower, the chapel. Liturgy class was a blur. He couldn't focus on the textbook. The lecture was a droning sound in the distance. Ladd began to think of the future. He looked across the classroom at David, then at Tyler, and knew how much he was going to miss his friends.

They had become his brothers. The seminary had become his home.

. . .

Promptly at three, Ladd knocked on the Rector's door. What Ladd had been anxious about since Tijuana was finally to happen.

But it was not the episode in Mexico that caused the axe to fall.

"Mr. Franklin, the faculty has determined that it is in your best interest and the best interest of the seminary that you do not return to St. John's after this semester."

That sinking feeling in the stomach returned, and Ladd's face flushed.

"It is the mind of the faculty," Father Proctor continued, "that you do not have the right attitude toward the Magisterium of the Church. It is the belief of the faculty that you would not be happy in the priesthood or effective as a teacher, since you do not have wholehearted convictions about the Church's official teaching."

The reasons took Ladd completely by surprise. He had no response.

"I am sorry to give you this news; but, as a faculty, we think this is for the best. A number of the professors spoke of the strong gifts and talents that you possess; but the faculty is convinced that you would not find the priesthood fulfilling."

Ladd had no arguments to address this position. He got up to leave.

"If there's anything I can do to help you in the days ahead, just let me know."

"Thank you, Father." And Ladd went to the door.

He found his way to David's room, knocked on the door and, standing on the threshold, said, "I just came from Father Proctor's room. I have to leave the seminary."

"What?"

"I'm to be expelled at the end of this term."

"What for?"

"The faculty thinks that I do not support the teaching of the Church."

"Oh, this is all wrong," David exclaimed. "You're a better person for the priesthood than I am. Listen, Ladd, have you told this to anyone yet?"

"No, I came right down to your room from the Rector's office."

"Well, don't tell anybody, absolutely anybody. We've got to think what we are going to do about this."

CHAPTER 16

Ladd lay awake for hours that night. He knew he would miss the friends he had come to know at Regina Cleri and St. John's - especially David.

He wondered if he should learn not to speak his mind. Perhaps his insights were not that brilliant and would be better left unsaid.

How would his parents take the news? His sister, Laura, would tell him he was better off out of the seminary.

He turned over in his bed and heard the distant melancholy whistle of a train, probably crossing the intersection of Oak Park Road in Menlo Park. "Hear that lonely whistle, calling cross a trestle, my mama done tole me . . ."

. . .

The Archbishop maintained a residence on the seminary grounds, and David knew the prelate was scheduled for a meeting there with several suffragan bishops on Monday. He would find a way to talk to the Archbishop. He might also get a chance to meet some of the other members of the hierarchy.

On the weekend, David slipped into the refectory and asked one of the kitchen Sisters if he could help them in serving the bishops at their luncheon break. Sister, surprised by this unexpected thoughtfulness, accepted David's offer, although she didn't know exactly how she would use the extra hand.

Monday came and David was enlisted to carry china and silverware from the professor's refectory to the residence dining room.

David's second trip across the Theology yard coincided with the arrival of the Archbishop and his priest secretary.

"Father Ratelli, may I see you for a minute?"

"Yes, what can I do for you?" the priest answered.

The Archbishop had already entered the house.

"I'd like a chance to talk to the Archbishop sometime today. It would be only for a minute or two."

"It looks like you're carrying supplies into the residence. The Archbishop will be busy once the meeting starts. You might try to catch him now."

David didn't know if he was prepared on such sudden notice. But this was the opportunity.

He reached the Archbishop at the foot of the stairs in the residence lobby.

"Your Excellency, could I speak to you for a moment?"

"What is it?"

"I am a seminarian and I have a friend, also a third theologian."

David plunged on because the Archbishop was moving up the steps.

"The faculty is about to expel him. His name is Ladd Franklin. I think it would be a great mistake. Ladd could be one of your best priests. Everyone knows that he is very talented."

"I don't interfere with the decisions of the faculty. That is their job - to determine who is qualified."

"But, Archbishop, I wish you could at least look into it or have one of your staff look into it."

"Talk to Father Ratelli about it, son."

"Thank you, Archbishop. My name is David Carmichael."

David knew he wouldn't be able to get out of the seminary to see Father Ratelli at the Chancery in San Francisco. On the lobby table, he left the tablecloths and silverware he had held during the conversation with Archbishop McHenry and went directly to the driveway circle where the priest secretary was still gathering briefcases and several manila folders from the Lincoln Continental.

"The Archbishop told me to bring the matter to you . . . Can I help with those materials?"

"Here, take these file folders and follow me. I'm getting things ready for the meeting, so we had better talk while we're walking."

David started again, "I told the Archbishop that the faculty here is expelling a classmate and it is a big mistake because this seminarian, Ladd Franklin, is really a good man. He will be a great priest."

Father Ratelli was clearly distracted with all the details of the meeting.

"Send me a brief letter with the name of the seminarian and the basic facts."

"At the Chancery?"

"Yes, but it would be a good idea not to tell anyone that you talked to the Archbishop about the subject. It would make the situation awkward."

Father Ratelli went on into the residence living room.

David was glad he had a chance to greet several other Ordinaries and auxiliary bishops as he left by way of the front steps. He was in awe of them.

. . .

Before he left the seminary grounds, Father Ratelli checked the roster of students' rooms on his own without consulting the seminary office.

He climbed the stairs to the third floor and knocked on Ladd's door.

Ratelli felt he had to see the seminarian in question and size him up, at least briefly.

Ladd came to the door.

"I'm Father Ratelli. Are you Ladd Franklin?"

"Yes, Father," Ladd answered. Ladd and the seminarians all knew who the young secretary was.

"Your name has come to my attention. I understand that you are being asked to leave the seminary."

"Yes, at the end of the semester."

Ladd told the priest that the faculty didn't think he had the right attitude and that he questioned the teachings of the Church.

"Do you?"

"Do I question the teachings of the Church? Yes, if I don't see the reason for a particular teaching, I question it."

"Can you give me an example?"

"The other day, I asked our Apologetics teacher if it wouldn't be better to cooperate with the other Christian religions, and try to bring us together rather than always refuting them and keeping them at a distance?'"

"Do you question any of the articles of the Apostles' Creed or the Nicene Creed?"

"No." I just want to understand the reasons we teach what we teach -- and can we do better."

"Do you love the Church?"

"Yes."

"Do you want to be a priest?"

"Yes."

"I will have to leave now. I think it will be best for everybody if you let our conversation remain between the two of us. In fact, at this time, it will be better all-around if neither you nor the faculty talk to anyone about your expulsion."

It was the same advice David had given. David seemed to think like bishops and bishops' secretaries.

"A faculty is in the best position to know the seminarians. Bishops expect them to make the right decisions and bishops do not want to undermine the faculty's authority, the priest secretary added."

As the priest left the room, he turned to Ladd and said, "I will look into this further."

. . .

Gordon had enrolled at Catholic University of American in Washington, D.C. for the fall semester. He would live across Michigan Avenue from the C.U.A. campus at Theological College and receive spiritual formation there. His classes would be at the university.

Each day, he walked to the campus between Gibbons and Graduate Halls, passed Albert and the Mullen Library to Caldwell Hall and McMahon, and the administration building.

Gordon was impressed with the beauty of the university complex, the brick and field stone buildings, the expanse of lawns, and the splendor of color in the fall foliage throughout the Nation's Capital.

Students were not permitted to have automobiles at Theological College, so on weekends Gordon took the Michigan streetcar down

North Capitol Avenue and visited various sites; the Smithsonian Institute, the Mellon Gallery, the Lincoln, Washington and Jefferson Memorials, and the White House.

Through his attorney-father in California, he obtained a gallery ticket to a joint session of Congress addressed by President Roosevelt.

Among his teachers at the university were such celebrated churchmen as Monsignor Fulton J. Sheen, Father Ignatius Smith, Dom Vernon Moore, and Monsignor John Tracy Ellis.

He came to know priests, Religious Sisters, Brothers and seminarians from nearly every state in the union.

In his priesthood, he knew that he would have a "home away from home" in most dioceses of the United States because of these acquaintances.

. . .

That same fall, Tyler's mother moved from Tucson to San Francisco to be near her son. At that point, Tyler appealed to the Bishop of Tucson to allow him to study for the Archdiocese of San Francisco. Although Arizona Bishop Leroux was reluctant to lose a good prospect for the priesthood, he granted Tyler his request.

Tyler would now be ministering in the same diocese as the many friends he had made in the seminary, but his love for Arizona made it sad for his native state.

. . .

The weeks had passed. Ladd was psychologically in a state of suspension.

It was difficult to give undivided attention to class work, to liturgy, even to sports when he knew he would be asked to leave the seminary at the Christmas break.

He found a note under his door on a Monday morning, directing him to report to the Rector's office at two o'clock that afternoon.

This was it. From past experience, he knew that expulsions take place immediately. He suspected that the faculty had decided to dismiss him now, rather than waiting until the end of the term. It was just as well. Ladd could make provisions for continuing his studies at an outside university or finding work between now and the new semester.

At two o'clock, he knocked at the door of Father Proctor's office and heard the familiar baritone voice:

"Come in, Ladd."

Ladd thought to himself "That is the first time he has called me by my first name. He is trying to let me down easy."

"Sit down, Ladd. I want to talk to you about this matter of expulsion."

"Yes, Father."

"The faculty has reconsidered and decided to let you continue your studies for the priesthood, if that is your wish."

Ladd's heart stopped.

"I don't think the Archbishop would want me telling you this, because he wanted you to understand that this is a faculty decision, not his; but his office interceded for you and asked the faculty to reconsider. I have discussed the Archbishop's intervention with the faculty. I must say that a large majority of the professors stated that they were personally relieved that the Archbishop had made this decision. I feel the same way. I believe we may have been hasty in making our original decision. The faculty is of a mind that you are a good candidate for ordination and we wish you well."

Ladd was too overcome to respond. Stammering a muffled thank-you he added, "I will try to do my best."

He supposed that the conversation had been concluded, so he rose from the chair and began to back out of the room as quickly as he could - before the Rector could change his mind.

Ladd went directly to David's room, because he knew it was through David's intercession that the expulsion had been reversed.

When David heard the news, he was probably happier about it than Ladd.

"That's great, Ladd. I knew the Archbishop would think that way. Father Ratelli must have given you a good report."

As Father Ratelli had recommended, reports of the impending expulsion had not circulated among the student body. Nobody lost face.

CHAPTER 17

Tyler's perfectionism was intensifying in the last semester of the Deacon year. His room was the neatest in seminary. He was not satisfied with "A-minus" grades.

For the final examinations before ordination, he began to "cram", studying late into the night, making last minute reviews of his outlines before each test. Inevitably, overload set in.

In the last week of May, ten minutes into Dogmatic Theology finals, Tyler experienced total blockage.

He had made a cursory reading of the ten essay-type questions and then returned to the first to begin his answers, unable to retrieve the points he had meticulously outlined the night before.

He moved to the second question and the block was there also. His learning had been mechanical, not a grasp of information absorbed as knowledge.

The more he reached, the more the facts withdrew. The first flush of panic spread over Tyler.

So important had succeeding become that, for the first time, the temptation to cheat crossed his mind. This was against everything in his nature, but all he needed was a jump-start. If he could see the first section of the outline on the grace tract, the rest would come back to him.

He despised himself for what he was thinking, but if he failed this exam, he would be brooding over it for weeks.

He stood up, asked the professor prefect if he could be excused to go to the bathroom. Once outside the classroom, he hurried to his own room, found the outline paper he needed and scanned it.

What he had expected proved true. The first few paragraphs brought the whole sequence of outlines back to his memory.

Tyler did well in the exam, but the feeling of guilt clung to him.

. . .

The final months before ordination were particularly hectic for the ordinandi.

Each seminarian began practicing Mass on makeshift altars, rehearsing baptisms by pouring water on dolls, and deciding on the design of a personal chalice all the while taking final and oral exams.

When David was practicing anointing with the simulated oils of Extreme Unction, Ladd, straight-faced, needled him. "You should be rehearsing anointing for Confirmation and Ordination. You will be a bishop someday."

"Knock it off," Secretly, David liked the remark.

The faculty had the uncanny ability to keep the deacons guessing as to whether they would be approved for priesthood ordination up to the last moment. The anxiety built day after day even though invitations had already been mailed, vestments purchased, first Mass preachers selected. By ordination morning, the candidates were shaken, on edge and at the lowest weight they would be for the rest of their lives.

The anxiety broke out on Ladd in the form of a rash on his hands and forearms.

The affliction had its benefits, however. The doctor, Roger Guerrero who served the seminary from San Jose, ordered Ladd to see a dermatologist in San Francisco.

The treatments required three Thursday visits to the City from mid-April till the end of May.

Despite the precariousness of final approval for ordination, Ladd managed to sneak in three movies, "Going My Way," "A Tree Grows in Brooklyn," and "Wilson" during his trip to San Francisco.

. . .

Tyler felt the pressure more severely. Around March, he began to feel he couldn't keep up with all that had to be done, finding it more difficult to concentrate. As the date of ordination drew nearer, he failed to complete assignments, lost confidence in himself, and eventually doubted that he could carry out all the demanding duties of a priest.

Tyler began to reflect on other jobs he might do for a living - jobs that would not require decision-making like driving a truck or taking toll fares on the Golden Gate or Bay Bridges.

Tyler was paralyzed and finally poured it all out to his priest confessor.

"I think I should leave the seminary, Father."

"Do you want to be a priest?" Father LeMay asked.

"That's all I've ever wanted to be."

"Well then, plunge ahead. God will see you through."

Tyler held on.

PART II

CHAPTER 18

On the morning of ordination, the class of 1946 boarded the Southern Pacific commuter train at Menlo Park at 6:30 a.m.

This was the day toward which their last eleven years had been aimed - nearly half of their young lives. Most of them were gaunt and pale after eleven years of studies and deprivation. The pressure had been building.

Ladd was relaxed. David was tense, but looking forward to the big day. Tyler had hardly touched the early breakfast served the ordinandi in the small refectory.

During the past months, a panic attack was gradually enveloping Tyler. But he was "holding on" as his confessor had advised.

The commuter rolled through Redwood City, San Carlos, San Mateo, Burlingame, San Bruno, South San Francisco, and into the Third & Townsend Streets Station.

From there, the soon-to-be-priests took a chartered bus through downtown San Francisco to O'Farrell and Franklin and Holy Trinity Cathedral.

In the church's basement or lower hall, the three friends picked out a corner and began to vest, adjusting their amices around the shoulders of their cassocks, then the long white linen alb bound at the waist with the cincture, the maniple on the left forearm, and finally the deacon stole over the left shoulder and crossed on the right side at the hip.

When the procession started to the upper church, David, Ladd and Tyler, who were of nearly equal height, were together in the single file line.

. . .

At the end of the procession, in the liturgical position of honor, walked Jose Gutierrez "by the grace of God and the favor of the Apostolic See", Archbishop of San Francisco."

At the appearance of the Archbishop, the Cathedral choir broke out with a robust "Ecce Sacerdos Magnus," ("Behold the High Priest").

The Archbishop walked the length of the middle aisle, trailing the long magenta train of silk, which, as the prelate entered the sanctuary, was gathered and folded on the arm of a boy train-bearer, who then sat at the foot of the episcopal throne.

When the prelate had re-vested for Mass the ordination rite began with masters of ceremonies, deacons, subdeacons, acolytes, gremial bearer, bugia bearer and other ministers at their proper places around the ordaining prelate.

The candidates were called forth by one of the ministers.

"Those to be ordained priests, please come forward."

One by one, each answered: "Adsum - Present" and walked to the Archbishop where he bowed in reverence.

When the candidates were in their places, the seminary rector addressed the Archbishop:

"Most Reverend Father, holy mother Church asks you to ordain these men, our brothers, for service as priests."

The Archbishop asked: "Do you judge them to be worthy?"

The rector answered: "After inquiry among the people of God and upon recommendation of those concerned with their training, I testify that they have been found worthy."

Archbishop: "We rely on the help of the Lord God and our Savior Jesus Christ, and we choose these men, our brothers, for priesthood in the presbyteral order."

The Archbishop then addressed the congregation in the duties of a priest:

"These men, your relatives and friends, are now to be raised to the order of priests. Consider carefully the position to which they are to be promoted in the Church.

"It is true that God has made His entire people a royal priesthood in Christ. But our High Priest, Jesus Christ, also chose some of His followers to carry out publicly in the Church a priestly ministry in His name on behalf of mankind."

He then focused his attention on the twenty-three young men:

"My sons, you are now to be advanced to the order of presbyterate. Meditate on the law of God, believe what you read, teach what you believe, and put into practice what you teach.

"When you baptize, you will bring men and women into the people of God. In the sacrament of penance, you will forgive sins in the name of Christ and the Church. With holy oil you will relieve and console the sick. You will celebrate the liturgy, praying not only for the people of God but for the whole world.

"Always remember the example of the Good Shepherd who came not to be served but to serve, and to seek out and rescue those who were lost."

Then each one of the candidates approached the Archbishop and, kneeling before him, placed his joined hands between those of the prelate, who asked:

"Do you promise respect and obedience to me and my successors?"

David and each of the men to be ordained responded:

"I do."

Finally, the Archbishop said to each:

"May God Who has begun the good work in you bring it to fulfillment."

During the litany imploring the intercession of the saints, the twenty-three stretched out prostrate, face down, on the marble sanctuary floor in a gesture of humility.

The choir continued the long list of saints: "St. Peter . . ." and the congregation answered: "Pray for us."

"St. Paul . . . Pray for us . . . St. Andrew . . . Pray for us . . ."

. . .

While David wanted to concentrate on the precious moment that was occurring, Tyler was still living in a fog. Often, when a person is at the ritual crossroads of his life, he is so preoccupied and anxious about the rubrics that he misses all awareness of the moment.

This event on a June morning in 1946 was the goal and objective of most of his conscious life thus far. This ceremony would determine the course of his life from now on.

. . .

David felt the strong hands of the Archbishop on his head. That solemn moment!

It was in that very moment he became a priest, the moment when he was given what is not given to angels - that he should now be able to offer God to God.

The Archbishop, then, placed his hands on the shoulders of each new priest in the sign of peace: "Pax tecum." "Et cum spiritu tuo," they responded."

. . .

At the end of the lengthy invocation, the Archbishop stood and prayed:

"Come to our help, Lord, holy Father, almighty and eternal God; You are the source of every honor and dignity, of all progress and stability . . .

"Lord, grant also to us such fellow workers, for we are weak and our need is greater . . . Amen."

After this essential prayer of consecration, the Archbishop anointed with chrism oil the palms of each man as he knelt before him.

The ordinandi then offered their first Solemn Mass with the Archbishop.

. . .

At the conclusion of the Mass, the parents and families of the newly ordained approached the altar rail and knelt to receive the first priestly blessing of their sons and brothers.

David felt the catch in his throat and the tears welling as he cupped his hands on his mother's head and then his brother's and gave them his first priestly blessing.

Tyler's emotions were on the surface also.

Though his mother felt warm pride of the moment for what her son had accomplished, she was in control of her feelings.

Tyler wept, openly.

Ladd received a kiss from his mother and sisters, and boisterous hand clasps from his father and brothers.

The swell of the Cathedral organ flooded the church, continuing the recessional hymn, "Another Christ, Anointed Priest Thou Art."

The twenty-three had entered the Cathedral not much more than boys; now, two and a half hours later, they left as "presbyters", that is "elders".

CHAPTER 19

His mother and brother's ordination gift to David was a personal chalice.

David had selected a chalice, a model of which he had found in a Belgian religious art catalog.

Its base and cup were gold plated, the base quadrangular, the cup a bowl rather than the traditional tulip shape.

The stem of the chalice was ivory, its four sides adorned with gold plated medallions with the images of Christ: Mary, the mother of Jesus; St. Francis, the patron of David's archdiocese; and St. Elizabeth, the patron saint of David's mother.

On the bottom of the base was welded his widowed mother's wedding ring.

. . .

It was a memorable occasion for the Carmichael family, relatives and friends and for the Catholic community of the Napa Valley. David offered his first Mass. Charcoal and aromatic incense, the parish choir, resplendent chasuble, dalmatic, and tunic, the sermon by a renowned Doctor of Canon Law all symbols that illuminated the Mass.

David had rehearsed carefully for his first Mass. He had never been asked to join the seminary choir and was never comfortable about his singing voice.

But he did sing the opening prayer, the "Collect," and intoned in Gregorian Chant the "Gloria in Excelsis Deo" and "Credo".

It was the Preface for the Sunday liturgy that tripped him up. He had practiced it well but when the time came, Archpriest Father John

Wells opened the altar missal to the page marked by a slender red ribbon.

Then David realized that it was the Sunday within the octave of the Sacred Heart - a special Sunday with a preface of its own. David didn't recognize the notes at all. The Preface is a complex chant for a beginner, and David complicated it even more.

He stumbled through it and pressed on to that hushed moment of the consecration of the unleavened wheat wafer and the wine into the Body and Blood of Christ.

David was in the first fervor of ordination when a priest is often closer to the Lord than at any other time.

He whispered the all-powerful "Hoc est enim Corpus Meum" and "Hic est enim Calix Sanguinis Mei," holding his breath. "This is My Body; This is the Chalice of My Blood."

Later in life his hands would be casual upon the White Wafer of Bread. But at this instant he was consumed with the awesome ability that had been given him.

His young hands trembled as he placed the consecrated Hosts on old and young tongues at Communion time.

A reception followed in the parish hall and with hands still moist from the chrism oil the day before, he blessed long lines of relatives and friends, some of whom, in the old tradition, kissed the palms of his anointed hands.

. . .

At six o'clock the next morning, as promised, David said his first low Mass at the Sisters' convent where he had attended school just twelve years before.

Strangely enough, this single quiet Mass at dawn in a convent chapel impacted the new priest even more forcibly than the splendid liturgies of the two previous days.

Perhaps it was because, without distraction, he could focus intimately on the enormity of the Mass.

In keeping with long-standing custom, the Sisters had prepared breakfast for their new priest. And by equally long-standing custom, they did not sit and eat with him, but hovered about, making sure that everything was proper.

. . .

That the brand new priests were really not yet "elders" was apparent in the fact that they vacationed after ordination at Santa Cruz beach, swimming in the surf, riding the giant roller coaster at the boardwalk, enjoying restaurant dinners, staying up late, and sleeping late.

It was a time of liberation after 11 years of Spartan existence.

Once they were in their parishes for the first time in their lives, they could come and go as they liked as adults. True, there would be the 11 p.m. curfew, but they could call up one another and go out to a movie after evening marriage and convert instructions.

They would even have access to a refrigerator in the rectory kitchen any time, day or night.

The morning San Francisco Examiner and Chronicle would be available at the breakfast table; in the evening, the San Francisco News and Call Bulletin. No more ban on listening to the radio.

. . .

The Archbishop, in his private office at the Chancery, handed business-sized envelopes to each of the newly ordained shortly after their vacations ended

The priests were anxious to slit open the envelopes to find where they would be living and working for the next several years. It could be anywhere in 13 counties of Northern California, but the Archbishop was talking and they judged it was not appropriate to be looking into their envelopes at that moment.

Each was handed a sheet of "faculties," which enumerated the powers they possessed in exercising their priesthood. Other pages of instruction and regulations were circulated to the 23 young men as the Archbishop proceeded to give fatherly advice about observing the curfew hour, being faithful to their daily Mass and prayers, reading the Breviary, keeping up their studies, obeying their pastors, and being kind to the people.

The advice was, for the most part, muffled by the overwhelming curiosity about what was contained in the envelope that lay on the desk before each of the new priests. Finally, they were dismissed with a blessing from the Archbishop and herded into the corridor outside his office.

Tyler caught up to David and Ladd as they left the Chancery building. The three friends tore open their envelopes together.

"The Most Reverend Archbishop is pleased to appoint you to . . ."

"I'm going to St. Luke's here in the City," David said. "Where is that?"

Ladd, the San Franciscan, said, "That's a parish out in the Sunset District. I'm going to St. Gregory's, in the Richmond District."

"What's yours say, Tyler?" asked David.

"Mine is Holy Rosary in San Bruno."

"That's good," Ladd said. "We'll all be close together."

"I wonder what our pastors will be like."

"I've got Father Gerald Archer for a pastor," David said. "Whom did you get, Tyler?"

"It's Father Todd O'Reilly. I remember hearing that he is a saintly guy that the people like very much. Who's the pastor at your place, Ladd?"

"According to the appointment letter, his name is Father Richard Preston. I don't know who he is, do you?"

David and Tyler didn't know him either but would soon find that Preston had a reputation for being demanding of his assistant pastors.

"I heard Gordon's boss will be Monsignor Everett Montgomery at the Cathedral. I bet Gordon will be sent away soon for studies and get a special office job in the Chancery," David said.

. . .

Father Todd O'Reilly, Tyler's pastor, was a distinguished scholar, a quiet man whom Tyler, over the months, came to revere. He was a thoughtful, caring priest who returned the affection for his new assistant.

At the downtown Cathedral, Gordon admired the Rector, Monsignor Montgomery, who served as Vicar General.

The Chancellor and other heads of diocesan departments immediately recognized Gordon's talents.

For his pastor, Ladd had drawn Father Preston, an energetic, well-disciplined man who prided himself on his strength and his appearance.

"Father Preston likes to think of himself as younger than he is," Ladd told David. "I've heard him claim to parishioners that he's 45 years old. I think he must be counting the years in Centigrade, rather than Fahrenheit."

Preston was also a rigorist who considered it his duty to acclimate the young priests with strict regulations.

Among other rules, he enforced the 11 o'clock nightly curfew, which Ladd had, on several occasions, come close to violating. Twice, only by leaving gatherings of his priest friends abruptly, did he make it home to his St. Gregory's rectory minutes before the clock struck the curfew hour.

On a Monday night in early September, he was delayed in a traffic log-jam, caused by an accident at Park Presidio and Geary Boulevard, and arrived at the rectory at 11:10. He tried the key in the front door but the dead bolt had been thrown. The pastor had engaged the lock at the back door also.

Reluctantly, he pushed the front door bell, listening to the chimes ringing inside. But nothing happened.

He rang again. Still, no answer. He knew the pastor was home upstairs. Father Preston had warned him about coming in late.

This time, after five more minutes, he pushed the button repeatedly as if in an emergency.

Finally, a light came on in the inner hallway and Ladd fearfully jumped away from the door and back behind the high shrubbery near the entrance.

Father Preston slid the dead bolt, cracked the door open slightly, saw no one and walked cautiously out to the door-step.

In his pajamas, bathrobe and slippers, the exasperated pastor strode to the street looking up and down the sidewalk to find the intruder.

It was not pre-meditated, but Ladd could not resist the temptation. He darted out from behind the shrubs, into the house, closed the door and shut the dead bolt.

In his compassion, hearing the doorbell ring furiously after long intervals on four occasions, Ladd finally opened the door and admitted the pastor. Without a word, Father Preston marched upstairs. Ladd knew there would be more to it than that.

The report was circulating in the Chancery Office and the Cathedral the next morning.

Gordon Caprice was one of the first to hear.

. . .

The most unnerving moment in the early days of David's priesthood was on the first Saturday of his assignment at St. Luke's Church.

He had not yet turned 25 years of age, and he was now sitting in a confessional box to hear men, women, and children pour out their most intimate sins and failings.

Would he be able to give the proper advice? Would he be able to judge the sincerity of the sorrow and the firm purpose of amendment of life of each penitent?

On this first Saturday of July, David heard the first penitent come in and kneel in the compartment to his right. He slid open the panel and heard a woman's voice on the other side of the screen.

"Bless me, Father, for I have sinned. It has been over a year since my last confession."

Why did his first confession have to be from someone who was away from the sacraments for so long?

The penitent began disclosing her sins over the past twelve months. It had been an adventurous twelve months. The woman cataloged nearly every sin that David had studied in Moral Theology. To this litany of offenses, the woman added some sins of her past life, already confessed. This practice gave scrupulous persons a feeling of certainty about God' forgiveness.

David was sweating with anxiety by the end of the confession, hardly knowing what to give in the way of counseling.

He mumbled a few words of encouragement gave 20 Our Fathers and 20 Hail Mary's for a penance and read the prayer of absolution, by which God forgives sin through the instrumentality of the priest. He had to read the absolution from a card, because he had not yet memorized it.

Through the screen, from the woman came the formula for the Act of Contrition, "O my God, I am heartily sorry for having offended Thee, and I detest all my sins because I fear the loss of heaven and the pains of hell . . ." At that point, David was finishing the absolution prayer in Latin.

With as gentle a voice as he could muster, he said, "God bless you," and slid the panel closed.

Taking a deep breath, he opened the panel on the opposite side. It was a child's voice, and he thanked God.

The confessions went on till near dinner time. But there was nothing to match that first one.

David felt like a veteran when he emerged from the confessional.

. . .

The following Wednesday night, David attended the St. Luke's Parent-Teacher dinner as their guest of honor.

The parents of the parish school wanted to welcome their new assistant pastor. And they looked forward to hearing his reflections on his ordination and his first days as a parish priest.

At the end of the meal, David rose and described the emotion of the day of ordination and all the days in the early fervor of priesthood. He told them how unsettling it was for him to be sought out for advice by people so much more experienced than he.

"People three times my age are calling me 'Father'."

David recounted the uneasiness he had in hearing confessions.

"As a matter of fact," he said, "wouldn't you know that the very first confession I heard was by someone who had to confess just about everything in the book. Some sins I had not even heard of before. I think I am ready for anything now, after that first confession."

This brought gales of laughter from the audience.

The Parent-Teacher Group president went through a long list of housekeeping agenda items with the members, and Father Gerald Archer, the pastor, was called on to say the usual few words.

As the pastor concluded his remarks, a lady who had come in late raised her hand at one of the tables at the back of the room.

When she was acknowledged by the PTG president, she stood and spoke to the crowd.

"I have just arrived. I am very sorry that I was not able to be here for the dinner and the speeches. I wish I could have heard the talk by our new priest. I feel very close to Father David because I know I had the honor of being the first one to go to confession to him."

A chorus of chuckles swept through the audience growing into uproarious laughter, as the crowd, in unison, craned their necks to see just who the woman was.

At the head table, David flushed and wondered if he had inadvertently committed the grave sin of breaking the secrecy seal of the confessional.

He took a sideways glance at his pastor and saw that he was shaking his head slowly from side to side and stifling his own laughter.

David had learned a lesson early in his career about off-hand remarks about the sacrament of the confessional.

CHAPTER 20

The first Sunday sermon was another pressure cooker.

David prepared his homily carefully, taking some paragraphs from what he thought were particularly effective "practice sermons" from seminary days.

He was confident about his ability to preach - probably over-confident. He wanted to be interesting. He did not want to see people glassy-eyed and slack-jawed, paying no attention whatever to what was being preached. He would be devastated if he saw parishioners looking at their watches during his sermon - shaking them as though they were wondering if the watches had stopped.

Although he had never said it openly, David was convinced that his sermons would be better than most of the ones he'd heard in churches.

His first sermon came at the 9 o'clock Mass on the second Sunday of July. He talked about Holy Communion. He emphasized reverence for the Blessed Sacrament.

"Jesus is moving in our midst today. He is walking on Geary Boulevard and 23rd Avenue, just as surely as He walked the dusty roads of Judea, Samaria, and Galilee. And how are we responding?

"What kind of friend are we to Christ . . .?"

To illustrate Jesus residing in the tabernacle on the altar, he quoted the lyrics of the song Sister Loretto had referred to in his second grade and which Perry Como had made popular again: "I'm Just a Prisoner of Love".

He was sure that this would appeal to the young people. And he suspected that although they did not necessarily listen to a preacher when he is talking to adults, adults listen to a preacher when he is speaking to young people.

Out on the front steps of the church after Mass, David was pleased to hear the complimentary remarks about the sermon. The affirmation came from all sides, young and old, men and women. He did not realize at the time that parishioners tend to overstate their appreciation, as they meet the preacher when they are leaving Mass. Especially they are inclined to give all the encouragement they can to a "baby priest."

. . .

Shortly after 3 a.m., the phone rang in David's room. It was Children's Hospital. A young infantile paralysis victim had just been brought into Emergency. She was near death. Could a priest come and give the last sacraments?

It would be David's first Extreme Unction.

Clearing his mind from a deep sleep, he fumbled into his clothes and raced down the stairs.

He unlocked the door to the sacristy in the church, found the tabernacle key, went immediately to the altar, and placed a single consecrated Host in his new gold-plated pyx. Looking more like a pocket watch, he carried the pyx in a small leather purse-like case, which hung under his coat jacket from a leather strap around his neck.

He drove through the fog along California Street. In the middle of the night, there was ample parking in front of the hospital.

David was met at the reception desk by a young nurse who ushered him to the door of a private room. There, he was stopped and required to put on a surgical smock, face mask and gloves.

David entered the room and found the patient to be a woman somewhere in mid-twenties. He took two other ordination gifts from his pocket - a reversible purple and white stole and his sacramental ritual book. He had not yet remembered even the brief essential words of anointing the sick.

The young woman was conscious.

"I have come to help you with some sacraments. What is your name?"

"Cecilia, Father."

"I know that these sacraments are going to help you to feel better, Cecilia."

In his mind, David recalled the sequence in which the sacraments should be given.

"Would you like to go to confession?"

"All right, Father."

Cecilia made the Sign of the Cross and began her confession. "Bless me, Father, for I have sinned . . ."

, "That was a good confession, Cecilia. I would like to give you Communion now."

Because he knew it would be difficult for the patient to swallow the full white wafer of consecrated Bread, he broke off a fragment and consumed the remaining portion himself.

"This is the Lamb of God, Who takes away the sins of the world. May the Body of Christ bring you to life everlasting. Amen."

He placed the Host particle on the tongue, and then read from the ritual: "May the blessing of Almighty God, Father, Son and Holy Ghost, descend upon you and remain with you forever."

David knew he had to speak slowly and clearly, not just because Cecilia was distracted by anxiety and physical pain, but because his own voice was deadened by his face mask.

Again, he fumbled through the pages of his ritual to find the words for the Sacrament of Extreme Unction.

David unscrewed the oil of the sick cylindrical container from the oil stocks, removed the surgical glove from his right hand, dipped his thumb into the oil-soaked cotton and began in Latin: "Through this anointing and His most holy mercy, may the Lord forgive whatever sins you have committed through sight."

He repeated the ritual on the other senses, the ears, the nose, the closed lips and the palms of Cecilia's hands. Because the rubrics allowed it, David omitted the anointing of the feet.

After imparting the Last Blessing, David said:

"Now you have all the sacraments that you need, Cecilia. I am sure that you are going to be fine. You are in good hands with the doctors and nurses at this hospital."

Cecilia's voice seemed stronger. "Thank you, Father."

"I will be back to see you. And I will be praying for you and remembering you in my Mass."

David turned to leave and found the nurse waiting for him just outside the door.

"You take off your surgical gown, mask and gloves, and put them in this container, Father. Also, you'll have to leave that book and vestment you are wearing around your neck, along with those metal containers you're holding. Cecilia's disease is highly contagious."

"I just received all these things as gifts for ordination a couple of weeks ago," David said.

"I can sanitize these metal containers and get them back to you, but the other things will have to be left with us."

With the help of the nurse, David scrubbed his hands with disinfectant.

"Will you give me a call at St. Luke's when I can get back my pyx and oil stocks?"

"Yes, Father. It will just be a couple of days. Thanks for coming in the middle of the night."

. . .

As is the time honored custom, the newly ordained were assigned the youth club, the altar boys, given a list of Communion home calls, addresses for sick and shut-in parishioners, several impending marriage preparations, and a good number of other duties which veteran priests like to pass on to rookies.

Ladd described Pastoral Care as all the work a pastor doesn't care to do.

. . .

The new priests relished the novelty of the priesthood and the reverence they were accorded: the happy days of Christmas season, the smell of Douglas fir trees in the rectory, the decorated church, the Fathers' Club Christmas tree sale in the school yard and the warmth of the Christmas Eve Mass on a cold San Francisco midnight.

In the spring, it would be the Holy Week ceremonies.

Most of all, it was the affection that spontaneously bonded parishioners with their parish priests.

These were the heady experiences of the first year after ordination.

CHAPTER 21

Father Archer assigned David to give the Wednesday night Lenten series on marriage.

David was, as usual, conscientious about preparing the series - half hour talks each Wednesday night for six weeks.

As the weeks went by, David was convinced that he was giving the faithful valuable advice in married life.

On the last night of the series, he made it a point after the service to go to the front of the church to talk to the parishioners and to wish them a happy Easter.

The parishioners expressed their appreciation of the series, asked him about the hours of the Holy Week services, and were affirming of his work as assistant priest in their parish.

Then along came Mrs. Gillespie, a faithful morning Mass parishioner. Not holding back, she said, "Father, thank you very much for the very interesting series of talks you have given on the Sacrament of Matrimony. After 42 years of marriage, I wish that I knew as little about marriage as you do."

This cooled off David's estimation of his own abilities as a preacher.

. . .

Three times a year, David substituted for Father Mario Martinelli at the County Jail. He liked this assignment. The inmates were among the most attentive and prayerful congregations whom he served all year.

David entered the visitor's gate. He had become accustomed to the routine. Open the suitcase of vestments, the Mass kit for inspection. Pass through the metal detector, sign in, and receive a visitor's badge for the lapel.

The alarm sounded when he went through the detector. David emptied his pockets of loose change, his rosary, comb, keys. Still the buzzer sounded.

"Take off your belt, Father."

David tried again. The same result. Then he remembered the St. Christopher medal and chain around his neck, under his clerical shirt.

"You might as well take off your shoes also. It might be the shoe nails."

This time he passed through with no alarm.

The recreation room had been cleared of Ping-Pong and pool tables, and a hundred and fifty metal folding chairs were placed in two sections with a wide middle aisle. A simple table faced the chairs.

David unfolded a linen corporal on the table, put two beeswax candles at the front corners of the make-shift altar and arranged his chalice and wine and water cruets.

He had forgotten to replenish the wine cruet and the bread wafers after his last Mass away from the parish church. What now?

There was no time to go back to St. Luke's or even the closest parish church. The prisoners were already filing into the hall and the movement from the various cell blocks was on a rigorous time schedule.

There could be no Mass.

"Do you have any wine around the offices?" David asked the guard monitoring the inmates' entrance.

"No, no liquor is permitted anywhere on jail premises."

"Could we get some bread from the dining room?"

"I'll try," said the guard.

"How am I going to handle this?" David wondered. He went on lighting the candles. "How am I going to tell these prisoners that, after all this, there will be no Mass?"

The guard returned. "Padre, this is the best I could do - grape juice and a hamburger bun."

"Oh, oh," David thought. "What about validity? I guess the buns are made from wheat flour. To be valid, the bread must be wheat and grape juice is sometimes permitted in the case of alcoholic priests. It could work, he thought to himself. "Let's do it", David said to the guard.

At the sermon, David reminded the inmates that Jesus was born homeless, that He had a contract put out on Him by the authorities when He was only a few days old, that He had to flee with Mary and Joseph like undocumented aliens across borders into Egypt. At 33 years of age, as an itinerant preacher, He was arrested by the temple police, imprisoned, put through a fraudulent trial and executed – all for being an outspoken preacher.

At Communion time, David had not anticipated so many approaching the altar to receive the Sacrament. Halfway through the line, he had to start breaking the hamburger roll into smaller pieces.

He knew that some of these men had not been able to receive Communion for years.

The devout expression on their faces impressed the young priest.

He continued to break the bread into smaller and smaller fragments until there was virtually nothing left but crumbs.

Then they were gone. And there were two men still in line.

One of the saddest things David could remember was the look on the faces of those two who had waited so long for Communion and could not receive.

David left the jail thinking of the two prisoners.

. . .

David told no one about the grape juice and hamburger bun Mass, but some way or other, perhaps through officers at the County Jail, the episode became known.

Gordon's father, George Caprice, heard the story related at the monthly meeting of Guardians of Doctrine, a group of Catholics who had banded together to preserve orthodoxy.

At his office the following day, George composed a letter to Archbishop McHenry:

"Your Excellency:

I know that you are pre-occupied with many concerns. I do not want to add to your burdens, but I feel obligated to inform you of the action of one of your priests.

It is my understanding that Father David Carmichael used ordinary bread and grape juice instead of unleavened bread and approved sacramental wine at a recent Mass at the San Francisco County Jail.

If I am correct regarding liturgical law, this was not only an illicit deed, but an invalid consecration.

With sentiments of esteem, I am

Respectfully yours,
GEORGE CAPRICE
Attorney at Law"

. . .

The following Monday morning, Agnes, St. Luke rectory housekeeper, buzzed David on the intercom, "Father, the Archbishop's office is on the phone."

David went to the hallway and picked up the receiver. "Hello."

"Father Carmichael, this is Monsignor Roach. The Archbishop would like to see you at the Chancery this afternoon at two-thirty. Are you clear?"

We'll see you here at two-thirty."

"Thank you, Monsignor."

David returned to his room. "I wonder what this is all about. Maybe it's a new assignment. Maybe the Archbishop wants me to do some graduate studies."

After lunch, David showered, put on a clean white shirt with French cuffs, cross-engraved cuff links, his new suit with clerical vest, and polished his best shoes.

At the Chancery Office, he was invited to wait in the reception area. At two-thirty promptly, the Chancellor appeared and ushered him into the Archbishop's office.

"Good afternoon, Father," the prelate said, holding out his hand and, at the same time, motioning David to a chair across from his desk.

David took the Archbishop's hand and made a motion at kissing the episcopal ring. "Good afternoon, Your Excellency."

"Father Carmichael, it has come to my attention that you have offered Mass using grape juice and ordinary bread."

David was surprised. This wasn't what he had expected.

The Archbishop continued, "At least this is the report I have received. Is this true?"

"Well, yes, Archbishop. I did. But it was an unusual situation," David recounted the circumstances at the jail. "It was a matter of the prisoners having Mass or not having Mass . . ."

The Archbishop interrupted, "It would have been better to forego the Mass."

David's instincts told him to be silent and take the rebuke.

"You know, it is a serious matter to expose the Sacrament to nullity."

"Yes, Archbishop."

That apparently was the end of the conversation. David rose hesitatingly from the chair.

"And how are things going otherwise at St. Luke's?" The prelate's tone seemed to soften.

"Fine, Your Excellency."

"Give my regards to Father Archer."

"I will, Archbishop."

"God bless you now and be very respectful of church regulations."

"Yes, Your Excellency."

David found his way out of the Chancery wondering, "Now, how did he know about that?"

. . .

The following Sunday, three seniors from Cathedral Girls' High School stopped David in front of St. Luke's after twelve-fifteen Mass.

"Would you say our Student Body Mass this month at Cathedral High?"

"Do the principal and your teacher know you are asking me?"

"Yes, we're supposed to line up the priests this time. The Mass is at the gym Friday morning at nine-thirty."

"Friday morning? Yes, I can be there. Do I have to bring vestments, chalice or anything?"

"No, the teacher in charge has everything ready."

"Okay, I'll see you then."

On Friday, David arrived at the Cathedral gymnasium at 9 a.m. Sister Hyacinth had prepared the altar on the basketball court.

The first of the students were filing into the high stacked gym bleachers. "Sister, do you think we could turn things around on the altar so I could face the students during the Mass? It would give them a better look at what is going on."

Sister was taken aback, but had no objection.

When the student body was assembled, David explained why he had turned the altar around and then began to put on the vestments, giving the significance of each.

"This first vestment is the amice. It goes around the shoulders and tucks into the collar.

"Next is the alb, coming from the Latin word 'alba' meaning white. It is a long white garment resembling the togas worn by the Romans at the time Jesus said the first Mass at the Last Supper with His friends the night before He died.

"These vestments are something like the street clothes Jesus and the Apostles were wearing at the Supper.

"The only difference with my 'toga' and theirs is that theirs did not have a zipper like this one." David was convinced that one way to hold the attention of the young was to use humor.

"By the way, speaking of the Last Supper, do you know what Leonardo Da Vinci's last words were? . . . No? Leonardo's last words were, "O.K. everyone get on the same side of the table, if you want to be in the picture."

This brought some laughter from the students. And faculty members began to look at each other uneasily.

David went on, "The next vestment has a name familiar to you. It is called a stole - worn around the neck and down the front of the priest, a symbol of teaching and preaching authority. It is cinched at the waist by this cord - called a cincture.

"The maniple which I am pinning to my left sleeve is like a napkin for the meal.

"Finally, this outer vestment is called a chasuble. That's also from a Latin word, `casula', meaning a little house or tent. It is so full and ample you can see why it has its name."

For the benefit of the Hispanic students, David added, "The chasuble reminds us of a serape or a tilma.

"What we have here is a table, because this is a continuation of the meal that the Lord had with His friends the night before He died. The altar table does not have to be an elaborate marble altar like in the cathedral up the street or a basilica. It can be a simple table like this or even a card table.

"Now we begin the Mass . . . In nomine Patris et Filii et Spiritus Sancti. Introibo ad altare Dei . . ."

As the Mass proceeded, David added commentary. "Remember, since what we are doing here is a continuation of the Last Supper, we have a tablecloth, a dish, a cup, food and drink, wine and water, a napkin and even candles, although we have plenty of light in this gym - candles not for atmosphere, but because the first Masses were illegally said in hiding in the dark underground catacomb tunnels where there was no natural lighting. We use candles because they symbolize Jesus, the Light of the world."

As he poured two or three drops of water into the wine in his chalice, David explained, "Christ did this at the Last Supper because it was the custom of the Jews to add water to the wine at the Passover meal. Also, the water represents our humanity being added to the divinity of Jesus, the Wine."

As the Mass continued to the end, David hoped that the eyes and thoughts of the students did not wander off from the liturgy as much as usual.

. . .

Priests who offered Mass at the high school had a standing invitation to break their fast from midnight with breakfast at the Cathedral rectory.

David walked across Franklin Street to the priests' residence and was served scrambled eggs, toast and coffee but no bacon -- it was Friday.

He was deep in Bill Leiser's column in the sports section when, unexpectedly, Archbishop Gutierrez came through the dining room door. David rose to the Archbishop, setting aside the Chronicle Sporting Green. Vicki, the cook, was ready with a cup of black coffee for the Archbishop.

The prelate was not one for small talk. There was an awkward pause. To break the silence, David said, "Your Excellency, I have just come from Cathedral High. We had the monthly student body Mass."

"Umph," was all that came from the opposite side of the table.

Another pause . . . and David pushed on, "So that the students in the gym could see what was going on better, we turned the altar around and I said Mass facing them."

The Archbishop looked up from his coffee. "You did what! Permission is never given for that. You must follow liturgical rules. Don't do that again."

The silence began again. Now David thought better about making more conversation. He knew he should go back to reading the paper. He sat quietly until the Archbishop finished his coffee. With a slight nod, the prelate left the room.

It was just as well that David had the opportunity to inform his superior of the altar turn-around on his own.

Subsequently, he learned that George Caprice and G.O.D. (Guardians of Doctrine) had been informed of the Cathedral High School Mass and had written a letter of objection to the Apostolic Delegate, the Pope's representative in Washington, D.C., with a copy to the Archbishop.

David, thinking back to his earlier meeting with the Archbishop on the "grape juice" prison Mass, said out loud to himself, "Strike two."

CHAPTER 22

Ladd Franklin's life at St. Gregory's was a kaleidoscope of emotional events.

In June, July and August, the Richmond District is fog-bound. Many San Francisco families head for Russian River, Boyes Hot Springs or Lake County, all north of the City; but, like clock work when school begins, the first week of September means hot weather has arrived in the City.

When he could get away, Ladd drove to Ocean Beach to get some sun and swim close to shore in the cold breakers. Signs were everywhere warning of the dangerous undertow.

On Saturday morning of Labor Day weekend, Ladd lay on the warm sand listening to KYA on his transistor radio. Patti Page was halfway through "The Tennessee Waltz" when Ladd heard shouting down at the water's edge.

A crowd had gathered. Two men were carrying a limp body up the beach away from the breakers. Instinctively, Ladd ran to the scene, as one of the men began artificial respiration on the girl, about twelve years of age.

Ladd worked his way through the on-lookers. "Excuse me, I'm a priest. Please let me through. Excuse me." The crowd made way for him.

As the rescuer tried to revive the girl, Ladd knelt beside her. He tried to recall what he should do.

First, give conditional absolution for sins, he decided. "If you are capable (of receiving this sacrament), I absolve you from all censures and sins in the name of the Father and the Son and the Holy Ghost."

As he finished the formula prayer, a wave much stronger than any that late morning washed all the way up the shore to Ladd's knee.

Vaguely thinking it an omen, Ladd scooped a handful of sea water and poured it on the young victim's forehead. "If you are not baptized I baptize you in the name of the Father and the Son and the Holy Ghost."

Anne Grenfeld never regained consciousness. She was pronounced dead on arrival at Mount. Zion Hospital. Anne was Jewish.

. . .

That evening, Ladd visited the Grenfeld home. He was uneasy approaching the family and felt awkward about the baptism. But he knew he should tell the parents.

"I am very sorry for the loss of your dear daughter . . . I feel I must let you know that I baptized Anne conditionally at the beach. I hope this does not offend you but from my point of view, I thought it was the right thing to do, not knowing her religion."

Ladd was fumbling for words. "It does not change your daughter, of course. She is what she is . . . And I am sure she is with God."

The Grenfelds were not offended.

"Father, we are grateful for your concern. And your effort to help is appreciated."

Though Ladd knew Christians, including Catholics, had on many occasions through history treated Jews shamefully, he had by his family and by his Catholic school teachers been taught reverence and respect for Jews and for all other faiths.

. . .

It was the custom at St. Gregory's to celebrate All Saints Day on November 1st, with a special Mass for the students of the parish. It was also a tradition for the third grade students to dress in the costumes of their patron saints or their favorite saints.

The procession formed in the school yard. The third graders had a privileged place in line, just ahead of the altar servers and Father Ladd, in his vestments.

As they waited for the signal to start, Ladd observed a little St. Catherine of Siena here and a St. Thomas Aquinas over there - saints of every race and gender.

Then, just as the procession began to move, he saw St. Therese, the Little Flower, punching out St. Francis of Assisi! Holy and religious clothing does not always reflect holiness on the inside.

Ladd moved quickly to restore order among the elect and the procession and liturgy continued peacefully.

. . .

Sister Hermogene had invited Father Franklin to speak to her 8th grade class.

Ladd entered the St. Gregory classroom on a Friday morning. As was their custom, the entire class stood and recited, on cue from the usual hand gesture by Sister, "Good morning, Father."

"Good morning. You may sit down now," Ladd said to the class.

Sister Hermogene spoke first. "Father, I want you to talk to those boys especially, who will never get into high school if they don't start getting more serious about their school work. They are not attentive in class. They are not completing their homework assignments as they should. I don't know what we're going to do with them."

It had not been that long ago since Ladd had heard his own 8th grade teacher leveling the same accusations at his class.

"Well, you should all take your studies very seriously," he said to the eighth graders. "Your education is very important. I know from experience what can happen to you if you are a poor student."

Sister Hermogene was nodding her head. This is exactly the advice she wanted the young assistant pastor to give.

Then Ladd continued.

"I almost had to leave school in the 8th grade because of pneumonia. It wasn't that I caught it; it was because I couldn't spell it. In high school, my S.A.T. scores were B.A.D."

This brought laughter from the boys in the class. They could identify with that.

"Of course, I came from a very poor school, a very tough school. Our football team was brutal. The linemen were like animals. After they sacked a quarterback, they would go after his family."

Sister Hermogene didn't know what to make of that comment.

Ladd went on to say, "So, you had better get serious about studies, or you could turn out to be like me."

This didn't strike Sister as being an encouragement toward a priestly vocation.

"Well, thank you, Father. It was good of you to visit our class."

Ladd gathered that this was the end of his address to the students. He excused himself and returned to the rectory.

. . .

Although the long hours in the confessional could be draining, Ladd found the sacrament of penance one of the most gratifying of his duties.

He even found humor there. Toward the end of a long Saturday afternoon, a young voice on the other side of the screen finished the catalog of her tender sins. Ladd gave her a gentle instruction and added, "For your penance, say three Hail Mary's."

"What, Father?" It must have been one of the youngster's first confessions.

Ladd repeated, "For your penance, say the Hail Mary three times."

The young girl seemed somewhat puzzled. Then very carefully, she began. "Hail May, Hail Mary, Hail Mary."

An adult then entered the box two penitents later. "Bless me, Father, for I have sinned . . ." The young man listed his transgressions and then began to hem and haw, obviously finding it awkward to admit to a final sin. After beating around the bush for several moments, Ladd knew the young man was too embarrassed to speak. He put the question directly to the penitent: "Have you slept with a woman?"

"I may have dozed off a few times," the voice responded.

. . .

David had guessed right. Just one year after ordination, Gordon Caprice was summoned to the Chancery Office and informed that he was to return to Catholic University to study Canon Law.

In the September that Gordon began his courses, his sister Willow, who had completed undergraduate studies at Stanford and had volunteered for four years as a veterinary assistant, enrolled in the graduate school of Foreign Service at Georgetown University.

Willow loved travel and had, for some time, planned to study for service in the United States Diplomatic Corps.

Both Gordon and Willow were happy to be together in the same city where Gordon had spent some undergraduate years, and where Willow was a stranger.

The sister and brother cultivated new friendships in their respective universities and much of their social life revolved around the new acquaintances. Still, Gordon made it a point to call his sister frequently, to visit her on the Georgetown campus and occasionally to take her out to dinner at Harvey's or one of the other upscale restaurants in the District of Columbia.

Frequently on weekends, they toured the sites of the nation's Capital together. Willow took Gordon to the Mellon Art Gallery. Gordon persuaded Willow to join him in a tour of the F.B.I. headquarters. They visited the Franciscan Holy Land Shrine together, the Smithsonian Institution and took the White House tour.

Their father in California had connections in high places in Washington. As a result, Willow and Gordon spent time with congressional leaders Representative Jack Shelley of San Francisco and Senator Leveret Saltonstall of Massachusetts.

On a Sunday afternoon in late spring, the two enjoyed a garden party at the home of Vice President Alben Barkley where they had a chance to chat for a few moments with President Harry and Bess Truman.

Gordon was proud of his sister. Willow charmed everyone they met. She became well known in the Capital's political circles. Willow realized this wouldn't hurt her chances of getting a diplomatic post at the completion of her studies.

With his priest friends at Catholic University, Gordon, for recreation, played basketball and, in the early fall and late spring months, golfed.

When afternoons or evenings were free, he saw Bay Area natives Bob Feerick and Fred Scolari play for the Washington Capitals' basketball team and enjoyed the first-base skill of George McQuinn of the Washington Senators. The Senators were humorously known as "first in war, first in peace and last in the American league."

Gordon did witness Hall of Fame talent in Sammy Baugh, when his father at home could push the right buttons and pull the right levers to get Gordon tickets to the sold out Washington Redskins' games. Season tickets were almost exclusively handed down to family members in last wills and testaments.

Through these years, Gordon absorbed the canon law of the Church and Willow grew in age and grace and beauty before God and men.

At the end of her first year of graduate studies, Willow returned to San Francisco for a year of internship at the Federal Building on Golden Gate Avenue.

CHAPTER 23

It was not all work for the new parish priests back home. They got together for cards, for a movie on Market Street or in the neighborhoods.

On a Sunday in mid-October, David left after the 12:15 Mass and met Ladd and Tyler at Kezar Stadium to see a brand new San Francisco 49ers pro football team play the Chicago Rockets in the recently formed All-American Football Conference.

The three were especially thrilled to see former college stars like Elroy "Crazy Legs" Hirsch play the home-town team featuring Johnny Strykalski, along with Frankie Albert and Norm Stanlee of Stanford University fame.

David especially liked football season. He had a favorite time of the year and a not-so-favorite time of the year.

He liked the months from Palm Sunday, usually in late March or early April, through to the day after New Year's Day.

He would just as soon leave out of his life the dreary months from January 2nd until Palm Sunday. But then Lent was meant to be dreary with penances and enjoyable things given up in sacrifice.

The only redeeming features of cold, rainy Januarys were the Professional Football League Playoffs.

Palm Sunday meant the beginning of the much treasured Holy Week - Holy Thursday, Good Friday, Holy Saturday and Easter Sunday. This time of year breaks the grip of winter - much like the feeling of a chest cold breaking up or a fever subsiding. The frail sun of winter takes on new warmth.

These days lead into spring and the baseball season. The comfortable voice of the Giants' Russ Hodges could be heard coming out of homes from the Presidio to Hunter's Point, from San Rafael to San Jose. For David, all was right with the world.

Then come the easy days of summer, the crisp months of fall, the football season, the interior warmth of the end-of-the-year holidays, and around again to the uninviting days of winter.

. . .

"Ladd, do you dream much?"

"Yeah, I usually dream."

"I have this recurring dream," David said. "Or a kind of theme which keeps returning. The dreams are different happenings in different settings, but there is always the element of frustration.

"I'll be backing up my car and I am looking in the rear view mirror and I see I'm coming closer and closer to hitting a car behind me, and I keep trying, but I can't hit the brake. My foot can't find the brake.

"Or I'm saying Mass in front of a big congregation on Sunday and I can't find the right page in the missal. I keep turning the pages back and forth. I know the people are getting restless, but I just can't find the right place. It goes on and on. I'm frustrated, even panicky. Ladd, do you think recurring dreams indicate some deep psychological thing about me?"

"Maybe so," Ladd answered. "Maybe you are basically frustrated. Do you think you're frustrated?"

"Well, I am always trying to get everything done. I guess I want to have things in control." He wasn't going to tell Ladd that he was always hoping to be a bishop, but it looked less and less that he would ever make it.

Ladd thought, maybe you're reaching for affirmation? For intimacy?

. . .

On a later occasion at U.C. Berkeley, David asked a psychology graduate student majoring in dream analysis how she interpreted his recurring dream.

Without knowing his father had died when David was five, she suggested, "You may be longing for a lost father."

This surprised David. "You know, I've never really experienced trauma over my father's death. I can remember loving my father. But I think I was too young to understand the loss. I was only five."

"Though you may not consciously recognize it, you can subconsciously still be grieving over this void in your life. This may sound strange, but I recommend that, now and then, you visualize yourself as a five year old again and take that young David in your arms on your lap and console and comfort him."

David would follow through on the suggestion.

. . .

What did it mean for David to be a priest?

It was to model his life on priests he had known in his parish as a youth - to serve the people, young and old, by punctual Masses, sermons that would not be boring, to do whatever the pastor wanted him to do.

His class came out into the ministry without a great number of specific plans, but rather to serve pretty much as the pastor and older associate priests asked them to serve -as second or third assistants.

In June 1946, one definition of priesthood was: "A priest is justice on a ball diamond; fortitude with a breviary in his hand; formerly known as the boy around the corner, he is a member of each family, yet belonging to none, he penetrates secrets, shares sorrows, heals wounds. He has the trust of a child, the kindness of a best friend, the authority of an encyclopedia and the versatility of a commando."

David's concept of ministry was to follow the teaching of the Church. Unanimity existed in the Church. Priests of David's vintage didn't advert to conflicts in theological opinion. They had some vague idea that there were differences between the followers of Duns Scotus and Thomas. But these were of historical interest only and had no practical application to the 1940s and '50s.

David was simply ordained to be a priest and everybody knew what a priest was.

The movie, "Going My Way," had won an Academy Award the year before his ordination, and Bing Crosby's portrayal of Father O'Malley was pretty much the accepted role of priesthood. Priests did not reflect on or anguish over their essence or function. "You could commit yourself with confidence to a celibate existence for life, be respected for it by a people who rarely question it, and expect to die serenely in the warm arms of Christ, whom you had served as your one Master."

David's duties as a parish priest were unambiguous. He was housed with two other assistant pastors, plus a priest in residence.

He was expected to bring Communion to a rotating list of shut-in parishioners each day, to be responsible for training and assigning altar boys, to take "duty" in turn during the day and night. There was one phone in the hallway on each floor of the three-story rectory. Each priest had a scheduled daily morning Mass.

His evenings were filled with instruction to individuals in preparation for marriage, convert lessons and counseling. Weekends were busy on Saturday with endless confessions, Sunday morning Masses back-to-back, starting at 6 a.m. through the 12:15 and five or six baptisms Sunday afternoon.

David spent a good deal of time trying to get lay people involved in "Catholic Action," the Jocists (Young Christian Workers and Students), and the Christian Family Movement.

Whatever stress there was for assistant priests was usually the stress of a "difficult pastor," which David did not experience. He had a hardworking and much loved pastor in Father Gerald Archer.

. . .

This was the world David, Ladd, Tyler and their classmates experienced in the early years of their ministry.

Life for the Class of 1946 had been stable, predictable and sure-footed. They knew the Church comfortably as it had been since their childhood, essentially as it had been for the past four hundred years.

One author went so far as to say: "If one looked outward away from it . . . one touch of change could shatter it. No wonder we protected it as long as we could with a sense of its brittleness; and some left it when it broke."

Suddenly, as 1961 turned into 1962, Father Patrick Peyton conducted the Rosary Crusade with 500,000 faithful at the Polo Grounds in Golden Gate Park, Archbishop Jose Gutierrez died, the new Archbishop Colin Costello arrived, the Cathedral burned down, the Vatican II Council began.

The world would never be the same again.

PART III

CHAPTER 24

Ladd left the rectory to get some fresh air. He drove downtown to Sixth Street, just off Market. Walking allowed him to look into the store windows and watch people in the street. Market, between Fourth and Tenth, was an image of blight, compared to its glory days. Still, it was relatively safe at this time late at night, with plenty of people and plenty of street lights. The Muni street cars and busses were still running.

The shop windows displayed an abundance of upscale merchandise in the Emporium, and even more so as Ladd turned north on Powell, toward Union Square, past Macy's and I. Magnin's.

What most caught his attention in the midst of the luxury were the drifters on Market Street, unfortunate transients, unkempt, hungry, some talking to themselves, some suffering the effects of substance abuse. Even worse were the destitute elderly bag ladies pushing a supermarket shopping cart holding their total material possessions.

Up and down the side streets and alleys, the homeless huddled under straggly blankets or newspapers, sleeping in shop doorways. Ladd knew that in other parts of the city at that moment, others, young and old, were trying to find rest in abandoned cars, buildings, and gas stations, in underground parking garages, and along the docks of the Bay, even in dumpsters.

On Post Street, Ladd watched an old man nursing a cup of coffee in an all-night doughnut shop. Below Union Square, a young mother with her small children was trying to do their laundry in a public restroom.

Ladd witnessed in one California county, unclaimed bodies of those who died homeless being sent to a county crematorium. There, the ashes were dumped without ceremony into an unmarked plywood-covered pit.

These scenes were eating away at Ladd.

. . .

Ladd had preached several times about the need for the government at the federal, state and county levels to do more for the homeless. He had asked Father Preston to make the parish hall-gymnasium available for the homeless to sleep at night, but the pastor refused. "It will disrupt the parish schedules. It will interfere with the sports programs for the school children. The parishioners will think we are bringing some criminal elements into the neighborhood. And we will have astronomical insurance problems and lawsuits when trouble develops among the transients."

Ladd had talked enough. "It's time for me to do something," he thought.

That Friday night, he took his sleeping bag and drove downtown to the Tenderloin to sleep with some of the homeless.

The rains had not yet reached the City, but Marin County was experiencing a deluge. On the car radio, a newscaster was saying, "Most of the streets of Larkspur, Corte Madera, and San Rafael are flooded. Hundreds of families have evacuated their homes. The Salvation Army is providing shelter, blankets and hot coffee."

Then, in a casual off-hand comment, the announcer departed from his script to remark, "Isn't that Salvation Army a great organization? They are always there when people need them."

The thought crossed Ladd's mind, "That's true about the Salvation Army. Have I ever heard a spontaneous comment like that about the Catholic Church? We should be out there with the people during catastrophes."

It was a mid-March night and, though San Francisco's weather is rarely severe, a biting late winter wind swept the intersection of Golden Gate Avenue and Leavenworth. Ladd huddled with a dozen other men and women, most of them braced against the cold under ragged blankets, cardboards and newspapers.

Somehow or other, the ABC television affiliate, located just down the street on Golden Gate Avenue, heard that a local priest had joined the homeless and sent a reporter.

"What is the message you're trying to send by sleeping here, Father?

"I didn't intend to make it a protest. I just wanted to be present to these men and women, to let them know that there are others who are concerned about them."

"Do you think the community should be doing more to help them?"

"Yes, I think there should be more decent shelters provided. And we have to find a way to generate more jobs. These people are not lazy. They're not welfare-cheats. Most have lost their jobs through no fault of their own, but because of downsizing. They're not out here because they want to be. There may be some drifters who prefer being out on the streets, but that is not true of most of these people."

As the cameraman panned along the line of his companions, Ladd continued.

"I am from a relatively poor family myself. But through all my life, I've had enough to eat and a warm bed at night. I wanted to experience for myself what it means to be homeless."

Ladd slept only sporadically through the night, awakened with a stiff back and neck, and drove back to St. Gregory's in time for the seven-thirty Mass.

· · ·

At the outset of the Vietnam War, Ladd backed the United States government's position. He assumed that America was doing the right thing in protecting a small nation in South Vietnam against Communist aggression by Hanoi.

But, as the conflict wore on, he began to listen to the growing protests by responsible people.

Disillusioned by the seeming official cover-ups, he decided to change his political party affiliation. He wanted to register as an Independent; but there is no such category in California, so he registered as "Declined to State".

· · ·

Ladd Franklin's growing interest in social and political issues was beginning to draw attention.

At the request of the Social Justice Commission, on the occasion of the assassination of Martin Luther King, Jr., Ladd addressed the Supervisors at a memorial service in City Hall.

"As a response to Dr. King's Letter from the Birmingham Jail, I offer ten new commandments;"

"1st Commandment to All of Us:
Thou shalt not differentiate Europeans, African Americans, Asians, Latinos, Native Americans.

2nd Commandment to the Government:
Thou shalt not make city and county budget cuts to hurt the poor simply because they are voiceless and powerless.

3rd Commandment to All of Us:
Thou shalt not contribute to the hate crimes, which are multiplying all around us.

4th Commandment to Legislators:
In this time of increasing unemployment, thou shalt not blame immigrants for taking away jobs.

5th Commandment to All of Us:
Thou shalt learn from fourth graders in San Francisco public schools this past Friday who, when asked to name their top 20 heroes - my Mom and Dad, Nelson Mandela, Michael Jackson, Harriet Tubman, and you, Martin.

6th Commandment to Myself:
I shall confess, Dr. King that I strongly disagreed with your opposition to the Vietnam War, and then realized you were far ahead of all of us.

7th Commandment to Myself:

Thou shalt rejoice with American Blacks who, one day might have a national holiday for you, Martin, knowing, as a Catholic, the joy I experienced when John Kennedy was the first Catholic elected president.

8th Commandment to Myself:

I shall appreciate some small part of the discrimination you experienced, Dr. King, when, as a boy, I felt I should be ashamed to be part Italian.

9th Commandment to Myself:

As a Catholic priest, thou shalt try to see to it that not all the statues in our parish churches are white-faced.

And 10th Commandment to Myself:

As a Catholic priest, I shall feel comfortable with a name that used to be awkward to Catholics, Martin Luther.

Sincerely yours,
Your Brother
Ladd Franklin"

. . .

One of his classmates, Terence Ripley, invited Ladd to exchange pulpits for one Sunday. Terence had been assigned to St. William's in Pacific Heights, the most affluent parish in the city.

Ladd was reluctant. He did not feel comfortable preaching to a wealthy congregation.

But Terence persisted.

"It would be a good change of pace for you, Ladd."

Ladd finally agreed. But he would say the things that he believed.

When the weekend for the exchange preaching came, Ladd mounted the pulpit at St. William's and began:

"Sometimes the things we priests preach about seem so unreal and out of touch. Often even the gospel story seems so distant and from another time and planet. What about today?

"It is today, September 11, 1963. President Kennedy has sent out a proclamation . . . that the whole nation should be enrolled in a census, and so Mary and Joseph travel to San Bruno to comply with the law.

"There is no room in the motels, so Jesus is born homeless in a garage in an obscure village named Brisbane. 'The birds have nests and the foxes have holes, but the Son of Man has not a place to lay His head.'

"A few days after His birth, because the Child is considered a menace to those in authority, Jesus, Mary and Joseph are obliged to flee like undocumented aliens across borders into Mexico.

"When it is safe again, the Holy Family returns to their home, not here in Pacific Heights, but in Hunters Point."

Ladd noticed some restlessness in a middle-aged couple in the second pew.

"The young Jesus eventually attends Nazareth Junior High School and encounters all the experiences of today. He finds He has to 'just say no' to hashish and other drugs in the school yard.

"As an adolescent, He must learn how to relate to women. There is something special, something different, about this young man.

"Grown to manhood, He has a sense of power and self-possession. As He talks to a group of people in Golden Gate Park, young children cluster around Him spontaneously. They know there is someone very lovable here.

"We come across Him addressing a large crowd at the Cow Palace. He is talking about people whom we may look on as different, Blacks, Latinos, Asians, Gays, and He is saying, 'These are My brothers and sisters. These are all children of your Heavenly Father.'"

At this point, a man near the back of the church stood up and left by the side aisle.

"On the east steps of City Hall, Jesus is approached by reporters and asked if He is a Democrat or a Republican, and His response is, 'Render to Caesar the things that are Caesar's, and to God the things that are God's.'

"He multiplies loaves and fishes at the Saint Anthony Soup Kitchen.

"This Jesus has power like no one else. He meets a man with tuberculosis at City and County Hospital, and cures him. As with the leper in the Gospel, Jesus does not just cure him, He reaches out, touches him and cures him. There is no outcast in Jesus' world. He embraces everyone. Can you imagine what this meant to the leper! This was probably the first time since he was a child that anyone had touched him tenderly and lovingly.

"From Twin Peaks, Christ looks down on San Francisco and weeps over the city. To the street gangs in the Mission District, He says, 'He who takes up the weapon will die by the weapon.'

"He weeps also at the breakdown of family life. But, at the same time, He reaches out in compassion to the divorced and separated. 'The bruised reed I will not break the smoking flax I will not quench.'

"Jesus understands, but He has some hard sayings. Some of His teachings embarrass us and make us feel awkward. We are tempted to turn away and no longer walk with Him.

"Because His words are demands and challenges which we do not like to hear, will we, some Good Friday afternoon, take Him outside the gates of the city to San Quentin Prison and gas Him?"

There was a hush among the pews.

As he stepped down from the pulpit, Ladd wondered if he would be invited to St. William's again.

CHAPTER 25

"Dave, I'm thinking of leaving the priesthood. I was attracted to it because I wanted to help people. But I don't think I'm really doing that."

"Ladd, you should talk to Father Mike Buckley," David suggested. "I think he'll understand how you're feeling."

Ladd knew Buckley from priests' retreats. He trusted his judgment.

Ladd drove to El Retiro and described to the Jesuit priest how he felt he was losing his sense of purpose.

"Jesus Christ was like a newly ordained priest but he died when he was a priest for only three years. We who are called to follow Him sometimes have to suffer a different kind of martyrdom - a prolonged, protracted, often routine ministry that goes on for 25 or 35 or even 65 years. And, during all that time, the fires of glamour and novelty in priesthood can burn down to embers. I think I am at the embers stage right now."

Buckley had encountered this feeling many times before.

"Ladd, one of the experiences that a priest must learn to assimilate is that of the seeming public irrelevance of the Church.

"We priests are asked to bless civic occasions. Politicians and business people may treat us with respect - even deference. Parents send their wayward children to us for counseling. But in so many of these occasions, we can be filled with a sense of artificialities, of expected social contrivances, while the serious business of living is elsewhere. Have you noticed how many people change from the tough hard language of business or politics to the more artificially pleasant, awkwardly respectful or contrived heartiness when they begin to talk to us?

"This kind of atmosphere around our 'life'," Father Buckley continued, "has a way of draining off our sense of purpose. We don't feel a part of real life."

"Yes," Ladd said, "I'm going through one of those low periods when the things I do in my parish don't seem to give me the enthusiasm I used to feel. Sometimes I doze off while listening to the seemingly endless story of a penitent in the confessional. That happens more and more frequently to me now. Worse than that, I fell asleep while giving instruction to the penitent."

"Yes, Ladd, one of the most debilitating things that can happen to a priest is that imperceptible loss of zeal. The demands upon you can be so enormous and so varied that what was once a sense of unconditional dedication gives way to something like a weary adjustment to life."

"To be a priest today can be to live with an enormous sense of incompleteness. You may experience a sense of failure to meet all demands - even though each demand in itself is reasonable. Trying to meet every expectation leaves you fragmented and exhausted, and yet you have to stir up that sense of commitment. Otherwise, your life will become unbearable.

Ladd continued to struggle with his vocation. On their day off together, he mentioned his anguish to David.

"I sometimes have that nagging feeling of the road not taken. Should I have lived a married life with a family? Am I missing the real world?

"Dave, I think I've made a decision about one thing I've been agonizing over. You know, for a long time, I've had questions about whether I was really doing what God is calling me to do as a priest. There seem to be so many people suffering out there, needing my help, and I'm spending my time on men's club activities, parish fund-raisers, and taking care of the parish buildings. Half my time goes to the four 'Ls': Locks, Lights, Leaks and Litter."

"Those are the things that have to be done to keep the institutional Church going," David said. "And speaking practically, that's how the Gospel has survived through the centuries."

"I know that," Ladd said, I don't say everybody has to feel the way I do to be following the Gospel values, but, for myself, I think of the people who are suffering around the world are the kinds of persons God wants me to help.

"I wonder if the Church is missing it original purpose - we seem to have drifted away from the words of the Gospels. For example, I was puzzled again on Ash Wednesday. At Mass, right after reading these words in the Gospel, 'When you fast and do penance, do not disfigure your faces like the Pharisees do,' I immediately proceeded to bring the congregation up to the sanctuary and disfigured their faces with ashes on their foreheads. It's a small point, I know; but it seems to be symptomatic. Is religion out of touch with the real world?" My morale -- and maybe some other priests' morale - is very low because of this and other conditions in the Church."

"Ladd, religion is not irrelevant today. Just listen to the conversations you hear around you. Every once in a while, I make it a point to tune in on what people are talking about at the next table in a restaurant, or people waiting in long lines for the cashier in a department store or supermarket. So often, they're talking about something they're doing in their Church or some moral issue that society is debating today. Really, religion and morality are very much on people's minds.

"And when polls are taken on who are the most admired persons, Fulton Sheen, Billy Graham and the Pope are usually in the top ten. The things in the Church are in the main stream.

"People are so overwhelmed by technology and change, when they encounter a priest who is contemplative, who is not tortured by the same demons that are devouring their own souls - the effects are altogether startling.

"Religion still has what the people are hungering for.

"Let me tell you what happened to me last week", David began. "From time to time, on Friday and Saturday nights, for exercise, I drive to the Mission District and walk along Mission and Guerrero Streets the two nights of the week that one can safely walk in a neighborhood after dark because the cruisers are circling between Army Street and 15th. As you know, many of the cruisers park their cars along the curb with their car radios blasting music. This one Friday night, as I walked south along Mission and got to about 23rd, I noticed one young man, probably about 19 years of age, tall, very fine looking young man, sitting on the hood of his Ford pickup, leaning back against the windshield and checking the cars as they drove by; his car radio was blaring KJBS.

"I was dressed in my priest clothes, collar and all. As I came closer to his car, he jumped off the hood and I noticed he had a clipboard in his hand. He was taking a survey and he stopped me and asked if he could put some questions to me. I said, "Yes," and the first question was: 'Do you accept Jesus Christ as your Savior?' The second question was: 'Do you believe that the Bible is the inspired Word of God?' The third question was: 'Are you born again?'

"I told him that I had heard that expression 'born again' many times, but I wasn't really sure what it meant. He explained that it meant reaching a point in your life where you totally let Jesus Christ take over on how you conduct your life. I told him that I certainly subscribed to that as a principle, but I hadn't been able to accomplish it yet.

"The point I'm making here is that, in one of the most improbable settings, a young man was thinking religion. The things of the Church are the yearnings in the human heart. You are needed, Ladd, everywhere - by the rich and poor, here as well as by the suffering people overseas.

Ladd nodded his head admitting this truth. David continued.

"A report I read recently revealed that priests have the same levels of emotional well-being as married men of the same age and education.

"In a Loyola University study, celibate clergy, on average, scored higher on work and life satisfaction than did comparable samples of married men.

"Only a few priests said celibacy was a serious problem for them and some said they'd probably leave the church to get married.

"Surveys consistently reveal that religious ministry is the most reverenced of all professions and occupations in the United States and the Churches are the most respected institutions.

"On the ever present point about frustration in not seeing our ministry really taking hold and affecting the people, I believe it is because we have been called to be ministers after the ages of faith have passed - in a world that is more and more secular.

"And yet, paradoxically, there is a disposition in people today toward God.

"Remember, Ladd, when we used to glory and be proud when we saw Catholic Davy Concepcion blessing himself before stepping up to the plate or Hank Lusetti, before a foul shot.

"Have you noticed how many football players today stay on their knees for a moment in the end zone after a touchdown? Prize-fighters, after knocking out an opponent, making it a point first of all to thank God! Even rock stars, winning Grammies, thank God.

"These seem usually to be players who are Evangelicals, members of the Assembly of God, or athletes for Christ, rather than Catholics. It occurs to me that we should not regret this. We should be happy that they're thinking about God. "We can learn from these religions. They are touching people who are feeling lost, overwhelmed, frightened in a complex world.

"But to get back to your problem, Ladd, have you talked to your spiritual director?" David asked.

As a matter of fact, Ladd hadn't. He would take David's suggestion and discuss the matter with his confessor.

. . .

The following Thursday, Ladd slipped into the confessional at St. Thomas Aquinas Priory and pushed the buzzer for Father Malachy Wood, an elderly Dominican whom he had known since seminary days.

Ladd made his confession, then asked the priest, "Could I have about fifteen minutes of your time in your room, Father?"

Malachy led Ladd to his quarters, where they settled into two rather worn upholstered chairs.

"Father, Ladd began, "I am having trouble with my vocation. I wonder if I am really doing the work I should be doing.

"What particularly makes you doubt, Ladd?"

"Well, let me give you one thought that has been going through my head. It is a recurring thought and it came up again this spring during Holy Week . . . Did you happen to see Franco Zeffirelli's TV miniseries, 'Jesus of Nazareth'? They showed it just before Easter."

"No, I haven't seen it."

"I saw two or three episodes," Ladd said.

"In the morning newspaper on Holy Saturday of that week, there was a picture of some local demonstrators, young and old, carrying crosses, protesting for the poor at the Federal Building downtown. They were blocking the entrance, so they were arrested for trespassing. The police treated them very gently and respectfully as they herded them into the police van.

"A photographer from The Chronicle had been out to our parish, St. Gregory's, taking pictures of the Good Friday liturgy for Saturday's paper.

"In the picture, I saw myself robed in beautiful vestments with the other vested servers clustered around me.

"Those two photos reminded me of two episodes in the 'Jesus of Nazareth' TV mini-series. The photo of the police and the hunger protestors recalled the scene of Christ being arrested in the Garden of Olives.

"In the other photo of the Good Friday service, standing there in my vestments, I looked very much like the high priests, Annas and Caiaphas, standing in the Sanhedrin as they condemned Jesus.

"It made me wonder: who was closer to Jesus - those people arrested demonstrating for the needy, or me, robed like a high priest?

"With all the beautiful ceremonies of the Catholic religion, have I wandered far from the simple teaching of Jesus of Nazareth? I think there is a danger of our Church letting our beautiful traditions, the stained glass windows, the holy water, the incense, distracting our minds from the central simple lesson that Christ was teaching.

"Are we satisfied that we are authentic Christ-followers because of these rituals, rather than carefully living His teachings?"

Ladd wondered if any of this was making sense to Father Malachy. The spiritual director recognized the sentiments very well. He spoke quietly:

"Periodically, through the centuries, there are times when we are inclined to 'purify' the Christian faith, to bring it back to its original charism, to what it was in the ministry of Jesus before 'Christianity'. This is what St. Francis of Assisi tried to do in the 13th century - what the Protestants wanted to accomplish in the 1517 Reformation. Possibly this was the intention of the Enlightenment movement in the 1700's and Modernism at the turn of this century.

"We have that gnawing feeling that our religion must be scraped clean of the human complexities encrusting the simple message of Jesus of Nazareth."

"That's it!" Ladd said, encouraged that the priest understood his question exactly. "I worry about whether some of the ceremonies that I am doing as a priest would be better set aside for corporal works of mercy, the healing, the reconciling that Jesus seemed to spend His time doing."

Father Malachy listened patiently. When Ladd was finished, the Dominican spoke. "It is apparent that you have given this a lot of thought, Ladd. And I can sympathize with your feelings – I've had them too. But remember, anxieties about the irrelevance of our priestly work can be misleading and can even be temptations. Have you thought of any alternatives?"

"Well, I have thought about joining Catholic Relief Services. Do you know the organization? It works with the poor around the world."

"Yes, I know CRS, Ladd. Why don't you look into it further? Make sure it is the kind of ministry you want to do. Pray over it. Give it some time. It is a big step. Don't make a hasty decision."

Ladd was glad the priest had not dismissed the idea as unrealistic or foolish. And he certainly wasn't being hasty. He had been thinking of this move for more than three years.

"I will give the priesthood one more chance. Maybe I can save my vocation in the Relief Services overseas."

. . .

A week later, Ladd asked for an appointment with Archbishop Colin Costello. Archbishop received him graciously. Ladd went through the same account he had given to Father Malachy.

The prelate heard him through without interrupting.

When, finally, Ladd asked if he could have a leave of absence from the archdiocese to serve as a priest with CRS, the Archbishop gave Ladd his reply.

"In the years I have been a bishop, I have found that a diocese must be generous in offering its priests who wish to work in missionary countries that desperately need priests. If you have given this matter due consideration and prayer, you have my permission to give it a try."

Ladd was surprised that the approval had come so easily.

"The permission is granted for three years. At the end of that time, I will want to review it with you," the Archbishop said pointedly as he shook hands with Ladd.

Ladd left the Chancery Office elated.

He contacted the New York headquarters of CRS the next morning. He would join the relief agency staff immediately.

CHAPTER 26

Ladd was welcomed to the New York CRS headquarters by the General Director, Raymond Washburn.

"It's good to have you on board, Father Franklin."

Washburn motioned Ladd to a sofa, flanked by end tables covered with photos of worldwide CRS projects. Citations and humanitarian awards and a mixture of what appeared to be Washburn family photos adorned the walls.

"It's good to be here," Ladd said, as he shook the director's hand. "This is the kind of work I've wanted to do for a long time."

"When can you join us?"

"Actually, I am all set up at Holy Angels rectory here in New York already. I can start anytime you have an assignment for me."

"Your job will be to visit CRS projects around the world and to submit reports on progress and needs.

"You can work out of both our New York and San Francisco offices. The best way to start for someone coming on staff is to get an overall view of what is going on in the field. I would like you, two weeks from now, to represent CRS at the World Conference on Religion and Peace in Nairobi and to get acquainted with our projects in Kenya and Morocco."

. . .

In keeping with the poverty level of the people with whom he would be working, Ladd asked for a very modest room in the New York rectory. For transportation, he used the busses or the subway.

When he was working out of the San Francisco CRS office, he used a four-wheel drive International Scout. There were times when he regretted its manual transmission at the crest of Mason or Powell Street hills. When the traffic light changed from red to green, exceptional hand, eye and foot coordination was required to release the brake, depress the clutch, shift into low gear and accelerate the gas pedal, all at the same time - especially when a cable car was looming three feet behind.

. . .

In ten days Ladd had his briefings on Africa, received the necessary visas and shots and took off from Kennedy to Frankfurt, with a connecting flight to Nairobi.

As Ladd deplaned and read the Departures monitor in the Frankfurt terminal, he marveled at the amazing capabilities of the airlines' computers. No matter what part of the world you are going to or coming from, the computers will unerringly schedule your connecting flight to be at the absolute other end of the terminal from the gate at which you arrived.

During the next week, Ladd had his first taste of the Third World in Kenya and a rural district of Morocco. Had he bit off more than he could chew? Could he stomach living among open sewers and grinding poverty?

He returned to the San Francisco CRS office and took up residence in a down-scale district parish south of Market. There, he split pastoral work with CRS obligations.

CHAPTER 27

In early summer, awaiting his next CRS assignment, Ladd enrolled in a five-day seminar on sexuality and celibacy. Hearing the lectures and in the frank discussions with other participants, he became aware of the possibility that a celibate priest could have a deep friendship with a woman. He faithfully listened to the nuances and the usual cautions, but became convinced that, for a psychologically well-adjusted priest, such a friendship could be valuable for growth and for a more effective ministry.

During the workshop, this kind of relationship began in Ladd's own life. Willow Caprice was working in the San Francisco office of the State Department.

Both were devoted to their work and, every two weeks or so, they would share a meal or take in a concert. They were very honest about their friendship and occasionally he brought her along to social gatherings at the homes of parishioners.

Both admitted to being attracted to each other but in a completely platonic way. And they were able to discuss occasional tensions. They had worked out an appropriate expression of their fondness for each other. Neither of them, in any way, intended for Ladd to leave the active ministry. Both were comfortable with their friendship.

Ladd considered their relationship to be a "gift of God".

But Ladd was devastated one day when he had a visit from one of his best friends. He had spent a lot of time in the presence of this layman and his family, and had a strong love and regard for them. Ladd's friend was ill at ease, but finally got to the point. He wanted Ladd to know that the whole parish where he was living in residence was talking about him and Willow Caprice. Some people were considering a petition to the Archbishop; some had gone to the pastor to complain about it; some had even left the parish.

Ladd was shocked and hurt. What bothered him even more was the caution his friend gave him just before he left.

"Father Ladd, we love you and will continue to love you even if you leave. But either you should stop dating this lady or leave and marry her. The things you are doing now are a scandal to the people."

Ladd did not think the criticism was justified. As the summer went on, he became more aware that his closeness to Willow brought growth as well as happiness. Her thoughtfulness about little things shamed him - and made demands on him. He began to discipline himself to notice personal things about her - her birthday, the things that brought her happiness, a kind of candy she especially liked - the way she noticed and remembered details about him. He discovered in himself a certain callousness and male self-centeredness which hurt her. As a result, he tried to be more sensitive.

Willow pointed out, gently but candidly, the ways in which he habitually "put down" women and the subtle tinge of clericalism that colored many of his relationships with lay people.

Ladd found that getting close to someone made him vulnerable to criticism. This was new to his experience.

Still, he liked what was happening. He felt more in touch with a whole range of feelings, his own and others'. He saw some of his behavior patterns for the first time and slowly began to change them where he found them selfish.

In all of this, Ladd sensed that his priestly ministry was being helped. Awareness of his own weakness made him more compassionate toward the shortcomings and sins of others.

He was careful not to "talk down" to parishioners at weekend liturgies and he went out of his way to call priest friends to congratulate them on good things they'd done or offer condolences at a time of death in their families.

Ladd felt gentler, more out-going, more alive, and very grateful to the Lord for Willow's role in his growth.

. . .

Willow, too, felt that she was benefiting in healthy ways because of guidance Ladd would offer as she struggled with her faith and prayer life.

"Willow, you ought to try Centering Prayer. To do this systematically, you take up a position and a deep breathing that quiets and relaxes your body. Then you close your eyes. Half of the world disappears because we think mostly by what we see. Then try to slow down the normal flow of thoughts by thinking just one thought. Choose a sacred word of one syllable that symbolizes your intention to be in the presence of God, calm and deep within you. That word can be simply "God" or "Lord", like the mantra "OM" in eastern religions.

Willow listened carefully, but had some questions. "It sounds like an exercise in doing nothing."

"That is what is meant by wasting time with God," Ladd assured her. "I used to find prolonged visits in the church burdensome. But then I learned you can just be present to God without having a thought. After I discovered this, prayer became liberating, no longer laborious.

"Centering prayer calls you to be comfortable as you pray. Willow, you may find that comfort inside a church, or sitting outside in the fresh air, in the warmth of the sun. Remember that St. Ignatius, for his Spiritual Exercises, suggests that a good posture of prayers is reclining.

"You know, Willow, when you see a couple riding in a car or having dinner in a restaurant, you wonder if they are husband and wife or maybe just long-time, close friends. They are not saying any words. They are enjoying themselves. They don't have to be talking. They're just content to be with each other. That's how it is with centering prayer. You don't have to be reciting formula prayers. Just be present to God. Words aren't necessary.

"If I am too busy to have regularly scheduled personal prayer time, I know I am too busy.

"Prayer is different from one person to another, and it is different at different times in life for each one of us. But whatever form my prayer takes, when I return to a regularity of prayer life, I get a feeling of being very clean and uncluttered. And the people seem to sense that I am more connected to God."

Willow and Ladd continually exchanged ideas and suggestions like this.

. . .

As time went on, however, Ladd was having second thoughts. He was finding that the earlier intentions both he and Willow had expressed about the relationship were a bit unreal. There was a dynamic at work that wasn't always easy to manage. The "appropriate expression" of their fondness for one another had progressed to the point where he wondered about its appropriateness. And about the "fondness" it expressed.

Eventually Ladd found himself avoiding any mention of Willow when he talked to priest friends. She was a part of his life that he felt more and more wary about sharing with anyone. He suspected people wouldn't understand, least of all his brother priests.

Willow found this new attitude difficult to understand and was hurt by it. He tried to explain his thinking to her without much success. They usually ended up arguing. This became one more source of tension between them. And Ladd sometimes felt trapped.

Then Ladd had received the permission to work with CRS. He was excited about the opportunity. The one drawback was that his assignments would take him a far distance from Willow. This meant a real pain of loss for Ladd, but there was the challenge of a new situation in a ministry he saw as more meaningful.

He felt more capable of facing the new work, thanks in large part, he knew, to the self-confidence gained from his relationship with Willow. She'd been good for him.

What he didn't anticipate was Willow's reaction. She fell apart unable to reconcile herself to seeing him only infrequently. And any talk of how grateful he was for her part in his growth seemed to make things worse. Where he felt freed up by the love and esteem they'd given each other, she saw it as simple desertion.

Ladd finally confided this to his sister. She knew Willow and liked her. She wasn't surprised at Willow's reaction.

"You have to understand, Ladd, relationships are different for a woman."

As she talked, Ladd began to realize how little he understood the complexities of any man-woman friendship, let alone a friendship involving a celibate man.

. . .

David was asked to serve on the Priestly Life and Ministry Committee of the National Conference of Catholic Bishops.

Meeting monthly over a period of a year as a writing committee, the members developed a document, Human Sexuality and the Ordained Priesthood - A Reflection Guide.

David and a fellow committeeman, Father John O'Callahan, were asked to develop the chapter on relationships between priests and laywomen.

David recalled Ladd's friendship with Willow Caprice, and asked Father O'Callahan to draw up two scenarios, one on the positive elements of that relationship and the other on the problematic aspects, as he remembered them.

Fictitious names were used in the two case studies, and David had asked Ladd for permission beforehand to use the relationship between Willow and Ladd as a model.

. . .

As much as Ladd wanted to take part in world-wide humanitarian work for the poorest of the poor, he felt a strong twinge of regret earlier when he had to leave St. Gregory's. He had enjoyed parish work and had become an integral part of the Richmond District. The parishioners, too, felt the pain of separation. They loved this parish priest and asked him back for a weekend of liturgies and receptions.

Ladd gave his farewell homily at the Sunday Masses. "Though there is the sorrow which Shakespeare speaks of in this parting, there is some measure of sweetness also, because goodbyes such as this one have been the occasion to bring us together in ways that are rarely possible.

"You can be sure that I will be keeping you in my thoughts and prayers. And I ask you to do the same for me."

Ladd would describe all of this for David.

"I don't know if I was a very good parish priest, Dave. I gave my farewell sermon to the congregation and told them that the Archbishop had permitted me to join CRS to work for the poor, and I was sorry to be leaving St. Gregory's. But, I told them, it was really Jesus who brought me to you people in the first place. And now it is Jesus who is taking me away from you." And then the choir sang, 'Oh, What a Friend We Have in Jesus.'"

CHAPTER 28

Even in the early 1960's, with the opening of the Second Vatican Council and the consequent momentous shift in relationships between priests and their bishops, events seemed always destined to go wrong when David was in the presence of Archbishop Costello.

The Archbishop's priest-secretary was on his day off. Costello needed someone to drive him home for lunch. David would drive him.

Driving his car to the Archbishop's special entrance at the back of the Chancery building, David picked up the prelate and started for the episcopal residence.

"I want to stop off for a moment at St. Martin's Hospital," the Archbishop said.

David turned the car in the direction of Hayes and Stanyan Streets and parked in front of St. Martin's. The Archbishop always took work home with him at lunch. As he stepped out of the car, his brief case fell from the seat beside him on the floor; the prelate hadn't noticed it.

David called out to the Archbishop, but he was out of ear-shot. Even if he had heard David, his response obviously would have been "Well, pick it up."

The contents of the brief case had scattered on the floor in front of the seat.

David was in a quandary. He couldn't just leave the mess of papers and file folders where they were. But David knew the Archbishop, when he got home, would take one look at the contents and conclude that David had taken the opportunity to retrieve the contents of his brief case, looking at confidential correspondence and documents to learn what was going on in the archdiocese.

He decided to scoop everything up and placed the contents as best he could in the brief case.

When the Archbishop climbed back in to the car, David tried to explain what had happened and hoped that his boss believed him.

. . .

A month later, David waited in the reception lobby for ten minutes before he was summoned into Archbishop Costello's office. The Archbishop did not waste time with words.

"Father Carmichael, I would like you to take over the diocesan newspaper, The Observer, as editor."

Because he was convinced by this time that the Archbishop questioned his judgment and good sense, David was taken by surprise. He was elated by this expression of confidence in him. He would be head of a department.

"You will want to do some studies to prepare yourself for the job. See what courses are available at San Francisco State, the University of San Francisco, Stanford, or the University of California, and enroll in this coming semester. I would like you to take over the position two months from now, so you will have to do some on-the-job learning. Do you have any experience in journalism?"

"No, Your Excellency, not really. I wrote a few articles for the seminary magazine. The only other qualification to be a journalist is that I had a paper route in Napa when I was a boy."

David thought some levity would be in place at this point but the Archbishop showed no humor in the remark. Archbishop Costello generally operated on the principle that a stern demeanor would keep an appropriate distance between himself and his subordinates. It might help him to exercise his authority more effectively.

David understood the posture. He used the same device when he was teaching eighth graders in the parish school.

. . .

David chose the University of California, and crossed the Bay Bridge to Berkeley the following Monday. The spring semester was getting under way. He found four classes that would fit into his schedule.

Over the next year, including summer session courses and some evening classes, David commuted to Berkeley.

The main challenge of his first visits was to find parking. He was not familiar with the City of Berkeley. His knowledge of the University of California was limited to a passing knowledge of football coaches, Stub Allison and Lynn "Pappy" Waldorf, the Golden Bears' Stadium, and Tightwad Hill overlooking the stadium.

Now he drove Bancroft Way and Telegraph Avenue to Sather Gate, wandered up and down the side streets until, at the top of Hearst Street, he found the university Newman Center. He managed to negotiate a parking space from the Paulist Fathers who staff the facility. In a few weeks, he became familiar with Wheeler Auditorium, Robert Sproul Plaza, Hillgard Hall and the milkshakes at Dad's Creamery.

He had long been familiar with the tall needle-like campanile tower, visible from the East Shore Freeway, on the countless times he drove from San Francisco home to Napa. When he was studying at St. John Vianney Seminary in Menlo Park, he was told by students at nearby Stanford University in Palo Alto that Stanford's Hoover Library tower was built deliberately three feet taller than the University of California campanile.

At first, the journalism classes did not seem to be practical or helpful. Classroom lectures were not meaningful, because he was getting the answers before he knew the questions. As the months went by and he was learning the actual practice of being an editor, the instruction began to make more sense. He was getting the answers now when, at least, he knew some of the questions.

But it was mainly through on- the -job that he was learning the profession; the editing, the "cutting from the bottom", and the necessity of putting the essence of the story in the lead paragraph. He would learn to measure column inches, crafting headlines to fit column widths along with the importance of avoiding "tombstoning" headlines, the difference between hot type and cold type, the pasting up of camera-ready pages for off-set printing.

These things were mechanical and eventually learned.

The difficulty came with circulation and advertising. Maintaining the forty to sixty ratio between editorial content and advertising and generally coordinating a creative and sometimes sensitive staff was no easy task for an editor, let alone a priest.

But more challenging than any of these was dealing with the turbulent times.

. . .

Two months after David was on the job, the associate editor invited him and the rest of the editorial personnel to a lecture by a Father Hans Küng, theologian.

The Observer staff had front row seats at the Jesuit University of San Francisco gymnasium, which was jammed to the top of the bleachers and folding chairs covering the entire basketball floor. David was amazed at the turn out.

Father Küng was an eloquent speaker, well known to David at the time.

Küng's topic was ecclesiology, what the Roman Catholic Church should be. What he was saying mostly made sense to David. It did not seem to be inflammatory and only marginally unorthodox. Half way through the address, the theologian turned to the subject of female Religious Orders. He spoke of the slavery of the women Religious, the need for fundamental changes in the exercise of authority in convents. David thought these remarks were reasonable, but he was completely taken by surprise when whole sections of Sisters, mostly in the upper bleachers, rose to their feet, clapped their hands and shouted in agreement.

For David, the sudden outburst was like the first small cloud on the horizon, signaling the tumultuous storm that was to come.

The Vatican II Council was beginning that September, and David and The Observer would be caught in the raging tides of change in a Church which had not been altered substantively in four hundred years.

The Observer was caught between a liberal editorial staff and a conservative archbishop-publisher.

One of the columnists would write that the worst tragedy that ever occurred in the Catholic Church was the Council of Trent. David knew this statement would anger the Archbishop, but he also knew now that it is totally unprofessional and intolerable for an editor to tamper with the words of a signed column.

Although David agreed with most of the positions of his editorial staff, the great struggle was deciding how far he could go printing stories which he knew were contrary to the publisher's convictions. Diocesan newspapers were becoming less and less house organs, less propaganda. Still, basic changes in Church liturgy and challenges to Church authority were highly sensitive.

One Friday, an article reporting a protest against a Midwest Cardinal Archbishop was positioned on the front page below the fold. David knew it was potential trouble. Two days after that issue was published and had somehow reached the Midwest, phones began to ring. There were objections from the Cardinal's Chancery Office. David received a personal call from a priest friend protesting the story, objecting to the prominence given it on page one.

David pointed out to the callers that it was a news-wire story from the United States Bishops' News Service in Washington, D.C., and that it was noteworthy that a Cardinal of the Church would be publicly challenged by members of his flock.

A day would come when news stories such as this were common place in the Catholic press, but at this moment there was no calming the anger.

Two days later, the intercom buzzer sounded in David's office.

"Cardinal Desmond is on the phone for you, Father."

David had no doubt about the nature of the call. Reluctantly he picked up the phone, "Hello."

"Is this Father Carmichael?"

"Yes."

"This is Cardinal Desmond."

"Yes, Your Eminence."

The prelate did not seem angry. He was very much in control.

"I have read an article in the San Francisco Observer this week to which I would like to respond."

"Yes, Your Eminence. I am sorry if this story was offensive to you. We did not mean it to be that way."

"The article was slanted and inaccurate. I would like an article, which I will send to you, printed in The Observer in the next issue, and I would like that article to be placed on the front page, just as the original story was placed."

"Your Eminence, may I say that we have had very little reaction about that article here in Northern California. I think that most of the readers of the paper hardly noticed it and have forgotten it, if they read it at all."

"Nevertheless, I want to see this article, which I am sending to you, published just as the first article was published."

"If I may say so, Cardinal, I really think that doing this will simply highlight the story and prolong whatever controversy there is about it."

"Be that as it may, you will receive the responding article special delivery within the next day or two. Thank you, Father, and God bless you."

The Cardinal's article ran in the following issue.

David would hear from his own archbishop about the matter.

Tight spots such as these occurred virtually every Friday, The Observer's publishing day.

. . .

The San Francisco Giants were in the thick of a national league pennant race. Gordon Caprice had obtained three tickets to a night game through his father. He invited David and Tyler. They accepted readily, after making some appointment changes.

As they had guessed, coming from George Caprice, the seats were good ones - box seats near home plate, along the third base line. That was the warmer side of Candlestick Park. As they looked across the diamond, they could see San Francisco fans on the first base side bundled in blankets. Others probably tourists, were dressed in light blouses, shirts and Bermuda shorts, since it was still summer. They turned blue as the fog drifted over the stadium.

The game was tied going into the seventh inning. Then Russ Hodges' voice boomed over the public address system. "If the priests from Holy Trinity Cathedral are in attendance, would one of them please report to the press box?"

Gordon was the Cathedral priest, so he left the box seat and climbed the stairs toward the announcers' booth.

Not more than five minutes later he was back.

"The Cathedral's on fire."

David and Tyler were stunned.

"Well, let's wait until the end of the inning to see if the Giants score, David said."

Gordon gave him a look of disbelief.

"Only kidding," David said as the three hurried up the steps and out to the parking lot.

As Gordon drove onto the freeway that leads eventually to Franklin Street, they could see the San Francisco sky to the north filled with an orange glow.

They exited at the Golden Gate Avenue off-ramp and were, in another three minutes, halted at O'Farrell Street where the entire block was circled with fire equipment. After double parking near Christian Brothers High School, the three ran to the Cathedral rectory. They were blocked from getting any closer to the fire. It was obvious that the church was completely gutted.

Gordon called one of the firemen over to the barrier. "I am a priest stationed here at the Cathedral. I would like to get into the church to see if I can retrieve the Blessed Sacrament."

"The Archbishop was already here and did that," the fireman replied.

"Do you know what started the fire?" David asked.

"I heard it was a large vigil light candelabrum someone overturned."

The fire, fed by heavily waxed wooden pews, swept the interior of the church from sanctuary to vestibule. It was the end of the venerable red brick edifice in which David, Ladd, Tyler and Gordon had been ordained only sixteen years before.

. . .

On a late November morning in 1963, David climbed out of his car in the Chancery parking lot. His secretary caught sight of him from the first floor Observer front office and called from the window, "Come in quick. We've just heard on the radio that President Kennedy has been shot - in Dallas."

David joined The Observer staff around the editorial room television as Walter Cronkite described the gun shots in Daly Plaza and the race of the presidential motorcade to Parkland Memorial Hospital.

Not more than 15 minutes later, a simple announcement. "The President is dead."

That weekend, David joined the rest of the world, glued to their television sets, reliving the tragedy. He would see live on television, the shooting of Lee Harvey Oswald, a somber Jackie Kennedy at the coffin in the Capitol Rotunda, and the sorrow-stricken funeral cortege to the funeral Mass followed by the burial, just below the Custis Lee Mansion at the National Cemetery.

With the image of little John Junior saluting his father indelibly etched in his mind, David wrote an editorial - a letter "To a President's Son".

"Dear John:

"Today, young John, you saluted your father on the way to his burial. It was your third birthday and you could not understand. But you did well to salute him. And someday, you will understand why.

"One day you will recognize that God gave to your father all the qualities that other men admire. He had exceptional intelligence. We marveled at his grasp of facts and his clarity of expression.

"Your father seemed to have a natural empathy. It just wasn't in him to be small in dealing with others. He was the kind of man who would have had compassion even for his assassin.

"Though he was rich, he was one of us. Though he had every reason to, he never took himself too seriously.

"He was young, and our civilization puts great store on youth. God had given him handsome features and an attractive personality.

"He was apparently the kind of father all fathers want to be -- loving you and your sister, and loved by you. More than anyone else in our memory, your father seemed to have all the qualities we expect in a hero. And with it all, he was self-effacing -- this enhanced everything else.

"To all appearances, God had been unbelievably generous to your father. But to whom much is given, much is asked. A man like this doesn't just happen. He is forged out of suffering and sacrifice.

"God had asked him to carry many crosses. He had suffered the loss of a brother and a sister in the prime of life. He had seen another sister burdened with a serious affliction. He had been called to endure heroic hardship in a World War. In illness he had come so close to death he was anointed. As a father, he had suffered the loss of your brother, Patrick. Though he served in an arena where deeds are sometimes sordid and principles ignored, this was a man demanded by his times.

"Like you will be in a few years, young John, the world today is awkward. It is an adolescent asked to grow up faster than it can. It needed a leader with intelligence far above the average; it needed a youth to keep up with the missile-speed times; and most of all, it needed someone with stability to temper the wild currents that are sweeping across the world and the passions inflaming the hearts of nations. He helped us in bewildering times.

"You do not understand any of this now. But may you salute your father all through your life. May you do more than that - may you resemble him."

CHAPTER 29

As the Church came open to the world, Scripture scholars began to reject the traditional image of the historic Christ, questioning the very words and miracles attributed to Him in the Gospels. As barriers came down among the Christian denominations and theologians questioned the "eternal" inaccessible teachings and disciplines of the Roman Catholic Church, some of the American Church hierarchy began to be challenged not only for their support of the Vietnam War but for their very authority. The foundations of David's life were shaken. At times he would awaken in the darkness of the night in anguish. He was inclined to accept the new concepts that were sweeping through the Church. But then the thought tortured him: "Am I losing my Faith?"

It was a time of tensions and conflict; conservatives against liberals, clergy against clergy, some laity against other laity, some parishioners against some pastors, priests against bishops and demonstrations in front of churches and outside chancery offices.

His staff continually pressed David to report these tensions and protests. He knew these events were at the heart of the Church's life in the middle and late '60s and into the '70s and should be reported.

David knew whatever hope he had for clerical advancement was rapidly eroded every Friday.

Priests Senates, unheard of in recent centuries in the Church, were being formed in every diocese, including San Francisco. Such associations were almost the equivalent of clerical labor unions.

. . .

Through it all, Archbishop Costello was remarkably patient. On occasion, he let David know his displeasure about a story or column that appeared in the previous issue of The Observer. But he never interfered. He did not exercise prior censorship or impose editorial policy.

There was one exception. That had to do with the proposed new Cathedral.

After four years, ground was broken for a new hyperbolic peraboloid cathedral, conceived by Pierre Luigi Nervi of Rome and Pietro Belluschi from MIT. It was a marvel in concrete design, rivaling the creative architecture of the Cathedrals of Liverpool, Tokyo and Rio de Janeiro.

Artistic critical acclaim was unanimous. San Francisco Chronicle's columnist, Herb Caen, praised the innovative design and typically had a nickname for it: "Monsignor's Maytag" because its unique structure resembled, to him, the interior agitator of a washing machine.

Ladd, back in the Bay Area for an interval at the San Francisco CRS office, led an active group of clergy, Sisters and laity opposed to the construction of the $17 million cathedral in the face of pockets of grinding poverty in San Francisco and throughout the Third World.

Ladd eventually organized a town hall meeting to let the protestors' views be known. The Archbishop directed David to attend and to defend the project.

Though he agreed with the opponents for the most part, as editor of the diocesan newspaper, he knew he had to uphold the policy of the archdiocese.

Ladd's reading of a position paper signed by 27 of the protestors introduced the open forum and drew enthusiastic applause.

From the floor, speaker after speaker addressed the issue, some truculent, some reasoned in their comments, some outraged.

David rose to respond:

"Catholics are not doing enough for the poor and the oppressed. We cannot speak for members of the Church everywhere in the world, but from what we see of the Church in affluent America, we are convinced that many of us are not giving sufficiently of our time and possessions to help the less fortunate in our midst and around the world.

"Let it be clear that this is the conviction of the archdiocese.

"We think that our Christian witness for poverty will most vividly and effectively be seen in the austerity of our lives as priests and people, in our detachment from luxuries, in the places we live, in the pouring out of ourselves without stint.

"The letter, moderate in wording, composed by Father Ladd Franklin and the twenty-seven signatories about poverty and Holy Trinity Cathedral deals with a subject which is debated in almost every age of the Church.

"The concern of these protestors is a commendable thing. This is what the Gospels are all about. Their bringing their convictions to the attention of the Archbishop is appropriate. This is what the Vatican II meant when it said that all the people of God must be heard.

"As far as the cathedral itself is concerned, we think the essential point debated is whether the money involved is better spent for the cathedral now under construction or for other purposes.

Some splendor is appropriate to feed the aesthetic hunger of the poor and rich alike. It was the poor who built the cathedrals of Europe and looked on them as one of the few signs of solace and hope in their wretched lives.

Ironically, whether or not the spending of resources on these edifices in those times was wise and socially responsible, it has come about that these same cathedrals, centuries later, are the principal attraction for tourism, Europe's strongest industry and the backbone of the economy for lower-income persons today.

As a matter of fact, building a new cathedral is precisely what the people contributed this money for. No matter how we might argue the matter theoretically, these people have given this money for a specific purpose. To use their contributions otherwise would be to disregard their intentions.

In some ways, houses of worship of God are more necessary now than ever because of the danger of a complete secularization of society. An emphasis on worship is needed because of a dangerous slippage in a sense of the divine, a sense of the transcendental.

We believe that, as construction continues, those in charge will keep very well in mind changing needs and build into the cathedral neither more nor less than what is consonant with the urgent needs of the times and what is suitable for man's aspirations in giving praise and worship to God.

Building houses of worship and helping the poor are not mutually exclusive. They go hand in hand. The more people honor God (and for many this includes material things, such as the building of churches) the more they express their love for God, the more they will love and do for the poor. (Though he spoke this forcefully, David wondered if this was true).

Though there have been societies without money and without walls, a society without prayer and a visible religious structure is unknown.

We know that no one is arguing for the elimination of cathedrals. The point at issue is whether a cathedral as expensive as the new one now under construction is necessary.

David's words were well received by most of the large audience. But the debate raged on for nearly three hours.

. . .

Once the cathedral was completed, Ladd, as spokesman for the protestors, presented David with the layout for an advertisement to be run in the dedication commemorative issue of The Observer. It presented in detail the ways the $17 million could be more responsibly spent according to Gospel values.

David knew this would be explosive. But he did not know how to refuse the advertisement. It was the honest expression of the beliefs of a segment of the archdiocese's clergy, Religious and laity.

He decided to run the advertisement.

Someone who knew about the proposed ad had apparently contacted Archbishop Costello in Chicago, where he was attending the spring meeting of the National Conference of Catholic Bishops. A phone call came to David's office.

"David, I have heard of an advertisement that you are planning to run in this week's Observer criticizing the new cathedral. I think such an advertisement is entirely inappropriate in the commemorative issue."

"Archbishop, would it be permissible to put it in the regular news section of The Observer, rather than in the Cathedral dedication supplement?"

"It is inappropriate to publish such an advertisement at this time, and I will expect it not to run."

That was that. The publisher had spoken.

David knew he had to give a call to Ladd and the advertisement's proponents, telling them that the ad would not appear.

Some of the protestors were incensed. The treasurer of the protestor's group verbally accosted David. "It looks like The Observer is still a house organ. Be sure to send us back the money we advanced for the ad."

Now David knew he had the displeasure of both sides.

He had known that already.

David suspected that the one who put in the call to Chicago to the Archbishop about the cathedral protest ad was Gordon. Working upstairs in the Chancery Office, he would have been one of the few to know about the ad.

Later, David realized that he should not have made that rash judgment. Gordon disagreed with him on many things, but Gordon was never devious or unfair. If he was going to report the advertisement to the Archbishop, he would have leveled with David about it beforehand.

It turned out that an employee of the paper's printing company for The Observer was a member of Guardians of Doctrine, and had called Archbishop Costello in Chicago.

. . .

It fell to David's lot to edit the archdiocesan newspaper in some of the most turbulent years of the Church.

In the '60s and early '70s, authority was being challenged at every level - government, parents, military, school, and the Church.

The religious community was particularly divided. Ecumenism was bringing a measure of unity among the separated denominations, but the chasms were widening internally within the individual churches. The divisions were along liberal-conservative, progressive-traditional lines.

Church newspapers particularly were feeling the heat of the conflict. Most Church ministries were accomplished quietly out of the glare of publicity. But the journalists' work was front and center for everyone to see. The Observer's hits, runs and errors were up on the scoreboard week after week.

CHAPTER 30

Rumors were circulating that Archbishop Costello was about to name a small number of Monsignors. As usual, a guessing game began as to which priests would be honored. All but one of the department heads were already Monsignors. The speculation centered on two older pastors who seemed to have been passed over in the last round of Monsignors. Others included Gordon Caprice and David Carmichael.

"You'll be wearing the red soon, David," Tyler said as the two headed out to see a re-issued movie they had both missed the first time around, "Lawrence of Arabia".

"I doubt it," David replied.

"Well it's an automatic for heads of departments. Will you still remember your old friends when you're part of the inner circle?"

"If I'm ever in the inner circle, I'll be way out on the periphery."

. . .

The following Monday, David received the weekly envelope that came down from the administrative offices on the fourth floor in the Chancery building. This contained the announcements that were to be printed in The Observer's second page "Official Column" each week.

David opened the envelope and found the usual list of events for the Archbishop's calendar. There was an additional page enclosed with a heading at the top: "Monsignors Named."

David felt that hollow feeling he remembered experiencing coming through the entrance gate at Regina Cleri Seminary the first week of September each year, after summer vacation.

He read the list, his eyes running rapidly down the page

His eye ran down the page.

Father Arthur Walkman, Domestic Prelate - a major rank.

Father Egidio Pozzi, Domestic Prelate.

Father Gordon Caprice, Papal Chamberlain - a lesser rank but, in Rome, an attendant to the Pope."

David thought back to all the other times he had lost out to Gordon, even from junior seminary days. He was disappointed, but he wasn't going to let anybody see his dejection. He passed along the Official announcements to the type-setters without comment.

One of The Observer staff retrieved the Monsignor list from the copy basket of the composing room.

"The boss didn't make Monsignor," he informed the other staffers in the editorial room.

"That's too bad. Even though I don't think much of the title, I think he should have gotten it."

"Should we say anything to him?"

"Maybe we should just say nothing, like it isn't all that important anyway."

"Well, I'm going to talk to him," said the associate editor.

He knocked on the door to David's office and walked in.

"I just saw the new Monsignor appointments list. I want to say for the staff that we all think you should have been on the list."

"Well, thanks, Tom. I don't think many diocesan newspaper editors will be made Monsignors these days."

"Well, we think you deserve it."

David secretly wished he had received the honor, but he harked back to his seminary formation and said, "We're not supposed to be looking for advancement or human awards anyway."

. . .

David gave no sign of being disappointed however, inwardly, he was hurt. He had worked hard, perhaps too hard. And now, he did not have the confidence of his superior, the Archbishop.

Although he usually kept his wounds to himself, he had to share this upset and confusion with someone. He would talk to his spiritual director, Father Michael Buckley.

Buckley was ten years younger than David. David knew him to have a keen mind and clear understanding of human nature.

As he rarely had done before, David poured out the full story of his disappointment. Without interrupting, Michael listened through to the end.

He did not try to dissuade David from the fact that he had been publicly disciplined. He took another tack. "Of all the terrors and demons within us, David, one of the worst is fear of personal failure. I recall Raissa Maritain writing in her Journals that she and her husband Jacques made a visit to the bedside of the dying Charles duBos - a major, if unrecognized, French intellectual. Both Maritains were enormously struck by one of the last comments of duBos on his deathbed. He said, 'The mark of every great life is failure.'"

Buckley let that thought sink in, and then he continued, "Perhaps duBos was thinking of Nietzsche dying in madness, or of Mozart dying in poverty with his music trivialized, or Aquinas and Chaucer with the Summa and The Canterbury Tales forever unfinished.

"You know, David, there is a tradition of weakness in the Church. Think of the Apostle Peter; Mary Magdalene; Augustine; and Francis of Assisi from a dysfunctional family.

"Just about any one of us can tell a personal tale of frustration, misrepresentation and failure. Worse yet, some of us are excessively fearful of failure. We give undue weight to the threats posed by risk and to the cost that the possibility of failure will exact from our lives."

"Yes, I'm one of those," David said. "I think too much of succeeding and advancement."

Buckley waited for David to continue, but he was silent.

"We must recall even Jesus failed, failed in His prophetic mission to Israel, thwarted by the legitimate civil leaders of His time. Then He was deserted by His friends and repudiated by His people. Actually, Jesus is discovered in failure. The failed Jesus is what Mother Teresa calls 'His most distressing disguise.'

"David, how do we define success or failure? Think of Socrates. He went to his death with calmness and poise. He accepted the judgment of the court; discoursed on the two alternatives suggested by death; found no cause for fear; drank the hemlock poison and died.

"Jesus was profoundly upset with terror and fear; he looked for comfort from friends and an escape from death and found neither. He finally accepted His death in silence and lonely isolation.

There was a pause for a full minute. Then David said, "I know. My priorities are all mixed up. But because my standards are what they are, I am really feeling low."

"David, be sure to learn from the experience. This is a time for growth in you. One of the most liberating discoveries we can make is that you and I will work out our salvation not despite our weaknesses and failures, but precisely because of our weaknesses and failures.

. . .

In the spring of the seventh year after his ordination, Tyler was called into the Diocesan Superintendent of Schools' office.

Monsignor Sheridan greeted him warmly and Tyler suspected why he had been summoned. "We would like you to teach at one of our high schools, starting this fall, Tyler."

Tyler's mind went back to his seminary spiritual director's advice - "Better to let the archdiocese decide what your work will be, rather than picking and choosing for yourself. Be careful what you ask for in assignments. You might get it! The only thing worse than not getting what you want, is getting what you want."

Tyler accepted. He enjoyed his ministry at Holy Rosary, but getting into special work seemed to be God's will for him.

In September, he took up his new duties at Padre Palou High School. His subject assignments were English, World History, Freshmen Religion and Latin. He had received graduate education in theology only. The other subjects he would have to study as he went along. He would stay one page ahead of his students.

Palou was a college preparatory four-year senior high school, all male, with forty to fifty students in each class.

Tyler asked veteran teachers for guidance. The one piece of advice they unanimously agreed on was: "Don't smile until Christmas." In September, Tyler considered that an exaggeration. By Thanksgiving, he knew it was literally true. Like Arizona coyotes, teenage boys are tolerably good individually, but in packs they can be ferocious.

Tyler remembered teachers he had during his own student days. He admired those who seemed at ease in the classroom and could deal with their students with humor and loose-reined control. What he didn't realize was that those teachers had developed that skill only over a period of many years.

For the first two weeks, freshmen are as frightened and as unsure of themselves as a new teacher is. But soon they begin testing the beginner to see how much they can get away with. If they detect any chink in the armor, the pack attacks. To a 14-year-old, this isn't unfair or cruel; it is fun.

Tyler, from the start, tried to treat the ninth graders as young men; but these are boys. After weeks of assigning punishments, five thousand "lines" or after school detention, "jug," Tyler finally got the hang of it.

One had to be young to carry the schedule of Tyler and his colleagues; five teaching periods a day, with four separate preparations, yard supervision at recess and lunch period, coaching the junior varsity football team, the parents' club, and the semi-annual school plays. Along with Mass in the chapel and correcting homework, – it meant a sixteen hour day. Tyler found himself crowding in the required reading of the breviary from eleven to midnight on school days.

Teaching was a relentless occupation. The hour-by- hour schedule was unyielding. There was no place to hide. Tyler's "parishioners" were there every day - in a 40 x 65 foot room. And the students were gloves-off candid and direct. It was a good job for Tyler to have early in his priesthood. After that, every assignment would seem easy. Every mark of respect wholeheartedly appreciated.

CHAPTER 31

Drought, famine and civil war were ravaging Ethiopia.

The flight from Rome arrived in Addis Ababa near midnight.

Mickey Leland of Texas met Ladd at the terminal and invited him to accompany the U.S. Congressman three days later on a flight to the refugees at the Sudan border. Ladd, knowing he would be returning to Addis in three days, accepted the invitation.

First, however, Ladd flew from the capital's international airport in a Cessna Caravan 9-seater toward Mosawa Port, Eritrea. Although there was a critical drought in other parts of Ethiopia, steady showers were flooding the Addis airport as the Cessna climbed to the north. (The city averages twelve inches of rain a year, as compared to San Francisco's average of nineteen inches, and the California Central Valley's – America's grocery basket) seventeen inches. Droughts recur in Ethiopia largely because the twelve inches of rain are not captured in dams.)

Ladd suspected the CRS chartered plane was overloaded with passengers and baggage. As he said the Liturgy of the Hours during the first part of the flight, his prayer intention was that the plane would make it over the next mountain range. It struggled to gain altitude and, finally, labored over the lowest of the peaks.

. . .

The passage from the Book of Exodus, which Ladd read from the breviary during the flight that day, told of Moses and Aaron petitioning the pharaoh to permit the Israelites to leave Egypt. The passage struck

Ladd all the more forcibly as he realized that the arid peaks and valleys below him were not many miles away nor that different from the land of Moses and Aaron.

And timely and meaningful were the words of the hymn Ladd read at Evening Prayer that night:

> "O Lord, who in the desert fed
> The hungry thousands in their need
> Where want and famine still abound.
> Let your relieving love be found;
> And in your name may we supply
> Your hungry children when they cry."

The northern landscape reminded Ladd of Yosemite, Yellowstone and the Grand Canyon. Was it the Ice Age, with glaciers grinding relentlessly through the terrain, that fashioned the spectacular crags, valleys and flat-top mountains in the Horn of Africa?

The pilot circled low to attempt a landing at the Port of Mosawa, but it was fogged in. The plane climbed out of the valley and headed north to Asmara.

After a fifteen kilometer drive in a Land Cruiser out of Asmara, Ladd worked at a distribution center and saw face to face those fragile, patient women and children, diseased, undernourished, with distended stomachs, faces tormented by flies.

Ladd's mind suddenly went back to a prose/poem about a similarly devastated mother. "The mother gently frames the skull of the child wither hands as if to heal his softened brain. He sits resigned, bound in hunger, the home he carries with him as a snail his shell . . . his body feasts upon itself, shriveling mouth making no sound, eyes devoid of pleading, ribs and flesh a woven mesh. This is no image of a Rubenesque apple-cheeked, placid Madonna, offering a child, plump and warm as rising dough."

Ladd helped the local CRS workers hand down from high lofts 110-pound sacks of wheat and other grains to be given, one sack each to a family as their subsistence for the next 30 days - along with a portion of soybean oil for caloric content, and powdered milk for protein and calcium.

Those who have the least are the most appreciative. The mothers, most of them very young, acknowledged Ladd's appearance with warm smiles. There was not the slightest hint of loss of pride in receiving this help. One could not find more nobility, dignity, and grace elsewhere. The children were shy but wide-eyed, watchful of Ladd and his colleagues, these newcomers to the scene. If the Eritreans were offered a hand in greeting, they stepped forward and shook the hand with complete trust. Some had walked on foot for five days to reach the center.

Ladd wondered if happiness can be measured. It is an intriguing question: With all the physical sufferings and deprivations, is there perhaps more genuine serenity, more experience of the profound realities of life found among the long lines of the hungry in this pitiful distribution center? There is something in the spirit here one does not find among the affluent.

CRS, together with counterpart humanitarian agencies, was stressing development in order to meet not just emergency needs, but to equip the people to deal with catastrophes in the future.

Ladd's party visited wells being drilled at various points in the valley, bringing from the water table, deep below the surface of the earth, uncontaminated water. Like the woman at the well in Samaria, Eritrean women balance on their heads bottles, jars and plastic canisters from dwellings miles away.

The drilling of wells and the development of a series of micro-dams was critical in this land of drought. Water pollution was increasing everywhere around the globe. One of CRS' slogans was "Give a person a fish and you feed him for a day; teach that person to fish and you feed him for a lifetime." Ladd suggested changing the slogan to "Give a person a fish and you feed him for a day; teach that person to fish and you give him mercury poisoning."

Regularly, along the way, Ladd's van was halted at the check-points by the government security forces. Three or four men at every station, bearing military rifles, checked to see if the driver had the proper credentials. They question Amel and Yemi, the Ethiopian CRS employees traveling with Ladd. They were on the look-out for guerrillas attempting to overthrow the socialist government of Dr. Mengistu. These insurgent rebels are also Marxists. Banners and monuments to Lenin, Marx and Engels are found throughout Ethiopia.

Travel advisories from the State Department cautioned Americans not to travel in these regions. With sporadic violence, the rebels interrupted the work of humanitarian agencies.

At a storage depot near Asmara, behind an equipment repair garage, Ladd helped cannibalize seven trucks destroyed by a rebel ambush the previous month. The trucks which had been carrying thousands of metric tons of grains, were completely burned out. All that remained were twisted steel and broken glass. Parts that could be saved were minimal.

In Adigrat, Tigre, Ladd's plane landed on a runway that was not yet intended to be a runway.

Disembarking, he was told that the landing strip was still under construction. His was the first airplane to attempt a landing. The runway was filled with ruts, potholes and jagged boulders.

A thousand government troops were slain by the rebels in Adigrat two weeks before Ladd arrived. It was one of the most intense trouble spots in Ethiopia. At the cathedral, Ladd met one of the two Sisters of the Assumption Order who were captured by the rebels and kept in custody four days before being released earlier in the month.

When the CRS party returned to the airfield, Mark, the pilot, had moved the plane from the unfinished runway to a second airstrip, somewhat smoother, but with a length of only 3200 feet. Mark conjectured that if he could get up to 70 kilometers per hour on the ground at take-off, the entire party could make the flight. Otherwise, he would have to stop in the midst of the take-off and let half the passengers off. This would necessitate two shuttles to Makelle.

As the Cessna raced down the runway, fingers were crossed. At the last moment, the plane lifted off successfully a handful of feet short of the end of the runway.

Just outside of Makelle, Ladd rode to a hilltop and suddenly came upon what resembled a biblical scene of some 800 to 1000 men, women and children carrying rocks through a valley to the construction site of a giant reservoir. This is a voluntary work project; the people are enthusiastic, grateful to be engaged in productive work. It was an unforgettable sight.

. . .

Outside the Makelle distribution center, Ladd encouraged the Salesians in a reforestation project planting 120,000 trees to honor the memory of the 120 thousand men, women and children who died there in the famine three years earlier.

The Cessna lifted into a brilliant sky at midday, passing over Lallabella, with its ancient underground churches visible from overhead at 2000 feet. From there, on towards Addis Ababa, the plane circled the Blue Nile Falls where the river proceeds northwest to join the white Nile on its way to Cairo.

. . .

The delay at Asmara was causing the CRS flight to return 45 minutes late to Addis Ababa. Ladd might miss the departure of Mickey Leland's plane on his humanitarian visit to the Ethiopian-Sudan border.

As they taxied to a stop, Ladd jumped from the Cessna and went directly to the commuter gate. He found an agent at the chartered airplane's desk.

"I'm Father Ladd Franklin. I'm to accompany Congressman Leland on his flight."

"I'm sorry, Reverend, that flight took off just five minutes ago. The Congressman inquired about you and waited for you."

. . .

That evening, Addis Ababa was swarming with U.S. military personnel. Ethiopia's government radio announced: "A search is being organized for the airplane carrying Mickey Leland of Houston, Texas, a member of the Congressional Select Committee on Hunger, and a party of 15, lost somewhere between Addis Ababa and the Sudan border."

Ladd was shaken. He feared for the congressman and wondered why God had protected his own life.

Ladd offered Mass at 10 o'clock on Sunday at Holy Savior Church for the safety of the congressman and his traveling companions from the U.S. Embassy and the United Nations, along with refugee program staffers.

Two hours after the Mass, word was received that the drowned plane had been sighted against a mountainside near Gambia. The first reports indicated that thirteen bodies had been discovered. Little hope was held out for the survival of the other three.

Military rescue teams, medics and other personnel flew out to the crash site the next morning to recover the bodies and to return them to the Embassy in Addis Ababa.

The aircraft had crashed near Fugnido, just five minutes short of the displaced Sudanese settlement camp and scant meters below the summit of the last mountain.

CHAPTER 32

Tyler was jogging outside the Serramonte Mall. It was Christmas time.

As the Upper Peninsula winter wind grew colder, he moved inside and walked along the shops, relieving the boredom of exercise. Every imaginable product was on display and every fourth or fifth store seemingly featured footwear. At the central plaza, Tyler stopped to watch the faces of the small children as they met Santa Claus - a disarming variety of facial expressions.

During an interval between children, Santa rose from his throne and walked over to Tyler. "Aren't you Father Stone?"

"Yes . . . Santa."

"I thought so," Santa said. "You taught me World History at Padre Palou High and gave First Communion to my little brother and sister."

"Oh," Tyler replied. "I didn't even know Santa was a Catholic . . . but then I should have remembered he's a bishop - St. Nicholas."

When his former student had returned to his chair, Tyler continued to watch the children - some delighted, some fearful - as they climbed on Santa's lap.

Tyler moved on to Toys "r" Us, more crowded than ever in the holiday season. As he observed the children with their parents, he was fascinated by the range of emotions. All were excited, but several of the children were crying afluent children in the midst of this wealth of Play Stations and Nintendo games. Perhaps those crying were tired or had been told they couldn't have this or that present. He wouldn't have given it a second thought but, fresh in Tyler's memory was the conversation he had recently with Ladd about Ethiopia and the house of abandoned and sick children tended by Missionaries of Charity. He had remarked how surprisingly resigned and even contented the little ones seemed to be. "I don't remember seeing any of the children crying," Ladd had said.

A Christmas present for them was a full meal of wheat cakes and a cup of powdered milk.

Even with all the misery and degradation, Tyler thought, if you could measure serenity and peace, would you find more there in the famine, or here among the abundance of Toys "r" Us?

It was the old paradox, the more we possess, the more the anxieties, the more the expectations, the more the disappointments.

On the other hand, wasn't it Pearl Bailey who said, "I've been rich, and I've been poor. And rich is better."

. . .

In Manhattan, just a week before Christmas, Ladd crossed Rockefeller Center. The traditional New York City community Christmas tree was lit. On one of the side streets, four or five people had clustered spontaneously. They didn't know each other, but they started singing Christmas carols. Ladd stopped and began singing with them. Soon there were six or seven more people. Then the number rose to twenty or thirty, and then over forty. And, for more than an hour, the strangers all coming together, feeling very close, sang "O Holy Night," "Come All Ye Faithful," "We Three Kings," all the carols they could think of. Ladd was impressed. He hadn't anticipated this on the streets of New York City.

But that's what Ladd liked about this holiday. Christmas was always full of surprises.

Ladd had, at times, questions about the divinity of Christ. Was He truly God? Who really was the historical Christ? What about the virgin birth?

These questions seemed to be muted when he heard the simple warmth of "O Little Town of Bethlehem."

Then it all seemed possible that the Infant could be born as serenely enriching and undamaging as light passes through glass without breaking it during that night which made Mary a mother though it left her a virgin.

CHAPTER 33

Ladd took off from San Francisco and landed in Tokyo at two-thirty in the afternoon, Tokyo time. He had lost a day crossing the international dateline. The Pan Am 11B flight was smooth, except for violent shaking of the plane near the Aleutian chain - "a little turbulence," the palliative voice from the flight deck described it.

Ladd's final destination was the World Conference on Religion and Peace Assembly in Beijing. This was an opportunity to get a feel for Asia generally.

. . .

On the evening of the opening day, Ladd was elected Vice President of the Conference. He addressed the full assembly of the morning of the third day:

"Together, we represent a portion of the family of humans far greater than any single government or any other single entity represents. Historically, political leaders cannot make major breakthroughs for peace. Political leaders tend to be centrists. They dare not take bold steps. Through the centuries, breakthroughs for peace and justice have been led by religious leaders or those armed only with moral authority.

"I call upon the religions of the world to unite and to advocate the following platform for peace:

1. Urge your nation to commit itself to unilateral, verifiable agreements to halt testing, production and deployment of all new nuclear weapons systems. The warheads that are being manufactured now will have no other effect than to 'make the rubble bounce.'

2. Declare your nation opposed to a policy of first-strike, the initiation of nuclear attack.

3. Each country must develop a national Department of Peace, financed proportionately to its Department of War.

4. Resolve to work seriously for an effective United Nations or other international authority truly representative of the world's people, granting veto power to no nation, small or large. Preserve each country's internal sovereignty. But give to that world community the moral and military authority to require nations to settle their disputes through negotiation, rather than armed conflict.

"Now I speak as one accepting the principles of Gandhi, Martin Luther King, Abraham, Buddha, Mohammed, as well as Christ:

"I believe political party platforms should declare war a mental illness. We are now building weapons beyond belief and beyond bearing. War and the trappings of war are an embarrassment of the human spirit.

"What was it Anatole France said:

> 'The governing classes do not really want war, but they want to keep up a continual menace of war. They do not want the cannon to be fired, but they do want it to be always loaded.
>
> 'A people living under the perpetual menace of war and invasion is easy to govern. It demands no social reforms. It does not haggle over expenditures for military equipment. It pays without discussion, and that is an excellent thing for the financiers and manufacturers for whom patriotic terrors are an abundant source of gain.'

"We do not despair, and we do not withdraw.
With Isaiah, we want to `repair the breech.'"

. . .

Ladd learned in conversations that though Buddhism has the greatest number of followers by far in China, most of the adherents belong simply through tradition, custom and the momentum of the centuries. Buddhism and Taoism, as religions, do not always affect conduct.

Among the young there is an interesting fascination with western Christianity. Twenty and thirty-year-olds who engaged Ladd in conversation were disposed to talk at length about western religions.

One young student thought the most admirable characteristic of Christianity was that it "despised wealth". Ladd told him he did not know exactly what he was referring to, unless it was Francis of Assisi or the vow of poverty taken by men and women in Religious life. Ladd added that Christianity does teach the spiritual is more important than the material and that wealth should be shared with those in need.

The interest of the Chinese in Christianity intrigued Ladd in the light of the preoccupation that many Westerners, particularly the young, have had in Eastern religions in recent decades.

CHAPTER 34

Tyler taught high school for eighteen years. After the first two years, he began to feel that he had a handle on the job. He was more at ease in the classroom and had developed the reputation of being "in charge".

Once he reached that point, he realized that he did not have to raise his voice or give penances. Once he got the knack of it, keeping discipline seemed as easy as riding a bike or swimming.

Though the schedule was still relentless, Tyler had come to enjoy teaching and felt that sense of satisfaction that teachers experience. He could see the young students in his charge developing into men.

Most gratifying was what he would come to experience as the years passed by. So much of what he taught and formed in these young men had no immediate result; but there was a delayed-action effect. In later years, students, even those for whom he had not had much hope, came back to visit him; and now they were solid citizens, successful in an occupation or profession, dependable husbands and fathers.

. . .

The Archbishop assigned Tyler as pastor of one of the larger city parishes, All Saints in the Sunset District of San Francisco. Parish life - that is what Tyler really had been prepared for in the seminary.

Two thousand families were registered in the parish exactly one square mile in size. Homes in Tyler's parish, built mostly in the '30s and after the war in the '40s, stretched some 18 blocks from 30th Avenue to the Great Highway and the ocean.

All Saints was a small village within a large city.

Typical of the "Avenues," the houses stand cheek-by-jowl, seemingly sharing exterior walls with neighbors to either side, little or no yard in front, and a garage beneath.

In the early days of the '50s, Sun-setters rarely locked their front doors.

Shopping in the same neighborhood stores, riding the "L" Taraval streetcar (which, because of the increasing Asian population, was known as the Orient Express), joining the same parish organizations, sending their children to the parochial school, the parishioners came to know each other as in a small town.

Out "on the avenues," the weather was moderate, particularly breathtaking sunsets in the fall, generally light rains in the winter, gentle springs, and fog, always fog, in the summer. As the weather report always said, "fog along the coast, extending inland night and morning."

It was for this reason Mark Twain had written, "The coldest winter I ever spent was a summer in San Francisco."

The residents of the Sunset were basically blue-collar and middle-income white-collar families. It was a time of families with four, five, six or seven children. All Saints School had three classes at every level from kindergarten to eighth grade.

These were the happiest times of Tyler's life, filled with house-to-house visitations, bringing Communion to the elderly in the convalescent homes, and visiting the sick members of his parish in hospitals scattered throughout the city. He tried to visit each classroom at least briefly each week.

Prayer life could be regular in parish ministry. This included rotating the morning Masses with his assistant priests, saying the daily 45 minutes of the Divine Office, the public prayer of the Church, and the breviary, with its psalms and passages of Sacred Scripture. Tyler made it a point to spend at least some quiet time each day in the presence of the Blessed Sacrament in the church, not reciting formula prayers or fighting off distractions, just "being present."

Tyler recited the rosary walking the parish dog, "Dogma," or driving to hospital visits. The seminary had impressed upon Tyler and his classmates, as seminarians, that there were five ingredients to an effective priesthood: Prayer, Work, Study, Leisure and Friends. And that the greatest of these was Prayer.

The beauty of All Saints Parish was that it had the feeling of "family." Tyler came to know and love the people and they him. Because it was a family, there were the inevitable joys and sorrows that families experience like the joy of being welcomed in every home. Though he had no blood family of his own, he was, in some ways, an intimate member of 2000 families.

The sorrow, feeling the pain of the tragedies of each family, the loss of jobs, the marriage separations, the deaths were also part of his newfound "family." He was devastated for months when three children of involved parish families were killed in separate accidents in a span of six weeks. In parishes this close-knit, the shock-waves roll through the community.

The sad days of funerals and lost parishioners reminded Tyler of William Butler Yeats:

"The old priest Peter Gilligan was weary night and day,
For half his flock were in their beds or under green sod lay.

Once when he nodded on a chair at the moth hour of eve,
Another poor man sent for him and he began to grieve.
I have no rest, no joy, no peace; my people die and die.
And after cried he, `God forgive; my body spake, not I.'"

Even tragedies were opportunities for bringing something of value to the people. Tyler could help them survive and even grow. And they were making him grow. He was learning here at the cutting edge of life. At the times of painful human loss and separation, he was seeing the reality of maxims he had learned in the seminary and repeated as teacher. "God writes straight with crooked lines."

From the candid, stinging reaction of a mother who had just lost her teenage daughter in death, Tyler learned not to try to console with senseless words like "It is God's will."

"It is not God's will," the mother had retorted.

In her faith, she knew that God did not cause tragedies. In a world distorted by original sin, God insisted on allowing freedom, allowing humans and all creation to function freely without His intervention.

. . .

And Tyler had come to feel more at home with death and fragility. When he had toured Laguna Honda, San Francisco's primary public home for the aged, years before as a seminary student deacon, he had silently and fervently prayed that he would never be assigned as chaplain to a place like this. But now, as pastor, visiting the aging, even in the most unpleasant vile smelling rest homes, he found a source of growth, personal maturing and inspiration.

Tyler spent quality time with the elderly. He consoled Erika Zambini and her convalescent home companions with reminders that Albert Schweitzer was still performing medical operations in his African hospital at the age of 81; that Winston Churchill was elected Great Britain's Prime Minister at the age of 65 (he was 70 years old when he addressed the English crowds on V-E Day); that Golda Meir became Prime Minister of Israel at the age of 71; that George Bernard Shaw was 94 when one of his plays was first produced (at 95, he broke his leg when he fell out of a tree).

"Erika, though we live in a society that puts great importance on physical attraction and, therefore, cherishes youth, we remember that many of the most beloved and renowned figures of the Bible were people of age, Methuselah, Moses, Noah, Zachary, Anne, Elizabeth, Nicodemus and Joseph of Arimathea.

"Do you remember that poem:

> `Strange that some of us treasure everything old,
> Gold, lace, wine, houses, trees, ruins --
> Everything but old people!
> Age is opportunity no less
> Than youth itself, though in another dress.
> And as the evening twilight fades away,
> The sky is filled with stars invisible by day.'"

. . .

The call came at 3 o'clock in the afternoon. It was a message relayed from a parish across the park, where the priest on duty was out of the rectory on another sick call.

A prominent founder of a leading California department store chain had suffered a stroke and was near death in Sea Cliff.

Tyler gathered up his sick call kit and headed for the upper economic class district at the edge of a Richmond district parish, overlooking the entrance to San Francisco Bay.

Tyler rang the doorbell of the impressive three-story residence and was met at the door by two fashionably tailored young women.

"Grandfather is very sick. We thought he should have a priest immediately."

"Fine," Tyler said. "I will give him the last sacraments."

"I'm afraid it will frighten him terribly if he knows what you are doing, Father."

Tyler tried to assure the granddaughters that the anointing of the sick was no longer reserved for sick people at the point of death. "It is really a source of consolation and strength, not a reason for fear."

"But grandfather is so old-fashioned. I am sure that if he sees we've called for a priest, it will hasten his death. Actually, we have blind-folded grandfather and told him that just one of his friends had come by to wish him well. Could you say the prayers very low so that he will not be able to hear what you are saying?"

"I really think you are being overly concerned," Tyler persisted. "Oftentimes, though we don't expect it, sick people experience a sense of resignation and calm in receiving the last rites."

But Tyler could not dissuade the women. They knew their grandfather better than he did.

Being assured that the dying man was well disposed to the Church and to the sacraments, Tyler entered the bedroom and administered the sacrament of anointing as surreptitiously as he could to the blind-folded, semi-conscious, dying tycoon.

. . .

Two years after he was installed as pastor, Tyler placed a questionnaire in his parish bulletin, asking his parishioners what qualities they thought were most important as a pastor. Parishioners were invited to fill out the form provided, return it to the rectory or place it in the collection basket the following Sunday. The response was overwhelming. The results were tabulated by the parish staff.

The qualities of a pastor most frequently mentioned by the parishioners were:

1. Teach spiritual things, teach the Gospel.
2. More contact with the people.
3. Holiness.
4. Love and warmth.
5. Less financial and administrative duties.

A second question in the survey asked: "If you were pastor, what would you do . . .?" In the order of frequency, the answers were:

1. . . . keep on doing what the pastor is doing now.
2. . . . be kind.
3. . . . get to know the parishioners better.
4. . . . practice and improve on celebrating Mass.

Far down on the list in 12th place was: If I were pastor,

12. . . .I would resign.

When Tyler received the final results, he pasted the top ten responses on his desk as a daily reminder.

. . .

The etymology of the word "pastor" is "pascere" -- "to feed."
Tyler was finding that the more he tried to be a good pastor, the more the parishioners "fed on" him. The demands on his time were incessant. He had to develop the attribute of "interruptibility."

. . .

Tyler had just sat down to his desk to prepare next Sunday's homily when the intercom intercepted him. "There's a man here who says he has to talk to a priest."
It was part of the foot traffic that dropped by parish rectories for all manner of reasons. A clerk at the Greyhound Bus Depot had once told Tyler, "The first question a transient asks when he drifts into town is, 'Where is the closest church?'"

The present visitor had a problem of conscience. He was a young man who was troubled by scrupulosity. He anguished over sin where there really was no sin.

Tyler took time to point out that he really wasn't culpable of any wrongdoing. It required close to an hour to persuade the man, but gradually the anxiety drained out of his face and he went away consoled.

Tyler went back to his room to take up the sermon preparation and, again, he was interrupted by the phone, "My husband is at St. Luke's Hospital. Although he doesn't know I'm calling, I think he needs to see a priest."

"Is he seriously ill?"

"I don't think he's going to last out the day."

Tyler drove to St. Luke's, recognized the parishioner, a foreman with a local construction company, infrequently seen at Mass.

Tyler talked quietly to the man and eventually asked if he wanted to go to confession.

"It's been a long, long time. I don't even know how to start."

"Just in your own words tell me any way you think you've seriously turned away from God."

Gradually the man recounted his sins. As Tyler said the prayer of absolution, he saw the tears of relief coursing down the rugged face of a hardened penitent.

That evening, Tyler still hadn't written the first word of his homily, but, as he looked back, he knew that these interruptions were the best things that had happened to him all day.

. . .

Tyler's life as pastor was a fast moving series of vignettes - some joy-filled, some sad.

All Saints was a conservative, highly residential parish in the Sunset district of San Francisco, with lower middle-class, parishioners, many civil servants. There were very few Blacks in that part of San Francisco. The district had, for some time, opened up to Hispanic, Filipino and Asian families.

Because the parish tended to be conservative, All Saints did not experience traumatic tensions of the changing Church.

Most of the tense moments were from progressive young associate pastors and seminarians doing their pastoral field work in the parish.

The families in the parish were not greatly impressed with the new currents in society. Still, Tyler was able to introduce delicate social issues; e.g., farm labor, disarmament, and liturgical reforms by presenting them not through social justice meetings or similar devices, but rather by calling discussion sessions "novenas" and holding them in the church.

. . .

Tyler would never forget the late autumn afternoon when repeated gunshots rang out on Taraval Street. Animosity had exploded in a convenience store between Asian and Hispanic street gang members.

Tyler heard the shots and raced in that direction. When quiet settled in, two young Vietnamese and one Mexican were dead.

What broke his heart even further that evening, when Tyler visited the ethnically different homes of the teenagers, he found on the walls and on the mantles of all three modest apartments the same pictures of the Sacred Heart and of Mary; he found the same good parents who had tried their best to raise their children.

How could Tyler judge this Hispanic family that had worked hard over the years to find some kind of decent life?

What could Tyler say to the Vietnamese family with four surviving children, frightened of what their neighbors might think. This, after a lifetime of fear, caught in an ideological struggle in Vietnam, fleeing to the south from Hanoi, traumatized by the war, drifting on the open sea as boat people. How could Tyler comfort them?

On the same evening, three days later, Tyler presided at the separate wakes of the young victims.

As he led the decades of the rosary, he became clearly aware that this prayer was not the mindless repetition of Hail Marys'. It was a prayer provided by the Church when people, in their enormous grief, could not form prayer words of their own.

. . .

Tyler gathered a number of parishioners together to establish a food closet to gather canned goods and household supplies for the needy within and outside the parish.

The food bank was in operation only two months when, during the night, a fire broke out in the trailers which housed the groceries and destroyed everything that had been gathered.

The parishioners and even neighboring communities rallied to the rescue. By the end of the week, the food closet committee had received three times the supplies that they had originally stored before the fire. It was a heart-warming expression of generosity from people of all faiths.

David had heard the news of the outpouring of gifts in Tyler's parish. At the following Sunday's Masses, he thanked all his own people who had contributed to the overwhelming response which had trebled the supplies, and he jokingly added, "I understand Father Tyler has planned the next fire for Thursday night."

. . .

Children preoccupied a good part of All Saints Parish life. Tyler visited the home of a young couple in the outer avenues because he knew they were expecting their second child. He had just arrived when the wife seemed to be going into labor. Tyler urged them to leave for the hospital.

The young father hurried his wife to their car, put their four-year old daughter in the back seat and started off for Seton Medical Center in Daly City.

When they arrived, there were no empty spaces available in the parking lot. The father circled the hospital grounds several times, looking for a place to park, with no success.

Suddenly, the time for giving birth arrived and the young mother and father were frantic. In a moment of desperation, the father pulled up to the emergency entrance and parked.

When he realized that the infant was beginning to come forth, he told his wife to keep sounding the horn in the hope that one of the doctors or nurses inside would come out and assist them. There, in the front seat of the car, he delivered the baby, with his young daughter looking on.

Finally, hospital attendants, hearing the automobile horn and the commotion outside, came out to the car and assisted in the final details of the delivery.

Mother and child did splendidly.

Some weeks later, when Tyler visited again to see how the family was doing, he and the parents overheard their four-year old daughter describing to some of her small companions how babies are born.

The little back-seat eyewitness to the blessed event explained, "Mommy just honked the horn and out popped the baby."

· · ·

Tyler was concerned about the content of religion class teaching which gradually changed after the 1960s. Priests ordained before the Vatican II Council suspected that solid theological content was lacking.

On a Monday morning in April, at the parish school, he visited the third grade and asked them about the coming Holy Week. "Do you know the meaning of Easter?" he asked.

A pupil in the first row waved her hand, "Easter is the day we are going to have my aunts and uncles over for a special dinner."

"That's fine, Shannon. But does anybody know what happened on the first Easter?"

Another young third grader raised his hand, "Easter is the day we have Easter eggs, rabbits and all kinds of candy."

Tyler was beginning to wonder if the children were getting any religious instruction at all.

Now, a little girl in the back was trying to get Tyler's attention, "Father, I know what happened on Easter. That was the day Jesus came back from the dead."

Tyler was relieved. "Yes, Megan, that's right." At least someone knew the real meaning of Easter.

Then Megan went on, "After He was dead three days, Jesus rose from the dead. He came out of the tomb . . . and then He saw His shadow and went back in."

· · ·

Tyler felt sorry for little children under 7 years of age who were taken by the hand by a parent and brought up to the sanctuary at Communion time and could not receive the consecrated Bread. When the priest, not being sure whether First Communion had been received, would extend his hand with the Host, the parent would hurriedly place a hand over the mouth of the child.

Tyler did not want the child to have come all the way to the Communion station and not receive anything, so he made it his custom to bless the child. This morning, when he blessed a little one about five years old with the Sign of the Cross, she blessed him back - the age of feminism had dawned.

. . .

Tyler was appointed diocesan chaplain to the handicapped, the disabled, the retarded. He found special satisfaction in the work. Every time he was associated with the handicapped, he learned from them.

Tyler often referred to them in his homilies. He told of one fleeting beautiful moment at the Special Olympics for the handicapped at Kezar Stadium. It was in the relay race when the runners were handing off the baton at the end of the first lap. One of the runners dropped the baton, and then all the other opposing runners stopped and turned around and waited for that runner to pick up the baton. It was a touching moment of compassion and unselfishness, overriding competition.

Moving incidents like this could overcome the sensitive Tyler.

. . .

On the evening television news, the sight of a young teenager being led away by the police after a courtroom sentencing, calling to his father, "Daddy, help me." The father, moments later interviewed by a reporter, remarked. "That's the first time he's called me 'Daddy' since he was a little boy."

Tender scenes reached deep down in Tyler's emotions.

There were times when even the lyrics of a song like Bobby Goldsboro's "Honey" made tears well up in Tyler's eyes.

. . .

The summer fog had rolled in over the avenues in mid-June and had stayed from morning till night through August.

But this Sunday afternoon, the overcast had broken, and Tyler found a place near the polo grounds in Golden Gate Park to sit and do some reading.

A few minutes later, across the lawn, a young father caught his eye. He was teaching three of his children, two girls and a boy, how to skate with in-line roller blades. The children, ranging from about five to nine years of age, would hesitatingly skate from their father, "Watch me, Daddy, watch me," and then come gliding back to him, clutching his arm or leg to stay upright.

It was a tender scene and, as he watched, Tyler thought one of the most difficult things about being a priest was not to have children of his own.

. . .

And Tyler brought his love for animals into his ministry. In October, on the feast of St. Francis, he invited the parishioners to bring their pets to the church.

In the plaza in front of the church and in the school yard, birds, dogs, cats, turtles, rabbits, guinea pigs, garden snakes - even a horse from the mounted police division, gathered for a special blessing.

Tyler in cassock and surplice, with holy water sprinkler in hand, stood at the top step of the church entrance and spoke to the animals and the humans:

"A ferocious wolf terrified the people of the town of Gubbio. St. Francis of Assisi became friends with the wolf and pacified him. As you know, Francis also conversed with the birds. He devised the first Christmas creche and brought live animals, a cow and a donkey, into his church.

"Many of you have seen 'E.T.,' one of the most successful movies of all times. That film has as its basic message the teaching of St. Francis on reverence for God's creation. Francis is, perhaps, the most popular of the saints. There is something about 'E.T.' and St. Francis that touches a deep chord in all of us.

"Though they sometimes seem to be at odds with each other, there should be no hostility on the one hand between people who work to save the whales or the seal pups in the northern territories and, on the other hand, those who are pro-life. They should work together. There is a gradation of hierarchy in God's creatures, but the principle arises out of the same basic reality - a respect for creation.

"As St. Francis says:

'If we have persons who will exclude any of God's creatures from the shelter of compassion and pity, we will have persons who will deal likewise with other humans.'

"Pope John has written:

'The dominion granted to man by the Creator is not an absolute power, nor can one speak of a freedom to "use and misuse" or to dispose of things as one pleases.'

"In a way, it is difficult to talk about this subject because I, like some of you, have looked on "animal rights" movements sometimes as an eccentric cause. But what we are concerned about is the killing of animals unnecessarily for luxurious clothing or accessories; the killing of animals for cosmetics production.

"Much is going on that we do not know of. One critical situation is Factory Farming: the torturous penning of cattle and sheep so that they cannot move or lie down.

- # Animals that never, in their lifetime, see daylight.
- # Hens that are, through day and night, kept in artificial light so that they will lay eggs continually and unnaturally.
- # Rabbits whose eyes are blinded in experiments. Some of these rabbits, I am told, recoil in such pain that they break their own backs.

"Dr. Albert Schweitzer has said, 'A person is truly ethical when he shrinks from injuring anything that lives.'

"And Ralph Chaplin writes:

'Mourn not the dead,

that in the cool earth lie;
But rather mourn the apathetic throng,
who see the world's great anguish
and dare not speak.'

"I know for the general public, this reluctance to speak out is not deliberate or intentional insensitivity. It is unknowing. These practices are hidden and out of sight.

"We are all compassionate by nature. No one of us wants suffering. Some experimentation is necessary for the good of humanity. But all of us should inform ourselves about the ongoing daily unnecessary suffering inflicted upon animals, and we should do what we can to correct the situation."

Tyler then moved among the crowd, sprinkling the pets and their owners with holy water. "Catholics can't seem to bless anything validly unless they scatter some water around. It is not a special magical water. It is just tap water blessed by a priest. The Church knows that we understand spiritual invisible realities better if we can see symbols that are visible and tangible - like a handshake as a sign of friendship, or a flag as a symbol of a country and patriotism. Holy water is used as a symbol of purification."

Tyler continued, "The blessing with water can be likened to a ship christening with the breaking of a bottle of champagne on the prow of the ship, or even the baptizing of a baby.

"The tranquility of St. Francis must be in the air here today," Tyler said. "Have you noticed how this mixture of animals - even dogs and cats - are getting along harmoniously?"

. . .

As pastor, Tyler was becoming more self-conscious in the way he celebrated Mass. He remembered that the parishioners in the survey had listed this as a priority. One morning after the convent liturgy, Sister Hyacinth offered advice to Tyler. "Try to say Mass more slowly. Say the words of the Mass as though you really meant them."

Tyler recalled the advice of Father Proctor, the seminary rector, when he and his classmates were learning the liturgy as transitional deacons. The rector had urged the seminarians "to say Mass like a bishop." At the time, that was a source of amusement to Tyler because he had seen Archbishop Costello rushing through Mass, mumbling, tracing seemingly meaningless gestures.

But that was another age before Vatican II. That was a time when priests and people instinctively believed that it was God who did the work, not the priest. That was the age of "ex opere operato," ("the power of the act comes from the act itself."). It was God who gave efficacy to what the priest did. The priest was merely the channel through which God's grace flowed.

In the spirit of the new age, Tyler was expected to say Mass in a way that his actions, his attitude, his mannerisms were all important.

In the earlier days, a priest could say a funeral Mass without personally knowing the deceased person in the casket, without even knowing whether the deceased was masculine or feminine. The Latin language of the Mass concealed the fact that the priest did not know the deceased or its gender.

But now, Tyler and all priests were expected to visit the family, to be with the sick person before death, to revisit the family after the burial for counseling and consolation.

Now they could not simply show up at the altar and marry a couple some Saturday afternoon. The bride and groom would feel that it was too impersonal for the priest not to know them personally and even socially prior to the ceremony.

The new emphasis was on personal relationships. It was now less the work of God and more the work of humans -- "ex opere operantis," ("the power of the act comes from the one who does the act."). John F. Kennedy had said in his inaugural address that "God's work must truly be our own."

. . .

Tyler recalled from his boyhood his grandmother's plump, aging arms and the fascinating way that the biceps hung down full and ample below the arm, rather than where bicep muscles should be.

Then one morning in front of his bathroom mirror as he combed his hair, the alarming realization to see the beginning signs of the same in his own arms.

Tyler had always been careful about his physical appearance. Because of his nearly round-the-clock duties at All Saints parish, he had little time for exercise. He would take up the offer from a parishioner for a free membership in the Sunset Health and Fitness Club. Three times a week, for forty-five minutes, he worked out on the Nautilus and the free weights. He conscientiously kept to this regimen not to develop a body builder's physique, but to keep up his health.

He also reserved an hour each evening for serious reading of current theological journals. He did not want to become a "body by Nautilus and a brain by Mattel."

Tyler frequented the club in his sports clothes. For the sake of being able to relax, he had decided that it would be better all around for the other members of the club not to know he was a priest.

Gradually he came to know several club members who exercised on the same days. His friends were acquaintances by first name only.

On a summer night two months after he joined, three of his acquaintances invited Tyler to accompany them for dinner to celebrate the youngest's thirty-first birthday. They jumped into a cab in front of the club.

"What do you recommend for a bar and entertainment?" one of his companions asked the driver.

"GoGo dancers?" the cabby suggested.

"Go for it," the man in the front seat exclaimed. "What do you say, Tyler?"

"Well . . ." Tyler was startled. He tried to sound casual. "Well . . . let's try it."

The cab made a U-turn and headed toward Carlton, just south of the city.

Tyler didn't know there were places like this. The bar was noisy, the booths and tables crowded. Hard-rock crashed off the walls. On a center stage, five smooth skinned girls undulated in leopard spotted halters and G-strings. The brassieres were worn so low they would serve better as gun holsters. Two were Chinese or Vietnamese. Asians often look younger than their years; some of these looked as young as eighteen. As the evening wore on, some of the dancers stripped further.

Through the smoky haze, waiters moved back and forth serving drinks. Tyler was both fixated and uneasy. Intermittently he tried to shield his face from those sitting nearby.

He felt a hand on his shoulder and turned to find one of the dancers smiling at him.

"Would you like a private show?" Startled by the question, Tyler swallowed and was trembling. She took him by the hand and led him out of the bar toward a flight of stairs.

Half way up, Tyler cleared his thoughts and muttered to himself, "What am I doing?" He turned back down the stairs and waited outside the bar.

When his companions were ready for dinner, they looked for him in the parking lot. He explained, "I wasn't feeling well. It was too warm in there."

. . .

The following Thursday, he would be able to get in his exercise only if he did it on the way to his hospital visits. This would mean wearing his clerical suit and Roman collar.

After his regular session of weight-lifting, Tyler did laps for twenty minutes in the Fitness Center pool, showered and entered the locker room. Three members were inside undressing, and carrying on a boisterous conversation. Typically, the conversation in the men's locker room setting was "gamy" with the off-color jokes and boasting.

Tyler toweled himself off and began to dress. First his shorts and a T-shirt. Then, as he began pulling on his black socks, his black pants and eventually his black clerical shirt, the conversation became quieter and quieter. Tyler could almost read the mind of each man, thinking to himself, "Oh, oh, what have I been saying in the past five minutes?"

One of the men had been a companion to Tyler on the night out at the topless bar. He had additional cause for embarrassment.

It came home to Tyler again that lay people are not always themselves in the company of a priest.

CHAPTER 35

At passport control in Ben Gurion Airport, Tel Aviv, the Israeli immigration officer did not stamp Ladd's passport. An Israeli stamped passport forecloses traveling in Arab countries. He was waived through customs and, at the entrance to the airport, was met by CRS volunteers, Jay Carreon and Joan Celetti.

The following morning, Ladd and Joan Celetti traveled to Bethlehem. Because it is a particularly agitated trouble-spot, they took a CRS van with plastic side windows, a precaution against rock-throwing. Palestinians did not always recognize the vehicle with the Israeli plates as a friendly visitor to the Bethlehem area, bringing humanitarian aid.

As Ladd and Celetti left an olive wood home shop to travel to Bethlehem University, word was passed along the grapevine that the police had raided a nearby store. For this reason, a lead car joined Ladd's van with a CRS banner flying from its right rear fender. The driver of Ladd's car draped an Arafat-type checkered headscarf or kofiyah on the dashboard. On two occasions, teenage Palestinians darted from the roadside, poised to throw rocks at the van. They drew back when they spotted the black and white headscarf.

. . .

Viewing the projects, Ladd again reflected that his priesthood was now addressing needs it was meant to address. He mused to himself, "This is finally the kind of work I should be doing."

. . .

At dusk, the party traveled the border between Samaria and Galilee to Lake Gennesaret, Lake Tiberias or the Sea of Galilee, as it is variously known in the New Testament. Though he had in his mind's eye an isolated body of water in the desert wilderness, the Sea of Galilee, for all the world, reminded Ladd of Lake Tahoe. The Tiberias' water reflects the brilliant azure of the Galilean sky, but it is seriously polluted. On the lake where Christ walked, young men streak by on water-skis. Beach umbrellas cover the rocky shoreline and 10-story high-rises have replaced cypress and oak forests.

Ladd's group circled the western shore and stayed at a kibbutz at Of Ginnasor on the north rim of the lake.

On the torrid July afternoon, Ladd and his colleagues swam in the Sea of Galilee with the water temperature ranging from 85 to 90 degrees.

. . .

On the second morning in Galilee, the tour headed for Cana, where the marriage feast had taken place. There, Ladd viewed descendants of the 12 to 16-gallon water jugs in which Jesus had changed water into wine. Each visitor was given a sample sip of current Cana of Galilee wine. "This wine is no miracle," Joan commented.

. . .

They headed west. At Nazareth, Ladd explored the Basilica of the Annunciation, completed in 1968, (the site where the Angel Gabriel announced to Mary that she was to be the mother of the Messiah) and toured the excavations revealing what is believed to be the original dwelling of Mary and, just around the block, the home of Joseph, which became the home of the Family on its return from Egypt. Here, Jesus is reputed to have lived as a boy and young man.

Ladd imagined the kitchen wall with marks on the door post where Joseph might have carved a higher notch each year as his foster Son grew.

From Mount Tabor, Ladd scanned the entire region of Galilee from the disputed Golan Heights to the Mediterranean Sea. Now the locations of the Bible would come to life for Ladd when he read or preached a homily.

The following day, Ladd's party left for the Gaza Strip. After an hour and a half drive through fruitful fields, suddenly they were at the border at Gaza. It was like entering an enormous outdoor prison camp. Here the Intifada began, ignited by the death of young Palestinians in a tragic automobile crash with a petrol lorry. Gaza City looked like a war zone. Buildings were deteriorating everywhere. Rubbish and debris lined the streets. Roadblocks of concrete and stacked oil cans impeded traffic. Small handkerchief-size flags commemorating Black Sunday floated from electric wires crossing the streets. Here and there, small Palestinian flags were seen. Armed Israeli soldiers were highly visible; bulldozed residences and shops; signs of retaliation.

In keeping with customary ritual, the driver switched automobiles at the border from a van with a yellow Israeli license plate to a car with a Gaza license, white background and black letters.

. . .

Passing through the hills of the West Bank villages, Ladd observed small children playing games, wearing Yassir Arafat scarves covering their faces, flashing the two-finger V for victory sign. The CRS vehicles were able to pass through the troubled regions safely because of signs written in Arabic script mounted in the windshields and back windows, identifying a humanitarian relief agency.

The driver placed in the side window a poster with the Islamic red crescent and the insignia of a doctor on call. Dr. Michael Sansur was with Ladd in the minivan.

Suddenly, at the entrance of Qabatia village, Ladd's companions were confronted by teenagers, rocks in hand. The cars now bore Israeli license plates. It was a tense moment . . . but the youths held their fire. Word had been passed throughout the village that a CRS contingent was arriving and there would be no rock-throwing until it departed Qabatia.

Ladd left Israel on a Sabbath morning, convinced that there was little hope for peace among the children of Abraham.

. . .

From Cairo, Ladd departed for the States. He was happy to be heading home.

. . .

There were others coming "home." As the plane was making its final approach into Kennedy, Ladd heard the young mother in the seat just ahead of him turn to her six or seven year old son and say, "Remember now, when we get to the terminal, run to your father first, and then the dog."

Ladd wondered if anyone would be waiting for him at the airport gate.

CHAPTER 36

While he was editor of The Observer, Saturday was David's day off. Faithfully each weekend, he would drive home to Napa from San Francisco to spend some time with his aging mother.

This Saturday, David took the opportunity to cover a news story in Santa Rosa and then doubled back to drive along Highway 12 east, through Oakmont and Kenwood, with the wineries and tasting rooms, straddling the roadway and vineyards, stretching to the east and west over Sonoma's rolling hills.

It was the Valley of the Moon, equal in beauty and in wine to the vineyards of Europe. Two places which visitors from the East want to see when they arrive in San Francisco are Carmel-by-the Sea to the south and wine country, Napa, Sonoma, Mendocino to the north.

David continued into Agua Caliente and Boyes Springs, a longtime summer vacation spot for middle-income San Franciscans.

Covering a second Observer story, David took copious notes at a meeting on the needs of Hispanic farm workers, held in the main conference room of the Sonoma Mission Inn, just around the bend from the central plaza and the last of the 21 California Missions established by Junipero Serra and the 18th century California Franciscans.

From there, David returned to Highway 12, slanting off east among the moss-wrapped evergreens and eucalyptus.

At the crest of one of the green, green hills of home, he crossed into Napa County at Carneros. Just west of the Napa River, David cut on to Highway 29 toward Vallejo and Fairfield. He wanted to cross the new George Butler Bridge, spanning the flooding stream of the Napa River, swollen by the winter rains. Finally, he turned on to Soscol Avenue and north to the old Carmichael family home.

Elizabeth Carmichael was devout, faithful to Sunday Mass and the Sacraments. At three o'clock every Saturday afternoon, his mother would say, "David, it's time to drive me downtown to St. Christopher's. I want to go to confession."

And David would say, "Mom, I am a priest now. I can hear your confession right here."

And she would always answer, "Not on your life!"

. . .

In his tenth year as Editor of The Observer, when divisions were fracturing the Church, David was appointed Pastor of Mission Dolores, the historical parish of San Francisco, south of Market, now mostly an enclave for a mixture of minorities.

David was happy with the appointment. It was the kind of parish he wanted to serve. Gradually, over a period of a year and a half, he introduced liturgical and social programs.

. . .

George Caprice wanted his concerns about the Church to be known by Archbishop Costello.

In the years that had transpired since the close of the Vatican Council, in Caprice's mind, things had gone dramatically from bad to worse. He directed a personal note to the Archbishop, requesting a meeting which would include selected members of Guardians of Doctrine. He also took the occasion of the letter to list "liturgical and other excesses occurring repeatedly in Father David Carmichael's parish, Mission Dolores."

The Archbishop responded, granting the audience, but stipulating, "It would be only fair to have Father Carmichael at the meeting to offer his response."

The meeting was set for a Monday afternoon. Archbishop Costello welcomed the delegation. "Mr. Caprice, it is good to see you again. Your son Gordon continues to do excellent work for us in the Chancery."

"Thank you, Your Excellency."

Caprice genuflected and kissed the prelate's ring, as did his four colleagues.

"Good afternoon, Father Carmichael."

David took the Archbishop's offered hand and thought it prudent also to kiss the ring.

There was tension in the room as the group settled in the hard back mahogany chairs semi-circled in front of the episcopal desk. David recognized two of Caprice's companions, a middle-aged couple, veterans in the campaign to save the Faith. He did not know the other man and woman, seemingly in their mid-fifties.

George Caprice was accustomed to getting right to the point. He saw no need for pleasantries. The Archbishop was just as happy to get things moving. And David wanted to get a chance to defend himself and get the meeting over with.

Caprice opened the discussion, "Your Excellency, we know that the Vatican Council accomplished some good things, but we believe that the Faith is losing ground. There are fewer and fewer people attending Sunday Mass. There is less and less reverence for the Blessed Sacrament.

"Now we have people holding hands at the Our Father, talking, hugging, even kissing at the Sign of Peace. There are fewer statues and crucifixes in the church, some crucifixes replaced with crosses without a corpus, fewer and fewer sermons on hell and purgatory.

"In many churches, the tabernacle has been moved from the altar to a side chapel.

"Everywhere there are guitars and tambourines, folk Masses, lay men and lay women distributing Communion, some people moving from one line to another to receive Communion from a priest, Communion under both the species of Bread and Wine, reconciliation rooms instead of confessionals. Many of these things are happening in Father Carmichael's parish."

Caprice continued, "Your Excellency, I see a gradual change from a law and order Church to a flexible Church; the blurring of lines of authority. Whatever happened to sin?

"I don't recognize our Church anymore. Actually, I think we are just trying to imitate the Protestants. There is a whole new vocabulary: charismatic, ecumenical, evangelization, immersion, lector, homilies instead of sermons."

The 50-year-old, whom David had not seen before, chimed in, "Archbishop, let me read you a poem a parishioner from Father Carmichael's church gave me yesterday. It's clipped from an eastern diocesan newspaper. The author is a Judy Wargs.

> "Twas the year '62
> And all through the Church,
> The bishops were saying,
> We must go in search.

> "Of a way to reform
> (Revolutionize, if you will)
> This traditional liturgy.
> It's too 'run of the mill'.

> "They turned 'round the altars,
> Tore down the rails.
> Christ on the Cross
> But where are His nails?

> "The pews stripped of kneelers,
> 'Mature' Christians stand
> To approach and receive
> Communion in hand.

> "You've got to participate
> In some ministry or other,
> Workshops, discussions,
> Let's all hug our brother.

> "A cry for the priesthood,
> For madam and mister.
> Who's that at the altar?
> Egad, it's my sister!"

"The parishioner who gave me this says she is not going to Father Carmichael's church anymore."

The Archbishop turned to David. "Father, we should give you a chance to say something."

David had heard these charges before. He knew what he wanted to say. He turned to the five seated beside him. "I can understand your anxiety. I was brought up in the same Church as you. I worry about the decline in members attending Mass. I worry about the lack of vocations in the priesthood and to the Sisters.

"The Church is changing. But the basic teachings of the Church have not changed. The Church is an organism - alive. It is bound to change in some ways. Only lifeless things are static and unchanging.

"In the past ten years we have been through a time of growth. It has been a time of adolescence in the Church, and adolescence is never easy. I think we are suffering the pains that accompany growth. Like adolescents, we are stumbling over our disproportionately large feet. It's like we're breaking out in an ecclesiastical acne; and that is painful."

"I don't think it's growth," Caprice broke in. "Look at the results, people leaving the Church."

"It is true that there have been excesses," David continued. "Some interpretations of the Vatican II documents have not been authentic."

"The liberal Catholics want to design their own Church contrary to the Holy Father," Caprice said in the direction of the Archbishop.

David countered, "We need liberal and progressive Catholics, who truly love the Church, to push us forward to new insights. And we need conservative, traditional Catholics for balance, to provide a challenge to new ideas, to insure that the faith of the Church is not diluted when old truths are expressed through new models. We are all part of one family."

The woman who had been silent to this point said, "The new things you are doing at Mass to attract people are just driving people away."

David knew the declining numbers at Mass was damaging evidence. He could only say, "Fewer people are going to Mass, but maybe the ones who are attending are attending for better motives than in the old days. They are not going just out of habit or because everybody else is going. Today they may be going because they see the value of the Mass. They are not going just because of the fear of hell if they don't go."

"You mean that it is better that fewer people are attending Mass?" Caprice exclaimed. "We must not accept blindly each new fad that comes along. `One who is married to the spirit of the times will soon be a widow.' The Church was a strong and growing Church before these fads."

"At the same time, we must remember that 'the good old days' are not what they used to be," David responded. "Nostalgia has a way of selecting the good memories and suppressing the bad."

David remembered something Martin Marty had said and tried to paraphrase it. "Nostalgia is remembering:

'The '20s with Russ Colombo, but without the Ku Klux Klan.

The '30s with Ella Fitzgerald, but not the Depression.

The '40s with the Andrew Sisters, but without World War II.

The '50s with Elvis Presley, but not the Korean conflict.

The '60s with the Beatles, but without Vietnam.'

"The Church of earlier times had drawbacks we tend to forget. Within the Church family, there are honest differences of opinion. The important thing is that we must try to hold the Church family together in the loving community for which St. Paul was always pleading."

David wanted to keep the momentum on his side. He pushed on. "Archbishop, let me mention a form of the Ten Commandments I offer to our parishioners to help them to weather the turbulence we feel in the Church today:

"1. The first Commandment: Thou shalt reverence the official teaching of the Church. Respect its 20 centuries of wisdom, Scriptural revelation, and tradition.

2. Thou shalt pray. Pray for Faith.

3. Thou shalt remember: our Faith is not primarily a set of regulations, but a relationship with a Person, Jesus of Nazareth, the same yesterday, today and forever.

4. Concentrate on the essential truths of the Church found in the Nicene and Apostles Creed.

5. Read the Bible regularly.

6. Develop a habit of serious study. Be open to ideas.

7. Receive the Sacraments faithfully.

8. Live the original Ten Commandments. The tablets given to Moses on Mount Sinai were not the ten suggestions.

9. Thou shalt concentrate on the heart of our religion, summed up in the words: 'Love God, Love One Another.' 'The greatest thing you'll ever learn is just to love and be loved in return.'

10. And the 10th Commandment: Thou shalt remember the Paschal Mystery - growth comes out of suffering. If we are confused in the Church, if we are troubled, if we experience a lack of direction, if we suffer in any way from uncertainty, whether we consider ourselves conservatives, liberal or moderate, we recall that suffering and anxiety are the life of a Christ-follower. We follow a man who carried a cross.'"

"Well, that's fine, Father. But the fact of the matter is that parishes are doing whatever they want," Caprice wanted to regain the initiative. "We've lost the sense of the transcendent in parishes like Father Carmichael's. Even the singing has deteriorated. Gregorian Chant is gone."

"I think the hymns reflect the mood of the people," David said. "In the 1950s, we were singing `Faith of Our Fathers'. Now, in so many Masses, we are singing `Be Not Afraid'. It is because we are caught up in change, and that can be frightening. I can understand that. But the Lord is saying to us: `Why are you fearful, oh you of little faith? I have planted my seed in each one of you and I am waiting for you to break the husks of fear. Fear not, I am with you all days, even to the end of the world.'"

The Archbishop realized that the meeting was not going as George Caprice and his companions had intended. "I think I have a sense of your concerns," the prelate said. "I will make it a point to review these matters with Father Carmichael and other appropriate pastors."

It was apparent from the Archbishop's words that the session was over. The group rose when the Archbishop stood. As the visitors filed toward the door, David sensed that the Guardians of Doctrine were not fully satisfied.

"Mr. Caprice, could I ask you to stay for a moment?"

"Yes, Your Excellency."

David left the Archbishop's office with the others. As he and the four went their separate ways in the Chancery parking lot, David wondered what was going on at that moment between Archbishop Costello and George Caprice.

. . .

The songs of the times seemed to mirror the divisions in the Church and in society generally.

Whenever David heard "Never My Love" by the Association, "Hey There, Georgie Girl" by the Seekers, Joni Mitchell's "Both Sides Now," Barbra Streisand's "The Way We Were," "We've Only Just Begun" and all the recordings by the Carpenters, these songs brought back sensations of the turmoil of the '70s. Their musical arrangements had a special feel all their own.

The songs of that generation had somehow slipped away from David's generation. Though David liked these melodies, they seemed to belong to someone else. He had always felt that current popular songs up until that time were his songs.

Everything changed in the late '60s and in the '70s.

. . .

A new entity was developing in the Church. Priests' Senates were forming.

The bishops of the world had gone to Rome for the Vatican II Council and put pressure on the Vatican for more "collegiality." They wanted the Vatican to share more of its power with the bishops in the governance of the Church. The bishops were successful.

But they had started something they had not anticipated. When they returned to their home dioceses, the "contagion" of collegiality came with them. Soon the priests wanted some of the bishops' administrative authority. Little by little, they were successful.

One evidence of that was the emerging of the Councils of Priests.

More than that, in some dioceses, clergy associations were formed. In some respects, even the authorized councils or senates took on the characteristics of labor unions, though they would be modified and tempered in the 1983 version of the Code of Canon Law.

In the mid-'70s, David was elected president of the Priests' Senate in the Archdiocese of San Francisco. Stomach-churning days of confrontation, of liberal priests against conservative priests. Though there were notable exceptions, lines were mostly drawn between younger clergy and older clergy. David, by nature, was not adversarial. He wanted unity. But now, at every Senate meeting, he had to preside over fierce encounters about the liturgy, about the selection of pastors, about compliance with Chancery regulations, about everything that affected ecclesial life.

He was pleased, therefore, at the February meeting when one of the older, more revered pastors introduced a motion which David was sure would be acceptable to both young and old, progressive and traditional.

Father Liam Cawley proposed, "I move that the Priests' Senate go on record as encouraging all the clergy to make every effort possible to attend the funerals of their fellow priests." The motion was seconded by Monsignor Melvin Defalco.

There was little debate; from the far end of the conference table, David heard a call for the question.

"All those in favor, signify by raising their hands," David announced.

The secretary counted the hands.

"All those opposed."

The secretary counted again.

"Abstentions?"

There were no hands lifted.

"The motion is defeated," the secretary announced.

David might have expected it. In that term of office the young outnumbered the old. At least this result was not as bad as the vote David had heard about in an eastern diocese where the proposal had been made to send a get-well card to the diocese's seriously ill bishop. That motion passed. But the vote was 9 yes, 6 nays, and 2 abstentions.

David was relieved when his term was completed. He did not like taking sides in a divided presbyterate. For this reason, during his presidency, he used, as often as he could, the secret written ballot, rather than the voice vote.

David was a reconciler.

. . .

David Carmichael knew that his life had been a good one. Although he came from a poor family with a widowed mother who worked in a Napa's Rough Rider pants factory until her 65th year, he had never really been in want. He always had substantial meals, a warm bed and decent clothes. Sometimes they were hand-me-downs from his brother Vincent, but they were always clean and well mended.

In adult life, David was careful that he dressed well. He brought his clerical suits to the cleaners to be cleaned and pressed regularly. On his days off, he wanted his mufti, his laity sports clothes, and his haircuts to be up to style - the right Levi's, the with-it athletic shoes, the longer sideburns.

However, he knew that he was not keeping up with the latest designer labels when one of his nephews, Bart, came to him one day and said, "Uncle David, tomorrow is Nerd Day in school. Can I borrow some of your clothes?"

Some years later, he knew he was assured of keeping up to style when he began to wear not "hand-me-downs", but "hand-me-ups" from each of his nephews who had grown to his size -- discarded trousers, shirts and jackets, many scarcely worn after purchase.

At length, David came to be convinced that a simpler, more modest life style was how it should be. In his meditations, he reflected often on the words of John Henry Newman, "I must say plainly this, that fanciful though it may appear at first sight, the comforts of life are the main cause of our want of love of God; the pleasure of sense, the feeling of security - these and the good life, if we are not careful, choke up the avenues of the soul."

. . .

In his early priesthood, David had been concerned about the model and color of the car he drove, the color-coordinated drapes in his rectory room. He was pleased if he was assigned to a parish in the better neighborhoods.

But now he changed. He now knew he should simplify his life, and Mission Dolores was the place to do it.

David had reached an age when relationships become more important than advancement and the world's understanding of success.

"Recently, I find myself more frequently wishing I had a family to go home to. At times, rather than watching TV alone, I go to the movies just to be in a big room, enjoying something with other people," David told his confessor.

"When I jog, I want to do it near the shopping malls, where there are people - also because, where I live, it is not safe to walk or jog after dark.

"Last year, I got a dog for the parish. Looking back on it, possibly it was because of loneliness. Now, not matter how late I get back to the rectory, this 50-pound black Labrador, "Dolores", is waiting for me at the door."

. . .

David enjoyed Mission Dolores Parish. He felt very much at home with the Latinos, the Blacks, the Filipinos, the Asian families, and the shut-ins. He spent long hours in home visitations, looking in on the parish school classrooms and talking with the children in the school yard.

The students particularly enjoyed his dog, "Dolores," and the dog looked forward to recess and lunch period for scraps of food and companionship with the children.

"Dolores" was very much a part of the parish family. It was one of the first graders who asked David, one day at recess, "What is your dog's name, Father?"

"Dolores," David responded.

The little girl pondered for a moment and then asked, "Was the church named after the dog?"

It was a satisfying time of life because, as a parish priest, he was dealing with persons directly one-on-one.

. . .

Archbishop Costello caught David in the corridor on a marriage case visit to the Marriage Tribunal.

"Archbishop Fulton Sheen is staying overnight at my residence on a stop-over to the Orient. He's arriving at the airport at 11:15 this morning."

The Archbishop handed a slip of paper to David. "This is his flight number. Would you please pick him up and bring him out to my house?" David regretted the sudden interruption in his schedule, but he was happy to get the opportunity to meet the celebrated Sheen. The Continental flight arrived on schedule at San Francisco International, and David was at Gate 26 to greet the visiting Archbishop.

He had rehearsed several topics to engage Sheen in conversation as they drove to the episcopal residence, so that there would be no uncomfortable silences. Sometimes famous speakers are not good at small talk. There was no need for concern. The celebrated Archbishop was gracious and easy to be with.

David accompanied the prelate down the escalator to the baggage claim area. As they waited for the luggage to arrive on the carousel, David saw in action the price of being a celebrity. As bystanders began to recognize the diminutive man with the dark piercing eyes and the finely tailored black clerical suit, gradually three or four sidled around to where he was standing. Then five or six more found reason to move near him. A young couple addressed the Archbishop, "Aren't you Bishop Sheen?"

"Yes, I am," and holding out his hand to take theirs, "How are you? It's good to meet you."

An elderly woman, like the woman in the Gospel with the issue of blood who touched the hem of Christ's garment, reached out surreptitiously to brush Sheen's elbow.

David would not forget this lesson about the consequences of fame.

PART IV

CHAPTER 37

Because of his statements on peace at international meetings and his participation in demonstrations on social issues, Ladd was invited by a representative of the Soviet TASS news agency to do an interview at the Russian Consulate in San Francisco.

Ladd passed through two check-point, bullet-proof glass doors into the inner offices at the exclusive Pacific Heights address. He was ushered in to meet the Consul General, who rose from a large padded chair behind his desk to greet Ladd warmly. After the usual pleasantries, the Consul General walked Ladd to an adjacent office where the TASS reporter was waiting.

"My name is Nicholas," the reporter said as he extended his hand to Ladd. The Russian's English was perfect, only the slightest hint of an accent.

"It is good to know you, Nicholas. I am Father Ladd Franklin."

Ladd was apprehensive. If this interview was going to be carried in the Soviet newspapers, he was concerned how he might be misquoted or quoted out of context. As he sat down, Ladd withdrew a hand-held recorder from his pocket and placed it on the coffee table in front of him. He wanted to have a fool-proof copy of exactly what he said in the interview and he wanted to send a message to his interrogator that he would, as a matter of fact, have this word-for-word record.

Nicholas countered by taking a recorder from his own pocket, placing it on the table next to Ladd's. Ladd guessed that Nicholas, also being a man subject to authority, would want to be able to prove to his superiors exactly what he said.

Actually, the interview turned out to be rather bland. Ladd felt that the questions called for easy answers, like hitting fungoes to the outfield.

Ladd agreed with Nicholas that it is difficult to consider how nuclear weapons can be used ethically or morally since they cannot differentiate between people who are military on the one hand, and patients in hospitals, children and the elderly on the other.

Other questions probed how the two nations can cooperate in peaceful efforts, attending to world pollution, poverty, hunger, famine, the poor, particularly in Third World nations.

Ladd made the specific recommendation of exchanging a thousand Russian students and a thousand American students each year.

At length Nicholas asked, "Do you agree that the United States has done things around the world that suggest Americans are trying to impose their form of government on others?"

"I have always believed the United States intervenes only when it thinks that it is preserving the freedom of weaker nations. Although we may misinterpret it, I suspect that when you, in the Soviet Union, intervene in places like Hungary and Afghanistan, you genuinely believe you are doing what is best for those countries."

"My last question," Nicholas said, "Do you think the new weapons which are being deployed by the United States in European countries will increase the danger of war?"

"Let me say that I do not know enough about the deployment of specific weapons, like the Pershing II or the Cruise missiles. My vocation is not military. All I can say is that the position of the American bishops is that there should be no increased deployment of nuclear weapons on either side. I do not know the details, but it is likely our government feels that we need these new weapons because of the Soviet's '20s."

"Thank you very much, Reverend," the man from TASS said, as he retrieved his tape recorder and returned it to its case.

"Thank you, Nicholas. It was good meeting you."

On the way, driving back to his residence, Ladd set his recorder on the seat beside him, rewound the tape and reviewed the discussion.

. . .

Two weeks after Ladd's interview by TASS appeared in Russia, Ladd was summoned back to the Soviet Consulate.

When he had been escorted into the Consul's inner office, Alexi Brosnick invited him to sit across from him at an expansive blond wooden desk.

"We read the report of your interview in the Russian newspaper, Father Franklin. I have been directed by our government, through the Russian Orthodox Church, to invite you to Moscow to meet with our peace committees in the Soviet Union. Would you be disposed to accept our invitation?"

Ladd had been expecting a rebuke or, at least, defensive responses to the statements he had made in the interview. The invitation to visit the Soviet Union hit him like a thunderbolt. He wondered what the Archbishop would think; but he did not want to delay a response to an attractive offer.

"I would be happy to accept," he said.

"The Orthodox Church is pleased to offer you hospitality for two weeks or more, if your calendar permits."

"I will have to consult my schedule, but I am sure it can be arranged. Can I get back to you in a day or two to firm up the dates?"

"That will be fine."

The Consul reached across the desk to hand Ladd a business card. "You can reach me directly at this phone number when you have settled on some dates."

"Thank you, Consul. I will give you a call before the end of the week."

An attendant appeared at the office door to see Ladd through the corridors and out of the Consulate main entrance.

. . .

On Friday, Ladd phoned the Soviet Consul General and scheduled the trip for early February.

Somehow or other, the United States State Department learned of Ladd's visit to Russia. A week before his departure date, he received a letter from the office of relations with the Soviet Union, encouraging him to visit the Department in Washington, D.C., on his way to Moscow. A day later, a letter came from the Soviet Union's Ambassador to the United States, Anatoly Dobrynin, inviting Ladd to a meeting at the Russian Embassy in Washington.

"This is pretty heady stuff for a poor kid from the Mission District in San Francisco," Ladd told David. "I wonder what I'm getting into."

"I think you're going to end up in a Gulag in Siberia," David said. "But we'll all be right behind you, Ladd, nice and safe here in the United States, praying for you."

"Get serious, Dave. All I'm going to do is keep my eyes open and my mouth shut."

"Have you said anything to the Archbishop about this?"

"No, I guess I should let him know I'm going."

Ladd made an appointment with Archbishop Costello for the following day. The Archbishop, to say the least, was surprised by what Ladd had to tell him.

"Are you sure you know what you're doing?"

"No, Archbishop; but I thought it was too good an opportunity to pass up. I may be able to get a few points across for the Church while I'm there."

"Have you let the Apostolic Delegate in Washington know about this?"

"No, I haven't even thought of that."

The following day, Ladd phoned the Delegation and explained the situation to the charge d'affaires in the Delegate's absence. "I will relay this information to the Delegate," the deputy assured Ladd.

On the first Tuesday in February, Ladd visited the State Department and had a 40-minute conversation with Raymond Smith of the Soviet Desk. Attending the meeting also was Charles Comstock, an intern with the State Department. The two officials took pains to be gracious, emphasizing that they wanted to help in any way they could. Obliquely, they suggested that Ladd should not take everything he was told in the Soviet Union at face value.

Ladd was startled by the next thing Smith said, "First of all, we have some good news for you. We have arranged a meeting for you this afternoon with President Reagan at three o'clock."

They must think I control the Catholic vote, Ladd thought to himself. Comstock gave Ladd the details of the presidential meeting. Then Smith went on to brief Ladd on things to be looking for during the Russian visit. He provided names of people to contact at the American offices in Moscow and in Leningrad. "Father, I advise you to request someone to accompany you from the Embassy for translation and interpreting purposes in both cities."

Smith also reviewed background on Russian history and Russian policy. Knowing the Catholic Church's position on the subject, he made it a point to quote Lenin on the principle of the end justifying the means. "If you want an omelet, you have to break a few eggs," was the quote.

As he left, Ladd handed to the two officials copies of personal letters which he had prepared for President Reagan and President Andropov.

From the State Department, Ladd went to the Soviet Embassy and spent thirty minutes with Ambassador Dobrynin. Also attending that meeting was Igor Lebedev, First Deputy at the Embassy.

As at the U.S. State Department, conversation at the Russian Embassy was cordial. Dobrynin expressed the desire for peaceful relations between the two countries, urging high level meetings and communications.

The Ambassador gave Ladd background on Russian history and something about his perception of relations between the U.S.S.R. and the Reagan administration.

In passing, Dobrynin mentioned that American commentators often refer to Soviet "quotations" which are not factual. He cited one instance of "Lenin's 12 commandments," which "never existed and Russians have never heard of."

The Ambassador became more intense: The Soviets do not subscribe to the principle of the end justifying the means. He said that, although the Communist government does not have a religious base and is atheistic, there is a very definite moral code to which Russian people and the Soviet government adhere.

Dobrynin added, "This is part of the Russian tradition and is found in all Russian families."

Ladd asked, "Does the Soviet government want to extend its influence along its borders and in underdeveloped countries for reasons of commercial gains?"

"Russia is totally self-sufficient and does not need businesses elsewhere. Nor is Soviet policy set by munitions manufacturers. As a matter of fact, Russian economy would profit more from peacetime pursuits than munitions manufacturing."

Dobrynin was a bear of a man, affable, a master salesman.

Ladd took his leave of the Embassy and caught a taxi to the White House.

. . .

Ladd waited only five minutes in a reception area before an aide led him to the Oval Office.

President Reagan immediately arose, circled the desk and shook hands with Ladd, motioning the priest to a sofa. Ladd recognized the ready smile and the down to earth approach. As the President seated himself at an angle facing the sofa, he said, "Father, I understand you have some ideas you wanted to discuss on our relations with the Soviet Union."

Ladd thought he had better set the stage by affirming the President at the outset. "I want to say, Mr. President, that the courage you evidence in standing by your convictions is admirable. It is encouraging to see you taking the first step toward easing tensions between the East and the West. I am sure the people of the United States appreciate your coolness under fire."

"Well, thank you, Father."

Ladd knew that his time was limited so he plunged on, "I hope that you are considering arranging a United States/U.S.S.R. summit as early as this spring, or perhaps a summer summit.

"If I may go on, Mr. President, I would like to list some other points that I think are important. First, to set up a schedule of regular, on-going senior-level meetings preparing for annual summits.

"I think it is crucial that you restore a spirit of civility and a privacy or confidentiality at these meetings, which will help offset posturing on either side.

"Another point, I would respectfully suggest a consideration of Prime Minister Trudeau's plan for involving the five nuclear nations at a summit meeting.

"I hope you won't mind me going through a list like this, because I know your time is very limited, Mr. President. I will give you a copy of these remarks when I leave.

"Finally, please prod your negotiators to a new and imaginative approach in the current arms control talks."

"Well, Father, I certainly subscribe to what you're saying and I wish you could say the same things to President Andropov. We must face reality that the U.S.S.R. is intent on spreading its influence and form of government around the world."

"Mr. President, have you had a chance to read George Kennan's recent article, 'Breaking the Spell', in the New Yorker magazine? He has some very interesting ideas regarding Russia's plan for world dominance."

"No, I haven't seen that article, but I will ask one of my aides to prepare a digest of the article for me. I am sure you are aware, Father, that there are many of our people, perhaps the majority, who are urging us to stay the course we are now pursuing. Also, I must point out quite frankly that there are national and international business interests, conglomerates and controllers of oil and other resources around the world that press us to take a hard line in our relations with the U.S.S.R."

"You know these facts much better than I, Sir. Still, wouldn't many of these corporations experience even greater profits by conversion to peace time production? Isn't it true that one billion dollars generate thousands more jobs in peace time employment than one billion dollars create in military related jobs? And would not less defense spending help balance the federal budget?"

"Though not under the seal of the confessional, I am talking to you this morning pretty much as to a father-confessor," the President said, surprisingly. "I know you realize, Father, that in political office you must be very sensitive to the convictions of the people. My long standing political constituents and the hard core of my supporters often feel 'betrayed' if I am 'soft on Communism.'"

Ladd appreciated the candid comment by the President. He said, "Haven't many of these supporters come to recognize the benefits that were realized by the opening with dialog with Communist mainland China?"

"Yes, that is true, but the people still want a 'strong' president. They want a leader who stands up to 'foreign enemies.'"

"Now, I'm talking to you as a father-confessor, Mr. President, and I ask, do you want to be that kind of president - a president that is 'strong' just for the image of strength, regardless of the rightness or wrongness of the issue? It seems to me that projecting this image appeals to the lower instincts of voters. You have the skills to challenge us to higher ideals."

"I will admit that I was surprised that the temperate and measured sanctions which I imposed following the Korean jetliner tragedy received wide acceptance and were commended by members of both parties," Reagan said.

Ladd wanted to press this point. "President Nixon's presidency has not been dealt with favorably by history. But nearly all commentators on world affairs are in agreement that his outstanding contribution to history was the opening of the door to China. And I think that most are in agreement that the centerpiece accomplishment of President Carter's administration was the reconciliation of Israel's Menachem Begin with Egypt's Anwar Sadat. The people hunger and yearn for peace. And anything a leader does for peace touches the deepest, most responsive, most enduring chords."

"Well, Father, you know that I am certainly committed to peace as strongly as anyone, but perhaps in the real world peace will come through strength."

"If we add more military strength, Mr. President, the Soviet reaction will not be to back down in fear. They will simply leap-frog us with more weapons. I certainly do not want our country to be subjected to an totalitarian regime. I understand there are things more precious even than life. And one of those, of course, is freedom. I do not subscribe to the slogan, 'Better Red than dead.'"

Ladd wanted to establish that he was patriotic and that he did not promote a mindless form of pacifism.

The President went on, "I know that the U.S.S.R. does not want global war. Our intelligence tells us that because of internal politics and Russia's own fragile economy, they, in no way, want to get into an armed conflict with the United States. That is precisely the reason they are fighting our proposal of a Star Wars defense in space. We know that their economy cannot support such a system. It is my hope that by accelerating our technology for a defensive network, we will force the U.S.S.R. economically to abandon the failed Communistic system and join the democratic nations of the world."

Ladd knew time was running out. He wanted to crowd in all his thoughts. "The peace we seek must not be a Pax Americana - a peace which is to the advantage of our country only at the expense of the people of other lands. Are we right in making every decision on the basis of national interest? We are members of the human family, as well as our national family."

The President broke in, "I have sworn an oath to work for the best interests of our nation."

"But it is in our own best interest if you can change the precarious situation that exists. Tensions of East and West are serious, but the long swollen tensions between the North and the South hemispheres are even more explosive. As long as the chasm between the `have' and `have-not' nations widens, there will be terrorism and it will eventually reach the United States."

The President had given Ladd more time than even Ladd expected. Reagan started to rise from his chair.

"One last thing, Mr. President. Please do not move away from the United Nations. We desperately need a federation of the nations."

Ladd wouldn't have this opportunity again. He pressed on with a litany of points he had rehearsed again and again. "Ohio does not attack Michigan. Texas does not invade Louisiana, because there is a federation of states. Cities are not allowed to exert violence against each other. Individual families on a block are not permitted to attack one another. We even separate children fist-fighting in a school yard. Only in the community of the world is it still permitted for one nation to settle its differences with another nation by what amounts to `fist-fights' and `street brawls'. Nations are the last entities on earth with a license to kill, a permit to use violence and war.

"We Americans guard our internal sovereignty jealously, and we should." Ladd concluded, "Each nation should have internal sovereignty, but we need an international authority with the capability of requiring nations to settle their differences through negotiation, rather than through armed conflict.

"That is why I hope that you will work for a strengthening of the United Nations to be more truly representative of the world's people. At least work gradually for a phasing out of the veto and reshaping of the Security Council, which now excludes all but the big powers."

The President stood and held out his hand to Ladd, "I know the best interest of the world are also our nation's best interest. I am grateful for your visit, Father."

Ladd handed him the list of the points he had made.

"You can be sure I will discuss these ideas with my advisors."

Donald Regan was waiting at the door as a presidential aide escorted Ladd from the Oval Office.

. . .

Ladd left Pennsylvania Avenue and caught the five o'clock shuttle out of National for La Guardia, New York.

A week remained before Ladd was due in the Soviet Union. He had another destination he wanted to reach before Moscow. At his request, the Russian Orthodox Church agent booked Ladd from J.F.K. Airport to Amsterdam.

. . .

As Ladd waited at J.F.K. for his departure, Flight 1259 from Denver arrived at the same gate. It was his lot to spend much time in airports and he made it his custom to study the faces of the passengers as they emerged from the runway, as well as the faces of the family and friends waiting to meet them.

It was one of the better moments of human emotions. Tensions and differences seemed to be swept aside for the time. Presumably, there has been separation for a considerable period. Children crane their necks to spot the awaited arrivers down the long passage. Faces of the welcomers light up with joy as the loved one comes into view. Hugs and kisses are given and accepted all around. Even teenagers accept the embrace of their parents and siblings with bashful affection.

So often on occasions like this, he remembered the many times young people would ask him, "Aren't you lonely, Father; you have no wife, no children. It must be a lonesome life." And Ladd would give them the instinctive answer, "Yes, I experience aloneness at times; but in the seminary they taught us to be aware of the presence of God as often as we could throughout the day and night. I haven't always done this as well as I should; but to the extent I have done it, my loneliness is diminished. When you analyze it, we are never really alone."

Still, Ladd thought someday he would like to be part of that spontaneous human warmth.

CHAPTER 38

The unspoken reason why Ladd had wanted to accept the invitation to visit Russia was that it would give him the opportunity to visit Willow Caprice.

Amsterdam was Willow's current foreign posting at a United States Consulate.

Ladd arrived at Amsterdam's Central Station in mid-morning and immediately looked for a public telephone and phone book.

He dialed the U.S. Consulate and asked for Willow Caprice.

Within a minute, a familiar voice came on the line.

"Hello?"

"Hello, Willow. This is Ladd Franklin."

"Ladd!. where are you?"

"I'm at Central Station here in Amsterdam."

"Oh . . . wonderful. Can you come to the Consulate? How long will you be here?"

"Two days. I'm on my way to Moscow."

"Moscow!. What are you doing there?"

"I'm a guest of the Russian Orthodox Church for meetings with Soviet peace groups."

"Come on into the Consulate, Ladd. We'll get together for these two days."

"I will be staying at the St. Nicolas Hotel on Spiustraat near the Central Train Station."

"I'll find it and drop by after work. Or let's go out for dinner. I'll meet you at your hotel at seven. Okay?"

"That'll be great. I'll see you then."

Promptly at seven, Willow arrived at the St. Nicolas and found Ladd at the registration desk in the lobby. Ladd was dressed in a business suit and tie.

Willow ran to him and embraced him spontaneously with a warm kiss on his cheek.

The two drew back and looked at each other.

"You look wonderful," they said in unison and both meant it.

In the next two days, Willow gave Ladd a whirlwind tour of the city of canals.

The outlandishly illustrated trams racing along Damrak, through Muntplein and beyond.

The Anne Frank House on the Prisengracht Canal, a well-tended reminder of the horror of the Holocaust. Each of the cramped rooms brought back memories of the world headlines of Ladd's seminary days.

Madame Tussaud's Wax Museum.

Ladd was somewhat more fascinated than tempted by the women in the windows of the red light district in the narrow alleys off the Wornestraat canal.

The touching beauty of the waterways, the massive St. Nicolas Church nearby the bustling pedestrian and street car traffic of Central Station.

The joints, the "skunks," the narrow twisting alleys.

The doll-like Dutch houses standing tall, row on row like slender passengers crowded on Tram 14 at Waterlooplein.

The swarming pigeons on visitors' shoulders, arms and heads, all of them plump from the fast food shops around Dam Square - plump pigeons and plump people.

The New Church and the Old Church, the West Church and the North Church, and no one in the churches - only occasional classical concerts or rock bands.

The tired sadness in the faces of the traveling foreign youth in faded jeans, carrying back-packs, the men bearded, the women fashionably unkempt, the open display of drugs.

The joyousness in the faces of the native Dutch, old and young, blond, ruddy from the weather of the northern tier of Europe.

The well stocked shops, the glass-enclosed "outdoor" cafes, the sausages, the McDonald's, the KFC's, the Dutch pastries, the FEDO's featuring small glass door cubicles like post office boxes for self-serving hamburgers, salads, pies and cakes - not unlike Horn and Hardarts in New York and the old Merry-Go-Round Cafe in San Francisco.

The perpetual hum of the trams and the grating sound of steel against steel, as the wheels strain against the curving tracks.

But where are the windmills and the dikes into whose holes little Dutch boys put their fingers? Where are the wooden shoes, except in the souvenir shops alongside the Dallas Cowboy T-shirts and outrageous postcards.

Amsterdam is action, movement, excitement, carnival. Ladd wondered, is it decadence or liberation?

His continuing flight to Moscow on Aerflot was scheduled for Sunday. Willow and Ladd attended Mass at St. Peter's Church. At breakfast, Willow asked, "Will I be seeing you when you come back through here on the way to the States?"

"No, actually, I am scheduled to go on flying directly to the Philippines."

Willow drove Ladd to the airport. They embraced on the sidewalk and said their farewells.

"Ladd, keep in touch. Let me know how it goes in Russia. And give my love to all when you get home."

"I will. Thanks for the good time."

. . .

On his arrival at the Moscow airport, as Ladd passed through passport control, he was asked for his international certificate of vaccination, approved by the World Health Organization. He had failed to include it in his passport packet. The Soviet immigration official directed him to stand aside, and made a call, presumably to another office in the terminal.

Five minutes later, a nurse appeared and led Ladd to an adjoining room. In English, the nurse explained that she would have to vaccinate Ladd against small pox.

"Please take off your coat and roll up the right sleeve of your shirt."

Ladd did as he was told, but he was apprehensive. He did not relish the picture of a husky, grim-faced Soviet nurse standing over him with what looked like a foot-long hypodermic needle, ready to puncture his right arm.

But the slight sting felt no different than vaccinations at home. He rolled down his sleeve, put the clerical suit jacket and heavy overcoat back on and joined the other passengers proceeding through customs.

Customs inspection was not perfunctory. Ladd was asked to open his suitcase, the smaller grip and his briefcase. Two officials ran their hands through everything. One of the officials came up with a paperback, which Ladd had brought along for light airplane reading and incidental background information on Russia. It was the novel, Gorky Park.

The official flipped through the pages, muttered a few words in Russian to his colleague and then pointed to the book, and looking at Ladd, shook his head from side to side. The book was confiscated.

There was also hesitation over a pair of Levi blue denim jeans, a precious black-market commodity in the Soviet Union. But the jeans were put back in place and the pieces of luggage closed.

Father Fyodor Platon, Dean and Pastor of Holy Savior Church, and a government interpreter, Raissa Kryshchuk, were waiting for Ladd at the customs exit. Raissa held a small rectangular sign: FATHER FRANKLIN in block letters. The two escorted Ladd from the terminal through the February cold to a waiting taxi. From there, twenty miles into central Moscow to the Hotel Ukraine.

. . .

Ladd joined Raissa and Father Platon for dinner, appetizers, pork, sturgeon and vegetables, in the hotel dining room, filled with an interesting variety of diners, Ukrainians, Georgians, Blacks, Japanese.

The temperature in Moscow was fifteen degrees below Fahrenheit when Ladd walked for a few minutes of fresh air in front of the hotel after the meal. His heavy clothes kept him warm. Only his face, around the cheeks and nose, felt the biting cold.

Guide Raissa Kryshchuk was a personable young woman, easy to talk with and comfortable in English. By profession, she was a church interpreter, fluent in four languages. Since she studied English in Stockholm, Raissa's English had a Swedish flavor.

. . .

On the third day, Ladd and Father Platon boarded the midnight "Red Arrow" train to Leningrad.

As the train cleared the Moscow suburbs, Ladd wanted to resume the discussion on ideologies. "It seems to me," he began, "that an analogy can be used to describe one difference between the United States and the U.S.S.R. Russia seems to have a clear concept of what is right and wrong in human conduct. There is very little hesitancy or doubt. Knowing what is good for human society, the government sets up a structure to direct its people in nearly every detail of human life. In many respects it is highly efficient. There is no litter on the streets, no graffiti on the subway walls, no unemployment, very little, if any, street crime. The government insists that this be the case.

"It might be compared to how a seminary conducted its life and affairs, especially in my days at St. John Vianney, before the Vatican II Council. Everyone knew clearly the theological and moral context in which the seminarians were to live. Rules and regulations were set down and, for the most part, the seminarians uniformly complied. It was an effective way of life. It got things done. For the most part, it was accepted without serious complaint.

"When you are in the Russian society, you have a feeling that you are living in a similar kind of structured, tightly ordered institution.

"The United States, on the other hand, starts from a very pluralistic view of human affairs. Although there is agreement on the importance of individual human rights, there is no common world view. For this reason, the government exercises much less control over its citizens. The consequence is a less structured society, possibly less efficient in many respects. Since there is disagreement on what is right and wrong in many areas, there are fewer rules and regulations to guide conduct in America.

"There is no visible pornography, even soft-core, in the media or elsewhere in the Soviet Union because it is seen to be harmful to human society.

"In the American scene, although most citizens would see little value to pornography, there is a serious regard for freedom of speech, freedom of expression, freedom of the press. Consequently, values are in conflict with each other and the question of pornography is only minimally regulated.

"Just as the U.S.S.R. might be compared to a seminary, the United States society might be seen as more analogous to an institution like

Stanford University, our seminary neighbor in Palo Alto, where there are a variety of philosophies, lifestyles and principles of conduct."

Ladd abruptly realized he was in a monologue, not a discussion. Father Platon had fallen asleep.

. . .

They arrived in Leningrad at eight-thirty the next morning, after being rocked to sleep on bed-bunks about the width of a book shelf, two persons to each compartment.

The weather was several degrees lower in temperature and somewhat overcast, after the brisk sunny days of Moscow.

The two were met at the Leningrad train station by Father Vladimir, Dean of St. Nicholas Cathedral, the young priest-secretary of Metropolitan Antonio, as well as Father Joseph Pavilonis, the only Catholic priest in Leningrad who served in the single functioning Roman Catholic church.

A Russian-made van drove them to Hotel Moscow.

Father Joseph asked Ladd for rosaries, scapulars and other devotional articles, but Ladd had none to give him. All he could give were some felt pens and chewing gum, which, according to the guide books, were appreciated as small gifts by the Soviet people.

Crowding the lobby and the corridors at the Hotel Moscow in Leningrad were throngs of teenagers, apparently high school and college age students from Finland, East Germany and some of the western provinces of the Soviet Union. They were remarkably like their counterparts in the United States. They dressed like teenagers in America, even some had punk-style haircuts. Many of the clothes were United States designer-label; the girls wore dramatic cosmetics. They were noisy in the typical teenager way, enjoying their companionship far away from home, laughing, teasing, rough-housing. The hotel officials didn't seem to exercise any particular restraint on their boisterousness.

Breakfast included white unflavored yogurt served in a drinking glass, choice of eggs served sunny-side up or closer to hard boiled in the shell in an egg cup, small slices of Russian black bread and white bread, not toasted. Oranges and apples were on the table. The coffee tasted very much as in the States. The hotel restaurant did not offer decaffeinated coffee. The cups, demitasse size, were filled again and again.

Ladd found the Hotel Moscow in Leningrad of modern construction, less than ten years old; the rooms modestly appointed, about the size and style of a budget motel in the United States. The television set was in black and white, even though color TV was common in Russia in the large cities. All programs were in Russian and much of the material is the kind of programming we would find in our public access channels. Three to five channels were offered in both Moscow and Leningrad.

Ladd's bed was a twin size, cot-like bed, covered with a blanket inside a bed-sized "pillow case" with a three foot oval hole in the middle, presumably for putting in or removing blankets.

. . .

As they rode into the entrance of Transfiguration Cathedral, Ladd noticed that the fence around the Cathedral courtyard consisted of cannon-barrels stood upright and driven into the ground, with chains linking the cannons. Father Platon remarked somewhat pompously, "May all the guns of the world be turned toward the ground as are the cannons in the fence of this cathedral."

The morning service was crowded, a liturgy of singing and reading of the Scripture, which lasted over two hours. The congregation stands throughout the entire service. There is no sitting or kneeling, but an abundance of signs of the cross, made with a motion from the right to the left shoulder, rather than the reverse as in the western tradition.

The liturgy reminded Ladd very much of the ritual and spirit of the Roman Catholic Church before the Vatican II Council, a sense of mystery and the supernatural.

It snowed through much of the day at Leningrad, not bitterly cold, but giving Leningrad a postcard wintry appearance. A constant concern of Californian Ladd was that he not slip on the icy sidewalks and streets.

He was having some difficulty sleeping because his body clock was totally out of sync with Leningrad time. Since there was an eight-hour difference in this part of the world, Ladd seemed to be getting up when New Yorkers were going to bed, and going to bed when New Yorkers were rising. After a few days, he became sleepy enough to make the adjustment and his sleep returned to normal.

In his sightseeing, he noted other non-Russian Orthodox places of worship in Leningrad were Baptist, a Moslem mosque and a Jewish synagogue. There were fourteen functioning Russian Orthodox churches.

On Sunday morning, Ladd celebrated the Sixth Sunday in Ordinary Time Mass at Our Lady of Lourdes Church.

It was a moving experience for Ladd to offer Mass, partly in Latin, partly in English, with people gathered early in the morning, still dark in February at 8 a.m.

Ladd's interpreter, Father Platon, translated his homily. At the Kiss of Peace, Ladd greeted all of the people in the congregation, and their warmth and affection were evident, even though they were startled that the celebrant priest left the altar and approached them for the handshake of peace. The Catholic Church in Leningrad followed conservative traditional practices. Ladd said Mass with his back turned to the people. All received the Sacred Host on the tongue; Communion was given only under the species of bread, not wine.

Ladd did not have a feeling of being under surveillance at any of his stops in the Soviet Union. In the intervals between meetings and state visits, he was free to roam anywhere he wished without accompaniment. He walked the city streets without fear. He felt that he could have walked the same deserted city streets at three o'clock in the morning without anxiety.

. . .

On the afternoon of his last day in Leningrad, Ladd took a walk along the Prospect Neva. He was approached by three young men in their early 20's. It turned out that they were students at the University of Leningrad.

Young Russians like to engage foreigners in conversation, especially Americans. Though he was not wearing his clerical collar and was bundled in a heavy topcoat, Ladd was obviously American. The student who seemed to be the oldest and the leader of the three said, in accented English, "Sir, we have guessed that you are from the United States. Could we talk to you for a few moments?"

Ladd was taken by surprise. He said, "Yes, of course."

They motioned Ladd to a bench in a small park alongside the Prospect.

"What do you think of Leningrad?"

"It is a beautiful city. I have been in meetings and have not been able to do much sight-seeing. But I have been impressed with the art collections at the Hermitage, especially the impressionists, and I have had a chance to visit the Summer Palace."

"What do you think of the Soviet Union?"

"Well, I have just been in the Soviet Union for a few days. It would be premature for me to make a judgment."

The youngest of the three students asked, "Why is it that Americans do not like the Russian people?"

"Oh, I am sure that most Americans like the Russian people very much. They may have some reservations about the Soviet government, but I do not think they dislike the Russian people."

"What reservations do you have about the Soviet Government?"

Ladd had heard that foreign visitors are monitored in a variety of ways. It occurred to him that even these young students might be sounding him out officially. He answered, "I don't think it is appropriate for me, a visitor very recently arrived, to express my criticism of a country that is my host. What do you young men think of the United States? Do you have any reservations about America?"

All three had responses immediately. "We do not like the way the CIA functions secretly in countries around the world - sometimes to undermine governments or to establish governments favorable to the United States."

Another responded, "We do not like the interference the United States made in the civil war in Vietnam."

A third student added, "The riots in Detroit and Los Angeles show that there is racism in America."

Ladd interjected, "Now, if you're going to make these accusations against the United States, perhaps I should reply to your question about reservations Americans have regarding the Soviet Union. We regret the lack of freedom that we see here. You do not have freedom of movement, freedom of assembly, freedom of religion, freedom of speech . . ."

The oldest of the three interrupted, "No, that is not right! It is a myth that we do not have freedom of speech in the Soviet Union. We are allowed free speech. We see in the American newspapers that you have protestors marching around the White House in Washington, D.C., carrying signs that say 'Down with Reagan,' 'Down with Reagan.' We can have the same freedom here in Moscow. We can have people marching around the Kremlin, carrying signs that say 'Down with Reagan,' 'Down with Reagan!'"

With this, the three students laughed.

Ladd was glad to see their sense of humor. The young in Russia are much more open to strangers and candid.

. . .

That night, Ladd and Father Platon caught the 12 o'clock train back to Moscow. In the capital, they registered again at the Hotel Ukraine.

Ladd turned on the television set in his hotel room. As he unpacked his suitcase, he heard the strains of America the Beautiful. Startled, he looked at the T.V. screen and saw a sequence of news footage, the mushroom cloud of America's atom bomb, homeless people sleeping in the streets of major United States cities, police dogs attacking demonstrators, and American policemen with clubs in hand chasing protestors. Behind all these depressing sights of violence, a chorus was singing "O beautiful for spacious skies . . . with amber waves of grain . . . God shed his grace on thee . . ."

Ladd wondered to how much of this anti-American propaganda were the Russian people exposed.

. . .

Ladd told Raissa that he would like to visit Roman Catholic priest Ladislaw Litov at St. Sergius Church. "You will not have to come with me this time, Raissa. I am sure that Ladislaw and I will be able to communicate. I understand that he can speak some English."

Ladd found the sacristan in St. Sergius Church and inquired of Father Ladislaw. The sacristan led Ladd into the sacristy just to the left of the main sanctuary. Ladd introduced himself as a Roman Catholic priest from the United States. When the sacristan translated the introduction, Father Ladislaw's countenance lit up in a broad smile. He was a man slight in stature, obviously in his late 70's or early 80's, dressed in the traditional black soutane.

The old priest embraced Ladd. Tears came to his eyes.

Ladd noticed that the priest motioned the sacristan to leave the sacristy on an errand. It was apparent that he wanted to talk to Ladd alone. As the sacristan left and closed the door behind him, Father Ladislaw motioned in the direction of the departing aide and shook his head from side to side warily.

The Kiev priest, it turned out, knew no English. How would they communicate? Ladd tried to dredge up his Latin from seminary days, but it was not much help. And the old priest's Latin was not much better.

"Non possum credere etiam meos collaboradoros."

Ladd took the halting Latin words as an explanation of why Father Ladislaw had dismissed the sacristan from the room before he started talking to Ladd. "I cannot believe or trust even my co-workers . . ."

The two struggled on with their long neglected Latin.

Ladd told the priest that he was bringing greetings from the faithful in America. "You are a brave man to work all these years in a difficult situation."

"It is a lonely life," Father Ladislaw replied. "The government says it has a policy of freedom of religion; but I really am not free. I cannot have instruction classes for the young. I cannot preach the Gospel anywhere outside this church building. It is almost impossible to get Bibles. The government limits the number that can be published. I would like to have rosaries and medals of the saints to give to my people."

"I have none of those religious articles with me," Ladd replied. "If you would write out for me your address in a way that mail would surely be delivered here in Moscow, I will send you rosaries and medals when I get back to the United States."

The old priest took a scrap of paper from the vestment case and wrote his name and address.

"I don't know if the Soviet post office will allow it to get through to you, but I will send you a package as soon as I return to America."

At this point, the sacristan returned from his errand. Ladd and Father Ladislaw gave each other a blessing, one in English, one in Russian.

CHAPTER 39

On the first full day back in the Soviet capital, Ladd and Raissa were driven to the residence of His Holiness, Pimen, Patriarch of Moscow and All Russia. On the way, their car was flagged down by a Moscow motorcycle policeman. The chauffeur had made an illegal left turn.

Ladd was astounded when the chauffeur got out of the car and berated the policeman. There was no citation made and no ticket given. Apparently the driver's federal government rating outranked the city police.

The secretary to the Patriarch, Father Boris, an imposing figure, met Ladd and Raissa at the door of Pimen's residence. The two were ushered into an elaborately furnished drawing room, remarkable for the icons that adorned three of its walls.

Patriarch Pimen, the counterpart of the Pope in the Russian Orthodox Church, was seated at an ornate ebony desk and rose as the two visitors entered.

Pimen was a relatively short, stocky man, dressed for the occasion in what Ladd would describe as a white embroidered Orthodox version of a house cassock. A gold reliquary hung from a chain below the Patriarch's graying beard.

Ladd wondered if he should kiss the Patriarch's ring, genuflect, or show some sign of reverence. Not knowing which was the proper protocol, he actually did nothing. He introduced Raissa as his interpreter. Father Boris remained in the room and seated himself with the others across the table from the Patriarch.

Through both interpreters, Raissa and Father Boris, Ladd gave a lengthy report on the work he was doing with CRS for the poor throughout the world.

As the audience proceeded, Ladd had a sense that the Patriarch, at an advanced age, was ailing physically and having a difficult time concentrating.

To lighten the conversation, Ladd said, "I am sure that Pope John Paul II would like to visit you in Moscow at some time, Your Holiness."

The Patriarch simply smiled. Father Boris said, "Many popes have wanted to visit Moscow."

Ladd gathered from that remark that he should not pursue the subject.

The Russians are gift-giving people. The Patriarch presented Ladd with a chain and chest cross, and a magnificently framed icon of Jesus Christ. (Ladd thought: How will I ever get all these gifts I'm accumulating, books, church music recordings, religious articles, into my suitcases?).

It was an awkward moment. Ladd had not thought to bring a gift for the Patriarch. He should have.

In desperation, he reached into the briefcase carrying prepared talks and journal notes taken at meetings, and retrieved the only thing that could pass for a gift - a clean, never-before-worn T-shirt, emblazoned front and back with the San Francisco "Bay to Breakers" marathon, 1984.

At least it was a gift that the Patriarch didn't already have. And at least the color was right - red.

. . .

Monday afternoon, his driver propelled Ladd in a government car to Number 36 Prospect Mira, the Boulevard for Peace. Seemingly there were no speed limits for official vehicles.

Ladd was escorted to a conference room on the second floor and seated at a table facing representatives of Soviet labor unions and the government, a medical doctor, several journalists and, speaking for the religions of the U.S.S.R., a Bishop Alexi Serge.

Oleg Hardin, Deputy Chairman, made the opening remarks. He expressed concern about Ronald Reagan's policies, the President's inflammatory language against the Soviet Union, and the increasing United States deployment of nuclear weapons, citing these as serious stumbling blocks to peace.

Ladd tried to keep the spirit of the discussions positive. He was convinced that if he did not put the Soviet representatives on the defensive, they would gradually be more open and come to realize that he was there to listen and that he was genuinely hearing their remarks.

He was tempted to put his tape recorder on the table, but decided that this might have a chilling effect on the conversation, so he left the dictaphone in his clerical suit jacket pocket with the tape running.

Up front, Ladd stated his loyalty to the United States. He made it clear again that the American people love the Russian people. Specifically he pointed out that the language of the United States administration had softened in the past several months, that there was clear evidence that America wanted peace. "Our common enemy," Ladd stated, "is nuclear war."

The doctor spoke up, "You know that this peace committee is not a government entity. It is completely independent and is supported from donations from all segments of our society."

The chairman asked, "How has the United States bishops' pastoral letter on peace been received by the government and the citizens of the United States?"

"For the most part, it was very well received," Ladd responded.

Ladd continued, "I want to say that Americans admire the moderation President Andropov has demonstrated in recent statements. Your President's invitation to 11 year- old Samantha Smith from Maine to visit Russia and to speak for peace was a very positive step. I am sorry to hear of President Andropov's recent illness and I will pray for his speedy recovery.

"I want to say in passing that I was very happy the other day to hear a Soviet official quoted in the media as saying spontaneously and quite casually, "I'll be in the office early Monday morning, God willing."

Several members of the committee managed a tentative smile.

The committee seemed to be looking for a statement from Ladd. "In many ways, the Church changed since the days of your revolution 1917. If both the Churches here in the East as well as the West are both seeking what is good for human society, why not lend each other our strengths, even though we may still have substantive ideological differences?

"I have a few suggestions I would like to offer at this time. First, is that in future summit talks and armed negotiation sessions, I hope that both sides will use proven professional conflict resolution facilitators. Secondly, it strikes me that it would be advisable to involve more women in these negotiations. They would bring a component which has been lacking in previous discussions.

"Thirdly, I urge the U.S.S.R. to consider the Brazilian Fonseca Pimentel renunciation of war treaty. I have also called this treaty to the attention of United States officials.

"Fourthly, in regard to the thirteen existing scientific and cultural treaties between the U.S. and the U.S.S.R., wouldn't it be a step in the right direction to reactivate the programs which have proven effective, for example, the student exchanges, the journalist exchanges, the joint environmental protection projects, and the cooperative space programs?"

As Ladd paused, a journalist from Izvestia interjected. "In all honesty, I must say that many of us see the United States as uncooperative and intent on dominating the world economically."

"The American people certainly do not want territorial, political or economic control over other nations," Ladd replied. "I realize that your country sees America as expansionist, and you know that we in the United States perceive Russia as threatening and expansionist.

"Our American leaders assert that the Soviet Union has international interests and commercial designs as well as a determination to control a warm water port, oil fields and other resources beyond your territory. At the same time, the American people recognize that the Russian people have suffered gravely from military invasions in recent centuries and have every reason to detest war.

"Both of our governments want to appear 'strong'. We in America honor strong presidents like Washington and Lincoln. You honor leaders like Peter the Great. But as each nation adds more military strength, the reaction of the other is not to back down in fear. It will simply try to outdo its adversary. The dangerous stand-off will continue."

One of the representatives of the labor unions stated, "I have read articles in United States newspapers that rejoice over Russia's grain shortages and also Poland's economic crisis. Is that the compassionate America, as your nation is often called?"

"I am not familiar with the articles to which you refer." Ladd admitted, "I do not deny that there are Americans who want to see the downfall of the Soviet Union. But that is not what I am here for, and I am sure enmity is not what you, as members of the peace committee, stand for."

From the far end of the table, the Orthodox Bishop asked, "Isn't America looked upon as the arms merchant to the world?"

"As a priest, Your Grace, I am not proud of that label, but I think both of our countries should desist from peddling arms to other nations. As I understand it, more than 600 billion dollars, calculated in United States money, are spent globally each year for munitions. This is incomprehensible while hundreds of thousands in underdeveloped nations are starving daily."

At this point, Chairman Hardin interposed, "Ladies and gentlemen, let us keep our discussion at a positive level. We appreciate, Father Franklin, the ideas you have proposed for our consideration. We are grateful for your visit to our offices, and trust that your stay in the Soviet Union will be an enjoyable one in every respect."

Ladd wanted to get in the last word in a positive vein.

"I think we all know that, at this point in history, we are down to the final options: coexistence or no existence. National boundaries are essentially arbitrary. Civil wars are the most agonizing wars. But all the people of the world are brothers and sisters; so all wars are civil wars. Soviet citizens and Americans are not different as people. We all laugh, bleed, fear, hurt and love. The Russian people and the American people have humanness in common. I am grateful for your invitation to address this committee. Spacibo and das vidanya. Thank you and goodbye."

There were handshakes all around. Ladd found Raissa and his designated driver waiting for him in the corridor.

. . .

That night, Ladd and Raissa left Moscow for Kiev and arrived to find soft drifting snow covering the downtown streets in a Christmas-like scene of Ukranian winter.

The two took part in vesper services with the Metropolitan presiding at Valdimir Cathedral, noted for its frescoes and lavish chandeliers.

At the end of the service, the Metropolitan turned to the people and welcomed Ladd to the City of Kiev, asking the visitor from the United States to address the people. Raissa translated. As he looked out over the congregation, so attentive to what he had to say, Ladd told the worshippers that their faces, young and old, looked just exactly like American faces.

"We are all brothers and sisters. I ask you to pray for understanding between the Russian Orthodox and the western Churches and between the American and Soviet people. I am overjoyed to be here in Mother Russia." That was a mistake. The Ukrainians do not consider themselves as part of "Mother Russia." Raissa saved Ladd by changing the translation.

It was a touching moment for Ladd to bless the people in Latin, and to hear them respond, "Spacibo," as one voice at the end of the blessing. As he passed down the main aisle in the recessional, the worshippers reached out to kiss his hand.

When Ladd emerged from Vladimir Cathedral, men and women workers were busy everywhere cleaning the new snow fall from the streets and sidewalks. Even at this late hour, women were working with labor crews, sawing down trees to replace them with newly planted trees on the main prospect of Kiev. Raissa pointed out that women are employed in all the occupations, professions and jobs in Russia.

The following morning, a five-person crew was painting the front facade of Ladd's hotel. They were industrious and skillful. But a day later, Ladd had a better understanding why there is virtually no unemployment in the Soviet Union. Now nine painters were on the crew, but they all had smaller paint brushes.

. . .

It was difficult for Ladd to keep up with the sumptuous food that was put before him at breakfast, lunch and dinner. He did not want to decline food as a guest of very gracious hosts, but when the entree came to the table after the many dishes that went before, Ladd had to think of some reason for not being able to eat the generous portions of meat.

Then Ladd recalled that the U.S. Bishops' Pastoral Letter on Peace states that the American bishops had pledged to abstain from meat on Fridays for the cause of nuclear disarmament and had urged others to do the same. He hoped it was a plausible excuse.

Ladd noted that here, as in the other cities of Russia, he saw no graffiti except a surprising K.K.K. scrolled on the main gate of the monastery in Zagorsk. He learned that Soviets seem to know a great deal about the American Ku Klux Klan and the Mafia.

That afternoon, as Ladd and Raissa were being driven to the hotel, the driver turned to them and relayed a radio news announcement that President Yuri Andropov had died. The bulletin stated that the Soviet leader had passed away at 4 p.m. the previous day. The announcement was solemn and brief. Back at the hotel, all the T.V. channels were presenting the same program, a tribute to Yuri Andropov, including classical music by a string quartet and a movie depicting episodes in the life of Lenin.

Since Ladd had a cough and a slight fever, he asked at the front desk if there was a house doctor at the hotel. Within ten minutes, a woman doctor came to his room to take his temperature. A physician was available for room calls 24 hours a day. All medical services were free in the Soviet Union, even to foreign visitors. When the doctor held the thermometer toward Ladd, he opened his mouth so that she could put it under his tongue, but the Russian system is to place the thermometer in the armpit.

The doctor selected from her kit what looked to Ladd like two horse pills. The medication killed his cold by the next morning.

. . .

The Russian people seemed to be very stoic about the death of their President. Very little was said about the subject, although there was a continual mention of his passing in the media. Raissa was brief in her answers to any questions on the subject of the burial service details or the election of a successor.

The Soviets were slow to admit health problems among their government officials. It is alleged that if a newscaster reported that the Soviet President was enjoying good health that meant that he had a heavy cold. If the reporter announced that the President had a cold that meant that he died last Wednesday.

Ladd learned from the U.S. Embassy that Vice President Bush and Senator Howard Baker would be among the United States delegation to the funeral on Tuesday.

The body was already at Red Square and the city was filled with soldiers. Red Square and the Kremlin were sealed off. Specified times were announced for queues to form to view the body. Separate times were set for official viewing by delegations from other countries.

As Ladd and Raissa returned to Moscow, the effects of President Andropov's death were evident. Police and military lined the prospects and highways. Substantially fewer people walked the streets. Many of the department stores and other establishments in the downtown area were closed. Although one could not enter Red Square, their driver took them around the perimeter of the Kremlin. New red bunting was flying from the buildings, a giant portrait of Andropov was mounted on the imposing green structure where his body lay in state. Long caravans of busses were bringing citizens from outlying districts to pay their respects to the deceased leader.

From time to time, an entourage of official-looking black limousines with headlights burning, sped into town, preceded by a police car, alternating blue and white lights flashing.

. . .

On the final morning of his stay, Ladd found several stores open and did some shopping. These department stores were for tourists only and articles could be purchased with foreign currency. Other department stores accepted only rubles and kopecks. The tourist stores, Ladd found, gave the best value to attract foreign currency, especially dollars, into the Soviet Union.

Raissa expedited Ladd through immigration control and customs. Under her watchful eye, the customs official overlooked the icon the Patriarch had given Ladd. Icons are not to be taken from the Soviet Union.

Ladd stayed overnight at Heathrow Airport, London, and departed at 12 noon, British time, connecting in New York, for BOAC flights to San Francisco and to Manila.

Five center section seats of the 747 were unoccupied, which allowed Ladd to stretch out and catch some sleep in the last leg of the flight over the Pacific.

CHAPTER 40

Tyler respected David's judgment. During a period of particularly virulent sexual temptations, he visited his friend and brought up the subject.

"Dave, I wonder if I'm wired wrong. I find myself always fantasizing about young girls, high school age. It's been like this since I was a teenager.

"Then, I used to watch Michelle Benedict out the window of our house on Park Avenue in Tucson. She was a blonde.

"I remember losing my breath and feeling my heart pump when Michelle entered the Old Pueblo drug store where I was a stock boy. I could hardly speak to her.

"Sometimes I think if I could have had a friendship with Michelle instead of just watching her from a distance, if I had grown up with her through high school years, I might have developed mature sexual appetites, even if I had committed some sins with her along the way.

"In the comics, I was fascinated by April Kane, the beautiful teenage girl in - was it in Flash Gordon? I wanted to see Hedy Lamarr in the movie, 'Ecstacy.' I would have seen the movie if I had the courage.

"At the library, I sneaked looks at topless girls in National Geographic. But alone, not with other kids.

"Also, in the balcony at the Lyric Theater, I can remember reaching across my 13-year-old cousin, Sabrina, who was budding into womanhood, to give Bobby some popcorn, only so I could brush Sabrina's breasts with my arm.

"I know I liked teenage girls. And that, of course, was normal.

"During vacation from the minor seminary, I envied students my age roughhousing on the campus at Tucson High or swaggering along Sixth Avenue. It's only now I realize I was envying them. Maybe subconsciously I was regretting that I never had a free-living boyhood like they were having.

"I never sowed wild oats -- though I thought about it a lot. I was thinking it and wanting it. As far as sinning is concerned, I might as well been doing it. I think I'm a hypocrite.

"When I was a counselor at summer camp, there were times I would find a pretext to go into the girls' locker rooms. I read books like Urban Fleege's `Self-Revelation of Adolescents' and Kinsey's books on sexuality. Even though I had this attraction, it didn't enter my head that I might be psychosexually under-developed. I just liked young people.

"It wasn't until I was about thirty-five that I began to recognize it when people began to talk about sex so openly. Research studies began reporting that some Catholic priests were repressed in their sexuality.

"Sometimes I think we have been brought up with a Jansenistic view of sex. We were never taught that sex was anything but a sacred gift of God. Still, looking back on it, I think we acquired a subconscious, somewhat wharped fear of the subject. We didn't deal with it naturally and confidently.

"Often I found myself marveling at the off-handed, open approach our high school students had toward sex. It's true this casual approach sometimes led them into regrettable experiences, but in a way their attitude seemed healthier.

"I began thinking back on my life. I thought a lot about girls in our class when I was in puberty. I was sexually attracted to them like my schoolmates.

"But then what happened? Did I get stuck in that early adolescent state of mind - attracted to teenage girls?

"At the minor seminary from the ninth grade on we were in an all-boys high school; for the next eleven years we were taught only by male teachers.

"We were lectured regularly on `custody of the eyes,' `don't even look at girls,' stay out of the `occasions of sin,' `he who lusts after a woman has already committed adultery in his heart.'

"On vacation, when a girl would look at me and smile, I would remember the school's counselor warning, 'Don't feel flattered. Girls will smile at a telephone pole if it is wearing pants.'

"I think all of us tried to put 'bad thoughts' out of our mind the minute they entered; and if we didn't, we made sure to confess it. Even when we were out of ear-shot of adults, we didn't talk about sex.

"All those years I struggled and I thought I was really weak, because I didn't think my classmates were having any of the temptations I was having. But was all that struggle good? Was it healthy?

"I think all of you and my other friends think of me as a self-confident man, well in control of myself, serene. But things are not that confident within.

"I have a low self-image. You know how little children are. If an adult stranger waves at them, they assume that no adult would be saying hello to them. They invariably turn around to see who it is that's being waved at. I am the same. In some ways, I feel inferior to adults. I think I don't belong.

"I took sexual development totally out of my life from puberty on. Maybe I am still thinking sexually like a 13-year-old. This makes me angry. Did the Church really know what it was doing in bringing us up this way?"

Tyler tried to control his voice. There was a long pause.

David finally broke the silence, "I think there is lot of truth in what you've said. But you have to think this through clearly, Tyler. Most priests have gone through the same seminary formation as you. They have not turned out the same way.

"There are many factors involved. I think the seminary authorities were giving good advice. But I think they were making some mistakes also. They did not realize the effect their directions were having on some seminarians.

"I guess they couldn't have been expected to know at the time. Even the medical profession didn't have the psychological information we have now.

"Still, there must be something to the Church's traditional positions on sexuality. Our society today has, for the most part, dismissed the Church's teaching - and the resulting current world scene is not admirable, increasing divorces, broken homes, teen pregnancies, social diseases.

"The matter is not a simple one.

"I'm sorry you're hurting. I'm sorry for the agony, the cover-up and probably the shame you have been feeling all these years.

"But you shouldn't feel shame. You are a good man, Tyler, a good priest. You are a courageous priest. You are a better man than I am."

CHAPTER 41

Ladd flew into Manila in the rain. The Philippine Islands were feeling the perimeter effects of a typhoon, even though it was not yet the rainy season, June to October.

As Ladd rode the airport van into Metro Manila, he studied the luxurious residential neighborhoods for the rich, the heart-rending barrios for the poor. The "middle class" make up fifty percent of the Manila population; five percent are rich and the remaining forty-five percent are well below the poverty level.

Ladd made notes for future development projects, rented an Avis compact and headed north to Olongapo to explore the possibility of introducing a CRS development project in that mountainous community.

Eventually no program was introduced. And that might have been providential, for if programs had been installed, they would have been wiped out in a relatively brief time.

Deep in its bowels nearby Mount Pinatubo was rumbling and about to shatter Olongapo, Angeles and Clark Air Force Base in the world's largest volcanic eruption in 80 years. The cataclysm would be ten time the size of Mount St. Helen's eruption. Dwarfing any thermal nuclear blast man has conceived, Pinatubo would leave 50,000 families without homes. Six hundred and fifty thousand would lose their jobs and a quarter of a million Filipinos would be displaced.

Clark was abandoned. And at Subic Bay, the base would close in six months. Even three years later, Pinatubo's soft gray powder lined the gutters of Manila two and a half hours away.

Ladd wrote his report, returned the rent-a-car at the airport and registered at a midtown motel.

. . .

At ten-thirty in the morning, Ladd was ushered into an audience at the residence of Cardinal Jaime Sin. As Ladd had passed through the front garden, he noted the scars of the bomb which exploded a few days before against the outer doors of the compound.

The Cardinal talked about his recent visit to the San Francisco Bay area, to San Jose, and asked questions about the Church in the United States. He is a vivacious man with a sense of humor always very near the surface. The Cardinal told Ladd of his impending journey to Moscow and to Lithuania, where he will meet with Mikhail Gorbachev, Patriarch Pimen, and Metropolitan Philaret.

. . .

Ladd checked out of the motel at 3 p.m. and boarded a 5:05 p.m. Philippine Airlines flight to Zamboanga, the major city at the southern tip of the Mindanao peninsula -- a region 60 percent Christian and 40 percent Muslim. At the airport, Ladd connected with a commuter plane to Jolo, one of the larger islands in the archipelago, stretching from the Philippines toward that part of Indonesia which was once Borneo. In the southern Philippines, a conflict has been waging for years with Muslims struggling for an independent nation. Kidnappings and terrorist acts by insurgents are frequent.

In Ladd's briefing documents is a travel advisory from the United States Department of State: "Americans are urged not to travel to the islands of Mindanao (except the cities of Davao, Iligan, and Cagayan de Oro) . . . travelers should be aware these areas are experiencing high levels of unrest and hold the potential of violence . . . Because unsettled conditions may also exist in some rural areas elsewhere in the Philippines, special care should be exercised at all times when traveling via public conveyances as well as private vehicles. Insofar as possible, road travel at night should be minimized and national highways should be used."

Security precautions are found everywhere in the Philippines, in Manila, as well as in the south - soldiers carrying rifles and dressed in jungle camouflage jumpsuits at the airports, around the hotels and in the streets.

On entering some urban buildings, Ladd was body-scanned with a hand-held metal detector. Hand carried luggage is checked scrupulously at the airport terminals.

During his final hours on the island, Ladd visited the new Notre Dame Elementary and Girls High School, which educates 2000 students, dressed in immaculate green and white uniforms. The older students at Notre Dame College also wear uniforms willingly, even enthusiastically. The uniform is a symbol of prestige education.

The students lined up in rows, single file, perfectly spaced and at attention, as Ladd addressed them.

At the end of his brief remarks, Ladd gave the "V" sign, a gesture universally recognized by young people. In just about all parts of the world, it stands for victory and peace. Many of the students, with infectious laughter, responded with their "V" sign. Others, good naturedly, held up their fingers in a sign which Ladd thought was "We are number one", the index finger pointing upward. Subsequently, he was told that the symbol is an "L" made by the index finger and the thumb. The "L" shape symbol was for Cory Aquino, and the "V" sign for her political opponent, Ferdinand Marcos. Ladd found he had been making a political statement which he had not intended.

In mid-morning, at a leprosarium, Ladd assisted the Sister-Director dressing the seeping wounds of victims of Hansen's disease. The patients range from very old to very young. Medication has now been discovered which completely cures leprosy, but there is much education to be done in the way of nutrition and hygiene to halt the spread of the disease in the Third World.

Crossing town in the company of a Muslim prayer official, Ladd blessed five pedicabs - the stylized bicycles with side-car for two or perhaps three passengers. Pedicabs are the mode of transportation for ninety percent of the population.

The vehicles are given through CRS to four or five people who qualify every three months. The new owner, from the income of his fares, gradually pays back the cost of the pedicabs. The purpose of the project is to establish people in an income earning small business.

Ladd reviewed the progress of a Church-sponsored credit union, then drove to the seaside and climbed precariously over a narrow bamboo passageway, amid the hovel huts, to the fishermen's association center. It defies understanding how small children and the elderly can navigate high bamboo bridge walkways with countless slats missing, and single narrow plank intervals requiring a tight-rope walker's agility and balance. Passage must be a nightmare in the dark of night and the rainy season. Ladd, with local staffers, helped organize a cooperative to purchase outrigger boats for the poor for commercial fishing.

On Monday afternoon, Ladd's team flew to Zamboanga and went immediately to a hospital on the outskirts of the city, where he toured a Muslim infirmary.

Ladd examined purses, dinner mats, throw rugs, and children's teddy bears made out of scraps of cut-away cloth from garments sized too large for the Filipino frame, sent from America in the Thanksgiving clothing drives.

Nuns in these deprived regions are inspiring in their dedication and in their simple lifestyle, often living in hovels with dirt floors, without adequate sanitation, clean water, or the minimum comforts the western world is accustomed to.

So respected are the Sisters in Mindanao that they are the only Christians who can routinely enter Muslim controlled territories.

. . .

In the late afternoon, Ladd flew out of Mindanao to Cebu in Visayas, boarding a connecting flight to Bacolod on the Island of Negros, Occidental, an area where political ferment and social unrest were intense.

Here Ladd met the renowned Bishop Antonio Fortich. He was the chairman of the National Cease Fire Committee, negotiating between the government and the leftist rebels. Committed to serving the poor and improving social structures, the bishop saw his residence set afire the previous year. He was now living in quarters at the Diocesan Chancery. Fortich pointed out the scores of shrapnel holes in the exterior walls of the courtyard outside his office. These the result of a bomb thrown into the compound just weeks before Ladd arrived.

Life is precarious for the Filipino hierarchy. Two other bishops had been involved in airplane accidents within the last few months.

· · ·

On his one-day stop in Manila, Ladd visited the Missionaries of Charity in the poorest section of the city. They serve the needy in the districts around "Smokey Mountain," a melancholy hill of garbage collected from Metro Manila, on which the poorest of the poor have built their dwellings and live off the refuse of the city.

CHAPTER 42

The next six weeks would convulse Ladd's life. He left Manila for Cotabato as a typhoon was approaching.

Arriving from the Cotabato airport in a UNICEF Jeep, Ladd was bunked overnight at the home of Archbishop Philip Smith, O.M.I., who remained in Tagaytay at the bishops' conference.

At the archbishop's residence, there was a knock at Ladd's bedroom door. It was two-forty-five in the morning.

A man, seemingly a non-Filipino, in his early thirties pushed into the room with a flashlight in his left hand and a revolver in the right. Perhaps it was the first time in his life Ladd was seriously frightened.

The gun was now at Ladd's head and the flashlight in his eyes.

The intruder was highly agitated. Either he was on drugs or needed drugs.

"Go stand in the corner."

Ladd got out of bed and moved across the room.

The robber set his flashlight on the night stand and distractedly scooped all the contents on the table into his pockets -- American and Filipino currency, small travel alarm clock and Rosary. As he did this, Ladd pointed at the beads and made the Sign of the Cross. The intruder must have been a good Catholic! He hesitated and replaced the Rosary on the night stand.

It seemed to Ladd that the robber was only half-hearted in his search for money.

There must have been something much more important that the trespasser was looking for. For an extended period of time, he rummaged through the closet, the drawers in the bureau, and Ladd's overnight bag.

Ladd was glad he had left his large suitcase with his CRS companions. Apparently finding nothing he valued, the robber angrily trained the gun on Ladd as he backed out of the room - and was gone into the night. Ladd vomited his breakfast later that morning.

It was just the beginning.

. . .

Completing his work as quickly as he could in Cotabato, Ladd took a domestic flight back to Manila and a JAL to San Francisco, where he had time only for a phone call to his family and to David. He flew on to Miami. He was due in Buenos Aires the next afternoon, so he booked the earliest flight possible, forgoing an overnight in Miami.

On Wednesday morning, Ladd landed at Aeropuerto Internacional de Ezeiza in the federal capital of Argentina.

He left springtime in the United States and arrived when Buenos Aires was enjoying fall in the southern hemisphere. As he stepped out of the terminal, he experienced the clear, clean breezes that had given the city its name. The feel of the cool morning air was not unlike Ladd's home in San Francisco.

A CRS staff member drove him to La Boca, one of the poorer sections of the capital. This was the harbor area and the quarter of early Italian immigrants.

For two days Ladd met with his agency's Country Representative and the co-workers, and visited three projects serving the indigent in the surrounding barrios. He would file a report to headquarters commending the effective staff at La Boca.

On the last evening of his stay in Buenos Aires, Ladd took the subway Linea C to the Centro. He stopped for an Aqua Mineral Villavincencio at the Obelisk of the Republic of Argentina - the crossroads of Buenos Aires, Avenida 9 de Julio and Corrientes. This "widest street in the world" - a triple thoroughfare - is surmounted by giant neon signs, "Sanyo", "Tome Sprite", "Whirlpool Electricodomesticos".

No people on earth take more time or pleasure in eating than the people of Buenos Aires. Every third storefront is an eating place and nearly half of those are confiterias featuring pizzas. The day runs far into the night with night life continuing into the small hours. There is a saying that "Argentineans' average hour for dinner is 10 p.m., but some prefer late dinners."

Ladd walked east to Plaza de Mayo, stood among the hundreds of well-fed pigeons, viewed the Casa Rosada, the "Pink House" of Government, famed for Juan and Evita Peron.

He accompanied a contingent of Argentina military as it marched from the Casa Rosada along the north side of the plaza to the nave of the metropolitan cathedral for the Changing of the Guard at the elaborate tomb of General Jose San Martin, Argentina's George Washington.

Ladd made visits to the nearby churches of San Roque, Franciscan, and San Ignacio, Jesuit. He noted that in all three churches the number of men attending equaled the women. Argentineans' faith is devotional with young and old giving veneration to the saints and running their hands over their statues.

Turning back toward the Lavalle pedestrian mall, as Ladd crossed Esmeralda, suddenly shots punctured the air above the roar of the traffic.

The 45-bullet came from Room 206 of the Regis Hotel, from the corner balcony directly above the intersection. Ladd heard the bullet hiss past his left ear and saw the impact of the slug at the base of the helado stand fifteen feet in front of him.

Ladd looked back over his left shoulder. At the second floor, he saw a figure pull back from the window. It could have been the same man that had broken into his room in Cotabato in the Philippines.

Immediately Ladd retraced his steps, weaving through the crowds, half running past the theaters and video game parlors on Lavalle to the broad boulevard of 9 de Julio.

He knew he would lose his assailant if he could reach the railway stations at Carlos Pellegrini and Corrientes, where Lines A, B and C intersect.

Ladd boarded the B Line running east, switched to the C Line south, transferred immediately at Avenida de Mayo to the first train to Playa Miserere. There he left the subway, walking north on Puejirredon, a short block to the train station.

He hadn't eaten since breakfast. Suddenly he had lost his appetite. But he should get something on his stomach. For one peso, he bought a tube of Garrapiñada from a street vendor, hailed a Black and Yellow

Cab, picked up his luggage at the terminal lockers and headed for the departure gate.

He suspected that going to the police would detain him in Buenos Aires for many days, and his pursuer would still be on his back. He had better keep on the run.

Ladd flew north out of Jorge Newberry on an Aerolina Argentinas 737. Below, millions of square miles of pampas were laced with the Rio de Plata, the Piranha, and other rivers like twisting fat snakes. The Pampas - the word recalled to Ladd boxer Luis Firpo - the Wild Bull of the Pampas.

Though Buenos Aires is indeed a city of Good Airs, with mid-April cool gusting breezes, from 10,000 feet, Ladd saw the yellowish brown pall draping the federal capitol, no different from Los Angeles or Mexico City. Below, the wrinkled South Atlantic is mud-colored. In the distance, countless small fires could be seen where farmers were burning the spent wheat and corn fields.

Ladd was puzzled that, though flying north at noon, the sun seemed to be shining from ahead of the plane. It should be from the south. Eventually he wondered, this being the southern hemisphere, if the sun made its course during the day from east to west in the northern sky.

Though he was ticketed for Sao Paolo, at the last minute during the half hour lay-over at Iguaçú Falls, Ladd slipped away from the transit lounge and hailed a taxi for Hotel Iguaçú Internacional. If anyone was tailing him, he hoped they had already reboarded the plane for Sao Paolo.

His hopes were not long lived. From the lobby of the Internacional, just before dinner, he saw his pursuer paying off a cab driver in front of the hotel. Ladd moved quickly to the back exit of the lobby and followed the signs to the upper course of the falls on the Argentina side, past Dos Hermanos falls and on toward the gigantic San Martin. There, the Rio Iguaçú (Big Water) pushes a massive white and chocolate-colored flood over a precipice a quarter of a mile wide, cascading through angry churning billows of mist 250 feet below.

As Ladd raced on, countless species of multicolored tropical butterflies scattered before him. Rainbows formed in the sky and in the mist at his feet, seemingly close enough to reach out and touch. All around him for miles, a hundred separate falls were crashing their burdens on volcanic rock, impervious to erosion. The Iguaçú cataracts have been here for millions upon millions of years. From all appearances, they will be here forever.

For visitors, the spectacle is breathtaking. For Ladd who had hardly time to look at the dramatic scene around him, the situation was breathtaking because of exertion and fear. If only he could reach the greatest of all the falls, the Gargantua Diabolo on the Brazil side. There, at the Hotel Das Cataractas Brasil, Angela Bettincourt, a CRS volunteer, could hide him and see that he reached the airport to fly to Sao Paolo or Rio. Hopefully his pursuer had no Brazilian visa.

He turned the corner beside Isla San Martin and found the course blocked! There was no way over the river. The only crossing was back at the Taneredo Neves bridge, miles away at the confluence of the Rio Iguaçú and the Rio Parana.

Ladd could not turn back without facing his pursuer. In desperation, he climbed over the chain of a "No Pasar" sign and headed on to a narrow path. A tapir and an ant eater scurried away in the undergrowth. A toucan and two macaws fluttered out of the foliage. Ladd wondered what other flora and fauna were unseen around him. He knew orangutans, scorpions, wild cats and snakes of countless varieties called this jungle home.

As he brushed swarms of butterflies from his face, Ladd found himself thinking what a paradise this would be for David's boyhood pastor in Napa, Father Claudel, the moth and butterfly collector. Above the roar of the falls, he fantasized himself as a Jesuit, pushing through the thicket on his way to the Mission Compound centuries earlier. He wished that were the reality now.

The path fortunately circled back to the Park Hotel.

Ladd went immediately to his room and considered his options. Should he place himself under the protection of the local police? Would they believe his story? What evidence did he have that he was being followed? He guessed that police systems in South America operated differently from those at home. Was he imagining the whole thing? Was it a conspiracy or a series of coincidences?

Ladd was scheduled to take a flight out of Rio de Janeiro to Miami. He just wanted to get back to the United States. Though he was ticketed to leave the next day across the river on the Brazil side at Iguaçú Airport, he decided to take a taxi immediately and try for an earlier flight.

At the terminal ticketing counter, he was told the only flight remaining that night was to Sao Paolo. From there, he could connect the following morning to Rio.

If it were a conspiracy, if a network of pursuers were involved, they would be expecting him in Sao Paolo, but on an earlier flight. Overnight in Sao Paolo might throw them off his track. He did not know if there was someone lying in wait in Sao Paolo. He did know there was someone on his trail here in Iguaçú.

Ladd was in Sao Paolo in an hour and a half. He found a hotel on Rua Aurora on the poorer side of old downtown, near the Parca de Repulica.

A rally was going on in the park dedicated to the founding of the Brazilian Republic. Loudspeakers were blasting "Igualdade, Dignidade, Ciudadania." Ladd deduced that the leaders of an activist organization, Central Workers Union, bearing the initials CUT, were urging the throng to do something about salary scales.

The amplifiers made sleep impossible for Ladd. He slipped out of the hotel side exit and eventually found himself on Rua Barco de Itapetininga. He felt more secure hidden among crowds. He was fascinated by scores of men, generally middle aged or elderly, carrying sandwich boards which, on front and back, listed job opportunities and phone numbers - everything from house painters to computer operators. He had to step around street people lying in shop front doorways, on sidewalks, some wrapped in blankets against early morning temperatures which could reach as low as 40° Fahrenheit this time of year.

Many were the Brazilian street children whom the American media have featured, apparently ranging from as young as nine or ten years of age. Some at the late hour were still up and walking the streets, asking for money. A trademark or characteristic of the young ones is to hold their arms completely inside their oversized T-shirts. Ladd made a mental note that CRS should start projects for the street people of Brazil.

As he picked his way through the endless throngs back to the hotel, he reflected that the Brazilian Portuguese word for people must be "Sao Paolo." People rushing everywhere, even at this late hour.

CHAPTER 43

On the VASP flight to Rio de Janeiro, Ladd was confident he had eluded his pursuer or pursuers in Sao Paolo. There was no sign of a stalker at Rio International Airport or on the bus coming into the Centro.

He took the subway at Cinelandia, jumped off at the Gloria station and climbed the winding cobblestone street to the octagonal-shaped Gloria Church on the Hill, the favorite worshipping place of the monarchy in the 1700s. Headquarters in New York had made provision for Ladd to stay at the historic church's rectory.

That afternoon, surrounded by ornate blue and white Portuguese tiled walls and overlooking the downtown skyline, Flamingo Park and Sugar Loaf, Ladd offered Mass privately and prayed for a safe resolution to whatever it was that seemed to be gradually entangling him.

Since he was sure he had shaken his "pursuer," Ladd would take advantage of the respite to follow up on some CRS inquiries.

He asked for and received a brief audience with the Archbishop of Rio, Ernesto Corporales, to discuss the possibilities of projects for the poor in the favelas of Rio, as well as Sao Paolo. The episodes that seemed to be plaguing him since leaving Moscow were very much on his mind, but he was reluctant to bring up the subject with the prelate. The nightmarish nature of the incidents or his perception of the incidents might jeopardize the plans he was proposing. Besides, the audience was very brief. A priest- secretary had requested that the informal meeting take place in the sacristy of the new Cathedral of Saint Sebastian where the Archbishop was to celebrate a Pontifical Mass on the occasion of Brazil's national Labor Day. The mammoth pyramidal edifice, completed in 1976, accommodates 20,000 sitting and standing worshippers.

The Cardinal received Ladd graciously, listened attentively, and encouraged the proposal. As he vested for Mass, he asked Ladd to see that a complete written description of the project be sent to him.

That much accomplished, Ladd summoned the courage to share with the prelate the harrowing events of the last few days. But as he began, a master of ceremonies stepped forward and gestured to the Archbishop to join the procession that was moving out of the sacristy past the stylized statue of St. Francis of Assisi and into the nave of the church.

"Goodbye and thank you, Your Eminence."

Outside the cathedral, Ladd took a bus to Favela Recinya Borel on the outskirts of downtown. Shacks and make-shift lean-tos cling to the hillside. This slum is notorious for clashes between the residents and the government police. Many have died or disappeared here. Though travelers are warned against visiting this section of Rio, Ladd figured, given the occurrences of the past week, he was as safe here as anywhere. No one would trail him in this neighborhood.

On every side, in fragile shelters and open sewers, he saw needs that his organization could serve. Possibly because he was wearing his clerical suit, no one accosted him or even approached him, as he wound his way through the favela.

Retracing his steps to the foot of the hillside, he saw a bus with the destination: Tijuca and Corcovado. Corcovado, Ladd knew, was the "hunchback" mountain at the top of which stands the 125-foot statue of Christ the Redeemer. The outstretched arms embrace all of Rio.

As much as he was conscious of the possible peril he was in, Ladd felt he could not leave Rio without visiting its most notable landmark.

Ladd boarded the cog train for the twenty-minute ride through dense jungle to the summit. The vista is like none other in the world. The 360 degree view from the base of the statue sweeps over all of Rio, Sugar Loaf, the Atlantic Ocean, the beaches of Copacabana, Ipenema and Leblon, more than 2300 feet below.

Returning to the lower station of the cog train, a young man with a Sony Camcorder stopped Ladd. "Father, do you want a video of your visit to the Statue of Corcovado?"

"No thank you," Ladd said.

"It's yours for free, Father. I take videos of tour groups. No one in this group wanted to buy a copy. I will just erase it. But you were in many of the pictures. So you can have it free if you wish."

Again, Ladd guessed it was his clerical suit that prompted the special consideration.

He accepted the tape. "Thank you very much. Obrigado."

Ladd had no way of knowing how crucial this film record would be a short while later.

. . .

At three-fifteen in the morning, the phone next to Ladd's bed rang, shattering the stillness that had finally settled over the Gloria region. Ladd sat upright, trying to remember what country he was in, fumbling to shut off an alarm clock, then realizing it was the phone.

"Hello," he mumbled.

He heard a man's voice talking to a third person at the other end of the line. The language was Portuguese. Then the voice of a third party, a woman, came on.

"Hello. Is this Father Franklin?"

The accent was both Slavic and Scandinavian.

Ladd wondered who knew he was here.

"Who is this?" he asked.

"This is Raissa."

"Raissa?"

"Yes, Raissa, your guide in Moscow. Do you remember me?"

Ladd's mind was clearing. He certainly did remember Raissa. And he recognized the English spoken with a Swedish accent.

"Yes, Raissa. What is this? Where are you?"

"I am in Moscow, but I cannot talk long. I am with friends here and I have a very important message for you. Can you hear me?"

"Yes, I can hear you."

"Do you remember when you were meeting with the Peace Committee in Moscow?"

"Yes."

"Did you have a tape recorder with you at that meeting?"

"Yes."

"Was it turned on?"

"Yes, but I just wanted to make sure that I had a record of what I had said in case anyone questioned me back in America."

"This is the important problem, Father Franklin. Please listen carefully to me. A security scanner detected that you were carrying a Dictaphone. One of the government agencies here thinks your recorder may have listened to -- picked up a conversation you were not supposed to hear. It was confidential remarks on the side. Do you still have the tape?"

"Yes, I have the tape somewhere in my luggage, but I haven't listened to it yet. I haven't been home since I was in Moscow."

"I must hurry, Father Franklin, but I want to tell you that on the tape may be something about the Pope in Rome. I cannot tell you anything more. They may try to stop you. Please do not tell anyone I called you. I must say goodbye now. Das Vidanya. Goodbye."

There was a click at the other end before Ladd could ask any more questions. How did Raissa know where to find him? Ladd had left some of his itinerary with CRS headquarters, including the Rio stay. Probably Raissa had contacted the New York office.

But what was all that about the tape? And about the Pope? Ladd didn't remember any reference to the Pope in the conversations with the Soviet Peace Committee.

He knew he would not be able to get back to sleep now. He turned on the light at his night stand, rolled out of bed and went to the closet for his luggage. He sorted through his audio tapes and found the cassette labeled "Peace Committee - Moscow."

From the side pocket of his Travel Gear suitcase, he withdrew his hand-held dictating machine, replaced his current dictation tape with the 90-minute Peace Committee cassette. Back in bed, he depressed the Play button and listened to the dialogue he had replayed so often in his head since those days in Moscow.

Ladd recalled again all the things he wished he had thought of fast enough to say during the Committee dialogue. It was pillow wit again.

But the debate on the tape was just as Ladd remembered it, all in Russian accented English and American accented English. He let the cassette roll to the end.

Fifty-five minutes into the tape, he did hear some muffled words which sounded like Russian, as though in an aside, apart from the give-and-take dialogue. Ladd didn't remember being aware at the time of the

FRANCIS A. QUINN

separate private conversation between two male voices. That exchange lasted no more than 30 seconds.

Other than that, the recording was substantially as Ladd had remembered it - a relatively cordial, if sometimes tense, encounter – but no mention of the Pope.

Where in Rio could he find someone who could translate the brief extraneous Russian language remarks? The Russian Consulate? Not there, certainly, if the substance of the private conversation was as Raissa described it. Maybe this explained the incredible series of "coincidences" beginning in the Philippines.

Just to be on the safe side, should he put in a call to the Vatican to alert them at least to the warning? What office in the Roman Curia? The Secretariat of State was all Ladd could think of. By the time he would shower, shave and visit the rectory office to get assistance in putting through a call, it would be mid-morning in Rome - a good time to phone.

A young priest at the reception desk punched all the right numbers to reach the Vatican office.

"Pronto," came the voice on the line.

"Is there someone there who can speak English?" Ladd asked.

There was silence for twenty seconds. Then an Italian sounding voice speaking English: "Yes, who is this calling?"

"This is Father Franklin of the United States. I am calling from Rio de Janeiro. I have what might be a very urgent message or may be just a crank call. I know it will sound like a strange story." Ladd went on to explain the background of the Moscow Committee meeting and then the details of the call from Raissa Kryshchuck. He wondered how much of his English the Curial official at the other end was understanding.

"What does the recording say about the Holy Father?"

"If it refers to the Pope at all, I do not know what it says because that is the part that is in Russian."

"Can you get the Russian words translated?"

"I will as soon as I can find someone with a knowledge of the language," Ladd replied.

"Please do that, Father, and then be sure to call this office again. My name is Father Benjamini."

Ladd heard the phone ring off. He did not know if the official had really understood the possible gravity of his message. He suspected that an international office like the Vatican Secretary of State received many calls sounding alarms.

Perhaps his call was just a crank call. He didn't know the meaning of the brief words of Russian. He didn't even know if the almost inaudible comments could be deciphered at all.

Tomorrow, he would leave for the States and do what he could as soon as he landed.

. . .

At breakfast, Ladd told the assistant pastor at Gloria Church that he would have to leave that day for the States. Would the young priest please help him with the language in making phone calls to reserve a flight from Rio to Miami as early as possible that day?

The flight was booked for 8:55 a.m.

"Would you also make a reservation for a flight from Miami to Rome? Give me at least six or seven hours in Miami." It had occurred to Ladd that once the tape was translated, a quick trip to the Vatican might be necessary. He would make the provision anyway.

Then Ladd thought, "Father, see if you can line up a flight from Miami to Rome, but through Amsterdam -- perhaps there is a KLM flight."

He decided he should get a duplicate of the tape and leave it with someone in safekeeping -- Willow Caprice in Amsterdam.

Ladd left the breakfast table to return to his quarters in the rectory to pack. As soon as he opened the door, he knew someone had been in the room since he left it an hour before. His luggage was open on his bed, part of his clothing on the floor.

He went through his suitcase. The money belt he wore around his waist while traveling seemed to be undisturbed. The passport, the credit card, the Brazilian reals, the American dollars, the travelers' checks were all there.

But the audio cassettes were gone.

Ladd's heart sank. He would rather they had taken the money belt. Hours of dictation, letters, reports were on those tapes.

Suddenly he remembered that he had never returned the Russian Peace Committee tape to the cassette collection. He went to the closet, felt for the pocket of his pajama upper. The cassette was still there.

Father Coelho gave Ladd the itinerary of the KLM flight. Ladd would phone Willow from Miami on the time of his arrival at Schipol Airport in Amsterdam.

Time was getting short for the flight to Miami. Ladd threw things back into his suitcase, put the cassette in the inside pocket of his clerical suit jacket, said quick goodbyes to his priest hosts.

He declined an offer to be driven to the Rio International Airport. He had come to know the Brazilian busses. They are the fastest transportation. All the drivers fantasize themselves as Emerson Fitipaldi or the late Ayrton Senna. They drive 15-ton omnibuses on wide thoroughfares or crowded narrow streets like sports cars scattering pedestrians in all directions.

Though he had to endure the extra details of an international flight - passport check, airport tax, security questions about luggage and customs documents, Ladd reached the departure gate in time.

. . .

Against unusually heavy head winds, the flight from Rio to Miami took nearly nine hours. On arrival, with quick passage through passport control and customs, Ladd hailed a taxi to the Miami Archdiocesan Chancery Office. He introduced himself to the receptionist and asked to see the Chancellor or Moderator of the Curia or any diocesan official available.

He was directed to a Father Liam Donohue. After the usual introductions, Ladd began, "Father, I have a rather unusual request. Do you know anyone here in Miami who is bilingual, English and Russian -- someone dependable, who could be counted on to treat information in a completely confidential manner?"

"Russian? Let's see. I don't have many Russian acquaintances. But I do know an old Russian Orthodox priest who has retired here. He's a serious, responsible type."

"Could you tell me how I might get in touch with him?"

"I'm sure he's listed in the phone book."

Donohue located the name, address and phone number, put in a call and made an appointment for Ladd immediately. The residence of the Orthodox cleric was some fifteen minutes away by cab.

Father Fyodor Konkov greeted Ladd at the front door of a modest residence in central Miami. Noting the formal black cassock, Ladd guessed he was an "orthodox" Orthodox. That would suggest reliability.

Ladd briefed the elderly priest on the reason for his visit and asked for and received a promise of total secrecy. He had rolled the tape on his dictating machine to a point just prior to the Russian language intervention, pressed the Play button and turned up the volume.

The Russian priest cocked an ear toward the cassette when he heard the mumbled Russian. Then he asked Ladd to play the brief passage again. Ladd studied the expression on the old cleric's face. It was mostly impassive, if anything, suddenly more serious.

"Can I hear that part once again?"

Ladd reversed the tape and played the segment a third time. Father Konkov looked at Ladd and said, "Whoever that is who is talking is saying that a day and time have been set for the attack on the Pope in Rome. I think he says the date, but I cannot make it out. It is not clear."

"Listen to it again, Father. I will make it louder."

The tape rolled again and the old priest put his ear to the cassette player. He shook his head. "No, I cannot understand the last part. The date is garbled."

Ladd knew now he had to take the flight to Rome and let the Vatican authorities hear the tape. He thanked the Orthodox priest and headed back to the airport.

After purchasing his reserved tickets and the two boarding passes at the KLM counter, Ladd put in a call to Willow's apartment in Amsterdam.

"Hi, Willow, this is Ladd. I am calling from the Miami Airport and I'll be flying into Schipol at nine o'clock your time tomorrow morning. I have something I want you to do for me, which I'll explain to you when I see you. It's a very confidential matter, and I'd rather not meet you at the Consulate or at your place, but somewhere we can talk privately and unnoticed. It's better if you don't meet me at the airport. Just tell me a place which I can find, and a time, and I'll be there."

"What's all the mystery, Ladd?"

"I'll tell you tomorrow."

"Well, you know the Rijksmuseum. Let's meet there - in front of Rembrandt's Night Watch at 11 a.m. That'll give you plenty of time to get into the city."

Ladd had seen no sign of his pursuers since leaving Rio. He could picture them huddled together listening to a dozen or more tapes of CRS reports and correspondence, not yet realizing that they missed the one cassette they wanted.

Even so, they would still be after him personally, not knowing whether or not he had already listened to the tape, caught and translated the side-bar conversation.

The rendezvous with Willow must be covert.

CHAPTER 44

At 11 a.m., Willow was standing before the heroic sized Night Watch, flood-lit, the centerpiece of the Rembrandt collection.

Ladd walked up from the side and touched her on the shoulder.

"Hi, Willow. It's good to see you."

"Hello, Ladd. What is all this cloak and dagger talk?"

"Let's walk around the halls. I'll explain while we're looking at the art.

"I have an audio tape which has some very important information. I mean crucial. Some people want the tape badly and have been following me ever since I left Moscow. In fact, one of them took a shot at me in Buenos Aires."

"Oh. What's the tape about?"

"The tape is the dialogue I had with the Soviet Peace Committee, but there are some extraneous remarks on the tape that talk about specific plans to attack the Pope. I haven't been able to get all the details translated. I'm on my way to Rome now to give the tape over to the Vatican offices."

"Do you have the tape with you?"

"Yes, that's why I wanted to see you. I want you to make a copy of the tape secretly and keep the copy in a safe place. I'll take the original to Rome. If anything happens to me or to the original, you can see that someone follows up on informing Vatican security or anyone there that has authority." Ladd continued, "I'm afraid everybody will think it is a bizarre fantasy or a hoax unless they hear the tape."

He waited until they were in one of the small salons where there were no visitors and no attendant. He took the cassette, now in a Gloria

Church envelope, and handed it to Willow who placed it in the small bag that hung from her shoulder.

"If you could drop me off a few blocks from the Embassy, duplicate the tape at the Embassy or wherever you can make the copy, and then see that I get my own cassette back. I'll wait on the corner where you drop me off, and then take a taxi back to the airport and leave for Rome."

Just over an hour later, a courier from the Consulate came in an official black Mercedes, spotted Ladd, who was signaling, and handed him a diplomatic pouch. The original tape was inside with a note:

"Be careful, Ladd. Put it into the hands of the right people at the Vatican and let them take care of it. Don't get involved any further. Love, Willow." Ladd asked the messenger for a piece of paper, scribbled a quick note:

"Thanks, Willow, I'll call you from Rome after I've made the delivery. If you don't hear from me in two days, tell your boss to follow whatever plan you think best. Love and prayers, Ladd."

Ladd placed the note in the pouch and gave it to the courier. "Please see that Miss Caprice gets this message."

. . .

Ladd was in Rome by 7:30 p.m. It was Monday night.

He went directly to North American College on the Janiculum, the United States hierarchy's major seminary in the Eternal City, where he had stayed on his previous visit. To the rector of the College, he explained his unusual situation from beginning to end, and asked his advice as to which Curial office he should present the tape.

It was agreed that, since he had already called the Secretary of State's office by phone, he should continue that contact first thing in the morning.

Ladd was given the room normally occupied by the Vice Rector who was away on sabbatical. This was originally the suite of the first rector of North American College, Archbishop Martin O'Connor. Again, as he kept the cassette within arms length and waiting for sleep to overtake him, Ladd rehearsed what he would say at the Vatican State Department in the morning.

. . .

At 8 a.m., one of the seminarians brought a house Fiat around and drove Ladd to the Secretariat. At the reception desk, Ladd asked for Father Benjamini with whom he had spoken from Rio.

In five minutes' time, a tall distinguished looking cleric, mid-forties, appeared in the lobby. "I'm Father Benjamini." Ladd suspected he was at least a Monsignor, but was using the more humble title.

"I am Father Ladd Franklin. You may remember I called you from Rio de Janeiro a few days ago."

"Yes, it was about the tape recording in Russian. You have made a quick trip. Do you have further information?"

"I have had the Russian excerpt partially translated. The sound quality is not good, but the content of the comments in Russian refer to an attack on the Holy Father. The Russian priest who did the translation believes that the words, unintelligible at least to him, refer to a date and time. I have the tape with me." Ladd took the tape from the inside pocket of his clerical suit jacket, handing it to the official.

"We have an East European and Russian desk at the Secretariat with staff fluent in the Slavic languages. I will take the cassette to that section. Follow this way, please."

Ladd accompanied the priest through a maze of corridors to an office deep within the secretariat. As they walked, Ladd, reading the dictaphone meter, fast forwarded the B-side of the cassette to the point of the passage in question.

"We have excellent audio equipment here," Father Benjamini said as they walked. "Perhaps the high fidelity will bring out the garbled words more clearly."

Ladd was impressed with the flawless English of the priest. He must have spent some of his diplomatic career at an English speaking nunciature.

Father Benjamini took the tape from Ladd and placed it in a state-of-the-art player.

The section of the dialogue came on which Ladd had heard so often in the past few days - the discussion immediately preceding the fragment of conversation in Russian. It was indeed much clearer than when played on Ladd's dictating machine.

But then the dialogue went on with no Russian language overlaying the committee discussion.

Ladd was startled. Where was the background conversation between the two deep male voices? In fact, there was approximately a 30-second lapse in the sound.

He looked at Benjamini puzzled. "Reverse the tape a few seconds, Father," Ladd said.

The priest pressed the rewind button briefly and the tape started forward again. The familiar segment of dialogue repeated, but then the blank again.

Ladd let the cartridge play on further. But he was sure they had passed the critical passage. He took the tape and placed it in his own recorder. The same section of peace committee debate sounded again without the Russian language undercurrent. Ladd was dumbfounded.

"I don't know what has happened. The conversation was there. Now it's gone." Benjamini also seemed puzzled.

Ladd wondered if the Curial priest was having doubts about the story. There was an embarrassing pause.

Then the secretariat official said, "Take the cassette with you, Father. Play it again in full. Perhaps the remarks are in another section of the tape. And give me a call when you find it."

Ladd left the State Secretariat's office and returned to North American College.

. . .

That night, Ladd had trouble sleeping. The events of the day kept churning through his mind. How had it happened? Had he been imagining the Russian conversation on the tape? No, the priest Konkov in Miami had heard it just as distinctly as he had.

Did he have the wrong place on the tape? No, that couldn't be the case. He had turned to the specific point on the tape counter of his dictating machine too many times before to be mistaken. And he had become familiar with the context of the Peace Committee discussion before and after the Russian language segment.

Finally, toward morning, he slept soundly, then awakened at seven-thirty. He joined three members of the seminary faculty in the priests' dining room for breakfast. Though he normally looked forward to tasting again the incomparable Italian continental breakfast rolls, this morning he had little appetite.

The Rector of North American College, his friend, was not one of the three at table. He saw no reason to bring the matter of the tape up to the others. They knew nothing about the tape in the first place, and yesterday's development was too disconcerting to relate.

Ladd drank a glass of orange juice, poured himself a cup of coffee from the espresso machine, picked up that morning's edition of the International Herald Tribune. It had been awhile since he had leisurely access to an English language newspaper.

"Are you going to the papal audience today?" a priest on loan as a spiritual director from the Archdiocese of Atlanta asked Ladd.

"That's right, it's Wednesday. What time is the audience?"

"I think it starts at 10 o'clock -- outside in the piazza of St. Peter's."

"Yes, I think I'll go. It will be my first with John Paul II."

Ladd estimated he had better leave immediately if he wanted any kind of favored position to see the Pope.

It was too late to contact the Monsignor at the old North American College, the Casa, the house on Humility Street, who was in charge of tickets to positions of preference for Americans at papal audiences. Ladd would shift for himself.

He put on his clerical suit, walked down the Janiculum hill, passed the international headquarters of the Society of Jesus, on to the Via Conciliazione, and into St. Peter's Square.

Crowds were already forming behind the barricades located in front of the Basilica. Ladd positioned himself as close as he could to the platform on which the papal chair had already been placed.

Rapidly during the hour and a half that followed thousands filled in the square behind and all sides of Ladd.

CHAPTER 45

Promptly at ten, a murmur began and crescendoed through the crowds. As the Holy Father arrived through the Arch of the Bells, no longer carried in the "sede gestatoria" or portable throne on the shoulders of papal attendants, but in what looked to Ladd like an oversized white, wide open Jeep Wrangler.

The motorcade began its customary journey, weaving through the crowds so that everyone could have a reasonably close-up view of the Holy Father. Some at the leading edge of each barricade were able to reach out and shake his outstretched hands.

As the procession passed Ladd's section, he saw the husky white cassocked prelate, vigorous in his motions, a radiant smile on a strong face with a peaches-and-cream complexion. Ladd was impressed.

He wanted to do some shopping at religious good stores for gifts to take home. When the motorcade had passed, he headed toward St. Anne's Gate. As he was leaving the square, passing through the Bernini colonnade, suddenly sharp explosions pierced the air. Ladd guessed someone had thrown fire-crackers into the crowd.

Ladd looked back toward the obelisk of Caligula and saw movement in the crowd around the papal vehicle. Then a rushing in that direction.

Ladd pushed his way through the confused faithful, some moving toward the Pope's motorcade and some hastening away. Papal guards were converging on John Paul.

Ladd first caught sight of the white clad Pontiff collapsed back in the arms of his secretary, Father Stanislaw Oziwisz. Blood was spreading on the mid-section and the right arm of the cassock and on the Pontiff's right hand.

A knot of bystanders was shouting and pushing its way towards a point about 30 feet to the left of the vehicle from where Ladd stood.

Confusion and panic were beginning to spread out from that point. The motorcade had come to a halt. Within moments, a siren shrieked in the square.

Now Ladd could see the pope mobile pushing its way through the crowds back toward the Arch of the Bells. Nearby, the apparent assailant had been wrestled to the ground. Ladd's mind was racing. "Was this the attack spoken of on the tape? Had Ladd failed by 24 hours to forewarn Vatican security?"

Several sirens were wailing. John Paul II was being removed from the white parade vehicle to an ambulance and rushed to emergency at Gemelli Hospital.

"What could have happened to my tape? How had the conversation about a papal attack disappeared?" Ladd forgot his shopping and turned his steps up the Janiculum to North American College. He was the first to bring the news to the faculty members and to students he met in the college corridors.

. . .

Ladd thought of Willow and wanted to tell her what had happened. From the rector's office, he put through a call to the U.S. Consulate in Amsterdam.

"Could I speak to Willow Caprice, please?"

The receptionist on the Consulate end of the line seemed to hesitate and then said, "Just a moment, please."

A desk officer came on the line. "Yes, can I help you?"

"I would like to speak to Willow Caprice."

"Who is this calling?" asked the Consulate voice, after a pause. To Ladd, it sounded like the officer had muffled the phone momentarily with the palm of his hand, as though to say something aside to a person nearby.

"This is Father Ladd Franklin, a friend of Miss Caprice."

"Willow Caprice is not here at the present time. Could you tell us how we can locate you in case Miss Caprice contacts us?"

"I am presently at North American College in Rome." Ladd gave him the phone number of the college.

"How long will you be at this address, Father Franklin?"

"Well, I don't know for the moment. Did you hear about the shooting of the Pope?"

"Yes, we just received word on the Telex."

"I might be here for a few days now," Ladd said, "to see how the Pope is and what happens next."

"Let me be sure we know how to reach you, Father." The Consulate official repeated the name of North American College and the phone number.

When Ladd hung up the phone, he was puzzled.

What did the Consulate official mean, "in case Miss Caprice contacts us"? And didn't the official seem overly anxious to know where Ladd was and how long he would be there?

For the next three days, Ladd stayed in Rome. The Pope had stabilized, but was still in danger. There were complications.

Roman authorities had the assailant in custody. His name was Mehmet Ali Agca. It was reported that he had Bulgarian connections. Also speculations about an Islamic involvement were spreading.

. . .

Ladd flew out of Leonardo de Vinci Airport on Monday. He would return home via KLM and United through Amsterdam. He wanted Willow to know all that had transpired.

From Schipol Airport, he took the shuttle to Central Station and called Willow at her apartment. There was no answer.

He boarded a tram to the U.S. Consulate. There, he was eventually ushered to the desk of a Philip Larkin - a high level officer, Ladd guessed, judging from the size and appointments of the office and its position adjacent to the quarters of the Consul General.

"Father Franklin, It is good to meet you. I am Phil Larkin."

The two sat in comfortable leather chairs, away from the main desk.

"I was hoping to see Willow Caprice. She is a friend of mine from California. I visited with her here in Amsterdam a few days ago."

"Yes, we know," Larkin began carefully. "We are hoping to get some information from you about Miss Caprice."

"Information? Isn't she here? Doesn't she work here?"

"She did work here. But the last we saw of her was last Monday. We do not know where she is."

"Have you checked her apartment? She may be sick."

"Yes, we've checked her apartment. Everything seems to be in order. Nothing seems to be disturbed. But it is obvious that she has been gone a few days."

"She left no word with the Consulate?"

"No, not a word." The official paused, studying Ladd's expression. Then he went on, "Why we are particularly concerned and why we have kept her disappearance quiet up to this time is that we have intelligence reports that indicate that Miss Caprice has defected to the Soviet Union."

Ladd was stunned.

"Defected? Not Willow. That's impossible."

Then Ladd's thoughts went back to the tape Willow had duplicated for him. He was about to mention this to Larkin, but caught himself. The Consulate had known nothing about the tape. Ladd wouldn't bring it up.

The missing conversation on the tape? No, it couldn't be!

Ladd wanted to go home.

CHAPTER 46

Ladd returned to CRS headquarters on First Avenue in Manhattan. He gave an oral report to associate director, Clement LaRoque, omitting references to Willow Caprice. From his written notes and from what he could recall from his stolen dictating tapes, he word-processed a summary account for the files in his own office.

Then he put in a call to David's cellular number in San Francisco.

"Hi, Dave, this is Ladd. I've just come back from Rome. How are you doing?"

"Things are going along O.K. here. How was your trip?"

"That's what I want to tell you, Dave. I've been through a scary few weeks since I last talked to you. But, first, I'm pretty broken up about Willow Caprice. You probably haven't heard. Did you know she has left the Consulate in Amsterdam and defected to the Soviet Union?"

"What do you mean?"

"Just that, Dave, she's gone over to the Communists."

"I can't believe it."

"I couldn't believe it either; but that's what she's done. And she really caused some trouble doing it. It's a long story, but I trusted her with an important audio tape that had to do with the assassination attempt on the Pope, and she betrayed me. That's what really hurts."

Ladd went on to tell David the details of his trip to Russia, through the Philippines, South America, Holland and Rome.

"I think I had the information on that tape that could have headed off the attack on the Pope."

David could hardly comprehend the harrowing account. "When are you coming out to San Francisco?"

"I'll be out there in a couple of weeks. I'll fill you in on the whole thing then. Willow's defection will probably be in the papers within a day or two, as soon as the State Department is sure it has all the details."

"Where is Willow now?"

"She's probably in Moscow. Neither government is saying anything at this time."

"This is going to be a terrible blow to the Caprice family, Ladd. Do you think I should talk to Gordon?"

"You should probably wait till the State Department gets in touch with the family. I think the Consulate considered my conversation with them totally confidential, so you should hold up on saying anything to anyone until the parents are informed and the facts are released to the media."

"Take care of yourself, Ladd. You didn't get into your new work to have people shooting at you."

"I know. I'd better let you go now. I'll be out there in two weeks or I'll give you a call before that if there is more news."

. . .

Ladd drove to the rectory at Holy Angels, where he had residence, and unpacked from his journey to four continents. The drip-dry clothing needed a real laundry. His clerical suit needed professional cleaning and pressing.

At the bottom of his luggage, he found the video tape given to him by the Rio de Janeiro photographer at Corcovado. He had forgotten it.

That evening Ladd and the associate pastor at Holy Angels, Father James Courtney, watched the tape on the VCR in the Holy Angels' common room. The camcorder had caught the sweeping panoramas of Sugar Loaf, the small sailing crafts huddled in Botafogo Bay, Copacabana, Ipenema, Leblon, the massive Maracana soccer stadium, the skyscrapers towering over Avenida Rio Branco.

Ladd had not been in Rio for carnival time leading up to Ash Wednesday, but the cameraman had spliced in several minutes of Mardi Gras festivities, with its giant mannequins, elegant floats and thousands upon thousands of costumed revelers.

Abruptly the camera panned back to the hunchback mountain Corcovado and the 125-foot concrete statue of Christ. Jim Courtney was amused to see Ladd in several scenes at the base of the statue. Ladd was amused too; he had not been aware of the presence of the photographer on his visit to the mountain.

As most people do, Ladd focused on his own image on the TV screen. He didn't think much of the color of the Guayabera shirt he was wearing that day; the wind had blown his hair out of place. Why didn't he stand up straighter when he walked?

Then it hit him.

"Whoa . . . what was that? Wait a minute, Jim. Wait a minute. I want to look at something again."

Ladd stepped to the VCR and hit the Rewind button. Then he pushed Play again.

"Jim, do you see that face just over my right shoulder?" He froze the shot.

"That's the one who was following me ever since the Philippines. He's the one that put a gun to my head in Cotabato and followed me through Latin America. It is not my imagination. That's the face. I've got to show this to the State Department."

. . .

The next day, Ladd took the 9 a.m. USAir shuttle from La Guardia to Washington National.

He had slept with the video cassette on the headstand next to his alarm clock radio. On the plane and in the taxi to the Department of State, he did not leave the video out of his hand. At Foggy Bottom, he asked for the only two names he knew, Raymond Smith and Charles Comstock, who had briefed him prior to his trip to the Soviet Union. Ladd gave his card to the receptionist, hoping that one of the two State Department officers would remember him.

After five minutes, Raymond Smith entered the lobby and shook Ladd's hand.

"Good to see you, Father Franklin. How was your trip to the Soviet Union?"

"Well, that's what I wanted to see you about. Do you have fifteen minutes or so?"

"Yes, let's go over to this reception room."

Smith was probably busy and disinclined to bring Ladd up to his office for a lengthy stay.

In the meeting room, Ladd went through the whole story from the Soviet Union to the Philippines to Latin America, Amsterdam and Rome. He finally caught Smith's attention when he described the gun and the hold-up in Cotabato.

"What I really came down to see you about this morning is this video tape. Last night, I looked at this tape for the first time. It is a video taken in Rio de Janeiro. In it, I'm sure, is a picture of the man who was pursuing me half way around the world."

"Do you know his name?" the official asked.

"No, I don't. Do you have a VCR here that I could show you that segment of the tape?"

"Yes, we have one we can use upstairs."

Smith led Ladd to the elevators and brought him to a lounge on the second floor. Ladd had rolled the tape to the point where his pursuer's face had first appeared. The television screen lit up with the scene of the milling visitors to the Corcovado shrine.

Standing at the TV set, Ladd pointed to the face of the man standing on steps just behind him. His face showed directly over Ladd's right shoulder. The image was sharp and clear.

Smith pressed the pause button and studied the screen.

"Just a minute I know that man. That's Warner Palm. That's one of our agents. He's posted in Amsterdam. He's on our side."

"On our side? He wasn't on my side," Ladd said. "He followed me in Argentina and Brazil. And he may be the one who took a shot at me in Buenos Aires."

"No, I know that face; that's Warner Palm. He's been with us for at least ten years. I've been stationed with him in Jakarta."

"Well, Warner Palm has an identical twin brother who was tailing me through South America. Did you say he's stationed in Amsterdam now?"

"Yes, he has a high level position there."

"Is it possible for someone here to check on him and his whereabouts the past six weeks?"

"That may be awkward - what are we going to ask Amsterdam? `Do you know the whereabouts of Warner Palm during the past six weeks?'"

"I'm sure that diplomats in the State Department can find a way to make the inquiry diplomatically," Ladd insisted.

It was obvious that Smith considered this an exercise in futility, but his forte was public relations. He indulged Ladd by snapping on the intercom and directing an aide to put the inquiry through to the consulate in the Netherlands. It was early enough to catch the Amsterdam office open on European time.

While they were waiting for a response, Smith was interested in knowing if Ladd thought the meetings with the Peace Committee in the Soviet Union were productive.

For the next fifteen minutes, Ladd gave the State Department official a detailed report of everything that transpired in Moscow, Leningrad and Kiev.

The intercom buzzed. Smith pressed the receive button. "Ray, we have some puzzling response from Amsterdam. They were at first reluctant to give me any information, but when I told them it was for you, they said that Warner Palm has not checked into their office. Actually, they admitted that his whereabouts had been unknown for several weeks, though he was seen at the Consulate briefly about a week ago."

"Thanks, Glen," Smith said and shut off the intercom.

Accustomed to concealing his feelings, the official showed no sign of surprise or upset, though Ladd knew that there had to be embarrassment for the Department of State not to be able to account for the whereabouts of one of its key agents.

Ladd felt more and more vindicated in his interpretation of events surrounding his journey to Latin America and Rome.

"If the State Department wants to know what Palm's been up to, they may want to take a look at this segment of the tape."

Ladd was about to hand the cassette to Smith, but thought better of it. This time, he would make a copy of the tape first and make sure there were no erasures.

. . .

"Ladd, I hope I didn't disturb you." Jim Courtney was on the Holy Angels rectory intercom. "There's a Philip Larkin on the phone from Amsterdam. Do you want to take it?"

"Larkin? Yes, he's from the U.S. Consulate." Ladd picked up the phone. "Hello, this is Father Franklin."

"Yes, this is Phil Larkin. I know it is late in New York, but I thought you would want to hear some information we have received. I understand you spoke to Washington about Warner Palm, one of our field men. I speak to you in confidence now. We have discovered that Palm has been a Soviet mole in the Consulate here. You were correct in identifying him. Intelligence informs us that he has returned to the Soviet Union. He is probably the one who persuaded Willow Caprice to defect. Looking back on it, they were very close."

"Yes, I was sure that was the face," Ladd said. "Do you have any news on Willow? Where is she?"

"They are probably together in the Soviet Union, but we do not know where."

"When are you going to give out a statement on this?" Ladd asked.

"There has been some leakage of the story here in Amsterdam already, so Washington is planning to release the barest details within the next 24 hours."

"Keep me informed whenever there is further news."

"Yes, we will," Larkin promised and rang off.

Ladd was broken. "Who's this Warner Palm? How could you do this, Willow? What are you thinking of?"

. . .

The first break came when a U.S. mole in Moscow got word to the U.S. Consulate in the Netherlands that Warner Palm was indeed in Moscow. Was he known to be in the company of an attractive American woman by the name of Willow Caprice? He had no information on that. The mole was directed to keep Palm in sight and to determine the whereabouts of the woman. A description of Willow was transmitted. The agent was also instructed to do everything possible to neutralize and discredit whatever the defectors were relaying to Soviet intelligence.

Officials at the State Department speculated on how much information Warner Palm and Willow had passed along to the Soviets. Ladd wondered how much Willow had told Palm about his own schedule after leaving Russia, so that Palm could follow him through the Pacific and through South America. That Willow could do this to him was heartbreaking. Their long friendship made that unthinkable.

The Department of State in Washington, the Embassy in the Hague, as well as the American Consulate in Amsterdam spent the next three weeks reviewing how much classified information the two defectors had in their possession. Palm's service had been much longer and his classification level higher. Though Willow's tenure in Amsterdam had been relatively brief, her obvious skills and personality traits brought her into confidentialities much sooner than one would normally expect. The damage to United States in lost intelligence and to the State Department in its credibility were incalculable.

. . .

At home in San Francisco, the news of the defection was catastrophic. The Caprice family's wide circle of friends and the archdiocesan family with which Gordon was so intimately identified were at first uncomprehending, then disbelieving and, at last, devastated.

The story was front page above the fold in both The Chronicle and The Examiner, and the lead story on the local television news. It was prominently placed in the national media.

Five weeks had passed, and neither Washington nor the U.S. Consulate in the Netherlands had received any further contact from the secret agent in Moscow. Then a cryptic message was relayed to the Hague office, "Warner Palm in two weeks of debriefing by KGB. Willow Caprice still under cover."

Whatever classified information Warner Palm possessed was now unrecoverable. The damage had been done.

Willow had likely undergone the same debriefing, perhaps in Leningrad or Kiev.

PART V

CHAPTER 47

The Bishops of the San Francisco Province gathered at the Metropolitan's Pacific Heights residence for their annual fall meeting.

Housekeeping duties consumed the morning session. Among the topics were financing the cost of asbestos removal from parochial school buildings, retro-fitting churches and other facilities against future earthquakes, providing a coordinated ministry to Latinos, and a province-wide response to the toughening state immigration laws.

In the afternoon session, the agenda consisted of a single item: the consideration of priests' names to be submitted for the office of bishop.

Each bishop submitted names and resumes of priests who had surfaced in his diocese as possible candidates, following a survey of clergy, Religious and lay leaders.

Prior to the meeting, each bishop had received and read the biographical sketches of the candidates submitted by the other bishops. After each name was raised at the meeting, a discussion ensued on the merits and qualifications of the nominee regarding his prayer life, moral character, leadership skills, pastoral experience, administrative abilities, and fidelity to the official teachings of the Church.

This was, in every sense of the word, an executive session of the province meeting, the bishops being sworn to total secrecy.

From the Metropolitan See, the Archdiocese of San Francisco, the names of Monsignor Gordon Caprice and Father Zachary Waterman were submitted for consideration.

Archbishop Costello elaborated on the written resume, which lay on the table in front of each of the prelates, giving high marks to Father

Waterman, a young priest who "though lacking some experience, has proven himself to be an outstanding pastor and preacher."

This was a new name to most of the bishops present, and the discussion was, therefore, brief.

Following the discussion, each bishop rose and placed one of three different colored marbles in a ceramic vase at a side table, a green marble for "approve", a red marble for "disapprove", and a yellow marble for "abstain".

The two youngest bishops of the Province served as tellers.

Having counted the marbles, Bishop Reinhardt announced, "For Father Waterman, five approvals and four abstentions."

The name of Monsignor Gordon Caprice was then introduced. Archbishop McHenry began, "I suspect that most of you are familiar to some extent at least with Monsignor Caprice, since he works in our Chancery Office and takes part in provincial tribunal matters.

"Monsignor is, of course, a very gifted and talented person. He has proven himself exceptionally effective, both in pastoral work and in administrative duties. I, personally, rely on him for the organization and supervision of our Curial offices.

"Monsignor Caprice is reliable, well adjusted, relates well to all age groups, is highly respected by his co-workers and is faithful to the Magisterium. He is a defender of orthodoxy."

It was apparent that the bishops knew this priest well. The discussion that followed was vigorous and enthusiastic. One of the bishops inquired about Gordon's health. The Archbishop assured him, "Physically and emotionally, Monsignor's health is robust. I cannot remember a day when he has missed work at the Chancery."

The vote was nine approvals, no disapprovals, no abstentions.

The senior among the suffragan bishops next submitted his nominees for consideration.

When all had a chance to discuss the complete roster of candidates, a letter was drafted to be sent to the Apostolic Delegate, the Pope's representative in Washington, D.C. This letter would include the names of the priests considered, a summary of the discussion, and the tally of votes for each nominee.

The Apostolic Delegation would receive similar lists from all 31 provinces in the United States. Eventually, these would be relayed to Rome for review by the Congregation of Bishops in the Vatican.

Finally, when a particular opening developed for a Diocesan Bishop or an Auxiliary Bishop, extensive confidential inquiries would be made of clergy, Religious and lay persons familiar with candidates under consideration. As the last step, a short list of three names, a "terna", would be submitted to the Pope for the final selection.

Though the bishops in their province meeting did not know it, this process would soon be underway for the Diocese of Fairview, California.

. . .

Bishop Joshua Kendrick of Fairview died suddenly in the early morning of Easter Monday. He had served the Northern California diocese for 23 years. When a decent interval of time had passed following the funeral, speculation began throughout the state on Kendrick's successor. Auxiliary bishops in the western states particularly stayed close to their telephones.

Gossip in the San Francisco area centered around Gordon Caprice, who continued to impress observers in his work as Chancellor.

But months went by and no diocesan bishop was named for the northern California diocese.

"Not to worry," said Ladd, "dioceses seem to run just as well or better when there is no bishop."

. . .

Bishop Kendrick had tended the Diocese of Fairview well. He was loved by the people and by the clergy and Religious.

David and Ladd, working at the time out of the CRS San Francisco office, traveled to Fairview to attend the funeral.

Monsignor Clem Quartermain gave the homily and spoke movingly of the deceased bishop's virtues.

At the end of the eulogy, Ladd whispered to David, "That was a good homily. At some bishop's funerals, it is a case of one bishop lying in the casket and another bishop lying in the pulpit. But this time the praise was all true."

. . .

David knew the Caprice family was mortified by the news about the defection. Willow's father was well known as a crusader against the Soviets. He was shattered.

David visited the Chancery to speak to Gordon. He found the Chancellor reviewing blue prints for a new parish church and rectory in Marin County.

"Gordon, you have a minute?"

"Yes, sure. Sit down, Dave."

"I know you must be confused about Willow."

"I don't know what got into her. She never gave us any inkling of leaning towards Communism."

Gordon was more overcome by emotion than David had ever seen him in all their years together. "I don't know what to make of it either, Gordon, but knowing Willow, whatever she has done, she has done it out of conviction of what she thinks is right."

"Yes, I know that's true. I just pray that she's safe wherever she is. I hope she gets in touch with us."

"She knows you are worried about her. I'm sure she'll contact you."

"If she's able to," Gordon said. "Did you want to see me about some business, Dave?"

"No, I just wanted to see how you were doing and let you know I'm keeping Willow and all of your family in my prayers." David wanted to distract Gordon with something positive. "You probably know everyone here is expecting you to be the new Bishop of Fairview."

"Thanks, Dave, but I've got other things on my mind. Just keep up the prayers for Willow."

. . .

Then one morning, through a circuitous route, John Barrington at the Amsterdam Consulate received a one-line message. "Caprice woman not a factor. Dead."

At that same moment, at the KGB headquarters, Warner Palm, in step-by-step detail, was describing his departure from the Consulate in Amsterdam.

"I had gained the confidence of a new co-worker at the Amsterdam Consulate. Her name, Willow Caprice. I knew that Ladd Franklin had made contacts with her. Returning quietly to the Consulate one morning, a little over two months ago, I came upon her duplicating an audio tape in the communications studio. She confided in me that it had something to do with the planned assassination attempt on the Pope. The tape, she said, implicated the Soviet because of a conversation surreptitiously recorded on the cassette. It was the very tape I had tried to recover in a pursuit through three countries.

"I told her that I would help her with the duplication because she did not seem to be mechanically inclined. I also remarked that transferring the recording to the new tape would require at least a half hour. Caprice left the room to write a note to her friend who was carrying the cassette. She wanted the note to accompany the original tape when it was returned to her friend. While she was gone, I managed to locate the incriminating segment and erased it.

"When Caprice returned with the note and a diplomatic pouch, I offered to drive her by the drop-off point for her friend who was taking the cassette to Rome. She accepted.

"Caprice went ahead to the consulate garage. I saw to it that a courier was dispatched to her friend with the altered tape and the note.

"Even though the woman became suspicious when I drove away from the route she expected and on to Vondelpark, it was there that I was able to knock her out, drug her and put her in the trunk of the car.

"I then reversed my direction and took the highway toward Utrecht. It had turned dark when I pulled off the roadway into a thick forest area.

"Caprice was still alive in the trunk, but still drugged. I gave her a lethal dose and buried her deep in the woods."

. . .

Two days later, a high level officer from the Department of State called the Caprice residence. Emily Caprice was home alone at the time of the call.

"This is Dennis Pendleton of the United States Department of State. I am in the Bay Area at the present time. Would it be possible for me to visit with you and Mr. Caprice this evening?"

"Mr. Caprice will be home after 6 o'clock. Is this some word about our daughter, Willow?"

"Yes, it is; but it will be best if we can talk together at your home. I have your address. Would 8 o'clock be a convenient time for you?"

"Yes, that should be all right with Mr. Caprice."

Pendleton rang the doorbell promptly at eight. George Caprice was waiting in the entrance hallway.

When the federal official had been welcomed into the residence, and the three were settled in the living room, Mrs. Caprice said, "Have you had dinner, Mr. Pendleton?"

"Yes, I've eaten. Thank you."

All three knew that it was not time for small talk. Pendleton spoke slowly, "I have flown out from Washington, because I am sorry to say that I have very sad news for you.

"We have just received word from our sources in the Soviet Union that your daughter, Willow, is dead."

Emily Caprice caught her breath in a gasping sound, "Oh, no!"

George, who prided himself on his strength and control, but who had suspected that there was a tragic reason for the personal visit, broke down in heavy sobs. From experience, Pendleton knew it was time for him to be silent and let the grief vent itself.

After a few moments, quietly, he related to the distraught couple the details of the abduction and death.

When the time came for Pendleton to leave the family alone in its sorrow, he assured the parents that the government would do everything in its power to bring those responsible to justice. He promised that his department would keep constantly in touch with them as further information was received. His office would be of assistance in any possible way they could in the days ahead.

"Willow was a brave young woman," he said. "We know that she fought valiantly against her assailant. She has served her country in an extraordinary way."

With repeated expressions of personal sympathy and assurances of support, Pendleton took his leave.

When the Department of State released the details of Willow Caprice's heroism and of Warner Palm's defection, the national media featured the story for more than a week.

Friends of the Caprice family from around the country sent messages of condolence.

Gordon Caprice was the principal celebrant at a Memorial Mass in the crowded cathedral. Archbishop Costello presided at the episcopal throne.

. . .

When Ladd heard the news in India, he was shaken to the core.

He thought back on the rash judgments he had made about Willow - and even the bitterness. He should have known that it was not in Willow to do what he had concluded. Along with his sorrow, there was a contravening stirring of relief, and pride that she was a heroine.

CHAPTER 48

The names of new bishops in the United States are released to the media on Monday, but are embargoed until nine o'clock East Coast time on Tuesday morning. As so often happens one way or another, rumors begin on certain Mondays that an announcement is imminent. This had happened already on two earlier occasions regarding the new Bishop of Fairview.

But this time, it seemed more serious. A priest chosen to be bishop by Rome actually has received the news at least a week or ten days before the public announcement, but he is under the pontifical seal of secrecy.

Though some persons start rumors and purport to know the identity of a new bishop, those who really know can't say. And those who say can't really know.

Bishop-watchers that weekend were keeping a close eye on Gordon Caprice to see if any of his actions would reveal that something exceptional was about to happen.

Some thought Gordon seemed more on edge than usual. At a finance council meeting on Friday, he seemed preoccupied at times. Uncharacteristically, he left the Chancery Office at 4:30 p.m. Monday afternoon when the rest of the staff left, instead of working on until nearly six.

· · ·

Tyler slept uneasily throughout the night. Again, for a countless time, he turned to find a more comfortable position, reversed the pillow to its cool side, and reflected on what it was that kept him awake. Was it the lettuce in the salad at dinner? Was it the unaccustomed glass of red wine? Often too much time sunbathing in the midday heat caused the buzzing in his ears and wide-awakedness at night. Typically, early September brought San Francisco 86 degrees that day.

It was 5:45 a.m. Tyler punched the "sleep" button on the radio near his head on the night stand. KABL was playing Barbra Streisand's "The Way We Were." He dozed and came awake again at the top of the hour, when Fred Lowery's voice broke through the music with the news.

"President Carter has sent another strong message to Iran for the release of the hostages. Ronald Reagan is winding up a campaign swing through the midwest in Milwaukee . . . a tornado cut a swath through western Kansas, leveling a recreational vehicle campground." Tyler dozed again.

Then a different announcer-type voice: "And in local news, investigations continue in the shooting at City Hall, at Candlestick the Giants win in the ninth, and a local priest has been named as Roman Catholic Bishop of Fairview. Details after these messages."

Tyler was wide awake.

He listened impatiently through the City Hall story and statistics on the number of new housing starts in the Bay Area.

Then, "Pope John Paul II has chosen a San Francisco priest to be the Bishop of Fairview. The post will be filled by the Reverend David Carmichael, who has served for twenty-five years in various capacities in the Archdiocese of San Francisco . . ."

"Dave! Whoa."

Tyler rolled out of bed and reached for the phone. Someone must have had a phone nearer to his bed. Tyler got a busy signal.

CHAPTER 49

At the hastily organized press conference, David told the media, "It is an exhilarating feeling to be asked to be a bishop. I cannot think of a greater honor than to be chosen to be a 'successor of the apostles,' to follow in the line of Peter and Andrew and James and John, and the bishops through the centuries, Ambrose, Augustine, Robert Bellarmine, John Carroll, James Gibbons. These first weeks and months are like a roller-coaster ride of emotions.

"And yet, I suspect there will be loneliness," David continued. "I've been told that once you are a bishop, two things will happen to you. You will never have a bad meal again, and you will never hear the truth again."

. . .

Hours later, alone with Ladd, David confided:

"Because of my nature, I think I will feel very isolated as a bishop.

"I remember hearing the reflections of one married man - I don't know where I found this. I believe it was in Daniel J. Levinson's The Season's of a Man's Life. I've saved it, because even though I am a celibate, his comments fit me perfectly.

"This husband said, 'Men, I have come to believe, cannot or will not have real friends. They have something else -- companions, buddies, pals, chums, someone to drink with and someone to lunch with, but no one, when it comes to saying how they feel - especially how they hurt.'

"Women know this. They talk about it among themselves. I heard one woman describe men as the true Third World people - not yet emerged. To women, this inability of men to say what they feel is a source of amazement, and then anguish, and then, finally, betrayal. Women will tell you all the time that they don't know the men they live with. They talk of long silences and drifting off and of keeping feelings hidden and never letting on that they are troubled or bothered or whatever.

"If it's any comfort to women, they should know it's nothing personal. Men treat other men the same way.

"This is something men learn early. It is something I learned from my father, who taught me, the way fathers teach sons, to keep emotions to myself. I watched him and learned from him. One day we went to a baseball game, cheered and ate and drank, and the next day he was taken to the hospital with yet another ulcer attack. He had several of them. My mother said he worried a lot, but I saw none of this.

"All I know is that most men don't confide deep feelings - and even the men who do -- the ones who can talk about how they feel - talk to women. Have we been raised to think of feelings and sentiment as feminine? Can a man talk intimately with another man and not wonder about his masculinity? I don't know. I do know it sometimes makes the other man feel uncomfortable.

"I know this is a subject that concerns me, and yet I find myself bottling it all up keeping it all in. I've been on automatic pilot for years now.

"It would be nice to break out of it. It would be nice to join the rest of the human race, connect with others in a way that makes sense."

"I have those same feelings," David said as he set aside the married man's reflections. "He could just as well be talking about me."

"Well, Dave, like the man says, maybe we all have difficulty sharing. Remember those melancholy words Leonard Feeney wrote about us:

'How and why a priest can happen is our own precious secret. It is the secret of men who climb a lonely drawbridge, mount a narrow stair, and sleep in a lofty citadel that floats a white flag.

"Singly we go, independent and unpossessed, establishing no generation, each a conclusion of his race and name, championing one another with a strange sympathy, to tender to be called friendship, too sturdy to be called love, but which God will find a name for when He searches our hearts in eternity.'

"Having companionship even with the priests will be more difficult now that I am bishop," David said.

"I won't be able to join a particular group of priests in our diocese for sports, for recreation or for support groups, because I don't want to give the impression of favoritism.

"There are times when I hate to face the desk in the morning because it seems that every day presents new problems, new demands. When the phone rings, it churns my stomach because it probably means another request or another complaint.

"At the same time, I do not want to be distant to the clergy and the people. One thing that must be hurting to a bishop is if the Bishop's Office seems alienated from the priests and the parishes, if there is a perception of the Chancery Office as a callous and mindless bureaucracy."

. . .

Before David left for his new diocese, the San Francisco Archbishop gathered the priests together, so David could say his goodbye to them.

Ladd was asked to introduce David's talk, "It was good of the Archbishop to bring us all together to wish our friend David well, as he takes up his new duties. We are all going to miss him. I don't know what kind of pastor he was at Mission Dolores. When he was leaving there, the parishioners even sent a car for him, but he managed to get out of the way.

"I understand that when you present the President of the United States for a talk, you do not make a long introduction. You simply say, 'Ladies and Gentlemen, the President of the United States.' I am told the same holds true for presenting a bishop. You do not make an elaborate introduction, and so I say, 'Ladies and Gentlemen, I present Bishop David Carmichael - the less said about him the better.'"

David expected that kind of comment from his best friend.

"I want to thank Ladd for his remarks. What can I say in response? Of all the introductions I have ever been given, that was the most . . . recent."

David dwelt on the nostalgia of the occasion and the spirit of long companionship.

"Whether we have come from the same diocese or religious order or not, been born and raised in the same state or country or not, these memories are understood by all of us.

"The memories of seminary days - though we may not have appreciated it at the time, the unusual opportunity for education, and the discipline of studies from our earliest years.

"The details might differ, but all seminarians have the same sights and smells and nostalgia -- the smell of tarweed and eucalyptus in September on the campus in Mountain View, the oak trees in Menlo Park, the long rainy days in January walking the cloisters, the depressed feeling when we drove back into the seminary grounds after Christmas vacation.

"The memories of our first parish, the families we have known and visited, the children we have seen grow up, as we have grown - and then to marry them and to baptize their children and to marry them. A member of all families and belonging to all. Knowing the joys of family relationships, working hard to make our celibate commitment creative and positive, rather than a reluctant hurdle on the way to ordination.

"Feeling the strength and companionship of fellow priests on days off, on vacation, in support groups, at rectory parties, on those `few days away' after Christmas or after Easter.

"Knowing that an ear-to-listen and the encouragement of a priest were always present not more than a rectory away.

"Our retreats together, the tempestuous, morale-building retreats of the '40s and '50s, the serious and tension-filled dialogue retreats of the '60s, the serious and reflective variety of retreats of the '70s.

"The life-long friendships made from being stationed together as associate pastors . . . and even friendships made with a pastor!

"The joy of seeing priests of an older tradition making an unflinching adaptation to changing times, attending workshops, reading, encouraging new ministries of the Religious and laity.

"To see the priests working so hard at measuring up to their calling, trying to serve their people whether it is patiently listening to a parishioner pour out his agony in the confessional or getting up from the dinner table to give someone the key to the hall.

"The perseverance of the priests in struggling with the demands of the priesthood, when so many of the psychological supports and human privileges which once came with the priesthood have been swept away.

"Admiration for the younger men answering the call to the priesthood today when real altruism, even heroism, is required, more than in former years.

"Sometimes the people, sometimes we ourselves can assume that priests have Faith. But the Faith a priest must have is a driving, compelling conviction that there is a God, that the Church is God's work. This Faith does not blaze up spontaneously. It has to be tended vigorously. I need to work at this.

"Sometimes the people and we, ourselves, assume that we priests love God.

"But a better question to ask is, 'Do I like God?' Do I have a taste for religion? It is possible for me to find the Scriptures boring, to find the Liturgy of the Hours irksome, even no longer to relish and enjoy the Mass. We may not realize it, but we may simply not savor the things of religion.

"We certainly love God - everybody loves God - but we may no longer really like Him, perhaps have never really liked Him. To like God, we have to know Him. It does not happen instinctively.

"We see priests all around us who have built into their lives the elements necessary to sustain their lives as priests, who seem to enjoy God, who make it a point to know Him day by day, by conversing with Him, by reading and knowing the Scriptures, by meditating, by being faithful to days of recollection -- by cultivating a taste for the things of God.

"This spills over into their whole being and personality. The people sense a godliness in them. They notice these priests are happy, have sensitivity for the poor, the powerless, the unattractive, for all who are suffering. They see the priests' warmth and kindness. When they see these priests, they see something godly.

"I am going to miss all of you in the archdiocese. I am grateful for your friendship. Let us keep up our prayers for one another."

CHAPTER 50

David's ordination to the office of bishop took place at Fairview's Cathedral of the Holy Spirit.

Just a century before, gold and silver miner, Bishop Emerson Clay, began construction of the imposing edifice.

At the time ground was broken, the Civil War had recently divided the nation, and the congregation sang, "Mine Eyes Have Seen the Glory of the Coming of the Lord."

As the cornerstone was put in place in 1886, the choir had sung, "Quam Delecta" and Gregorian chant.

That stone, laid at the southwest corner of the church, records that Leo XIII was Pope, Clay the Bishop, Grover Cleveland President, and Washington Bartlett Governor of the State.

David's consecration procession entered a church built in the form of a cross, with the long nave and the transept cutting across the sanctuary. The style is in the Italian Renaissance tradition. Brian Clinch, the architect, modeled the cathedral after La Eglise de la Trinite in Paris, a church which Clay had come to love during his visit to Paris after he was ordained a priest.

Cost of the entire church, furnished, was under $300,000 in the late 1880's. David would later see 1889 bills from the Seth Thomas Clock Company: labor to hoist and set the clock - $119.55, and laborer wage: $3.50 a day.

When the people in downtown Fairview saw the construction begin one hundred years ago, they had complained, "Why is the Bishop building the Cathedral so far out in the country?" Now, it is at the city's center.

The word cathedral stems from the Greek, "cathedra," meaning chair. The cathedral is the one church in the diocese which will have David's official chair. Here David will preside - the word has its root in the Latin, "sedes," meaning chair. This chair is intended to be the center of and to give unity to the third of a million faithful in 25 counties of Northern California.

As the procession moves to the entrance, the cathedral bells are ringing. There are four original bells in the tower, weighing from 1000 to 4000 pounds. The largest bell was a gift of Bishop Clay. Workmen had labored feverishly to install that last bell when the Bishop was ailing. They wanted him to hear it, but he died on Ash Wednesday, a few days before it was in place. The bell was first tolled to announce his funeral.

On this day of David's consecration, electronic carillon bells sound the hour and half hour.

In the transept and in the sanctuary, sun rays stream down on the procession through stained glass windows, fashioned 100 years ago in Innsbruck, Austria - gifts of prominent early Californians and organizations, Mrs. E. B. Crocker, Tessie Fair, Captain Thomas Dwyer, the Young Men's Institute, Ancient Order of Hibernians, the James Mackeys and David Lubin - the founder of Weinstock's department stores.

Mr. and Mrs. Augustine Coolot donated the large Last Supper window over the sanctuary. Above the Last Supper, carved angels and eaves cast shadows against the back wall. Actually, they are not carvings; they are not three-dimensional. The shadows are painted shadows. There is dispute as to the identity of the figures looking down on the ceremony from the south wall of the sanctuary. Teachers: St. Gregory, Pope Alexander, St. Augustine, St. Thomas?

The most impressive of the paintings is the 8 x 10 foot full size reproduction of Raphael Sanzio's Sistine Madonna. Only two such reproductions exist. The second is displayed at Stanford University, while the original is exhibited in the Royal Art Gallery in Dresden. The Raphael was a gift of the wife of the Governor of California, Mrs. Leland Stanford, who received permission for the exact-size reproduction from the King of Saxony. In Raphael's painting, to the left of the Madonna, Pope Sixtus is portrayed; to the right, St. Barbara was portayed. It was only 15 years before David's consecration day that John

Matthew, Director of the Crocker Art Museum, during the renewal of the cathedral, had delicately cleaned away the dust and grime, and revealed the cluster of angels above Pope Sixtus. The two cherubs at the base of Raphael's masterpiece have renewed popularity and are seen everywhere in the 1990s.

Stations of the Cross, along the sides of the nave, were rendered by a Franciscan monk from Southern California, the same artist who did the Stations, in rectangular form, rather than square, in the chapel of David's seminary, St. John Vianney on the San Francisco peninsula.

The church, on consecration day, accommodates 1300 of David's friends and faithful.

This will be David's cathedral, a home for the worker in nearby office buildings dropping in for a prayer and a refuge from the pressures of the work place, for a child on the way home from school, for an unfortunate drifter on the Goodwin Street Mall who has no other place to turn. And today it is the setting for the ordination and installation of the fifth bishop of Fairview.

. . .

For the ordination and installation, a cardinal, three archbishops, including the Apostolic Delegate, and thirty-four bishops are in the sanctuary.

Nearly four hundred priests, Sisters, permanent deacons and Brothers fill the section to the left of the main aisle. Faithful from the Fairview Diocese, as well as from San Francisco and the Napa Valley, occupy all the remaining sections, including the balcony.

David's mother, brother and his family and relatives to the third and fourth degree of kinship have reserved seats in the front rows, facing the sanctuary.

. . .

"Most Reverend Father, the Church of Fairview, asks you to ordain this priest, David Carmichael, for service as bishop."

Archbishop Costello asked in return:

"Have you a mandate from the Holy See?"

"We have."

"Let it be read."

The papal document appointment of David was read aloud to the congregation. At its conclusion, all responded, "Thanks be to God."

Addressing David, the Archbishop said:

"You, dear brother, have been chosen by the Lord. Remember that you are selected from among men and appointed to act for men and women in relation to God. The title of bishop is one not of honor but of function, and therefore a bishop should strive to serve, rather than to rule. Such is the counsel of the Master: The greater should behave as if he were the least, and the leader as if he were the one who serves."

"The Bishop-elect rises and stands, facing the Archbishop, who questions him:

"My brother, are you resolved by the grace of the Holy Spirit to discharge to the end of your life the office the apostles entrusted to us, which we now pass on to you by the laying on of hands?"

"I am."

"Are you resolved to maintain the deposit of faith, entire and incorrupt, as handed down by the apostles and professed by the Church everywhere and at all times?"

"I am."

"Are you resolved to be faithful in your obedience to the successor of the apostle Peter?"

"I am, with the help of God."

"May God, who has begun the good work in you, bring it to fulfillment."

The narrator describes David, lying face down on the floor of the sanctuary, as the long litany of the saints is chanted. "At the end of the litany, all will rise."

The Archbishop and the consecrating bishops stand at their places, facing the people. David rises, goes to the principal consecrator, and kneels before him.

The Archbishop lays his hands upon the head of the bishop-elect in silence. After him, all the other bishops present do the same.

Then the principal consecrator places the open Book of the Gospels upon David's head; two deacons, standing at either side of the bishop-elect, hold the Book above his head until the prayer of consecration is completed:

"God, the Father . . . You have chosen your servant, David, for the office of bishop. May he be a shepherd to your holy flock, and a high priest blameless in your sight, ministering to you night and day . . . May he be pleasing to you by his gentleness and purity of heart, presenting a fragrant offering to you."

"Amen."

The narration continues: "The principal consecrator puts on the linen gremial or apron, takes the chrism oil and anoints the crown of the new bishop's head.

Archbishop Costello hands the Book of the Gospels to the newly ordained bishop.

Archbishop Costello loaned him a chamois-lined skull- cap. David guessed that had some historical connection with the yarmulke, the skull-caps worn by rabbis. It was a natural association, since Judaism is the parent faith of Christianity. David suspected also that the skull-cap had been retained by the bishops through the centuries to cover the bald spot that most of them had by the time they were named bishops.

David, on occasions later when he addressed Jewish organizations, would take this vestment called a zuchetto from his pocket and place it on his head as he approached the podium.

At the time of the public announcement of his appointment as bishop, when David was first allowed to wear a zuchetto, Troy Warneke, a seventh grader at St. Catherine's School, presented him with a skull cap he had purchased at Paramount's Great America in Santa Clara County. It was the same shape as a bishop's zuchetto, the same magenta color, but it had a special feature, a bright silver propeller on top. David contemplated using this special "zuchetto" at some liturgy or other for the young, but the impropriety of it deterred him.

Next, the Archbishop places the episcopal ring on the bishop's right hand ring finger:

"Take this ring, the seal of your fidelity. With faith and love, protect the bride of God, his holy Church."

David's generation had been brought up in a tradition forbidding priests from wearing rings. It was a particular thrill the day Archbishop Costello presented David with the Vatican II episcopal ring, which the late Archbishop Costello had received from Pope Paul VI at the Council. The gold plated ring in the shape of a bishop's miter was not a closed circle. The band was open so that it could be fitted to the finger of any bishop, large or small. The figures engraved on the face of the ring were Jesus, Peter and Paul, especially appropriate since David's consecration day was June 29, the feast of the two apostles.

The inner surface of the ring was stamped with the coat-of-arms of Paul VI, a reminder that episcopal rings were originally signet rings, worn on the ring finger of the right hand. The bishop's coat-of-arms on the face of the ring, in earlier times, was pressed into the hot wax on the seal of official papers, in proof of the authenticity of the documents.

When David was a young priest, the faithful genuflected to kiss the ring of a bishop, but now that practice had fallen into disuse - a sign of the Church's attempt to do away with the excessive trappings of the episcopal office.

The consecrator next placed on David's head the miter - a double-peaked headpiece worn by bishops in solemn liturgies - most likely oriental in origin. The miter has two flaps or pendants hanging shoulder-length in the back. What the pendants symbolize, David never learned. He heard somewhere that, originally, they were used to tie down the headpiece during windy weather. He had never confirmed this. He did understand that the front peak of the miter represented the New Testament of the Bible and the back peak the Old Testament.

Ladd had remarked to David that the real reason for the miter was to make a bishop look taller and more threatening, so that he could exercise his authority more effectively.

Actually the miter has an unnerving similarity to the peaked cap worn by the Ku Klux Klan.

Lastly, the Archbishop gives the pastoral staff to David and says:

"Take this staff as a sign of your pastoral office; keep watch over the whole flock in which the Holy Spirit has appointed you to shepherd the Church of God."

Crozier is the name of a bishop's staff, designating him as shepherd.

In an effort to dispel triumphalism, the simile of bishop to people, as shepherd to sheep, has been down played since the questioning of all authority in the '60s.

David had chosen a simple wood staffed crozier, carved from oak. It was the gift of his classmates.

Although the mitre, the ring, and the crozier seemed outdated vestiges of the past, David would find them shields and confidence builders in exercising his new sometimes frightening authority.

He would use these episcopal emblems, not as the Scriptures say, because "the powerful like to make their importance felt."

The pectoral cross is suspended from a chain or a green and gold colored, braided cord, and worn on the bishop's chest. It is a reminder that Christians follow a man who carried a cross.

"The Archbishop leads the new bishop to the episcopal chair, assisted by the Apostolic Delegate. Bishop Carmichael, now seated, wearing the miter and with crozier in hand, faces the congregation. The new bishop has formally taken over leadership of this section of the Lord's vineyard."

On cue, but with ready spontaneity, the assembly breaks into applause.

. . .

Finally, David assumed the role of principal celebrant and proceeded to the conclusion of the Mass, with its solemn blessing:

"Lord God, now that you have raised me to the order of bishop, may I please you in the performance of my office. Unite the hearts of people and bishop, so that the shepherd may not be without the support of his flock, or the flock without the loving concern of its shepherd."

"Amen."

"Bishop Carmichael follows the long recessional line, blessing the congregation, tracing the sign of the cross alternately to the left and right, as he departs by the middle aisle."

That afternoon and evening were taken up with a public reception and dinner.

The next morning, May 14, 1998, the serious work began.

CHAPTER 51

Abruptly, the ordination to the office of bishop brought new, unexpected experiences for David - writing a small cross in front of his signature; people listening attentively to his words as never before, as though he had something especially profound and important to say; suddenly, priests older than David holding a door open for him to walk through ahead of them; having one's own episcopal chair in the cathedral.

He felt totally inadequate. He knew that he was no different, no more qualified than he was the day before. But the miter, the bishop's hat, and the crozier, the bishop's staff, mistakenly suggest talents and abilities one never had previously.

David grew up seeing bishops vesting at the altar, with an extra candle on the altar table at Mass. At solemn ceremonies, the bishop was surrounded by a train-bearer, bugia and gremial bearers, an archpriest, and a canopy over the throne.

The trappings were not without reason. The more reverence shown you, the more respect, the more affirmation given you, the more you try to live up to expectations.

Those symbols of office built through the wisdom of nineteen centuries, in some respects, served a purpose.

But they were extrinsic rewards. The rewards today are intrinsic, less visible, less tangible, but more authentic.

Coming to Fairview as bishop had something of the same exhilarating feeling as receiving his first parish as priest.

The first time he flew from Modesto, in the southwest, to Tulelake, in the northeast, and looked down on the 25 counties of the diocese, 60,500 square miles, David suddenly felt the heavy spiritual responsibility of all those people below.

Whenever he drove the Feather River Canyon to Susanville, Westwood, Quincy or Portola for a parish visitation, he sensed the history, the bonding with Bishop Killane and Bishop Clay, the first bishops who traveled this territory with horse and wagon - and the bonding with the Apostle Paul, journeying to Corinth, Ephesus and Antioch - or Thomas to India.

Then came the impact of his first ordination, when he cupped his hands on the head of a man kneeling before him and created a priest - an awesome moment. By the stroke of a pen, he could assign a priest and change his whole life.

. . .

The months raced by in a blur of impressions. The days brought one powerful new experience after another.

The most touching - the night he administered the Sacrament of Confirmation to 20 young leukemia victims, some in their teens, some as young as five or six, many bald from radiation, their faces white as their hospital pillows. The youngest were being advanced to Confirmation because they would not live to the usual age for the sacrament.

At first, David was apprehensive. He thought to himself, would these children be indignant, resentful toward a God who was allowing them to die so young? Would they have in their mind the atheist's cynical parody mocking the traditional religious hymn, "Praise God From Whom All Blessings Flow."

> "Praise God from whom all cyclones blow.
> Praise God when rivers overflow.
> Praise God when lightning strikes the steeple,
> Brings down the church and kills the people."

But no, there was no sullenness or bitterness, but rather faces filled with innocent wonder and awe at receiving this sacrament, this anointing - something special from God. It was a bittersweet moment - bitter because of their wasting sickness, sweet because of their unquestioning faith.

  #   David was heartened seeing the people of his diocese developing food lockers, dining rooms for the hungry, overnight lodging vouchers and low-cost housing for the homeless and poor - providing the corporal works of mercy when government agencies, because of budgetary constraints, were increasingly withdrawing from human services.

  #   From his own days as priest, David knew one of the most crucial needs for a bishop was to be close to his clergy. One opportunity that David had to know his priests and understand their interests occurred at the breakfast table during his parish visitations. He would note what section of the morning newspaper the priests picked up first. Some would go immediately to the main section. They had an interest in current events. Others would select the sports section first or the entertainment pages. Still others would reach immediately for the financial pages to study the previous day's Dow Jones averages.

The new bishop made it a point to know their interests.

One of the most difficult things in maintaining good relations with the clergy is selecting one priest for an important parish when five or six qualified priests have applied for it.

David was sure it was more difficult now than in Archbishop McHenry's time. When McHenry wanted to move priests around to different assignments, he would say to his secretary, "Give me my pen and I'll scatter 'em."

Now the process involved advertising openings, applicant interviews, and personnel board recommendations.

David tried to help the priests to deal with the new forms that were presenting themselves in a changing Church. For his own part, David was apprehensive about forming a diocesan pastoral council. There is that anxiety about sharing authority, worrying about losing control in handing decision-making over to others.

But the council, consisting mostly of lay persons, was of enormous assistance to David and forced him to face critical questions.

David knew he could be infected with an unhealthy clericalism.

He had to give example to his priests, for he had admonished them:

"Beware of a class system. We do not think we suffer from clericalism. But we are hesitant about handing over decision-making to the laity. The reason for this, we say is that we have to protect the teaching of the Church about ordained ministry; we warn about the 'unfortunate experience of trusteeism' in the American Church in the last century.

"It is important for us to know clearly what the Church's documents say, on the one hand, about the priesthood shared by all baptized persons and, on the other hand, the ministry of the ordained priest. We must guard against protecting turf. So much of our energy is spent on the 'Sons of Zebedee Syndrome' working to protect our own status, our right to make the ultimate decisions.

"We must learn how to give up some of the power.

"In retired clergy, we see the hurt of losing power. A retired priest may anguish because, although he can still confer all the Sacraments and do all the priestly things, he can no longer determine the color of the paint on the parish hall.

"All this can be likened to giving up the papal states. Historically, though the Church felt maltreated, when that happened, the Church actually grew stronger. Now we are being forced to concentrate on things more important than secular power: Teaching, Reconciling, Healing, Sanctifying.

"We are functioning more like the early Christian Church."

. . .

Among the recurring joy-filled events were the regular almost daily Confirmations in the spring. David intended to engage youngsters to be confirmed in a question and answer session, instead of giving a homily. He remembered again the seminary advice that if you direct your remarks at adults, the young people will not listen, but if you talk to the young, the adults will listen.

In his quizzing of the confirmandi, David planned to ask them if they knew the names of the insignia of a bishop. (He recalled the Sisters in Napa instructing his class to cut out pictures of croziers and miters for pasting in their eighth grade religion composition books. But he also remembered Ladd telling him what happened when, in his eighth grade Confirmation, he answered a question asked by the bishop and identified a "Monsignor" as the cross the bishop wears.)

David began to suspect that teachers of previous Confirmation classes now, as they did back in his grammar school days, were relaying his examination questions on to parishes preparing for upcoming Confirmations.

When he arrived at St. Kevin's Parish, he decided against questioning the candidates. He would talk to them directly:

"This evening, you are being initiated. Initiated into what? Into a family, a club, a gang - a gang of Jesus of Nazareth.

"All initiations have a ritual. One of the rituals that I will do with you a few minutes from now is to anoint your forehead with an oil. It is called 'Chrism'. Is it a magic oil? No, it is simply olive oil into which has been added balsam, an aromatic spice, to give it fragrance.

"You and I are flesh and blood. We understand invisible, spiritual things better if they are made visible or tangible, if we can see them and touch them. And so the Church uses a symbol, oil, for the spiritual gift you are receiving tonight.

"Oil has always been a sign of strength. Long distance swimmers like those who cross the English Channel or swim from Alcatraz to the mainland in San Francisco in the cold Bay waters, cover themselves with oil and grease for warmth and strength. On television this summer you saw some of the Olympic Games athletes, before entering an event, covering their arms and legs with oil to make their muscles more supple.

"This chrism oil I am holding is simply a symbol of spiritual strength and healing which you are receiving in this sacrament.

"I know that you need strength, especially at this time of your life, a very demanding time. You have worries and fears. I will not just smear the oil on your forehead. I will trace the oil in the form of a cross, because I know that you carry heavy crosses.

"You worry about the illness of one of your parents, or you worry about breaking up with a friend, or whether you're going to get into the high school you want to attend. Perhaps you are worrying about pressure to get into a gang or to do drugs. You're fearful of violence at school and on the street. You feel the weight of competition, competition for grades, competition in sports. You feel the pressure of the expectation of your parents. Or, perhaps, you sense a disadvantage of growing up in a single-parent family.

"My father died when I was six years of age, so I grew up in a single-parent family.

"The results of that fact may indicate you can grow up adequately in a single-parent family. Or I may be strong evidence of the dire consequences of growing up in a single-parent family.

"You are at an age when human sexuality is impacting on you powerfully. You wonder if you're attractive to the opposite sex. Do you find that you are comparing yourself to your schoolmates? Why am I not as good looking as this classmate? Why can't I be taller? Why am I not more popular?

"You feel the obligation to keep up with the current clothing styles and designer labels. You want a room of your own at home. You can't wait until you get your driver's license. Maybe you just worry about zits.

You are concerned about keeping up with the current fashions: the Nike shoes, the Chinos, the baggy look, the Abercrombie shirts – I know I am far behind the times in styles and designer labels. Not too long ago my grand-nephew, Jason, came to me and said, "Uncle David, tomorrow is nerd day in school. Can I borrow some of your clothes?"

"The sacrament you are receiving now is not just for Church, not just for Sundays. This Confirmation brings you strength really to help you in these everyday problems and worries.

"But I won't do something to you tonight that the bishop who confirmed your parents did to them, and the bishop who confirmed me did to me. He gave us a slap on the face right after he had anointed us to remind us that life is tough. If we are going to live as we know we should live, it is going to be difficult.

"If you do not find your life difficult, you should ask yourself, 'If I were hauled into court for being a Christian, would there be enough evidence to convict me?'

"University and college professors in History departments were asked to list the historical figures who, in their minds, were the world's greatest villains. When the results were tabulated, these names turned out to be the top ten most notorious.

"In chronological order: Caligua, Nero, Atilla the Hun, Catherine de Medici, Ivan the Terrible, Abdul-Hamid II, Hitler, Stalin, Mao Tse-Tung, and Idi Amin.

"What is it that these ten people have in common that make them stand out as the most evil in all history? I think it is insensitivity to the feelings of other people, being insensitive to what hurts others. In two words -- callousness, self-centeredness.

"About three years ago, a survey was conducted of students in high schools here in the Bay Area. The students were asked to identify not villains, but their heroes. Who came in first?

"In the first place (admirably) came Mom and Dad, then Joe Montana, Michael Jordan, Pope John Paul II, Mother Teresa of Calcutta, Mortal Kombat, Barry Bonds, Tom Cruise, and Number 10: Jesus Christ.

"Now, at first, we might be shocked that Jesus would come in last behind the others. But on analysis it is, I think, edifying that the young people listed Christ at all. I'm sure that most didn't even think Christ belonged in this category of contemporary heroes. Most would have disqualified Him spontaneously.

"Setting aside current-at-the-moment celebrities, five of the top names are self sacrificing heroes and heroines.

"Many people are concerned about the young generation today, but from my experience, I think that your generation is probably no better or no worse than young generations before you.

"As a matter of fact, in many ways I believe that young people today are better. Some young people are doing some very bad things. But I think there are temptations and pressures you deal with today that we did not experience - street gangs, drugs, and the powerful appeal of materialism and the 'good life.'

"When you resist these pressures, you become a stronger, more serious, more principled generation.

"I want to share with you a special Ten Commandments -- that is, not the Ten, but the Teen Commandments.

> The first commandment:
> Thou shalt be patient enough to obey. You will be giving orders yourself one day.

The second commandment:
Turn away from racial prejudice. Each of us or our parents or great, great grandparents were all immigrants.

Third commandment:
Don't show off while driving. If you want to race, go to Indianapolis or Daytona.

Fourth:
Get to church regularly. The Creator gives you the week; give God back an hour.

The Fifth Commandment:
Choose a date who would make a good mate. (That is, choose for your dates, someone you would be willing to spend your whole life with as a spouse.)

Sixth:
Respect God's beautiful gift of sex. Do not be afraid of it. Do not be obsessed with it.

Seventh:
Avoid 'following the crowd', be an engine, not a caboose.

Eighth:
Think twice about gangs. Choose your companions carefully. You become what they are.

Ninth:
Stop and think before you drink. (Or, as the current version would be:) Show some class, keep off the grass.

And, finally, the Tenth commandment:
Thou shalt remember the lyrics of the song, 'The greatest thing you'll ever learn is just to love and be loved in return.'

"That final commandment is a particularly crucial commandment. Those of us of an older generation worry about you young, because often you seem to have a sadness or depression about you.

"William Saroyan once wrote: 'It seems everything you learn after you're fourteen is either bad or sad.'

"It need not be that way. Your life should be a happy life.

"And it will be, if you know that you are loved. Because of the inevitable tensions in families, because of the necessary scolding at times at home, you may think that you are not loved.

"You are deeply loved by your parents, by your family, by your school, and by your God. Yes, God loves you. In fact, though you may not think so, God likes you just the way you are."

. . .

David felt somewhat uncomfortable when Father Tom Kettleman, his priest-secretary, accompanied him to Confirmation services. Out of all the people in the congregation and the clergy in the sanctuary, David was most conscious of this young priest who had heard the same thoughts at Confirmation again and again.

David and this young priest-secretary who served him so well as master of ceremonies were un-vesting in the sacristy after the Confirmation service.

David gently reminded Tom not to stand up automatically as the homily was drawing to a close. This would be a sure signal to the people that the talk was repeated almost word for word, Confirmation after Confirmation.

"Another thing I've been meaning to mention, Tom, whenever we are having a ground-breaking, please phone ahead. Tell them to soften up the ground a little bit in that spot where we're going to turn over the first earth.

"There is nothing more embarrassing than to have cameras and reporters all around and you can't make the spade dig into the hard crust of dirt. It is especially awkward if there is a little old nun next to you breaking into the soil easily."

. . .

Following the Confirmation, David had a chance to meet the newly confirmed and their families at a reception in the parish hall. Because it allowed him to be more like a parish priest again, David looked forward to these gatherings.

This afternoon, Confirmation had taken place at one of the poorer inner city parishes. On the way to the parish hall, as he walked through the school yard, David was edified and surprised to be surrounded by a cluster of elementary school age youngsters. They shouted their welcomes and pressed forward to shake the bishop's hand. It was an unusual show of affection. When he reached the other end of the school yard, David found that his episcopal ring was gone. So much for affection for the bishop.

Later, during the reception, one of the teachers somehow or other retrieved the ring.

CHAPTER 52

There were other light moments in David's life.

The Vatican II Council reactivated the ancient order of permanent diaconate. The morning arrived for the ordination of the first class of married men. This was an historic occasion for the diocese, as the fourteen candidates processed into the Cathedral of the Holy Spirit - a landmark event. For the first time in centuries in Roman Catholic churches of the western world, married men were receiving the sacrament of Holy Orders.

As in all ordination ceremonies, to insure validity, David, as a novice bishop, followed the ritual carefully. But there was one glaring oversight.

Tom Kettleman, the master of ceremonies, had stepped away from David's side momentarily to direct an altar server. David continued to read from the Pontifical. The text was for transitional deacons as well as permanent deacons, and David overlooked the rubric: "The following question is to be directed at transitional deacons only who are continuing on for ordination to the priesthood."

David asked the fourteen married men standing before him, "In the presence of God and the Church, are you resolved to remain celibate for the sake of the kingdom and in life-long service to God and mankind?"

David hardly noticed the somewhat confused, half-hearted response from the candidates. "I am."

Then David responded, "May the Lord help you to persevere in this commitment."

Without missing a beat, David continued on with the ordination and through the Liturgy of the Eucharist.

It was not until all had emerged from the church in the recessional and were gathered with the crowd in the plaza that several of the new deacons' wives confronted David. "Did you really mean to ask that question about celibacy?"

David was startled. "Celibacy? Did I say celibacy?"

"Yes, you did. You swore our husbands to celibacy."

"Oh, oh. That wasn't supposed to be in there."

David spent the next fifteen minutes circling the plaza, individually assuring each new deacon that he was officially releasing him from any promise he may have made about celibacy during the ceremony.

Several of the men stated that they had noticed the mistake and did not make the response, "I am."

Another one of the husbands replied, "I'm not sure I want to withdraw my promise of celibacy."

His wife, standing beside him, hit him on the arm. "Tell the Bishop you're only joking."

. . .

Early in the fall, David was invited to the "Holy Bowl", the traditional rivalry between the Christian Brothers and Jesuit high schools.

He found a parking space on the west side of the stadium and entered at one of the 40-yard line gates. He came out into the bleachers and found himself on the Christian Brothers High School side.

At about the middle of the first quarter, it occurred to him that, as bishop, he must rise above partisanship. Neither high school could be his favorite.

When half-time arrived, he followed the custom of the President of the United States at the Army-Navy game. He crossed the field to the Jesuit side of the stadium.

Over the course of ten years, attending the Holy Bowl, David was gratified to find that teams had scored 193 points when he was sitting on their side, and only 84 points when he was sitting on the opposite side of the field. He attributed all this to fervent prayer and the power of the episcopacy!

. . .

In the spring of the first year, David traveled to Mexico to ordain one of his new priests.

Virtually all the inhabitants of Tuxpan crowded the Church of San Juan Bautista for the ordination of Raul Ramirez on a warm January day. The sanctuary was filled with forty priests, some from the neighboring parishes of the Diocese of Ciudad de Guzman, some from Assumption Seminary in San Antonio, Texas, six from the Diocese of Fairview, where the new Father Ramirez was to serve.

San Juan Bautista is an imposing church for a small village. More than a thousand faithful, most of them standing, witnessed the ordination liturgy.

The prayers of the Mass and the homily were in Spanish. David had prepared the homily and practiced the Spanish translation many times before the ceremony. Hopefully, the congregation could understand his Gringo Spanish. Often Spanish-speaking people understood his English better than his Spanish.

David focused his attention on young Raul and began: "The five ingredients needed for a happy life are: Work, Study, Leisure, Friends and Prayer. And the greatest of these is prayer.

"The book which I am using at this ordination ceremony is called 'The Pontifical'. That comes from the Latin word for 'bridge'. In ordaining you, I am building a bridge. You are to be a bridge between God and the People. If you, the bridge, become uncoupled from God, the bridge will collapse.

"You must stay close to God in a daily prayer life. Parishioners sense it when a priest is not connected with God.

"Nor must the other end of the bridge become detached from the people. The people are the Church.

"There are some confusing concepts of what priests should be today in relation to the people. The clergy seem to have lost some privileges and position. The emphasis now is on servant leadership.

"'The concept of the 'prince-priest' is doomed,' says Father Ray Brown. And he goes on to say 'If I may use the term, I do not really think that the "pal-priest" is much of an improvement.'

"We have departed from an emphasis on spiritual asceticism and taken on a new asceticism of staff meetings, parish council meetings, and committee meetings."

At the end of the liturgy, David wanted to show his appreciation for the welcoming he had received. He would tell the people that he was "Mexican" in spirit. He tested his Spanish without a written text, extemporaneously: "Yo soy Mexicano" - "I am Mexican." And the congregation roared its approval.

Gaining confidence, he ad-libbed further. He wanted to let them know he was their brother. That's where he made his mistake. "Yo soy hermoso," he shouted.

He always did get those two words mixed up. He wanted to say, "Yo soy hermano" - "I am your brother," but he had shouted, "hermoso" - "I am beautiful!"

The crowd applauded and collapsed in laughter.

David was overwhelmed by the warmth and affection of the people. In the recessional from the church, following the ordination, the center aisle completely closed down with people moving from the pews to kiss the bishop's ring. It is not often that a bishop has the opportunity to visit the smaller villages.

It took David a half hour to move in the recessional from the altar, down the main aisle and back to the sacristy.

· · ·

And there were somber moments:

Federal agents were making sweeps along the Delta to round up illegal aliens. Word came to David that earlier this October morning, during a sweep, two fleeing young Latinos had jumped into the brown Delta waters near Lodi in an effort to escape. Neither could swim. Both had drowned.

That evening, David traveled to say Mass for the field workers at the housing center near Dixon. At an outdoor altar, as a still warm autumn sun was setting, David spoke to the crowd through a portable mike.

"We grieve the loss of these young men. How frightened and panicked they must have been to jump into the river, rather than be captured and sent back to a hopeless existence at home. We offer this Mass for the peaceful repose of their souls, and we promise to their families, loved ones and to you a continued remembrance in our prayers.

"I take this opportunity to express to you, the farmworkers, our appreciation for your labors day after day in the fields, which bring the fruits and vegetables to our tables. From this central valley, you provide the abundant nourishment which the people of the United States enjoy. It is a back-breaking work that not many of us would undertake. Que Dios bendiga a cada uno de ustedes. May God bless each one of you."

With a banner of Our Lady of Guadalupe slapping against the wooden standard beside him, David concluded the Mass, blessed religious articles brought to the altar, and joined the workers for a repast of tortillas and refried beans.

. . .

And there were the tragic occurrences in David's ministry.

As David left the cathedral following a Knights of Columbus Mass, a policeman called to him on the steps.

"There's a shooting at the court house, Father. I think several people are hurt. They probably could use a priest."

"At the court house?"

"Yes, just around the corner on 7ᵗʰ Street."

David rushed into the rectory, picked up his sick call kit and headed for the scene.

The block was cordoned off with barriers and yellow police tape.

The first policeman turned David away. "It's for your own safety, Father. There's still shooting going on." The officer in charge standing nearby over-ruled his colleague. "No, let the bishop through. Someone in there may want the sacraments."

As David entered, three rifle shots exploded from above. From the roof, the heavy body of a man somersaulted six stories to the pavement twenty feet behind David. He turned to see the man crushed to the street curb. His right leg had struck the bumper of the squad car and was severed just above the calf.

In violent injury, the last rites can be administered for a considerable time after apparent death.

David gave conditional absolution and anointing of the forehead. "Si tu es capax . . . If you are capable of receiving this Sacrament . . ."

The police converged on the site. The dead man was the assailant. He had been cornered on the court house roof by the SWAT team.

"Father, there are two more people that can use your help. Come on with me."

Behind the reception desk, on the third floor, a man and a woman lay no more than eight to ten feet apart, bloodied and sprawled awkwardly. They were the sole victims of a random, meaningless shooting. Again, David administered the last rites.

As bishop, he was still a parish priest.

. . .

David had set aside his book, just turned off the lights and was falling asleep when he heard the news bulletin on the clock radio at his bedside: "Sacramento Kings basketball star, Bobby Hurley, has been rushed to University of California Medical Center following an automobile accident near Arco Arena."

David knew that Hurley had attended St. Anthony's High School in New Jersey. If he remembered correctly, Bobby's father still coached there.

By coincidence, David had talked to the chaplain at U.C. Med that afternoon. The priest had told David in passing that he would not be on duty at the hospital that evening; he would be visiting his father.

With his clerical suit over his pajamas, David drove to the hospital and was escorted to Emergency by a nurse who recognized him at the elevators.

Doctors and nurses continued their frantic work over the injured athlete, but they separated enough to let the bishop to Hurley's side. When David saw the man on the gurney, he was sure he had reached the wrong patient. The Kings' guard was known as one of the smallest players in the National Basketball Association. This man had a sturdy chest and strapping shoulders.

But it was Hurley. To the crowds watching Bobby match up against the likes of Hakeem Olajuwan and David Robinson, he was diminutive, but among normal sized people, he was of good size.

Because the player was in a life threatening condition, David quickly administered the last sacrament as best he could in the frenzied activity all around him.

Due to his exceptional physical conditioning, Hurley withstood the early trauma, and the bishop was able to visit him in the company of his parents two days later.

David gave him one of the picture cards he regularly distributed to Confirmation classes as memento. "This is my Rookie Trading Card," he told the basketball star. "You know, you can get three of Michael Jordan's for one of these."

"I'll see that you get one of mine when I get out of the hospital," Hurley promised.

. . .

As a young cleric, David had read about meetings of the American Hierarchy. It was a heady experience now to be part of this. The November, 1986, General Assembly of the United States Catholic Bishops was tense as a taut wire.

For the first time in David's experience, camps and factions were appearing among the bishops. There was always a little of this; but now it was a pronounced part of the assembly.

In the Administrative Committee meeting on Saturday, six of the bishops tried to tone down the statement drafted on the Archbishop "Dutch" Hunthausen situation in Seattle.

The bishops wanted to be faithful to the Holy See, but, at the same time, they did not want to be making a judgment on the rightness or wrongness of Rome's decision about who should have the ultimate episcopal authority in the Seattle Archdiocese. Most felt they could not make a judgment because they did not have all the facts.

After much maneuvering and many proposals and counter-proposals, the statement was modified.

Though the final vote on the Pastoral Letter, Economic Justice for All, was to be the top priority of the assembly, it was obvious when Monday came that the discussion in the hallways, at meals, and in between sessions was mostly on Hunthausen.

At the Executive Session, the discussion was courteous and proper. Some assertive statements were made, but the emotion was not at a high pitch.

There was the traditional inclination to be supportive of the Holy Father, but, at the same time, most did not want to give the impression that they approved the split-authority arrangement in the Seattle Archdiocese.

In the long hours of discussion, the Conference President's statement to be released to the press became a version more compassionate towards Archbishop Hunthausen. A handful of bishops spoke assertively, questioning the justice of the process used in the investigation. Eventually it was agreed that the National Conference of Bishops should offer its good offices to help the Archbishop and Auxiliary Bishop Donald Wuerl in any way it could. Cardinal Bernardin, speaking for the four Cardinals, spoke in favor of the final draft, as did Archbishop Roach of Minneapolis-St. Paul.

The final vote was virtually unanimous. Several bishops -- feeling they were caught in an impossible situation, preferring that if what they considered a fair statement could not be made, no statement should be made - refused to vote for or against the document.

Media people were everywhere. David could not remember a Bishops' Conference that attracted more attention.

CHAPTER 53

His Holiness
Pope John Paul II
Vatican City
Europe

Holy Father:

Regretfully we find it necessary to write to you to report several events taking place in the Diocese of Fairview, California, which are in violation of official Church teaching.

The most egregious of these are a joint ceremony of Baptism involving the Roman Catholic bishop and bishops other than Catholic; an ecumenical prayer service for a state governor who supports abortions; a Jazz Mass which features secular music and questionable dancing -- all of these taking place in the Cathedral of the Holy Spirit.

We must cite also Catholic high school presentations on human sexuality, frequent liturgical aberrations, special ministry to homosexuals, engagement in political activities, such as the capital punishment debate, contrary to Vatican regulations.

We are calling on Your Holiness to remove Bishop David Carmichael from office for this conduct which is a scandal to the Faithful.

I have the honor to be your obedient servant.

Respectfully,
George Caprice
For Guardians of Doctrine

. . .

Richard Harris was to be executed at midnight, the first death penalty in 30 years now that capital punishment had been restored in the State of California.

David accompanied members of the diocesan Social Justice Commission to San Quentin to speak against the death penalty. Opponents and proponents of capital punishment gathered at the gates of the state prison in Marin County, on San Francisco Bay. State Police guarded the gates. Signs proclaiming both sides of the argument were mounted on poles along both sides of the entrance roadway.

A Dodge Ram pick-up kicked up dust as it rumbled past the protestors. Three teenagers in the cab of the truck shouted, "Burn Harris."

A Fundamentalist preacher was quoting the Bible in support of the death penalty. A TV news reporter asked David if he subscribed to the same biblical position. Before David could answer, the minister, spotting the Roman clerical collar, approached David, "The Old Testament says that if a man kills another, he himself is to be killed."

David responded, "That same quotation says that if a man commits adultery, he should suffer the death penalty. If we are going to be consistent, we'd have to impose capital punishment for a number of sins."

The Fundamentalist persisted, "The word of God is very clear, if a man takes another man's life, he forfeits his own."

By this time, television cameramen, radio microphones, newspaper reporters with their spiral pads had surrounded the two clerics.

"You're quoting one text out of the 72 books of the Bible," David responded. "The whole theme of the New Testament is for mercy, for rehabilitation, for redemption."

"The Old Testament Book of Leviticus says clearly, 'Whoever takes a life of any human being shall be put to death . . . Whoever slays a man shall be put to death.'

"If we are going to take that quotation literally, "David repeated", we will have to put many people to death to be consistent. The same book of the Bible says that adults who have sex during menstruation shall be put to death, and Exodus mandates execution for children who curse their parents and for people who break the Sabbath day."

But the Evangelical persisted, "You cannot deny it. The Bible says again and again, 'You shall give life for life, eye for eye, tooth for tooth, hand for hand . . . stripe for stripe."

"Again, that has to be interpreted," David responded. "To punish arsonists, are we going to set them on fire? Is the punishment for rapists going to be to rape them? The Jewish Torah tells the story of Cain, whom God forgave for the premeditated and unprovoked murder of his brother Abel. The modern State of Israel has never had capital punishment. This indicates how the Jewish State interprets the so-called pro-death penalty passages in the Hebrew Scriptures. As a matter of fact, the American Jewish Congress states that 'Capital punishment degrades and brutalizes the society which practices it . . . The death penalty is cruel, unjust, and incompatible with dignity and self respect.'

"Moreover, David continued before his adversary could reply, "the whole theme of the New Testament of the Bible is mercy and forgiveness, along with justice. You have heard that it was said, "An eye for an eye and a tooth for a tooth." But I say to you, offer no resistance to one who is evil . . . be not overcome by evil, but overcome evil by good.' 'Father, forgive them for they know not what they do.'"

"Your arguments," the Evangelical countered, "are exactly what is causing the downfall of society today. Because we are soft on criminals, crime rates are soaring."

David realized that he was beginning to shout to match the decibel level of his opponent. He moderated his voice, "Statistics may be debated, but there are many studies that indicate that the death penalty is not a deterrent to crime. A recent United Nations' study says that no conclusive evidence has been found on the efficacy of the death penalty to reduce crime. And Louis Freeh, the head of the F.B.I., just last February, declared that the death penalty does not deter capital offenses. In America, states which have abolished the death penalty have 4.9 murders per thousand. States which have retained the death penalty have 7.4 murders per thousand."

The preacher was not to be put off, "There are three kinds of lies: lies, damned lies and statistics. You can twist statistics any way you like. The fact of the matter is that you have more concern about the criminals than about the victims."

"You are right," David said quietly. "We should do more for the victims of crimes. I try to write letters to the families of victims. As a society and as a government, we should do more. But it is precisely to help save possible future victims that I am against death penalty. I believe that savagery begets savagery. Additional killing is not the way to prevent killings. Actually, many family members of murder victims do not want the death penalty for the assailants of their loved ones."

"I have figures that would contradict those statistics," the minister said. "We could debate this subject for hours, but the plain fact is that we have a capital punishment law in this state and the penalties which are called for by law should be applied."

"Yes, we do have the law," David rejoined. "But there is a question whether the law can ever be applied fairly and equitably. Seventy-five percent of those on death row were financially not able to hire a private attorney to represent them at trial. Persons from ethnic minorities constitute nearly 50 percent of the death row population, but these minorities make up only 18 percent of the general population.

"I think America should reflect on the fact that we are the only western industrialized nation that still has the death penalty. At this point, as far as capital punishment is concerned, we are in the company of such countries as the Soviet Union, South Africa, China, Iran, Iraq, Liberia and Nigeria."

"If a killer is executed," the Fundamentalist retorted, "he will not be out on the streets again, killing someone else. That's a fact. That is why the vast majority of the public is for capital punishment."

David knew that was a telling point to a television audience. "I most certainly believe," David argued, "that anyone who is a threat to society should not be out on the streets. If it is clear that a person is a threat to others, he should be incarcerated without possibility of parole.

And many states, for example Oregon and Florida, are now tightening up that kind of law for capital offenders. In this state, California, not one prisoner sentenced to life without parole has been freed from prison since the state installed the no-parole option in 1977.

"Also, as a matter of fact, the public is not as strongly in favor of the death penalty as some reports would have it. The Mervin Field poll has revealed that 67 percent of the people in this state, if given the option, prefer punishment to be life imprisonment without possibility of parole, coupled with assistance to victims . . . they prefer this punishment to the death penalty."

David sensed that his debater would appeal to the crowd that had gathered around and to the viewing audience on the basis of economics, so David tried to anticipate that point.

"Putting this subject on a purely economic level, I realize that the public sometimes is frustrated because so many tax dollars are spent to room and board capital offenders for a lifetime. Apart from the morality of the subject, it costs the state much more to execute a criminal than to imprison him without possibility of parole. Because of the eleven levels of appeal, court costs and other expenses leading to the death penalty can rise to $15 million, whereas even to warehouse the convicted person for a forty-year average life expectancy costs the state approximately $930,000."

A scuffle broke out about 100 feet west of where the crowd of reporters and spectators had clustered. Cameras and note pads hurried to the new conflict. David was relieved. He had said just about everything he could think of.

Three weeks later, Richard Harris was executed.

CHAPTER 54

David conjectured that three other episodes provoked George Caprice's wrath and brought about the charge that David was meddling in "politics."

The California gubernatorial campaign focused on Family Values. In the final televised debate between the two leading candidates at the State Capital, David was asked to introduce the Open Forum with a formal address on Families.

Not having experienced parenting first hand, David had to rely on textbook sources.

"Family is one of the most beautiful words in the English language. Our family gives us something to hold on to. Family is what helps us to have self-identity.

"When we were very small, if we were ever hurt or rejected or treated badly, it was natural and spontaneous for us to run home to family. There, we found protection and familiar surroundings.

"Family means the place where the wage-earner comes home, beaten and bruised from work and finds refuge and support.

"Family is the place you can be yourself. There is no place for sham or deception within the family.

"In a healthy family, members frequently interrupt each other's speaking. Communication is to the point that you do not have to finish your sentences.

"Theodore Adams offers beatitudes for the home:

Blessed is the home where each puts the other's happiness first.

Blessed is the home where children grow up and grown-ups do not act like children.

"And Leonara Zearfoss adds:

Blessed is the mother who knows how to comfort, for she shall possess a child's devotion.

Blessed is the mother who answers simply the startling questions, for she shall always be trusted."

David noticed that both candidates were taking notes.

"Since I am a celibate, I do not know what it means to have children of my own. Nevertheless, over the years, I have gathered thoughts about fathers:

The greatest gift a father can give to his children is the love he shows to their mother - the love he clearly shows.

Fatherhood should be open to failure. Weakness and human failures, honestly dealt with, are often the most effective source of love and learning in the children.

The deepest regret of fathers is that they did not spend more quality time with their children when they were young.

A father is a husband also. He must always nourish a private and personal relationship with his wife.

'All evidence of love is important, but there is no substitute for the direct expression of love in cuddling and embracing a child', a young father says. 'I never fully understood what James Joyce meant when he wrote, 'I desire to press in my arms the loveliness which has not yet come into the world,' until I sat cradling my newborn child in my arms.'

'And there are suggestions from the children, developed by the Adler Institute:

Don't spoil me. I know quite well that I ought not to have all I ask for.

Don't use force with me. It teaches me that power is all that counts. I will respond more readily to being led.

Don't correct me in front of people. I'll take much more notice if you talk quietly with me in private.

Don't tax my honesty too much. I am easily frightened into telling lies.

Don't ever think that it is beneath your dignity to apologize to me. An honest apology makes me feel surprisingly warm toward you.

"I recognize the incongruity of my giving 'infallible guidance' in family values, having never had to raise a family myself. I offer these as suggestions and will be grateful for whatever consideration the candidates may accord them as they now debate the issues."

The candidates took their places at the lecterns and, for an hour, argued traditional and contemporary family values along the lines the media had framed the debate throughout the campaign: society's changing perceptions of marriage and family, divorce rates, live-in couples, alienation of children, the influence of the Religious Right on politics.

The next morning there was unanimity among the California's newspapers that the contestants had stuck to the issues. The media declared the debate a draw.

. . .

The second "political" involvement occurred when Sadam Hussein once again challenged the United Nations' teams monitoring Iraq's mass destruction weapons, and the United States responded with a show of force.

David had his reservations about the military response, but he was called upon to bless an Army Reserve contingent departing from Travis Air Force Base. He prayed:

"All sides in the Persian Gulf conflict read some form of Sacred Scriptures, and pray to their own God.

"Each side invokes Your name, Lord, against the other under the many names humans have given You.

"With variations on Joyce Kilmer, we offer a Persian Gulf prayer for all military personnel if armed conflict erupts again.

> 'I march through sands that burn and smart.
> Jehovah's coolness on my heart.
> I may not lift a hand to clear
> My eyes of salty drops that sear.
> I thirst beneath the desert sun,
> Muhammad's wish that all be one.
> My shoulders ache beneath my pack,
> Lie easier cross upon Christ's back.

I long for home that war may cease.
May Buddha grant internal peace.
God, Thou dost suffer more to see
Thy many nations' enmity.
So let me render back again
These graceless, clumsy words. Amen.'

"As Lincoln did, 'fondly do we hope, fervently do we pray that this awesome threat of war may surely pass away.'"

Though David's role at the departure ceremony was to pray, a question came from one of the reporters, "What is your position on conscientious objection in this situation?"

"I believe that conscientious objection to serving in a combat position in the military because of the person's moral or ethical convictions is a perfectly acceptable stance. I also support selective conscientious objection. Although one may not have declared himself a pacifist on principle, I believe it is moral for a person to make an objection to a particular war. That person should be exempted from serving in combat duty. I wrote letters to that effect to the draft boards during the Gulf War, and I think the same policy can be applied at this time."

. . .

The more Bishop David came to be known in the northern California counties, the more hectic his life became.

Hour by hour, day by day, demands on his time swung between pastoral duties, requests for talks, administrative obligations. This led to the third and final brush with partisan politics.

David was invited to offer the prayer opening the second day of the Democratic National Convention at Moscone Center in San Francisco. He knew that he would not be invited again, so once he had the podium, he was going to take advantage of the opportunity.

"Heavenly Father," he prayed, "voter turnout has declined steadily in presidential elections since 1960.

"A recent poll quotes 21-year-old James Greenlee as saying, 'Early in my young life, I discovered that power and money are what really carry the clout in America.' Others surveyed expressed the same conviction.

"So often we hear the quote of former President Dwight Eisenhower: 'Someday the people of the world will want peace so desperately that political leaders will have to get out of their way and let them have it.'

"But it is not happening.

"I can understand how Christ did not want to address the party platform of the Roman state. He must have known that there was no use trying to influence political decisions. For this reason did He say, 'Render to Caesar the things that are Caesar's.'

"And so I have felt the temptation to withdraw from the system. To let the political parties go their way.

"But we must not withdraw. We know that ineptness in government is just a symptom of the disease. We call out for radical surgery.

"The basic illness is this: To be elected or to be retained in political office now requires enormous sums of money. The financing of campaigns must be changed. The administration and congress are talking about this, but not much is being accomplished.

"We must recommend a preliminary plank in the party platform not directly related to war and peace, but prior and essential to it all.

"The electoral process must be restructured so that campaigns are not financed by private money, so that political leaders are no longer beholden to those who have the power and the wealth to dictate policies for profits or to protect the status quo interests around the world.

"Political conventions come and go, but the melancholy fact is that a strong, silent human infra-structure controls the day by day decisions during the four years between conventions.

"Unless this system changes, we are all wasting our time here.

"Lord, we have taken the awesome intelligence You have given us and used it to discover unspeakable ways of killing each other. We have devised weapons which grow beyond belief and beyond bearing.

"Help us, Lord, to communicate the reasonableness of the cause of peace without polarizing nations with strident words. Others will follow us only if they see in us wisdom and forbearance.

"Make us ready to grant that our political leaders and our military personnel yearn for peace just as fervently as we do.

"Paraphrasing Thomas Merton, we say: 'Let us be joyful with the words that are given to us; not to force anyone, not to confute anyone, not to prove anyone absurd. We are the ministers of the solid persistence that is needed to cure all victims of absurdity, who lie dying of a contrived joy. Let us then recognize ourselves for who we are; peacemakers armed with a therapeutic love which some persons may fear more than violent revolution, for violence changes nothing. But love changes everything. We are stronger than the bomb.'

"May we recognize that we are now down to two final options: Co-existence or No-existence.

"We pray for total disarmament negotiations for nerve gas, nuclear, chemical and biological weapons. Do we judge rightly, Lord, when we say that if these negotiations use the bargaining chips of fear, deterrence, tonnage of throw-weight and national advantage, they will never succeed?

"Help us when we see fear and panic in our adversaries -- help us not to mistake the fear for aggression.

"In times of international tensions, give us intelligence to see clearly and to act responsibly.

"Grant us prudence in proportion to our power, wisdom in proportion to our science, humanness in proportion to our wealth and might.

"Gentle Father in heaven, the era of tribes came on earth and passed away. In earlier times, the world brought to an end unceasing tribal warfare by federating the tribes. Help us now to discern how the nation states, each internally sovereign, can be federated into an international community, a world authority, by which disputes will be settled, not by armed conflict, but by reasoned negotiation. Amen."

It was more a lecture than a prayer; but none of the convention officials could find it in themselves to interrupt an Invocation.

David did not want his part in the program to be a perfunctory routine to be gotten over with so that the "important" business of the convention could get underway.

George Caprice would see this "prayer" as the straw breaking the camel's back in political meddling.

CHAPTER 55

It was Memorial Day weekend and time again for northern California's Delta Jazz Jubilee– a celebration attended now by more than one hundred thousand.

And another bone of contention:

David had received photocopies of letters sent to the Apostolic Nuncio and to the Vatican protesting the "desecration of the Liturgy and the Cathedral" by the previous year's Jazz Jubilee Mass. The numbers participating were growing each year, so that what had begun as a single event had increased to three Masses. Acknowledging that he was no connoisseur of current music (for the longest time he thought Madonna was a painting in the Vatican Museum) and was not a student of jazz, David had observed Jazz Mass congregations in the past and found them prayerful and devout.

For years David had researched jazz and prepared a homily with quotations drawn from several sources - sources, to whom, as much as he wanted to give attribution, he could no longer identify.

On Sunday morning, he faced a thronged Cathedral. He hoped to legitimize the Jazz Mass:

"Dizzy Gillespie once said, 'You are a reflection of your music. Your whole life is so intertwined with music that you don't know where one starts and the other ends.'

"Anthropologists tell us that from primitive times, religion has been inseparable from music and dance.

"And Martin Luther writes:

'Music is a beautiful and lovely gift of God . . .

I give music the next place of honor after theology.

The devil doesn't stay where there is music.'

"David danced in the temple in a spirit of joy and freedom.

"During the Last Supper, the Gospel tells us that the Apostles sang hymns. Through the ages, we have sung at liturgies. From the beginning, religion has been associated with music. 'Play harp and lyre. Blow the trumpet,' says Psalm 81. And Psalm 98: 'With trumpets and sound of the horn.' A variety of instruments and dramatic presentations accompanied the Mass during the Middle Ages.

"For centuries, the pipe organ and Gregorian chant enhanced the liturgy. In the 1960s, guitars were introduced in Folk Masses. On Memorial Day weekend at this Cathedral, the music is jazz.

"Although they are accomplished performers, the musicians and choir know that this gathering is not a performance. It is a prayer. We recall the age-old maxim: 'Anyone who sings once, prays twice.'

"The word 'jazz' comes from the language of the bawdy houses. But Dixieland Jazz grew out of the Black Spirituals of the South. It is authentic Gospel singing. A Jazz Mass really needs no apology. This music which came from the Gospels returns very appropriately this morning to the liturgy of the Gospel.

"William C. Handy, pioneer of traditional jazz, could say at the turn of the century: 'It was the way that Methodist Reverend Cordie White sang 'Train's A Comin' that set the tom-toms beating in my blood.' While a modern day jazz artist, Charles Mingus, writes: 'I was born swinging and clapped my hands in church as a little boy.'

"West African religion and the Christian religion of the New World fused easily. The Church had inexpensive images and lithographs of saints like St. Patrick driving the snakes out of Ireland, which the slave could compare with Damballa, the Snake God. St. Anthony was associated with Legba, the God of the Crossroad - both were depicted as tattered men who related to the poor and to children. St. Michael was identified with Ogun, the God of War.

"The Black slaves sensed elements comfortable to them in the Latin Catholic colonies. There was something in the Latin culture of the Spanish, Portuguese and French which reminded them of the rhythmic West African music. The music of the Latin colonies, especially the Spanish, had a rhythmic life. The Moorish conquest of Spain had introduced improvisation and complex rhythms of African music.

"Jazz came out of religious camp meetings, spirituals, Gospel songs. It was first heard in the washboard bands playing religious hymns on the way to funerals, then picking up a hotter beat on the way home from the burial.

"Jazz music grew out of a feeling of oppression and a yearning for liberation from within. Religion and freedom of the spirit go hand in hand.

"Slaves of the South felt domination. And so their music, jazz, began as a mournful hunger for a better life. Jazz grew out of the cane rows and the levees - very much like our migrant camps along the Sacramento River and the Delta farmlands.

"In his recitation lyrics, Duke Ellington says, 'When the baby screams out after the doctor's first spank, are we certain the baby isn't trying to say "Thank God, I'm free?"'

"From the first moment of birth, we are alive with the pulse of life and the yearning to be liberated.

The baby feels that rhythm in life - breathing in and breathing out with a heart-beat in rhythm - 72 beats a minute.

"Jazz was a non-violent expression of rebellion, a sensing that something was fundamentally wrong. If you want to know the history of a nation, listen to its songs. There is something haunting about jazz. The music is externally jumpy and glad, but its inner taste is sweet and sour.

"As Manley Brayton has written, 'In jazz, gone are the tyrannies of written music and the fetters of the conductor's baton.'

"Jazz is characterized by virtuoso performance, improvising, variations, independence and individuality. These are precisely the qualities of the religious spirit: freedom from those restraints which keep us from being fully human.

"The blue notes of jazz can be thought of as the cracks between the piano keys. Jazz is a music form which interrupts the predictable pattern. It introduces syncopation. It accents the unexpected syllable.

"Jazz went counter to many of the regulations of music. It frightened some. It puzzled most people. Because it seemed to break through rules and conventions, some moralists attacked jazz. Not until 1925 did a brave-voiced preacher say, 'Jazz is not necessarily the pathway to hell.'

"As a matter of fact, the spirit of jazz is compassionate and caring. I understand that the police report that security is not a problem in Old

Fairview during the Jazz Jubilee, despite the tremendous throngs. The jazz patrons' mood is a friendly one.

"The history of jazz moves through the times of Buddy Bolden, Huddie Ledbetter, Kid Ory, Jellyroll Morton, Louis Armstrong, Bix Beiderbecke, Duke Ellington.

"Just as the Church, since it is a living organism, struggles with tensions between liberals and conservatives, traditionalists and progressives, jazz felt the same tensions hovering between institution and complexity, wanting to be avant-garde and wanting, at the same time, to go back to its roots. People like Fletcher Henderson and Chick Webb ushered in the jazz form which became known as 'swing.'

"In the mid-1950s, there was a reaction to the cool jazz era of complicated orchestrations and a return to earthy blues and the Gospel style. Rhythm and blues was an attempt to rediscover jazz's emotional roots.

"Just as our Faith did in the Second Vatican Council, music continually tries to find the road between our beginnings and our future.

"I am not a musician. I try to avoid all the singing parts of the Mass, because my singing voice does not really contribute to the liturgy. Still, I admire music from a distance. I do not think I understand jazz. It has always struck me as a highly specialized music form - a musician's music.

"But music touches the soul as few other experiences do.

"I have always wondered why teenagers are so obsessed with music videos, albums, records, tapes, CDs. I had been puzzled by this until a few years ago when radio stations like Magic 61 and KCTC began to appear. These stations play the original records of the '30s, '40s and '50s. When I hear a young Perry Como sing 'Till the End of Time' and Ella Fitzgerald sing 'A Tisket A Tasket,' all my juices begin flowing again. I know what it was to be young and filled with song.

"The word 'jubilee' comes from a Hebrew word, 'yobeel', meaning a ram's horn. The word 'jubilee' also has as its definition an occasion of joy. The word 'jazz' is a Creole word. It refers to a music that is creative, totally American, innovative. Its beat is boom-ching. It is syncopation, originally called ' ragging'.

"And it is a mixture of both joy and sadness. Dixieland and Blues. Our Delta Jubilee is Dixieland and joy. Happiness is the trademark of religion, not gloom. When there is a belief in a loving God, there is always hope. There is always song.

'Wherever the Catholic sun doth shine
There's plenty of songs and good red wine
At least I've always been told it's so
Benedicamus Domino.'

"In the early days of jazz, the music was associated with taverns, with bordellos; it had a sinful context. But Mary Lou Williams, a devout person who wrote many religious compositions, once said, 'Jazz is meant for bars and pool rooms and jails and the streets -- and for the churches.'

"Jazz authority, John Gentzel, has written, 'Jazz doesn't have to be baptized. It was made to be holy.'

"A good part of contemporary music in every age was written, first of all, for the churches, from Bach to Mozart to Dave Brubeck.

"One of the most recent joys was the Dave Brubeck Concert this past weekend in the Cathedral. He honored this church with the composition, 'Let Us Bow Down' in reverent variation on 'Pange Lingua.' I found the Mass, 'To Hope,' exhilarating and inspiring. As I watched this artist, I saw something very wholesome. The smile on Brubeck's face, which is not always seen in musicians as they perform. The obvious pride he had in his son who was accompanying him in the quartet. The obvious affection for his wife who arranged the music. There was something heartwarming about the closeness and intimacy of this family. I don't know if others noticed, but I was impressed by Dave unobtrusively bowing his head reverently during the words of consecration as the choral group sang the lyrics of his Mass.

"Contrasting with the joyous strains of 'My Rock and My Strength' and 'The Saints Go Marching In,' the Blues have a sad and woeful character:

'I go through life just catching colds and missing trains.'

'My Mama don tol' me when I was in kneepants; my Mama don tol' me, Son, a woman's a two-face, a worrisome thing who'll leave you to sing the Blues in the night.'

"But there is always, even in the Blues, a sense of hope and a sense of humor, sense of realism.

"Songs stir memories.

"I was teaching in a parochial school as a priest when Rock 'n Roll was emerging, and I was supervising Junior Proms when I first heard 'At The Hop' and 'Rock Around the Clock.'

"Then came the protest years in the Haight-Ashbury, Otis Redding's 'Sitting By the Dock of the Bay.'

"Three songs bring nostalgia in the years I recall, as a priest, serving in a parish in the Richmond District in San Francisco: 'Sweet Caroline,' Petula Clark's 'Downtown,' and one from overseas, 'Volare.'

I reminisce on the '70s and my first pastorate at Mission Dolores when I hear 'Send in the Clowns.'

And from the beginning, I have associated happy days in this diocese with many, many melodies: 'That's What Friends Are For,' 'Every Breath You Take,' and 'The Wind Beneath my Wings.'

"Popular music treats spiritual themes. Example: 'I Believe'. And Peggy Lee poses a deep theological question when she asks, 'Is That All There Is?' If you listen to the lyrics, Dean Martin preached an effective homily on married life in 'Memories Are Made of This.' True, there have been unfortunate messages that we adults did not catch about drugs in some of the music that was popular in our younger days, 'Slow down, you move too fast; you've got to make the morning last. Just kicking down the cobblestone, looking for fun and feelin' groovey.'

"But think now; the theme of 90 percent of the songs which we and our children have enjoyed is the theme of love. And love is at the center of the Gospels. 'Love Me Tender.' And something for us older folks - 'Somewhere My Love.'

"A movie critic at one time commented on a current album by the artist known again as Prince and saw it as Prince's struggle with the two faces of love, sex and God, which he describes as Prince's two obsessions. This critic, David Barton, describes the song 'Anastasia' as a rock-gospel prayer that casts Prince as some modern version of St. Teresa of Avila, who brought mysticism to the people. I think Prince would be very surprised by that comparison - and so would St. Teresa.

"Some have criticized songs such as Madonna's 'Like a Prayer,' describing it as a mindless clutter of random associations, 'quick cut sexual fantasy, and Madonna's seemingly incurable habit of equating liberation with lingerie -- a musical performance suffering from a severe case of satisfaction.'

"I believe these criticisms are unfair and miss the mark.

"Isn't it intriguing that Madonna is constantly fascinated with the symbols of her early faith: the crucifix, the rosaries, the statues, the candles, the stigmata of Christ and Francis. Could it not be that the lyrics reveal beliefs that this singer has been struggling with just below the surface, young adulthood, the age of reconversion, which must first go through the age of rebellion - even to a daughter named Lourdes.

"Lyrics of songs from jazz to elevator music to Rock and Rap have to do with love, even though often love is confused exclusively with genitality.

"God created our sexuality.

"Lyric writers may demean and diminish its meaning.

"But Duke Ellington, perhaps, understood it well when he wrote, 'Is God a Three Letter Word for Love?'

"The healthy thing is to take love and sexuality straightforwardly. Not to romanticize them, nor neuroticize them.

"A sign of maturity is when one gets over being in love with sex and begins to be in love with a person.

"I am called to be a celibate. I don't know if I really know what love should be. I think that genuine love is valuing another person for that person's own worth, wanting what is best for that person.

"Music is music. Charlie Parker, Scott Joplin, John Coltraine, Mary Lou Williams, Dizzie Gillespsie, Glen Miller, and the Rolling Stones all use the same eight musical notes as Beethoven, Bach and Mozart.

"After a concert, Albert Einstein once addressed these words to the young violinist, Yehudi Menuhin, 'Thank you. Your music has once again proved to me that there is a God in heaven.'

"If we truly understand God and music and our human nature, the Jazz Festival may do the same for all of us, may help us come closer to God.

"The Church feels very much at home in this festival, in this jubilee of jazz. Later on today, I will put on my Jubilee jacket and go into Old Fairview. It is where the Church belongs because of the God-given talents in the musicians, because of happiness in people who enjoy artistry and who enjoy being with other people. There is community, a being together. Old Fairview, for these three days, is an open-air cathedral. Some things that happen in the festivities shouldn't happen -- because we are all weak. The Church is a family of very human people;

strong and weak, sometimes good, sometimes bad. The Church is not a museum for saints, but a hospital for sinners.

"Why are so many of you attending the Jazz Jubilee? Is it because you love jazz? Is it to find some escape for the weekend? Is it to be where the crowds are? Is it to party? Whatever it is, the Church is with you. Our Faith and the Mass belong in Old Fairview with the Jazz Jubilee.

"We may not be experiencing the oppression of slaves or suffering an impoverished life in the cotton fields or on the levees. But each one of us carries his own personal cross. And our Faith is meant to be with us in times of entertainment, in times of depression and loneliness, in times when we are looking for escape in the crowds so that we can drown out the sounds of our pain - whether in the Cathedral of the Holy Spirit or on the cobblestones of Front Street.

"The Church wants to be there with its joy and its hope to remind us, no matter what our burdens, that one day the saints - and that hopefully means all of us -- will indeed go marching in."

. . .

Ladd, working during the late spring at the San Francisco CRS office, drove to Fairview to attend the Jazz Mass that David had talked about.

What was it about memory and songs of one's youth? He hadn't heard this song since boyhood, but the lyrics came back to Ladd word for word:

> "Missed the Saturday dance.
> Heard they crowded the floor.
> Couldn't bear it without you.
> Don't get around much any more."

He recalled the words as readily as any Catholic over the age of forty could repeat the rote answer to their childhood Baltimore Catechism question, "Why did God make you?" "God made me to know Him, to love Him, to serve Him in this life and to be happy with Him forever in the next."

"It seems to me I've heard that song before.
It's from an old familiar score . . ."

And yet, Ladd could not remember the lyrics to the hymns that choirs now were singing week after week at Sunday Mass.

Was his memory slipping on things of the recent past - or was he slipping away from the things of worship?

. . .

As David came out of the cathedral from the Jazz Mass, at the bottom of the front steps, he met a woman in the company of two young men. "David, I'm Melissa Auth. I used to be Melissa Ruther."

David was taken aback at being addressed by his first name, but then the recognition set in. "Melissa - sure, we were at school together in Napa."

"These are my two sons, William and Anthony."

"Good to meet you," David said, shaking the hands of the two young men. "It's really good to see you. Where are you living now?"

"I live in Woodland. The two boys live in Stockton."

"This is a wonderful surprise. You know, William and Anthony, maybe I shouldn't be saying this, but you two could be my sons. When we were in the eighth grade, I really had a crush on your mother. Who knows what might have happened if I hadn't gone to the seminary."

Just then, one of the church ushers hurried up to David's side, "Bishop, you've left your cordless microphone on. Everything you're saying is being announced on the public address system in the church."

"Oh, oh, what was I saying?" as David fumbled beneath his chasuble to turn off the microphone. "I probably upset some of the congregation already with parts of the sermon I just gave. There may be some more letters to Rome about the homily and about the off-the-record remarks on a live microphone."

. . .

That evening David recalled Pope John XXIII who allegedly always concluded his night prayers with the same words. Here was a man who had all the problems of the world on his shoulders. It is said of him that he ended his night prayer each evening with the same sentence: "It's your Church, Jesus; I'm going to bed."

David found the life of a bishop often stressful.

For this reason, he had made it a personal rule never to open an envelope after six o'clock in the evening. Most letters contain problems of one kind or another, and if they were serious enough problems, they caused David to lose sleep at night. He would save all late arriving messages till the morning when he could face them with more optimism and energy.

But waiting for him on his return to the rectory this Jazz Mass evening was a package of hand-delivered letters obviously from young school children. They would not be stressful.

The fourth grade class at St. Anthony of Padua School had written in their best Palmer method:

"Dear Bishop Carmichael:

My name is Dexter Westbury, and I am in the fourth grade. My religion teacher is Miss Collender. She told us to do this assignment, and here I go. I learned in school that you own all the churches in Fairview . . ."

"Dear Bishop Carmichael:

. . . I wonder what you do when you are yourself? . . ."

"Dear Bishop:

I like you. I hope you are pope next. If you are, get a Trans Am . . ."

"Dear Bishop Carmichael:

How are you? . . . Are you a Catholic? . . ."

David thought to himself, "George Caprice is probably asking the same question."

PART VI

CHAPTER 56

Tyler struggled with impure thoughts. He wondered when, if ever, this would no longer be a problem.

His confessor had told him, "The temptations against chastity will not end until an hour and a half after you're buried. It's part of the human condition." Tyler struggled on. He took cold showers. More and more he chose to go to confession anonymously, rather than face to face.

Tyler rose from his knees in the darkened confessional and started to leave. But the door wouldn't open. Either it was stuck or he couldn't find the handle for releasing the latch. He kept pawing around the door. He knew the priest confessor on the other side of the screen could hear the commotion. Panic set in. The priest would be coming out to open the door for him and he would be recognized. Tyler was terrified. Finally, fumbling around, he found the latch and the door swung open. He left the church immediately. He would say his penance later.

After going to confession, Tyler experienced a clean, liberating feeling, and firmly resolved that he would do better in the future.

Chastity, he was beginning to discover, was not a state of life, but a state of constantly becoming.

. . .

Ladd landed in Delhi International Airport at 2:30 a.m. India time. Even the atmosphere around Delhi airport gave Ladd the feeling of abject poverty, many of the people dressed in the long, flowing robes of the Indian women, the men in turbans, the women with the red circle dot on their foreheads. There is an overwhelming crush at the desks for transportation. Some people are sleeping on the floor of the airport entrance.

The next morning, Ladd passed the Rag Ghat, the memorial at the location where Mahandas Gandhi was cremated. Continuous crowds file past the shrine, touching the marble platform where the cremation took place. With the other visitors, Ladd removed his shoes and approached the site.

In Delhi, Ladd was exactly halfway around the world from San Francisco. As a matter of fact, he did not have to reset his wristwatch because of the 12-hour time difference. Then he discovered a 30-minute discrepancy. There are no time zones across the wide subcontinent of India, and the Standard Time for the entire country is one-half hour off the time zones of all other parts of the world.

In a CRS van, Ladd was chauffeured along the outskirts of Ranchi in a Suzuki Maruti soft-top (the Indian version of the Suzuki Samurai) scattering bicyclists, dogs and cattle. As pedestrians leapt for safety, Ladd felt uncomfortably like a British Viceroy of the 1920s, driving through a crowd of untouchables.

. . .

Heading east, Ladd made a lay over, landing in Calcutta at dusk - a city of seven million, with three million children. Eighty-five percent of these children are racked by malnutrition and other diseases. Many are orphans, destitute and the products of an unjust social structure, unloved, unwanted and uncared for. Calcutta is awesome in its population. The streets everywhere are thronged with people. This night was humid and over 90 degrees.

People in the warm, humid July nights swarm everywhere. Vendors line the sidewalks. Small children beg for money, mothers with children in their arms pulled at Ladd's sleeve for help.

Very late at night, with the heavy humid air hanging over the city, gradually the foot traffic stops and people sleep along the sidewalks and streets. This seemingly endless outdoor dormitory has an eerie, frightening look. Not all the sleepers are homeless - though many are. Some voluntarily sleep in the streets to escape the oppressive collected heat of their dwellings.

. . .

Ladd entered the House of the Dying, a former Hindu temple donated to Mother Teresa as her first facility, where the abandoned sick, in the last stages of life, are cared for. Here, Ladd conversed with young men and women: Belgians, French, Canadians, Swiss, Americans - youth from around the world helping the Missionaries of Charity comfort "the children of God" in their last days.

Ladd visited also Mother Teresa's institute for malnourished and sick children, some, at the age of 8 or 10 months, weighing only 5 or 6 pounds. The clinics are immaculate. The Sisters and the volunteers are forever mopping, sweeping, changing bedclothes.

Ladd remarked to his companion, the Country Director, "We do not know in America the overwhelming, crushing poverty we see here. The United States poverty is rather a poverty of the spirit. Perhaps our agony is a poverty of intimacy. We experience the anguish of alienation and loneliness. There is such a massive presence of humanity here in India, such bonds of family and extended family, I wonder if anyone can ever be lonely in Calcutta."

CHAPTER 57

The intercom buzzed in Archbishop Costello's office in San Francisco. "There is a Mr. Shortland on the phone for you, Your Excellency."

"Do you know what he wants?"

"He wouldn't give me any details."

"Why don't you have him speak to Monsignor Caprice or one of the others in the front office?"

"Mr. Shortland sounds very irate, and he insists in talking only to you, Archbishop."

Archbishop Costello punched the flashing button on his telephone console, "Yes, this is the Archbishop."

"I have a very important matter to discuss with you, Archbishop Costello. It has to do with one of your priests, and I must meet with you personally very soon."

"Can you tell me the nature of your call?"

"No, it is something that can only be done in a private interview. Otherwise there will be serious trouble for the archdiocese."

Alarms went off in Archbishop's mind. "I can see you in a 15-minute period tomorrow morning at eleven-thirty here at the Chancery Office."

"I'll be there," Shortland replied and hung up.

The next morning at eleven-fifteen, Philip Shortland was waiting in the reception area on the administration floor of the Chancery. At eleven-thirty, he was ushered into the Archbishop's office.

"Good morning, Mr. Shortland."

"Good morning, Archbishop," the visitor, a short stocky man, said as he settled himself in the chair across the desk from the prelate.

"I want to get right to the point." The man was obviously highly agitated, red-faced and on the outer edge of self control.

"I have a 17-year-old daughter, Amber, who attends one of your high schools, Queen of Angels. She has just informed my wife and me that she has been raped by one of your priests, a Father Tyler Stone."

Archbishops are accustomed to crisis, but this was staggering. His heart sank. His sadness went out for the young girl, imagining the trauma she must have endured, and with concern for Tyler, whom he knew and admired.

"Mr. Shortland, I am very grieved to hear this report. Can I ask you if you are reasonably sure about the charge?"

"I certainly believe my daughter. She has always been very honest with us. I want something done about this immediately."

"You can be sure that I will act on this immediately. I will call in Father Stone at once and tell him about the accusation. If I may have your phone number and address, you can be sure that I'll get back to you without delay."

"I want something done on this immediately," Shortland repeated.

The Archbishop rose from behind his desk, came around and placed his arms around the shoulders of the visibly shaken father as the two moved to the door.

"I am very, very sorry. We will want to help your daughter and your family in any way we can."

When Shortland had left the office, Archbishop Costello rang his secretary, "I want Father Tyler Stone to come in to see me at the first opening I have in my schedule."

The secretary scanned the desk calendar in front of her and said, "You could see him tomorrow morning at nine."

"That will be fine. Please get him on the line for me."

The intercom buzzed in Tyler's office, "The Archbishop is one the line for you, Father."

This was unusual, the Archbishop calling directly to one of the priests.

"This is Tyler Stone, Archbishop."

"Good afternoon, Father. I would like you to come in to see me at the Chancery as soon as is convenient for you. If possible, I would like to see you at nine in the morning."

"That will be fine, Your Excellency."

Tyler was about to ask if the Archbishop could tell him the purpose of the visit; but he thought better of that since the Archbishop had not volunteered the information.

The Archbishop rang off without further word, and Tyler began to run through the possibilities of what the Archbishop had in mind. Could it be that he was to be given a new assignment? He hoped not. He had not been at All Saints very long, and was very happy there. Could it be that some parishioner called in a complaint to the Chancery about him? Perhaps it was to discuss the details of the expansion to the parish hall, which Tyler was contemplating. But the Archbishop wouldn't personally put through a call on a matter like that. Tyler would simply have to wait 'till the morning.

. . .

The following day, the Archbishop, as he had promised, put in a call to Mr. Shortland. There was no answer at the Shortland residence, so he directed a second call to the office phone numbers which appeared on the business card that Amber's father had left him. "Carter Industries," a voice on the other end of the line responded.

"Could I speak to Mr. Shortland, please?"

"Could I ask who is calling?"

"This is Archbishop Costello."

"Just a moment. I will give you Mr. Shortland's secretary."

After a few moments, a second voice came on the line, "Is this Archbishop Costello?"

"It is."

"If you called, Archbishop, I was directed to refer you to Mr. Shortland's attorney, Stephen West. Do you have a piece of paper and a pencil? I will give you Mr. West's address and phone number."

The Archbishop took down the numbers given, thanked the secretary and hung up the phone.

So it has come to this, the Archbishop thought.

He immediately dialed Robert Campbell, the diocesan attorney, and gave him the story as it had developed thus far. "Bob, the matter is now partly in your hands. Please be sure to keep me apprised every day on developments. In the meantime, I have called Father Stone. I know that you will want to talk to Father also about his side of the story. I would like you to be here tomorrow morning at nine, the time he is scheduled to come to my office. There will be some questions that you will want to ask. And we must keep in communication with the Shortland family to help their daughter in any way she needs help."

. . .

Tyler slept uneasily that night. He racked his brain to think what the reason could be for the special meeting. He was up to date on paying diocesan parish assessments. Except for a rather generous sized checking account, he had deposited All Saints savings in the Chancery, as diocesan regulations required.

At 8:50 a.m. sharp, Tyler pulled his car into one of the visitor spaces in the Chancery parking lot. He took the elevator to fourth floor administration and announced himself to the receptionist. After a five minute wait in the lobby outside the Archbishop's office, Tyler was invited in.

Archbishop Costello rose from his desk chair as the priest entered, shook his hand and motioned him to a chair across the smoked-glass-top desk of the prelate. Archbishop Costello was a clean desk man. The surface carried only a pen in its onyx holder and an instrument which served both as a telephone and intercom. To the Archbishop's right was a side table with in-and-out boxes equally filled with correspondence - and along side a dictating machine.

"Good morning, Archbishop."

"Good morning, Father Stone."

Very formal, Tyler thought. "Father Stone", not "Tyler". Normally the prelate made it a point in one-on-one conversations to address his priests by their first names. This must be something serious. The Archbishop confirmed that suspicion with his next words.

"I want to talk to you about a grave matter that has come to my attention. A gentleman was here to see me yesterday, who made the charge that you have had a sexual relationship with his daughter."

The words sounded to Tyler as though they were coming from a far distance. He was thunderstruck. He wanted to speak, but he couldn't form words. He could feel his heart pounding, his face flushed and his mouth suddenly dry.

To fill in the embarrassing pause, the Archbishop said:

"Before I can do anything about this, of course, I have to hear what you have to say."

"Who is this? I can't believe what I'm hearing," Tyler asked.

"The girl is a minor. She is from one of our high schools, Queen of Angels."

The Archbishop was studying Tyler's reactions.

Tyler asked, "Who is she? What is her name?"

"Her name is Amber Shortland. Do you have anything to do with that high school?

"Yes, I teach a religion class to the seniors once a week."

"Do you know this Amber Shortland?"

"Yes, I know who she is."

The Archbishop let Tyler continue, but there was silence. After an agonizing moment, Archbishop Cotello asked the difficult question, "What do you have to say to this accusation?"

"I don't know what to say. I haven't done anything like that."

"You mean you're saying that you've done nothing improper with this girl?"

"No, I have not, Archbishop."

"What do you think would cause her to make a charge like this?"

There was another prolonged silence. The Archbishop wanted to believe his priest. "I have not talked to anyone else about this. Would you have any objection if I called in Mr. Campbell, the diocesan attorney? I have asked him to stand by. He may have some more questions."

"That will be all right," Tyler mumbled.

The Archbishop signaled the front desk to send Campbell to his office. In the intervening time, the Archbishop said, "Amber Shortland's father has turned the matter over to an attorney. That is why it is important for us to work through our own legal representative."

Robert Campbell, a tall, soft-spoken man in his mid-50's, was just down the hall. In a moment he entered the office, took a chair next to Tyler, who shook the attorney's offered hand in a state of confusion. When introductions were completed, the Archbishop backgrounded the lawyer on the facts that had so far developed.

"Mr. Campbell, I have explained to Father the charge that has been leveled. You may want to ask some questions."

The attorney faced Tyler and asked, "Do you teach at Queen of Angels High School?"

"Yes, I do . . . one class a week to the seniors."

"And do you know this Amber Shortland?"

"Yes, I know who she is."

"The accusation Miss Shortland is making is, of course, very serious, especially since she is a minor. Have you given the Archbishop a response to the charge?"

"I don't know what to say. I have never done anything like that."

"Can you think of any reason why the Shortland girl would make up such a story?"

"No, I can't."

"Could it be that you've given her a grade that she objected to? Any scolding in class?"

"No, I can't think of anything."

Campbell paused for a few moments to see if Tyler wanted to add anything. But he had nothing to say.

"Have you ever been alone with Amber Shortland?"

"No."

Campbell was asking questions like a lawyer, and Tyler began to feel he was on a witness stand.

"If we asked other students in the class about you or about any relationship between you and Amber, would they give us the same answers?"

"I would think so. I hardly know her."

The attorney, as the Archbishop had done earlier, allowed a period of silence to see if the priest wanted to think things through and talk further, but Tyler said nothing.

"You know, Father, in a situation like this the best thing for everyone concerned is to come out with the whole truth right from the start. You realize that there is an attorney-client privilege of confidentiality between you and me, and a priest-penitent privilege of confidentiality between you and the Archbishop. So whatever you say here is not subject to discovery."

There was silence again, and then Tyler said, "I don't know what to say. I didn't do anything like this."

The attorney waited again to see if there would be anything more forthcoming. After this pause, Campbell said, "I wonder, Your Excellency, if we could have Father Stone step outside for a few moments?"

"Tyler, would you wait in the next office? We'll call you back."

When Tyler had left the room, the Archbishop said, "What do you make of all this?"

"It's hard to tell. He appeared to be genuinely surprised. His answers seem to be sincere. However, typically in cases like this, there is initial denial. I would give him overnight to think the whole matter through. He may add to this story or have another story tomorrow."

"Well, I guess there's nothing more we can do right now, Bob, except I would like you to get in touch with the Shortland family to see if there is anything we can do to be of assistance to them and to their daughter."

"I'll see that that's done, Archbishop."

"Would you ask Father Stone to come back in for a moment?"

As Tyler re-entered the room, the Archbishop said, "I think that's about all we can discuss at the moment, Father. It is probably best for you to return to the rectory now and either I or Mr. Campbell will keep in touch with you."

Campbell added, "It is advisable for you to say nothing about this matter to anyone for the present in view of possible future litigation. Everything we have discussed here is privileged. None of it is discoverable in law.

"Also you should take a leave from ministry until we can get this matter cleared."

"Father," the Archbishop said, "you can go now. I know this has been a difficult time for you. I will be in touch with you very soon. Remember, you should not talk to anyone about this subject." Then, turning to Campbell, "It occurs to me that Father will feel a need to talk to someone. Isn't it possible for him to share this with a confessor or spiritual director?"

"Yes, that's permissible, but I would limit it to that."

Tyler, still flushed with heart pounding, backed out of the room, muttering his good-byes.

He wanted to talk to someone. He wanted to unburden himself to anyone who would be sympathetic, but he remembered the attorney's admonition.

He left by the back elevator or the Chancery, hoping he would run into nobody he knew. He drove back to All Saints or, rather, it was as though his car drove itself back. He was, for all intents and purposes, barely conscious of the traffic.

Tyler was drowned in shame. He didn't want to talk to his confessor . . . Now he didn't want to talk to David or anyone. He just hoped that it was all a dream and that it would suddenly go away.

. . .

That same morning, at his law offices, Stephen West interviewed Amber Shortland. "I have to get certain information from you, Amber. For the record, would you tell me just exactly what happened on the day you say Father Stone assaulted you?"

Amber was noticeably uncomfortable. "Father Stone handed back our homework papers and, on the top of mine, he had written that he wanted to see me after class."

"And did you stay after class?"

"Yes, I did."

"Where there any other students in the room?"

"No, they had all left."

"Were the classroom doors closed?"

"Yes, I think they were both closed."

"What did Father say to you?"

"He said that he wanted to discuss with me some questions about the Faith that I had asked in my homework paper. They were questions about Church marriage regulations and about the sacrament of confession."

"And did he answer your questions?"

"He started to, but then after a while he began to say he was sorry I was having doubts about the Faith, and he wanted to console me."

West waited for Amber to go on.

"He put his arm around my shoulder. He touched me, he fondled me."

Tears welling up in Amber's eyes, "And then he raped me."

"It is painful for me to ask you this question, Amber, but I must. Do you think you did anything to encourage the priest to do these things?"

"No, I tried to resist, but he was too strong for me. He forced me."

"All right, Amber, that is enough for today. I know it is difficult. I am very sorry this happened. You can be sure that we will do everything we can to be of help to you and your family."

When Amber was gone, Stephen West dictated a detailed summary from the notes that he had taken on a desk pad during the interview.

Eventually a trial date would be set for the end of March.

CHAPTER 58

Father Ronald Osborne of the Fairview diocese attended an Encounter program. He shared intimately with the other participants and had been profoundly affected.

During these sessions, those attending tell their deepest hurts -- hurts inflicted by a parishioner, one's father, a bishop; for Osborne it was a seminary professor, years ago -- a hurt that had never healed.

Now, in this sharing, he had finally identified the pain and had forgiven the one who had hurt him.

One of the tasks that the priests on these renewal weeks are asked to do when they return home is to write a letter to their bishop.

Ronald Osborne wrote to David:

"Dear Bishop:

I apologize to you and ask your forgiveness for the times I have criticized you. When you first came to the diocese, you started forming all these committees. I didn't think they were necessary and said so to my priest friends. I haven't agreed with some of the diocesan appointments that you have made, and said so.

I pledge to you, my bishop, that from now on I will not criticize you or my brother priests. If I should be in company where such criticism takes place, I will do my best to change the subject.

I want to tell you that I love you and from now on I will do my best for you."

After Ronald Osborne was back in the parish, at all the weekend Masses, in a homily, he told the people he was sorry for the way he had treated them.

"The distance I have kept separate from you; the anger and harsh words. I ask your forgiveness."

Toward the end of Mass, he knelt in the sanctuary. Young children came forward and anointed his forehead as a sign of the people forgiving him.

There were tears in the congregation.

People approached Ronald in front of the church after Mass, who had never spoken to him before.

. . .

David's ministry in the Diocese of Fairview was going well. He had a warm relationship with the clergy, as he had with Father Osborne, with the Religious Sisters and Brothers, as well as the people. But now and then projects that he tried and episodes which inevitably occurred in a busy, growing diocese, troubled the waters.

Two controversial episodes happened quickly when David tried to bring the various Faiths in the community together.

. . .

The first of these occurred when Monsignor Christopher Wright proposed to David that, as a gesture of interfaith cooperation, the diocese invite Protestant and Orthodox bishops in the locality to a joint baptism at the Cathedral of the Holy Spirit on Pentecost Sunday.

The idea was enthusiastically received by the Lutherans, Episcopalians and Greek Orthodox.

Planning began.

Word of the proposed event spread rapidly. Laity who spoke to David about the matter warmly endorsed it.

Still, a number of priests expressed concern. Would this ecumenical ritual give the impression that all baptisms are valid, that one religion is as good as another?

Bishop Paul Malloy from the Midwest wrote to David about the matter. "I have heard of your intention of having a joint baptism with other Christian faiths. This would seem to me to be very unwise and give the wrong impression to our Catholic people. Please reconsider the proposal." By that time preparations had advanced too far to reverse the plan.

As the day drew near, David decided that it would be advisable to make a public announcement, giving the reasons for the ceremony.

Questions were now coming from the media, and David would use the following statement to respond.

"The 'Ecumenical Celebration of the Sacrament of Baptism' will be a symbolic event celebrating the unity that exists in the four traditions through this Sacrament which they share. It is not intended that it will start a new form of practice or create a different concept of the Sacrament which we each have, or lead to interfaith baptisms. It is to be a single event recognizing that 'Baptism . . . constitutes the sacramental bond of unity existing among all who through it are reborn,' and that its grace strengthens our common Christian way of life. (Vatican II Decree on Ecumenism 22,23).

Special care is being given in the ceremony to emphasize that, while all share the grace of Baptism, we are separated by historic divisions that occurred both in the east and the west. It has been said that in spite of the differences that exist in varying degrees among us, 'it remains true that all who have been justified by faith in Baptism are incorporated into Christ.' (Vatican II Decree on Ecumenism 3). To illustrate the point, the four Bishops will jointly assist at a coordinated ceremony celebrating this, our common heritage of faith. However, when the Sacrament of Baptism is administered, each Bishop will separately baptize an infant of his own congregation, using the form that is proper to his Church. That Baptism administered with water in the name of the Father, the Son and the Holy Spirit is common to all.

Thus the Pentecostal celebration of Baptism is a fitting and appropriate expression of the degree of unity that has evolved over these many years of witness to the heritage we all enjoy. At the same time, it recognizes the differences that still exist and, while respecting the variety of backgrounds and customs, it is a step that will encourage deeper study and more fervent prayer that the complete unity, for which Our Lord prayed, will one day be realized."

On Pentecost Sunday, David hosted his counterparts in northern California, Bishop Arthur Maxwell, Episcopalian; Bishop Carl Hanson, Lutheran; and Bishop Anthony Nicholas, Greek Orthodox; at Holy Spirit Cathedral.

With respective parents and godparents standing by, in succession each prelate baptized a child into its own denomination. The rite was received warmly by the faithful who thronged the Cathedral.

The following morning's newspaper carried a front page photo of Orthodox Nicholas totally immersing a smiling naked infant, Alexandra, into the slightly warmed waters of the baptismal font.

. . .

The second unsettling occurrence involved a similar interfaith event and could be construed as still another intrusion into politics.

Representative clergy formed a long colorful line outside Holy Spirit Cathedral awaiting the prayer service for the newly elected pro-choice Governor of California.

As the procession began, loud voices broke out inside near the sanctuary. The sounds of a scuffle followed and then security officers carried a young man by shoulders and ankles from the congregation down the aisle and out the heavy main entrance doors.

The interfaith service proceeded.

As host bishop, David was invited to give the opening address to the new California Chief Executive.

"Governor, may I propose an examination of conscience. I do not stand in judgment of you. As bishop, I must constantly make my own examination of conscience.

"Do you find your life preoccupied with the following anxieties? Do you find yourself asking these questions:

"Will the tough stand I took in favor of immigration end my career? Am I losing ground in the Opinion Polls? Is that young popular mayor in Southern California planning to run for Governor?

"Is my life a life of meetings and mountains of reports and bills I will never have time to read?

"As a public official, do I find myself forever in receptions, surveying the room with my eyes to see who the important people present? Do I feel a relentless pressure to say 'hello' to the right people at dinners, shake the right hands, be within camera and microphone range when the media are present? Am I troubled about my family, the inevitable strains in relationship with my spouse, the distance that could develop between my children and me?

"But remember, Governor, there are joys also in your profession. Some of them are simple, forgivable human joys, such as being recognized in public.

"Some are deeper satisfactions - proposing difficult, unpopular legislation because you really know it was right; helping a voiceless constituent who interrupted your schedule, but who genuinely deserved your help; the joys of a loyal staff; life-time friendships made in the halls of government.

"In your examination of conscience, you might ask yourself: Will I have the patience and good sense in cabinet meetings to listen as well as to speak? Do I look upon my political colleagues as an opportunity to share ideas and not simply to air my own?

"If I have the label of 'conservative,' will I have the tolerance at least to study wholesome changes and the desperate social needs that are sweeping society? If the public thinks of me as a 'liberal,' am I sensitive to what are valuable traditional structures and frugal government? If I am known as a 'moderate,' do I confuse moderation with lethargy or cowardice?

"Am I mindful that it is the function of government to be compassionate for those who cannot help themselves, whether on Spring Street in Los Angeles, the Tenderloin in San Francisco, or the Crown Street Mall in Fairview.

"May I have the common sense to recognize that goodness and truth - and not re-election - are the priorities of the farsighted.

"As bishop, I do not know the complexities of market economy or supply side economics. I do not presume to speak on the specifics of government budgets.

"Nevertheless, I propose Ten Commandments:

The First Commandment:

The people are the ones you serve. Thou shalt not have false gods before them that is the gods of powerful lobbies and campaign contributors.

The Second Commandment:

Thou shalt not take the name of welfare recipients in vain.

The Third Commandment:

Remember to keep holy the state budget deadline day, June 15th, each year.

The Fourth Commandment:

Honor your election campaign promises.

The Fifth Commandment:

Thou shalt not kill the credibility of incumbent office holders.

The Sixth Commandment:

Thou shalt not commit a form of adultery in violating the solemn vows you have made to the people of this state.

The Seventh Commandment:

Thou shalt not steal from Aid to Families with Dependent Children, the unemployed, children at risk, newly arrived immigrants.

The Eighth Commandment:

Thou shalt not bear false witness against the opposite political party.

The Ninth Commandment:

At the expense of the weak and the voiceless, thou shalt not covet popularity or re-election.

The Tenth Commandment:

At the expense of budget justice, thou shalt not covet election to higher political office.

"And I propose Seven Political Beatitudes:

Blessed are the Poor in Spirit, theirs is the Kingdom of Heaven.

Blessed are you who insist that the government live within its means - you will have a budget completed by deadline.

Blessed are you who cut the fat out of the budget, but not the lean sinew and bone of the poor.

Blessed are you who are disciplined by your Party for following your convictions, rather than Party lines, you will overcome.

Blessed are you who mourn now because you are criticized by the powerful interests, you will be comforted by your conscience.

Blessed are you who hunger and thirst for the sake of the impoverished, those not likely to go to the polls on election day, for you will have self-esteem.

Blessed are you who 'live simply, so that others may simply live.'

"May the Good Lord, who is clothed in purple robes with planets in His care, never let you be carried away with your own importance.

"Take hope, Governor, the 'current' crisis of confidence in government is not current at all, but as old as government itself. There are times when we mortals lack confidence even in God's government.

"At the end of your career, history will not judge you on the number of terms you served, but by the quality of those terms.

"At the end of your career, may you be known not simply as a politician, but as a statesman."

. . .

As the clergy left the church in the recessional, they were met at the outside plaza by several dozen shouting pro-life protestors. David left the recessional and walked through the anti-abortion signs, past the baby doll nailed to a cross, to the leaders of the protest.

"I am with you," he said to the angry faces.

"You are not with us. You are a traitor."

"I am against abortion. I stand with you."

"You are a liar."

"Let's say a prayer together," David said.

"We will not pray with you."

One young protestor held out his hand to David.

"C'mon, we can pray with the bishop."

David grabbed another hand and began: "Our Father, who art in heaven . . ."

A protestor's voice from behind interrupted: "Why don't you say a Catholic prayer like the Hail Mary?"

As they finished the Lord's Prayer, David noticed the police patrol wagon at the edge of the plaza by the rectory.

He realized then that some of the protestors evicted from the cathedral had been arrested.

David hurried over and began to speak to the faces peering out through the wagon's back door window bars.

"I'm sorry this has happened," he said.

"Get out of here. You are one of them."

"I will try to help you."

"You're an abortionist. We don't want your help."

David turned and walked toward the rectory.

CHAPTER 59

Philip Shortland insisted on pressing criminal charges. His daughter Amber would not change her story and Tyler persisted in his claim of innocence. The District Attorney's office entered the process.

For the next several weeks, Tyler's life was caught up in a whirl of interviews, depositions, hearings and subpoenas. Grand jury indictments, the search for corroboration of evidence, physical examination of the alleged victim - these were all new to him. It was as if he were living in a foreign country.

In his first interview with which, at his attorney's direction he complied, Tyler repeated his contention that he had never been alone with the Shortland girl. In a second interview, he recalled the after school session alone with her in the classroom.

To Tyler, it seemed as if people in litigation were swept up into the lawyer's game. Attorneys had their own language - a legalese that mystified all non-professionals. One felt totally in their control. It was their game. People accused. People sued. People were accused. People were sued. Acquittals. Convictions. Financial settlements. Incarcerations.

In the rush of litigation, psychologists enter with their own expertise and their own technical language which mystifies all non-professionals - medicalese. They have woven a web of neurosis, psychosis, repressions, recalled memories. And all the while the persons involved in the litigation, hardly comprehending, are hurried along to life-affecting resolutions.

Tyler hoped that the clergy of the Church were not guilty of the same thing, drawing people into the web of their own technical terminologies.

Did the Church catch the faithful in the clutches of "mortal and venial," "divine law and natural law," "actual and sanctifying," "de fide" and "ex cathedra"? Did the Church have its own ecclesial-ese, punishments and sanctions, totally perplexing to the non-ordained?

. . .

Tyler's trial began March 28th.

An assistant district attorney, Harry Wembley, was assigned to the case and gave the opening statement to the jury, a panel of five women and seven men.

"We intend to show," Wembley began, "that this is a clear instance of a crime that happens all too often in our society. Amber Shortland is a young girl, barely seventeen, who has been sexually molested, yes, raped by an adult male. I know that you will not allow the special vocation of the defendant to deflect you from the heinousness of this crime.

"Since the defense has questioned Miss Shortland's credibility, we intend to establish by our witnesses that this young girl has no reason to fabricate the accusation she has made. She has described the abhorrent act forthrightly, and classmates and others will testify to Amber's veracity."

The defense's opening statement was similarly brief.

Robert Campbell faced the jurors, explaining how the defense proposed to demonstrate that there was no evidence whatever of this alleged crime, that the defendant was characterized by all who knew him as a man of exceptionally high morals and exemplary conduct, that the charges could have risen only out of misplaced spite and retaliation.

Testimony got underway as Wembley called four schoolmates to the witness stand to testify to the good character of Amber Shortland. The fourth witness, Marjorie Kearney, a senior classmate, stated, "In all the years I have known Amber, I have never heard her tell a lie. She is not the spiteful kind that would want to hurt Father Stone just out of maliciousness."

At length, Wembley called Amber to the witness stand.

His approach was gentle. "I know it is terribly unpleasant for you to do this, but I want you to tell the men and women in the jury what happened to you in the classroom after school on the day in question."

Amber recounted the sequence of events as she had detailed them before to her attorney, Stephen West, and in a later deposition.

Toward the end of her testimony, she was trembling and tearful, and the spectators in the courtroom could barely make out her words. But they could hear enough and observe her emotion to be genuinely impressed. It was obvious that the jurors were deeply moved.

Amber's voice trailed off at this moment of impact.

Wembley turned away from the witness and said quietly, "No other questions, Your Honor."

Campbell knew it would serve no good purpose for the defense to cross-examine. Judge Henry Orosco excused Amber from the witness stand.

. . .

Robert Campbell's plan of defense was an indirect one. He wanted to paint a picture for the jurors how unlikely it was for this priest, Tyler Stone, to commit a rape, given the background of his Church's deep convictions about human sexuality.

Campbell called as the defense's first witness, Father Ladd Franklin.

After the preliminaries of swearing in, name and occupation, Campbell asked:

"Father Franklin, are you familiar with the defendant?"

"I am. I have known him since we were thirteen years old, attended boarding school with him for eleven years and have served with him in ministry since that time."

Campbell: "This trial has to do with an accusation of sexual molestation. Could you give us in some detail the context of the Church's and Father Stone's position on human sexuality?"

"To start with," Ladd began, "I think we have to understand that many things conspire to make human sexuality an unnecessarily complex and totally confused element in the American society. Sexuality is simply a part of nature. Historically, world religions including Judeo-Christian teaching introduced a structured control of genital activity. Although, at times, burdensome and irksome, this moral control has benefited the human race for the most part, limiting excessive and destructive appetites."

Campbell wasn't too sure where his witness was going.

"In the course of time, however," Ladd continued, "this teaching on sexuality can slip into puritanical forms such as Jansenism. Then human sexuality becomes a hyper-sensitive subject. Taboos set in. Secretiveness sets in. All this serves to heighten interest and to whet sexual appetites. Repression and denial intensify desire. Sexuality loses its natural, unpressurized condition.

"In our own American society, young people growing up in this secretive, highly explosive climate of sex, can be traumatized by the subject. At the same time, all around them the media and advertising titillate and tease with suggestiveness, capitalizing on the mystery of the subject.

"On the one hand, our culture glamorizes and promotes casual genitality, but, on the other hand, our culture recoils if casual sexuality is pursued. All around us, society revels in the portrayal of illicit sex, but then society is shocked and brings harsh laws and punishments into play if illicit sexuality is practiced.

"In this turbulent, totally illogical climate, legal systems, attorneys, psychologists, counselors find a fertile field. Likewise, the media feast on the transgressions. In the end, all our society is in turmoil. And all this turbulence swirls about a subject that should be a simple, uncomplicated, radiant part of nature.

"Christianity has tried to make sense out of this situation with its teaching about Original Sin. As a result of the misdeeds of our first parents, our human nature is in a generally disordered state, including a disordered condition of sexuality. According to this teaching, our intellects are clouded, our wills are weakened and our human appetites have become unnatural and difficult to control. Many scholars question the concept of Original Sin now.

"If we do not posit some such premise as Original Sin, we can only conclude that on our own we have allowed elements in our society to complicate and muddle the whole matter of human sex so that it causes much more anguish than it ever should have.

"I think some young people who are brought up with strong traditional Catholic convictions about sin and sex, about turning away from sexual thoughts without sexual release, end up being persons who are in constant fever pitch of desire. Psychologically, it is as though they are constantly in that highly charged, loin churning condition just before orgasm.

"Because of their abstinence, that intensity which occurs momentarily in most men just before sexual release is, for the conscientiously sensitive, an ongoing state of mind. This makes temptation for them overpowering and ever present."

"Objection, Your Honor, I fail to see how these theological ramblings have any relevance to the case," Wembley complained from the prosecution table.

Realizing that such a line of testimony was questionable in this criminal case, Judge Orosco turned toward Campbell: "Counselor, can you tell us where you are going with all this?"

"We are simply trying to establish for the jury the attitude or mind-set Father Tyler Stone has in his approach to sexuality."

"You may proceed, but keep the testimony to the point."

In a pre-trial conference with the clergy witnesses, Attorney Campbell had decided that it would be advisable to level totally with the jurors in letting them know the context in which celibate priests, denied sexual release, can be helped to control their sexual drive -- a basic human drive, second only to the human drive to survive.

This trial rested on one element - credibility. The jury's decision would be made on which of the two, accuser or accused, seemed to be more honest. Campbell would lead his witnesses to be totally candid about their personal lives.

Ladd resumed his testimony: "I used to ask my teachers in the seminary - and I still ask my confessor from time to time - why is it a person in genital activity can feel so good, so happy, so close to someone if all this is bad.

"My classmates used to badger me about being Italian. It has been a long-standing joke about Italians that even though they may have been away from the sacrament of penance for many years, some begin their confessions with the words: 'I don't do nothing wrong. I don't hurt no one.'

"I used to laugh at that myself. But now I think, maybe, the Italians had it right. If they really didn't hurt anybody, they didn't do anything wrong.

"But this accusation which is being made against Father Stone - rape is a horrendous crime. It forcibly hurts a person in the extreme. And I know Father Stone. This kind of act goes against everything he is or believes in.

"Every kind of sexual activity also goes against the promise of chastity which a priest makes; that is an added dimension. Any deliberate genital act would violate his promise of chastity. It is a matter of integrity. And Tyler I know to be a man of his word."

Campbell: "No further questions, Your Honor."

The prosecutor, Wembley, was lost in Ladd's philosophizing. "No cross examination."

"Your Honor, I have asked Bishop David Carmichael to come from Fairview to be our next witness."

When David had been sworn in, Campbell asked the same question he had asked Ladd about how well he knew Tyler, and David's answer was the same as Ladd's.

"Bishop, could you tell us how you think Father Stone would react to sexual temptation - how likely or unlikely it would be that he would commit a violent sexual act?"

The prosecuting attorney objected again, but was overruled.

"Younger generations of priests may not have the same difficulties that Father Stone and the rest of us of an earlier generation might have in our relationship with women." David continued, "We have had to adjust a little on this, having been brought up in the 'solus cum sola' period. That is, we were not, as clerics, to be at anytime alone with a woman. That meant normally not having the Sacrament of Confession for a woman any place but in the confessional, not giving counseling without the office door ajar, never riding alone in a car with a woman. If you had to drive your mother somewhere, you asked her to sit in the back seat.

"I think there was some healthy aspects to the teaching going on at that time. We grew up with a reverence and respect for women. I do not think we were frightened of women or awkward in their presence. The relationship that a priest should have with a woman was quite clear in our minds, and it was not filled with anxiety or tensions.

"But we had a good deal to learn in some social relationships with women. I believe the younger generation is better at this now. Authentic relationships important for growth are interactions with women in ways that are responsible and appreciative, whether it be a mother, blood sister, a Religious, a relative, staff members, parishioner or friend.

"'Numquam solus cum sola' - never alone with one woman - was too mechanical. The idea must be changed into 'be sensible, be caring, be a realist.' In that way, our relationships with women will not be stunted, not romanticized, not neurotic, not wrongfully intimate.

"'It is not good for men to be alone' does not refer only to marriage. The paradox is that we priests who have been taught to love everyone, in reality, can find ourselves without an authentic friend.

"We know that we have to accept an existential loneliness. It is part of Christian belief that loneliness will persist until we are finally united with the Object of all our yearnings, God."

The prosecuting attorney saw that the attention of the jury had been caught by the candidness of the witness. Wembley moved from his chair on two occasions to retrieve a binder from a briefcase and to get a drink of water, but, in reality, to distract the jurors.

"From what you know of Father Stone," Campbell continued, "would you judge he suffers from excessive loneliness?"

David continued, "The saddest words you can ever hear a child say are the words: 'I have no one to play with.' Loneliness occurs at any age. I recall when Tyler was a ninth grader at Regina Cleri College Seminary, he had a room on the fourth floor. Sometimes at night, he told me, he would look out the window and, in the distance, he could see the headlights of the cars moving along the Bayshore Freeway between Sunnyvale and Mountain View. And he would think, as he saw those cars, those people are going home or coming from home, and he would be homesick.

"This need for emotional relatedness can become even more acute in later years when we no longer get so absorbed in the doing of things which helps drown out loneliness.

"When the sexual revolution came in the '60s and when psychiatrists began telling priests that they had been retarded in their psychosexual growth, I think some of the priests, in an attempt to correct the situation, went about it clumsily. In trying to adjust their relationships with women, they were like awkward adolescents. Some over-compensated and they made mistakes.

"This is the milieu of Catholic clergy that Father Stone has lived with.

"But knowing his intelligence, his conscientiousness and his self-discipline, he is one of the last persons I can think of who could commit an act of rape."

Bishop Carmichael was excused from the witness stand, again with no cross-examination.

. . .

Campbell had been ambivalent at first, but eventually coming to know his client better, decided to allow Tyler to testify. The defense advisors argued against this strategy.

Campbell knew the line of questioning was precarious, but he took the chance.

"Father Stone, do you think you have matured psychosexually?"

"I do not think I ever really adverted to sexual tensions systematically or scientifically. To be sure, there have been many battles and many wars. But I do not think I ever had a real battle plan or strategy. I just experienced the temptations and tried to deal with them, sometimes successfully and sometimes unsuccessfully, as they arose. I do not know that I ever did mature in this matter. Does anyone ever feel he has become satisfactorily adjusted in sexuality or genitality? If you are raised in a tradition of the teaching on original sin, you probably figure that there will always be need for more maturing and more growth. All of this is the result of `the clouding of the intellect and a weakening of the will', and the intense drives which we formerly knew as concupiscence.

"Rectory living also must be reviewed as to its effect on growth and maturity in the priest. If priests were obliged to live as lay people do, being on their own, obliged to take care of the many necessary daily temporalities which lay people must attend to, this might stimulate maturity in priests. There would, however, be many disadvantages for clergy in not having the growth that comes from the give-and-take of community rectory life.

"If there were optional celibacy, there would probably be relief from some of the stress that now exists. However, married life in the clergy, we know, would bring many new tensions. Clergy of other Faiths attest to this. Greely and Kennedy studies indicate no significant differences in sexual maturity between general male population and celibate clergy."

Tyler had anguished over these thoughts frequently and now the words brimmed over and poured from his lips.

"The hierarchical system of the Catholic Church probably has its effect on the growth of priests. It is important for the clergy to have a well adjusted attitude toward authority, an attitude that does not feed on resentment and, at the same time, is not abject or obsequious in its relation to authority. Inter-dependence, self-dependence, and self-control are important to maturation.

"If I am to share my personal feelings in these matters, it would be helpful to you to know such things as my Myers-Briggs profile. I am an ISFJ.

> I - A shade on the introvert side.
> S - Sensate: I go on what I observe - not intuitive.
> F - Feel - rather than think.
> J - Judge; I want closure - I do not like ambiguity.

"I have never been measured, but probably I am Type A: I try to do several things at once. I dictate letters while driving my car. I even floss my teeth while driving my car -- sometimes all three at the same time.

"Whatever sex information I received, I picked up from friends, and rather slowly because I was in a Catholic elementary school environment with a general reluctance to deal with the subject.

"Family influence is most critical. But my single-parent mother never spoke to me about sexual matters.

"I was not born on a farm and, although I was born in a city, I did not really grow up on downtown city streets, which environment might have made me more knowledgeable.

"I recall youthful fantasies about a beautiful teenage girl up the block. I know I had a crush on Carole Landis and Elisa Landi when I saw them in movies at the Congress Theater in Tucson.

"Catholic elementary school - no sexual education that I can remember, except the Sister principal warning the girls in our eighth grade class to stay away from carnival workers when the Foley and Burke Carnival was in town.

"I do not really remember any seminary instruction about sexuality, except 'there is no parvity of matter in sexual sins. Everything is grave. Everything is mortal.'

"Seminary professors probably followed the principle: The less we talk about sex, the less the seminarians will think about the subject.

"At this late date, I do not recall my thoughts about sexuality at puberty or adolescence.

"Seminary training -- and for me it began at the time of puberty - offers few opportunities for social contacts with girls. This is a formative period in life. Seminary instruction, as I remember it, had good emphasis on Christian moral codes about sexuality and genitality, but very little physiological or psychological instruction."

Judge Orosco called for an end to the day's proceedings. "We will be in session at 9 o'clock tomorrow morning."

Campbell welcomed the break. He would interrupt Tyler's testimony and call Forrest Winkler, psychiatrist, as his first witness in the morning.

CHAPTER 60

The defense psychiatrist was sworn in and, in answer to Campbell's questions, commented on Tyler's previous day description of his boyhood sexual education.

"Sexual awareness and growth in the early teen years could be fixed and frozen at adolescent level, unfortunately.

"It is generally agreed that the period of sexual awakeness is when we are 3 to 7 years of age; sexual fantasy and sexual preoccupation 13 to 16 years old; superficial sexual relating 16 to 20; and finally sexual integration.

"Among the manifestations of underdevelopment of a priest or any person, for that matter, is failure to achieve an integrated psychological identity. Sexuality is not integrated when we function at a pre-adolescent or adolescent level of psychosexual growth.

"Many celibates use strong psychological controls so that their public behavior will in no way stray out of bounds. These controls, however, drain away an inordinate amount of energy and time in one's life. To put it simply, sex takes more time and effort to handle and control and is productive of more anguish than it should in any adult life."

. . .

When Campbell resumed his questioning of Tyler, he attempted to establish a religious atmosphere. "What effect did Confession have on your growing up, Father Stone?"

"It probably depended a great deal on the adjustment or maladjustment of the confessor who counseled me. There was good spiritual direction in Confession, but not much in psychological growth, as I recall. I do remember this. As a seminarian, I would stop off in Phoenix on the way home from vacation to go to confession so I would not have to go to the parish priests at Santa Cruz in Tucson who knew me and my voice."

"Father, could you tell us something of how sexuality impacts your life more recently?"

"After teaching for awhile, I have been assigned as pastor of a parish which is very large. Because the ministry there began to consume more and more of my time, my biggest problem has been a growing feeling of isolation. I see classmates and priest friends less and less often. The net result is that I have been experiencing bouts of loneliness that seem almost adolescent - especially since they, at times, involve temptations to self abuse - which hasn't been a problem for years!

"The teenagers with whom I work possess a far greater casualness about the entire question of sexuality and sometimes seem much healthier for it, even though it is very clear that their overconfidence puts them in awkward situations at times, and even ruins a few lives. The ease with which young people live together before marriage is a real puzzle to me. On more and more occasions, I find myself on the defensive with the youth club officers and often hard pressed to come up with reasons that sound convincing. I'm not sure I'm convinced of them myself.

"It occurs to me that the New Testament didn't devote very many verses to the topic and it seemed to have other ethical priorities, and that is at least confusing, if not confirming, the general cultural context we see all around us.

"When I entered the priesthood, I knew what I was giving up and I felt O.K. about doing it. As a seminarian, we had little contact with girls, but the camaraderie of my classmates and the seminary structure made that seem normal. There were some clues along the way. I found myself fantasizing sexually from time to time; found myself making excuses to be near the girls' locker rooms at summer camp. As a young priest, I had experienced the goodness and attractiveness of many of the women with whom I had contact in parish projects, in the work for the grade school, some counseling and even in confession. But I'd never gotten involved with any of them. I'm not involved now. But something's different. I find myself wondering if I wish I were involved.

"I feel guilty about these things, but I guess I try not to think too deeply about it. I still seek out confessors who do not know me. And I rehearse ways to conceal what I really feel I should reveal to the confessor.

"I've even been tempted to slip into X-rated movies across town. And the erotic imaginings that come to me at night and increasingly at other times frighten me. Sometimes I am tempted to think it would be better if there were a real woman in the picture. I know that's wrong, but that, at least, might seem more normal - I keep fighting these thoughts."

Campbell became apprehensive. Honesty was the strategy, but this was stretching candidness to the extreme. Should he interrupt?

In the back of the courtroom, David was listening to Tyler's testimony carefully. He was deeply impressed. What Tyler was saying should be heard by all celibates. David resolved to see that Tyler's experience would be reported anonymously in a NCCB case study being prepared for publication, Human Sexuality and the Ordained Priesthood.

To his attorney's relief, Tyler moved to another point, Andrew Cusack's advice: "Having a good opinion of oneself, what the Early Christian Communities called 'the humility of self esteem' (the psychological words for the Theology of the human is made to God's image and likeness), is necessary for healthy adjustment of genitality. One who is constantly criticizing others has a low self-image and predictably has a genitality problem. The tongue that is a sword facilitates the drive of genitality. As priests, we are sexual to the extent we believe in ourselves. We are genital to the extent we do not believe in ourselves. To believe is to choose life; to not believe is to be 'driven' in life.

"If I finally manage that, I will get outside of myself and turn towards others. I will not be self-centered. I will be able to love someone, love others, thus have the foundation upon which God's love abides and flows outward. I will be vulnerable. I will love and be loved in return.

"Our lives as priests will, of necessity, be unsettled, tension-filled if we are not living according to the principles we believe in -- if we are living in the shadows. The latter creates a self centered consciousness; the former, a God consciousness."

Campbell: "What specifically do you do to safeguard your chastity?"

"To keep my life integrated with the principles I believe in, I need the help of a personal daily prayer life. I don't always follow this schedule, but I know it is what I should do.

"I try to live during the day in a spirit of prayer. Daily Mass with the people. Liturgy of the Hours and Scripture reading daily. Quiet time with God daily. Regular shared prayer with co-workers. Sacrament of Confession at least once a month. Visit with spiritual director at least every other month.

"I try to see celibacy as a positive and challenging commitment. If celibacy is creatively and positively lived, not 'tolerated' as a begrudging condition of ordination, celibacy can be understood without anxiety. Celibacy, that is, not enforced bachelorhood.

"Sex is, of course, a beautiful part of nature. Celibacy is simply meant to be a sign of total commitment. As priests, we see ourselves as fellow strugglers with the laity in trying to live up to Christian sexual ideals.

"There can be temptations to rationalize, to convince myself that I did not really understand the commitment I was making at ordination. Sometimes I am tempted to persuade myself that times have changed, that God does not want us to be diminishing our humanity, even that the Church is unenlightened and insensitive."

Campbell interjected, "Intellectually it is fairly easy to understand sexuality and celibacy, but a hard fact remains. In erotic moments, usually passion triumphs over knowledge. Chemistry overwhelms reason. No matter how psychologically adjusted you are, you will be tempted, simply because of the pleasure of genitality. What do you do when these sexual drives become strong in you?"

"I know what you are supposed to do," Tyler said. "Keep your sense of purpose and motivation strong. Keep your prayer life strong. Seek sound counseling and genuine friends. And avoid the occasions of sin - that is, stay away from the people, places, reading, videos and computer websites that you know attract you to have sex. Be particularly vigilant on vacation and days off. This is time-honored advice, but I think there is no other magic formula. Psychologists talk about co-dependence, but their advice coincides with the old fashioned advice.

"I must deal with the confusion and turmoil I am experiencing right now. Not in the sweetness and light of some of the resolutions I made in the first flush of early priesthood. Those realities were fine once, but now they are somewhere else.

"I cannot engage in genital activity, but I will neither be frightened by my sexuality or obsessed with it.

"God's way of loving is the only licensed teacher of human sexuality. God's passion created our passion. Our deep desiring is a relentless returning to that place where all things are one. If we are afraid of our sexuality - we are afraid of God.

"I remember Thomas Merton saying, 'We must make ready for the Christ, whose smile, like lightning, sets free the psalm of everlasting glory, which now sleeps in your paper flesh.'"

Campbell decided this would be a strong note on which to close. "Thank you, Father Stone. No further questions."

. . .

Wembley stood at his desk, "Your Honor, I wish to reserve the right to cross examine the defendant after the last defense witness has testified."

"Your request has been noted, counselor. Attorney for the defense, you may call your next witness."

"I recall to the stand psychiatrist, Forrest Winkler."

Campbell: "Doctor, we have heard rather moving testimony from the defendant on how he sees his own sexuality. Would you, in your expertise, judge Father Stone to be sexually well adjusted?"

"To measure healthy sexual adjustment, several factors must be taken into account.

"Today, studies stress the importance of not confusing sexuality and genitality. Though priests must abstain from genitality, they should not suppress their sexuality. If they are to be fully human, they must understand and live their maleness. This is necessary for them to be effective ministers as well as fully human. This is a new perception, not emphasized in the seminary training or in society's concept of priesthood in Father Stone's generation of priests. Pope John Paul II, himself, has said in a recent radio message to a meeting of the bishops in Dallas: 'If we were to study the human person without reference to sexuality, we would be overlooking a fundamental truth revealed to us in the Book of Genesis.'

"Each one of us grows up with many varying influences on us as to how we develop our understanding of our sexuality. Mothers and fathers influence greatly. Fathers may push for maleness in boys: sports, standing up for rights, machoism, guns, sowing wild oats in adolescence. Mothers may do the same or they may impress other characteristics which would normally be considered more female qualities, or, in some contexts today, more enlightened attributes of masculinity.

"Until recently, at least, maleness and femaleness have had commonly perceived characteristics. Male: dominant, aggressive, assertive, usually non-emotional. Female: tender, caring, emotional, generally not aggressive.

"In youth, boys tease girls; girls go to the powder room in two's or three's; boys are disruptive; girls jump up and down when they are overjoyed, hug each other. Some of these cultural mannerisms have been deliberately blurred in the last three decades.

"Hopefully, integrated sexuality gradually develops. There always remains the drive toward intimacy. And it can be stronger when older. Just as in romantic love, the physical attraction can hold a marriage together for about four years, the novelty of priesthood can overpower loneliness in ministry only for so long.

"Priests probably are having no more difficulty with intimacy than comparable married males in the general population.

"Erick Erikson's sixth stage of developmental tasks involves the struggle between intimacy and isolation.

"Our relationship with God is only as healthy as our relationship with other human beings. It is the opposite of self absorption. Old maids or crusty bachelors, as opposed to warm grandmas and grandpas. Admittedly, there can also be warm bachelors and crusty grandmas and grandpas.

"Lack of intimacy can lead to hoarding, self-centeredness and narcissism. Repression can lead to compensation - through chemical dependency, obsessive compulsive anger and outbursts, obesity, workaholism, and acting out.

"Intimacy is a call to innocent touch and a psychological nudity, the capacity to share our strengths, hopes, fears, sorrows, spirituality, secrets, feelings. It needs only be done with one or two in a lifetime. It is critical that there be a sharing of one's deepest feelings and experience with a spiritual director or capable confidante, a willingness to accept qualified counseling.

"One thing I know, profound companionship is a necessity in a priest's life as it is for anyone. The wonderful realization that someone really wants you to visit them. You are loved. Someone wants you around.

"A priest can otherwise be starved, shriveled up. He may be convinced he is never really loved. Guarded. Defensive. Not vulnerable. Unloving.

"But Father Stone, from my observation, impresses me as one who has come to terms with intimacy and with his sexuality, and would not engage in aberrant genital behavior, certainly not involving force."

. . .

The prosecuting attorney had one question he wanted to put to the psychiatrist.

"Doctor, would it not be true to say that a substantial number of psychologists consider the celibate life unnatural? Might not the blocking of natural sexual outlets incline a person to seek satisfaction in aberrant ways like molestation and even rape?"

"No, that is not the reality," Forest Winkler responded. "You may be familiar with Gabrielle Brown's, The New Celibacy. It points out that Freud was 'surprisingly open to the positive results of celibacy.' He observed that people can achieve happiness by transcending sexuality for a higher experience of love. And he took examples from the Religious life."

Looking at the jury, the psychiatrist added, "It is interesting that a non-Religious woman has written this volume, rather than a priest or Religious.

"Brown, a non-Catholic, envisioned celibacy as providing for a more intimate, more flexible experience of love and a more balanced approach to living fulfilled, progressive lives.

"As a matter of fact, she writes, 'Celibacy offers a freshness unique in human relations.' Perhaps this is what Mohandas Gandhi had in mind when he said that because of its celibate clergy, the Catholic Church would remain eternally young.

"Secular celibates, that is celibates not in a religious vocation, could learn from Brown's conclusions: 'That genital love is but one way of relating -- certainly not the only way. That sexual abstinence does not destroy sexual ability, nor should it cause either psychological or physical problems.'

"'Celibate prowess, not genital prowess, has been most often regarded in history as the real proving ground for the challenge of masculine strength' -- and we can add feminine strength as well."

This was not going the way the prosecution wanted it. Wembley cut the psychiatrist short.

"You are citing what would be considered a non-professional's opinion. Is it not true that most psychiatric authorities would hold that sexual repression leads to deviant behavior?"

"That is a complex question which does not allow a yes or no answer."

. . .

Wembley saw no point in pressing the psychiatrist or other defense witnesses further since their testimony was psychological and theological and dealt with Church discipline. In the first place, he did not feel competent to engage the witnesses in ecclesiology and, in the second place, he was confident that the jurors found the whole line of testimony incomprehensible.

But he did want briefly to cross-examine Tyler. "Father Stone, two of the witnesses have testified to your reputation for good conduct. Would you say that they are judging you on past performance?"

"I suppose so."

"Roughly during the time around the month of last October when the rape was alleged to have occurred, how often would Father Franklin and Bishop Carmichael be observing your conduct first hand? How often would they see you during that period of time?"

Tyler was not sure he understood the significance of the question. "Bishop Carmichael was in Fairview, so I didn't get a chance to see him more than every two or three months when some obligation would bring him to the City. Father Franklin is working out of New York mostly now, but I think he was overseas for Catholic Relief Services last fall."

Wembley pursued the point, "Would it be fair to say that these two witnesses did not have the opportunity actually to observe your behavior during the time in question?"

"Yes, that's right."

"And isn't it true that though we've heard from witnesses a good deal about the Church's teaching on sexuality and the exhortations it gives to its priests to control themselves, it is possible for a priest to transgress these rules and regulations?"

"Yes."

This time an objection came from the defense table; again it was overruled and the prosecutor was directed to continue.

"Isn't it true that some clergy have, as a matter of fact, violated their promises?"

"Yes, a small minority have."

"But some have, haven't they?"

"Yes."

"No further questions, Your Honor."

The case had consumed only two courtroom days, leading up to the closing arguments.

. . .

On Wednesday morning, Wembley, in his summation for the prosecution, stressed: "In this trial we have the word of one person against another, and we have heard witness after witness testify under oath that this young girl is a person of complete veracity, trusted by her parents, trusted by her family, trusted by her classmates, trusted by everyone who has come to know her. She is in no way known to be spiteful or invidious.

"There is no reason on earth why this young girl - still a child - is making up this accusation. She is not asking for money; her family is not asking for money. They simply want to make sure that the accused man cannot do this again to an innocent minor.

"I know I do not have to recall to you the fact that in testimony disclosed under oath the accused at first denied that he had even been with Amber alone. And then, sometime later, he admitted that he had asked her to stay after school, alone with him in the classroom.

"We have heard all kinds of Church theology and descriptions of rules and regulations controlling clerical conduct, but what does that say to the particular charge you are dealing with?

"It does not answer the question of what this one priest did in one given situation.

"For too long a time now, women have been subjected to this kind of treatment. For too long a time have their cries for help fallen on deaf ears. For too long a time have their accusations and pleading for help actually been shamelessly turned back against them. I ask you now not to let this happen once again."

Robert Campbell walked confidently to the jury box and began speaking immediately. He wanted no prolonged pause to allow Wembley's words to sink in.

"Indeed it is true that all we have here is the word of one person against another. The person who is making the charge told no one about it for over two months after the assault allegedly had happened.

"The person against whom the charge is made is known to be a man of outstanding moral character. Everything in his being and in his behavior militates against the idea that he could perpetuate such an act. His upbringing, his life-long training, the code of ethics surrounding his vocation and lifestyle shout out a loud denial to this charge.

"There is simply an accusation. There is no evidence. There is not even any circumstantial evidence that this act occurred. Can we, in justice, inflict what would be a horrendous punishment on a man when there are all kinds of reasonable doubts - indeed all kinds of compelling doubts?"

The summation was brief and to the point. Campbell returned to the defense desk satisfied.

That was it. Judge Orosco gave the routine instructions to the jury and sent them to their deliberations.

. . .

The hours went by. It was apparent that there would be no quick agreement among the twelve jurors. They did not send out for further clarifications from the judge.

Late in the afternoon, they did send out word that there would be no verdict that day. There would be an overnight.

The next morning wore on and still no decision. Neither attorneys, Campbell or Wembley, took this as a good sign. Things pointed toward a hung jury. In the late afternoon, the foreman sent a note to the judge that there still was no unanimity and that he saw no hope for breaking a deadlock.

The judge directed them to continue to deliberate, no matter how long it took them. There was another overnight.

. . .

At eleven o'clock in the morning on the third day, the bailiff brought word to the judge. The panel had reached a verdict. The jurors were instructed to return to the court room. The principals of the case and their attorneys were recalled.

When the twelve had resumed their places in the box, the judge asked, "Has the jury reached a decision?"

The foreman rose, "We have, Your Honor."

The judge, "What is your verdict?"

"We find the defendant guilty as charged."

Tyler held his bowed head in his hands. Campbell looked astonished. His strategy had been to present his client as disarmingly honest, but the tactic had failed. By his words had Tyler convicted himself?

The faces of the principals at the prosecutor's desk expressed relief, but not elation.

"The defendant is remanded to custody."

Tyler was escorted from the courtroom by two uniformed officers.

* * *

Sentencing, a week after the trial, was brief. Judge Orosco asked Tyler if he had anything to say.

"I just say that I've said all along. I've done nothing wrong."

The judge, mindful of the lack of clear evidence, set the sentence at six years, with possibility of parole in four.

Tyler looked at his attorney beside him. Campbell shook his head, but said nothing.

Tyler, shackled, shaken and showing the signs of physical and mental strain from his first week in custody, dressed in blue prison issue and flanked by male and a female officers, left the courtroom.

CHAPTER 61

Guardians of Doctrine flourished in Northern California. Representatives of the Fairview chapter had requested a meeting and were waiting in the outer reception area of David's office. The group was made up of six middle-aged men and women whom David had met singly or in groups on previous occasions around the diocese. They were dedicated church-going people concerned about the direction of the Church since the Vatican II Council. David felt comfortable with them. Their image of the Church was the same as the one in which he had been formed.

David was not surprised to find George Caprice accompanying the group. Caprice was still pursuing him and had, no doubt, alerted the Fairview chapter to be watchful of David's conduct.

The spokesperson, a stylishly dressed, slender woman in her early 50s, Sonya Redmond, introduced herself and her colleagues. "First, we want to thank you for agreeing to meet with us, Your Excellency. As you know, we are disturbed, as are many of the faithful today, about what is happening in the Church and in society generally."

"I share your concern, Sonya," David said. He wanted to establish that point from the outset. "I share the same beliefs that you do."

"Nevertheless, we are disturbed by a number of things that are going on in this diocese. Let me list some specific instances:

"First, we know that several priests in various parishes depart from the prescribed liturgical wording when they are saying Mass. We really wonder if some Masses are valid. "Secondly, it is unconscionable what is being taught in some of our Catholic high schools. We can document instances when speakers have been invited to these schools to talk about the use of contraceptives - even with graphic illustrations. These speakers know nothing about the Church's teachings on sexuality or are in outright opposition to those teachings."

As was his custom, David was taking notes as Redmond spoke. He wanted to be able to respond specifically and to refresh his memory if he would be required to take some action in the future.

"Thirdly, from our experience, we hear very little being preached about abortion from the pulpits of this diocese. And in this connection, we are shocked to learn that at least part of the diocesan insurance program subscribes to an HMO that provides benefits for abortions. "Also, on this particular topic, we protest the diocese granting permission for the use of the cathedral for the graduation of a nursing school that offers training in abortions.

"Fourthly, although we have never heard you advocate the matter publicly, it has been reported that you have made statements that could be interpreted as encouraging a study and discussion of the possibility of ordaining women to the priesthood.

"And, lastly, as you know, we object strenuously to the highly publicized joint Catholic, Lutheran, Episcopalian and Orthodox baptisms in which you took part at our own cathedral."

That appeared to be the end of the litany. David waited for comments from other members of the delegation, but no one spoke.

"I can understand your concerns," David began his response. "I share your beliefs and your insistence on the necessity of preserving the Church's doctrines and practices. Some of your statements have come as news to me, and I have taken notes to investigate.

"On other occasions, I have tried to respond to the other objections you have raised. I do not think we differ in our convictions, but we may prefer different strategies for accomplishing the same objectives."

George Caprice, who had seemed particularly uneasy during David's comments, interrupted, "We have heard this response before, Bishop; but the fact of the matter is that the Church is in serious decline."

"The Church in Northern California is experiencing the same patterns as the Church is throughout the United States," David continued. "The Church is a living organism. Only dead, lifeless things are unchanging. The Church is part of society, and society changes. Some of the changes, I admit, are detrimental. And these we must try to control. Other changes, though painful in the transition, may simply be growth. Growth is never easy.

"I am saddened, as are you, by the decline in attendance at Sunday Mass and the lack of vocations to the priesthood and Religious life. But, in some ways, we may be going through a golden age of the Church. It is more demanding today to hold on to the Faith when the currents are all against us. People today have to give a reason for the Faith that is in them. They are not going to Mass out of routine or on the momentum of people all around them. Those who are faithful are practicing their religion for better reasons, for more enlightened motives.

"I know that this does not seem to be a shining era, but golden ages are golden only to historians looking back on them. They are not golden for the people living through them. Things that are 'golden', things that have value, exact a price. They are not easy."

David had made these points before and he knew he was not convincing the small audience in the semi-circle opposite his desk.

"How can this be a golden age? The truths of the Faith are all watered down. Jesus spoke with authority," Caprice said. "He knew what the truth was and spoke it fearlessly. Most of our preachers do not speak with authority today."

"I'll admit that I do not speak with the certainty and forcefulness I did as a young priest," David granted. "Things are not as clear now."

"The clergy spoke of hell, sin and the commandments with much more conviction before the Vatican II Council." Caprice was not going to be put off. "Since the '60s, most of the priests preach almost exclusively one sermon: 'Love, love, love of neighbor.' But no instruction in doctrine is given in Sunday homilies."

"We should speak with authority," David responded. "But a preacher cannot force himself to believe. He believes what he believes and he must preach what he believes. I can't speak with authority just for the sake of speaking with authority. There has been much rethinking, questioning and review since the Vatican Council. We are trying to find our way.

"We need to pray for faith." David was speaking and struggling with his own convictions at the same time. "Faith is not mindless and unthinking and irrational. It is based on reason. We are, by reason and faith, convinced that Christ established a visible Church, that He gave it the truth and that He said He would be with that Church and protect it in truth till the end of time.

"When we know this, we can take the essential truths of the Church, the basic beliefs, and preach them with authority as Christ did."

"The only time the clergy take forceful stands today is when they talk about the environment or capital punishment or political issues," Caprice pressed on. "The Pope has made it very clear that the clergy should not be meddling in politics. Yet we have priests again and again making political statements and taking part in demonstrations. You, yourself, Your Excellency, have been guilty of the same thing."

"The Pope has said that the clergy should not run for political office," David replied. "He has not said that we are forbidden to make political statements. That word `political' is vague. I think that the clergy should refrain from attaching themselves to individual candidates or to particular political parties; but the Church must speak out on moral issues. And moral issues and so-called `political' issues often overlap.

"The word `political' comes from the Greek word `polis', meaning city or citizen. If we were to withdraw from discussions on war and peace, nuclear disarmament, abortion, immigration and refugee questions, we would be abdicating our responsibilities as spokespersons on ethical matters. We would virtually have to refrain from speaking on any `people' issues. The Pope, himself, is constantly making statements on `political' issues.

"I know that I have not addressed all of your specific points; but I will reflect on them seriously, and I will act on the information you have given me. I think we should meet periodically. I admire your love of the Church and your loyalty."

"Remember, Your Excellency, it is the bishop who is ultimately responsible that the traditions of the Church are safeguarded," Sonya Redmond interjected, surmising that the meeting was coming to an end.

Claudia, David's secretary, had buzzed several times. David did not respond to the intercom, but it was apparent that another appointment was waiting.

A younger woman, who had not spoken yet, squeezed in her intervention, "And it is the bishop who is responsible for the salvation of our souls. Also, one last thing, Bishop. We want to know how you voted on the letter about women."

David thought this subject might come up. "The Bishops' proposed letter on women's concerns, as you know, was introduced several years ago. It went through four drafts. Each draft was considerably modified in one way or another. What some women were saying in the first draft was no longer contained in the last draft.

"By the time that fourth draft came out, the statement really did not address what was in the hearts of many women well enough to make it advisable to issue a letter. It would do more harm than good.

"We couldn't have had a better bishop chairing the committee in charge of the letter - an open, intelligent, good man. He struggled to do everything he could to make that letter a success.

"The debate at the bishops' meeting in November was lively. No acrimony. The opinion of individual bishops changed back and forth as they heard the arguments. The real discussion was whether this fourth draft would serve the Church well and particularly serve women well.

"Eventually, enough bishops, 110, did not think it was proper to issue the statement as a pastoral letter. It was tabled. I voted against issuing the letter. Although there were many excellent features in the final draft, I felt publishing it would have been divisive."

As David began to rise from his chair, George Caprice said, "Can we say a prayer together, and would you give us your blessing, Bishop?"

David began to sit back in his chair, but thought better of it when the group fell to their knees. David knelt with them and, rather than beginning the prayer as clergyman, he asked Sonya to lead them, which, given the conservative background of the group, may or may not have been a politically correct request.

Sonya prayed, "Our Father, Who art in heaven . . . Hail Mary, full of grace . . . Glory be to the Father . . ."

David stood, made a circle of his hands and signed the cross over the six, "Benedictio Dei omnipotentis Patris et Filii et Spiritus Sancti descendet super vos et maneat semper. May the blessing of Almighty God, Father, Son and Holy Spirit descend upon you and remain forever. Amen."

There were subdued pleasantries as David led the delegation to the outer office and individually said his good-byes. He thought to himself, "These are good people who genuinely have the welfare of the Church at heart. I must not only listen to them, but really hear what they are saying."

CHAPTER 62

Tyler Stone's friends were profoundly shocked by the verdict against him. "I still can't believe it," David said. "I know that Tyler struggled with temptations in sexual matters, but I have never known him to act out."

Ladd was silent for a few moments, then wondered whether he should say what was on his mind and, typically, did. "I think Tyler was too good in a way. I don't think that during the eleven years in the seminary his vocation was ever really tested. Maybe things were too easy for him. It would be better for him to have had to wrestle with his vocation and with serious temptations before he was ordained. Then he could have made the decision whether celibacy was the life for him or not. Better for the testing to come before ordination than afterward."

A pall hung over All Saints Parish. Tyler's parishioners were quick to forgive him, but it was not easy to forget.

. . .

During the long days in prison, Tyler kept up his exercise regimen by doing laps on the Yard running track and working with the free weights. Most of his cell time was spent in reading and writing letters to his mother, priest friends and parishioners at All Saints who corresponded with him. His mother was a constant visitor. David and Ladd, whenever they could get to the Bay Area, were faithful in their visits to Tyler as was his spiritual director, Father Michael Buckley.

Those visits, extremely awkward at first, were now the consolation of his life.

Because his celibate vocation called for a life of aloneness, Tyler found the burden of isolation lighter than his fellow inmates. But it was a burden. For long hours, he contemplated on the state of his soul.

As he always had, he struggled with temptations to bitterness, temptations to blame others, to fix the fault of his present situation on his upbringing, temptations to anger, to recriminations against Amber Shortland.

He struggled to control ever present human sexual drives. He held fast to his lifelong practice of turning away from impure thoughts at the first moment they arose. When the temptations presented themselves, he tried immediately to absorb his attention in reading, in push-ups, in cold showers when he had access to showers.

He feared mortal sin. Since his boyhood he "dreaded the loss of heaven and the pains of hell." To be on the safe side, he requested the sacrament of reconciliation whenever a priest visited him. After each confession, conducted on the phone through the glass wall in a visitors' cubicle, his life again seemed clean and uncluttered.

. . .

As Tyler tossed and turned on his bunk, he was tormented by doubts. How can God allow this to happen to me?

How can my finite mind even comprehend the infinite God? The one we call God spans the universe, spans even "universes" which we can't conceive. Does God even know I'm here? I just pray for faith. But is my decision to pray for faith simply the result of a lifetime of brainwashing?

In the darkest hours, for the first time in his life he could remember, Tyler struggled with his Faith. The way things had turned out, was his whole life based on illusion? Were his life premises unreal?

Even, was there a God?

Am I just going along on childhood beliefs, like Santa Claus and the tooth fairy? Is God just some cosmic force out there in the universe?

Do I still think of God as an old man with a long white beard?

Subconsciously, am I still thinking of God as someone up there lying in ambush with a clipboard in His hand, keeping a record of every slip I make?

Have I related to God subserviently, as though He were a neurotic parent that I have to get on the right side of? I should know I can't make God happy or unhappy by what I do. He is happiness.

God isn't a manipulative parent who holds threats over me if I don't obey.

Maybe I've just dealt with God like a magic pacifier expecting Him to give me whatever I cry for. Or a slot machine that I back away from when it doesn't pay off.

Are you a merit badge God? If I do something good, You'll reward me. That's not love. That's a business transaction.

What am I doing in prison?

Why have You abandoned me?

. . .

Tyler was known to his fellow inmates and to the prison administration to be a priest. Because his conduct had been beyond reproach for the time he had already served, the authorities acceded to his request to say Mass on Christmas morning for the prisoners in the cell block. With the multiplication of Masses for the special holyday in his parish, the regular chaplain was not available for the prison.

In a tightly controlled procedure, inmates who indicated the desire to attend were escorted, small group by small group, into the recreation room where ping pong, card and pool tables had been shifted toward the wall to provide room for a make-shift altar and 15 rows of folding chairs.

Tyler opened his Mass kit, which had been kept in the custody of a guard, took out a small chalice, paten, vigil light candle, one cruet of water and a second cruet with less than an ounce of white wine, and placed them on the altar. Father Buckley had brought him missalettes for Advent and the Christmas season.

Looking over the blue clad congregation which had assembled, Tyler estimated the number of white wafers of bread he would need for Communion. He placed those hosts on the Communion plate.

Guards stood along the walls at five row intervals.

With the white side of his reversible purple-and-white stole around his shoulders, Tyler began the Mass, "In the name of the Father, and of the Son, and of the Holy Spirit. The grace of Our Lord Jesus Christ and the love of God and the fellowship of the Holy Spirit be with you all." Perhaps only a tenth of the inmates answered, "And also with you." But Tyler could see that the men, without exception, were attentive and devout.

Mass went on with Tyler reciting the Gloria, the song of the angels over Bethlehem the first Christmas night. He had asked two of the prisoners in the front row to do the readings and the responsorial psalm. One was a natural lector, the other stumbled through the words of St. Paul to Titus. After he motioned to the congregation to stand, Tyler proclaimed the Gospel, recounting the manger scene, the birth of Christ and the shepherds. In his homily, Tyler drew the parallels found in Christ's life and in the prisoners' own lives.

"There is a mural in a small church in Southern France which depicts a 33-year old Christ carrying His cross, and behind Him a long procession.

"We see in the single file line a housewife, and she is carrying a cross; and after her a king, and he is carrying his cross. Next comes a laborer and then a grandmother with crosses on their shoulders. Many others follow. We see among them a prisoner with his heavy cross. And at the end of the long, long line is a mother holding a tiny infant. And even the baby is carrying a cross. Whether we are here on the inside or on the outside, whether young or old, every one of us is hurting.

"The little One whose birthday the whole world is celebrating today is not really different from you. He had his problems right from the start.

"He was really a child of a single parent family. Mary was his only physical parent. And tradition tells us that Joseph, his foster father, died when Jesus was a young boy.

"When He became an itinerant preacher, He was hassled by the authorities. Eventually, He was apprehended by the temple police, betrayed by a companion, denied by one of his friends, deserted by the others, even seemingly abandoned by God, put through a fraudulent trial, executed and buried in a borrowed grave."

The Mass moved to the Prayers of the Faithful, with Tyler inviting the men to offer personal petitions. It took several moments for the first inmate to gather courage to speak up, "For my son, Jason, who is celebrating his fifth birthday tomorrow."

"Lord, hear our prayer," Tyler responded aloud.

"For my parole hearing next week."

This time a few of the prisoners, remembering the formula, joined Tyler, "Lord, hear our prayer."

There were other intercessions for a sick wife, that a girlfriend would be faithful, for a mother who died three weeks ago. "Lord, hear our prayer."

During the consecration of the Bread and Wine, a stillness settled in the room.

Then for the first time a majority of voices joined in a prayer - the Our Father; but Tyler noticed no joining of hands during the Lord's Prayer, as was the increasing custom on the outside.

"Let us offer each other the Sign of Peace."

In what he considered to be a special Mass, Tyler unliturgically left the altar and exchanged handshakes, sometimes the brotherhood three-fold hand clasp, down one side of the main aisle.

As he began to return up the other side, suddenly there was a commotion in the center of the chairs. A scuffle had broken out during the peace-giving. The violence poured out into the aisle where Tyler stood.

A prisoner lunged heavily back against Tyler, knocking him to the floor. Guards were scrambling through the over-turned chairs. As he raised himself from the floor and tried to restrain the convict nearest him who was flailing his arms, Tyler felt two heavy blows to his chest and stomach.

In an instant, the guard pinned the two most frenzied men to the floor, face down.

It was then that Tyler saw blood on his alb front and the white stole. And now, where he had felt the pounding, he felt deep sharp pain. The guard at Tyler's feet had wrestled a kitchen knife away from the heavier of the two attackers.

The young guard next to Tyler saw the blood on the priest's front and shouted to an officer at the hall door to call for help from the infirmary.

The color drained from Tyler's face. As he was eased down to the floor, he felt nauseous and lost consciousness.

Word of the prison attack swept through the convict community. Inmates who had come to know him during the six months were angry and asked to visit Tyler. The one who had done the stabbing, now in special confinement, protested that he had never meant to strike the priest. He was after the fellow convict who had insulted him and with whom he had a long-time feud.

As Tyler's condition worsened from stab wounds near the heart and the pancreas, he was moved to City and County Hospital. His mother was at his side each day. Visits from friends were strictly limited. David came from Fairview to visit him. The Archbishop and Gordon Caprice, as Chancellor, were allowed into his room. But, for the most part, Tyler was unresponsive. He came into consciousness only rarely.

. . .

On the last day of January, Tyler died. Archbishop Costello had anointed him two days earlier. Tyler briefly recognized the Archbishop and thanked him. A memorial Mass was said at Tyler's former parish, All Saints, with the upper grades of the parochial school in attendance.

The Mass of Christian Burial was concelebrated at the Cathedral by David, Ladd and most of the priests of the archdiocese, with the Archbishop as principal celebrant.

There were tears as the simple casket was carried out - and the recessional song, "Going Home."

. . .

On a fog bound Bay Area day in March, Amber Shortland visited her attorney, Stephen West, and recanted.

"I don't know why I said what I did about Father Stone. I guess I just wanted attention. And then later, as the days went by, I was afraid to admit that I lied."

PART VII

CHAPTER 63

Ladd made it a point whenever he returned to the Bay Area to visit David in Fairview. David felt comfortable and relaxed during these times with his friend.

Ladd brought David up to date on his most recent activities with CRS, and David reciprocated with details of his life in the northern tier of California counties -- never as adventurous as Ladd's foreign exploits.

At lunch they would retell old stories of seminary days, laughing at the antics of the "characters" among their schoolmates and the faculty. And they would share enthusiastically the current antics of these "characters" in the ministry.

Turning serious, but trying to keep it somewhat light-hearted so as not to alarm, Ladd said to his friend, "Dave, what are you up to in this diocese? I hear there are people trying to depose you."

"Who told you that?"

"On two occasions, I've heard that George Caprice and others have written letters to Rome about you 'liberalizing' your diocese. You know you could be eased out."

David dismissed the thought casually, "Oh, there are many bishops that are being reported to the Vatican for the same reasons. It is the continuing story of the traditionalists and the progressives in the Church. For the health of the Church we probably need both for the sake of checks and balances."

But inwardly, David did not take Ladd's words casually.

Ladd said, "I don't think George Caprice reasons clearly. He is so far behind the times. It probably was only a couple of generations ago that his ancestors began walking upright."

"Though I do not agree with him on some matters," David countered, "I know that George Caprice is highly intelligent and has the good of the Church at heart. His ideas should be listened to."

Ladd admonished his friend, "Well, take it easy, Dave. We don't want you censured or banished."

. . .

The letter arrived on a Wednesday morning. The return address was the Apostolic Nunciature, Washington, D.C. There was an interior envelope with the coat of arms of the Holy See in the upper left hand corner. It was addressed simply "Most Reverend David M. Carmichael." Understandably, David set aside the other correspondence and opened the envelope from Rome.

> "Your Excellency, it pleases His Holiness, Pope John Paul II, to invite you to a private audience on June 4th. The Holy Father requests also that you make arrangements for a meeting with the Congregation for the Doctrine of the Faith prior to the audience at a date convenient to your schedule.
>
> "With fraternal best wishes and blessings, I am Sincerely in Christ."

And it was signed by Octavio Cardinal Brunelli, Secretary of State.

David knew that over the years, as had most bishops, he had received photo copies of letters sent to the Apostolic Delegate or Nuncio and/ or to the Vatican, complaining about various statements, policies and practices in the diocese.

David could think of no other reason why he would be summoned to a special audience and instructed to meet with the office for the Doctrine of the Faith.

In the ensuing weeks, he pondered on questions that the Vatican might raise and how he might respond. On the more complex questions, he consulted with his Vicar for Theological and Canonical Affairs.

. . .

Having settled on a June 2nd interview with the Secretary of what had long been known as the Holy Office, now the Vatican Department charged with responsibility for the preservation of doctrine, David left Fairview for Rome on May 31st. He arrived midday Wednesday at Leonardo Da Vinci Airport.

A cousin of Ladd's, Father Luigi Boldonado, met him at the terminal and drove him in his Fiat the long way around on a sight-seeing route, which circles Rome, past EURA, a modern development in the Eternal City, eventually to Trastevere and up the Janiculum.

David entered North American College where a room had been prepared for him.

The College overlooks St. Peter's Square. From his window, David could see the sunset just left of Michelangelo's Dome. Even though the College is situated high on Janicolo, still the Basilica's Dome towers above the six-story seminary.

From the top floor of the College, David had a 360 degree panorama of the Eternal City - the Victor Emmanuel Monument to the east, the towers and domes of countless churches, punctuating the horizon; Castel Sant' Angelo guarding the entrance to Vatican City at the Tiber.

David's arrival in Rome coincided with a visit to the Vatican by President Bill Clinton and Hillary Clinton.

On Thursday, David was invited along with two American Cardinals living in Rome to attend the reception of the President by Pope John Paul II. Secretary of State, Warren Christopher, and Raymond Flynn, U.S. Ambassador to the Vatican, were among the civic and Church dignitaries present.

In the reception line, David had a chance to exchange pleasantries with the President and Mrs. Clinton. The President later addressed a general assembly of Americans in Rome, paying particular tribute to the North American College seminarians for the commitment of their lives to the service of others.

David joined the faculty of North American College in a private tour of the refurbished Sistine Chapel, its ceiling and murals restored to their brilliant original colors. Leaving the Sistine Chapel, the North American group took a privately escorted tour of the Vatican Museum, the high audience hall above the vestibule of St. Peter's Basilica and several sacristy-like rooms, where a newly elected Pope is first clothed in the white cassock, store rooms for papal tiaras (triple crowns), historic miters and special chalices, gifts from heads of states around the world, including the diamond encrusted chalice used by the Pope at St. Peter's for Easter and Christmas Masses.

That evening, as he was going to sleep, David experienced another instance of "pillow wit." He thought of something he should have said to the President when he had the rare opportunity. Apart from personal political preference, he wished he had said, "If you want to go down in history as a statesman, I have the three word formula to guarantee that. Those three words are: `Be totally honest.' Political figures get in trouble not so much because of their misdeeds; but because of their attempts to cover up. The public resents, above all else, dishonesty.

Later, David would pick up a copy of USA Today and read from Michael Medved's column a speech he encouraged President Clinton to make to the American people at the very outset of the Monica Lewinsky episode - if the sexual allegations were indeed true:

"Perhaps it was arrogant of me to believe that once I arrived in the White House I could instantly overcome my weaknesses and transform myself. I now understand this transformation is only possible with a humble spirit and the assistance of an all-merciful God.

"I have begun the process of rebuilding and overcoming self-destructive behavior patterns with the help of qualified professionals and clergy. In the course of this private reconstruction, I do not expect your pity, but I welcome your prayers.

"In this spirit of healing, my legal representatives have reached an out-of-court settlement with the women involved. As part of the agreement, I acknowledge the pain I have caused them and ask their forgiveness.

"We must re-establish the essential distinction between private failings and political accomplishments, between personal shortcomings and the public agenda. Restoring this necessary dividing line will decide more than the fate of one administration. It will determine the future of our democracy."

David noted that up to this point, the President did not make such a speech.

"'Oh, what a tangled web we weave, when first we practice to deceive.'"

. . .

At midmorning on Friday, David presented himself at the offices of the Congregation for the Doctrine of the Faith. He was immediately ushered into a conference room and greeted by Archbishop Pietro Canelo at the far end of a carved mahogany board-room table. The Archbishop was sitting in for Cardinal Robert Rettleman who was on an official visit to Calabria. Sitting two to the left and one to the right of the Archbishop were three priest staff members. All four were fluent in English, though the Archbishop's words were heavily accented.

After introductions, the Archbishop began, "It is good to see you, Your Excellency. You are welcome to Rome. The Holy Father has asked this congregation to discuss with you certain questions that have been brought to our attention. We know that you will be very helpful in clarifying these questions.

"The first subject concerns the joint ecumenical celebration of Baptism in your cathedral church. We have received the statement you published explaining your reasons for the ceremony. Still, we want to state that this rendered a disservice to ecumenical dialogue and caused not a little surprise and some confusion among both the clergy and faithful.

"We trust that Your Excellency realizes that this congregation would have been most willing to act in a consultative manner in order to ensure that all the implications at every level could have been examined. Likewise the members of the Pontifical Commission for the Promotion of Christian Unity would also have gladly assisted Your Excellency in the delicate aspect of the ecumenical dimension.

"The second matter has to do with an ecumenical prayer service in which you participated for the Governor of the State of California. It seems that there are questions in the minds of some of your faithful regarding this service, since this governor was in favor of abortion."

The Archbishop paused.

"Your Excellency and Fathers," David began, "I cannot add anything to the statement which I sent you on the ecumenical baptisms.

"I assume that you know the details of the second event involving the governor. When arrangements were made for the interfaith service, I do not think the subject of abortion was in the minds of any of the planners. If we had anticipated that the ceremony would eventually become associated with the question of abortion, I would not have taken part and it would not have been held in the Catholic cathedral. When the abortion issue was raised, preparations were well underway.

"Religious services quite often are conducted in connection with government inaugurations. The prayer service was not intended to honor a public official, but to pray for God's help for the new administration. It was an opportunity for representatives of all Faiths to come together, asking God to give the new governor understanding and enlightenment. In no way was it meant to condone the Governor's position on the abortion issue. The prayers and remarks of the service were petitions for divine assistance, not praise for the governor. It goes without saying that our diocese preaches and teaches the Church's pro-life position."

The oldest of the priests who obviously was American spoke up, "We understand there was police action during the ceremony."

"Yes," David said. "Whenever a governor or a president or any high official is present at a function, there are law enforcement officers with all the attendant security equipment and precautions. These, as you can imagine, are somewhat out of character in a church setting. Before the ceremony, the Cathedral priests were asked if some people who were insisting on sitting in the pews which government officials were scheduled to occupy should be removed. The police were directed by the clergy not to remove them, but to make other provisions for the officials.

"I knew if there were loud disturbances, the police would, no doubt, remove protestors during the ceremony. And they did. Although I observed one of those protesting being removed, I did not learn that anyone had been arrested until I arrived outside the church after the service.

"I was very sorry about the arrests. I went from the cathedral to the local police department and to the county jail to tell the authorities that the Church did not want the arrested persons detained or any charges brought against them. As I understand it, the arrests were made by State Police. Actually, those arrested were almost immediately released.

"About four weeks later, I attended the arraignment and again asked that whatever charges had been made be dropped. The charges were eventually dismissed.

"Those who made the protest are sincere people. They are to be admired for their dedication to the defense of the unborn. Different members of the Church have different strategies, but the basic convictions for most of the faithful about this matter are the same."

The Archbishop pursued the general subject, "It has been brought to our attention that this subject of abortion is not preached forcibly in your diocese."

"I know that our clergy and Religious firmly uphold the Church's teaching on the sanctity of life. Perhaps the misunderstanding about the forcefulness of the preaching may be because of differences of opinion how best to communicate that teaching - the differing strategies to which I have just referred.

"I believe we must, in our position concerning abortion, acknowledge the very real difficulties that face women in some pregnancies. And when we preach, we want to make sure we are not causing women to brood over past sins for which there has been genuine remorse, confession and forgiveness.

"Our diocese insists that an individual, separate human being is present in the womb from the beginning of a pregnancy and these defenseless innocent beings should be protected, but we weaken our argument if we refuse at least to recognize the realities that some women face. We should emphasize counseling and provide for adoptions.

"Our approach must be compassionate and it must be intelligent. If we say we defend human life, I think we must stand for a consistent ethic regarding all human life. I realize that theoretically a nation has a right to defend itself against an unjust aggressor, even to the point of killing in war. But, given the unspeakable weapons we have today which kill massively without distinguishing between combatants and women and children, I think we should be pacifists as far as nuclear weapons are concerned."

The youngest priest sitting immediately to the left of the Archbishop interrupted, "But what if situations in which nations are faced with a Hitler, or situations as in Bosnia-Herzegovina?"

"I don't know how to answer that," David said. "Maybe passive resistance, as practiced by Gandhi in India, until the oppressors finally come crashing down of their own weight as the Soviet Union eventually did. I really don't know the answer. But I think Christ was a pacifist," David added.

"Was He?" the young priest persisted. "Didn't Christ use force when He took up whips and drove the money-changers out of the temple?"

"I know," David said. "I wish He hadn't done that. It clouded the whole issue.

"But the overriding message of the Gospels is peace and reverence for life. And we must be consistent. Not just abortion - granted that we are talking about the most helpless of innocent beings in that instance. Even though we have traditionally taught that a state has the right to practice capital punishment, to execute in self-defense for the sake of society, when we consider the way the death penalty is mostly imposed on the poor and the powerless, I believe we should really mean it when we preach the consistent ethic or the `seamless garment' of life, and we should oppose the death penalty as it is now implemented.

"I'm sorry that I have taken a tangent from the original question, but these thoughts may explain why you have reports on preaching that is `soft on abortion.'"

When David finished his recitation, he hoped "no one dared ask any more questions" on the subject.

Since there was momentary silence, David decided he would take the initiative on another related matter. "I know you have received letters about the Sierra Hospital School of Nursing graduation at our cathedral. Because the cathedral is on the central plaza of the city and adjacent to the State Capitol, many public events like graduations take place there. The public's mind does not link an event like a general hospital's graduation with teachings contrary to Church. In any event, the Divine Providence Sisters have recently acquired Sierra Hospital, and medical practices and procedures now comply with Church doctrine."

There were no comments from the curial officers.

The Archbishop went on to another topic, "Would you tell us something about the report that one of your parishes sponsors an organization promoting homosexuality?"

"Over an extended period of time," David said, "I have consulted with the clergy and Religious at All Souls Church, who have been trying to minister to the homosexual community since the mid-'70s. The members of this small group, I am told by the clergy there: emphasize liturgies, educational sessions, outreach to the poor, and other human services. They are not a group with an aim to make public protests to the teachings of the Catholic Church.

"I recall that on one occasion recently when a public protest was mounted in Fairview by a militant homosexual group from southern California, the All Souls group refused to join, typical of the non-confrontational posture and the good will they try to practice.

"As I understand it, the Vatican document on 'Pastoral Care of Homosexual Persons' did not single out any particular group by name. The criteria which that document details are that we should not assist groups proclaiming against the teachings of the Church, and that we should deal with homosexuals with compassion. I believe the All Souls' unit meets those criteria. The members see a need for the Church's ministry and a need for an organization in which they can experience mutual support, rather than alienation.

"I trust that All Souls is trying responsibly to do a ministry as Christ did when He reached out to those whom society sometimes alienates and often harasses, in order to restore them to wholeness through His healing presence.

"The program is certainly not seen as an endorsement of a homosexual lifestyle. In reaching out to them, All Souls hopes to help them to discern God's will in their lives through a love for the teachings of the Church. The parish wants, of course, to follow the guidance and direction of the Holy See. In consultation with our presbyterate, our Vicar of Theological and Canonical Affairs and others, I am continuing to monitor the ministry.

"I admit that there may be persons attending these gatherings who do not endorse some of the teachings of the Church on sexuality and, as individuals, may publicly express those convictions; but I think through the All Souls project, we have a good chance of bringing to them the truth and wisdom of the Church's teaching."

"Some of the reports that we receive are not as benign as you describe the situation." This was from the priest who had, up to this time, not spoken.

David could only reply, "I will continue to monitor the program."

"What about the homosexual men's chorus which gave a concert at your cathedral?" the same priest persisted.

"In many dioceses in the United States, as you know, various activities are held in the mother church, the cathedral, including sacred drama and sacred music." David thought the same thing might be true of Italy, but said nothing.

"After reading an article about the concert, I asked the cathedral staff about the event. I understand that the chorus had been engaged for this program several months before Christmas last year. The music sung at the concert, I am told, was for the most part sacred music, much in Latin, and Christmas carols.

"About people being ejected from the church, a priest who was near the back of the cathedral stated that ushers are always told to treat everyone courteously, that they knew of no one who was forcibly pushed. I cannot personally vouch for that.

"The cathedral requires a rental fee, which covers heating and other utilities, preparation for events, janitorial needs and insurance. The rest of the money collected for admission goes to the organization that puts on the event. The homosexual community may promote and encourage the chorus. I do not know.

"It could be true that, when the cathedral was full, those people who came to the concert without tickets were turned away. The ushers may not have allowed people to enter. As is true of most downtown churches, the cathedral is closed daily to everyone from 6 o'clock in the evening until 6:45 in the morning for the 7 o'clock Mass. The people know this is the case, and do not come to the church during the night to pray.

"That particular chorus, I understand, sings in many churches in northern California."

"Bishop," Archbishop Canelo cautioned, "I would commend to your reading the document on Sacred Music in the Church."

"Yes, Your Excellency."

"Speaking of music in the church, there is the question of your Jazz Masses. The letters on this are numerous."

"There are varying opinions on the appropriateness of the celebration of the Eucharist with jazz music," David responded. "Much of the difference, however, revolves around individual tastes. Let me simply say that, for many people, various artistic idioms can be very reverential. The jazz music used is moderate, mostly traditional folk spirituals. My experience over the years at the Jazz Mass has led me to conclude that this is a legitimate form of worship in the Church. The congregation is extremely attentive and prayerful. The throngs attending increase each year, so that we have been obliged to add two more Masses on the Jazz Festival weekend.

"Some years ago, I received a letter from the Congregation of Divine Worship regarding the Jazz Mass. The letter stated that this could be a legitimate expression of praise and thanksgiving to God at Mass, so long as care was taken to ensure the reverence and dignity of the Rite. I can assure you great care is taken by those involved in the planning to make sure that the sacredness of the Mass is preserved. Polka Masses and many other similar forms of liturgy have been celebrated with the Church's approval. These are cultural liturgical forms which various people find devotional."

The younger priest was the delegated stenographer. Throughout the session, he was conscientious in his note taking. His summaries and his interpretations would be the basis of the permanent record.

"We have kept you a good long time, Bishop Carmichael. There are just two more matters to be discussed. The first has to do with a presentation on AIDS to two of your high schools, which your local secular newspapers featured. We understand that these instructions included the use of condoms."

"As to the AIDS program, sponsored by Golden State Hospitals of Northern California," David responded, "I am told that those offering the instruction were cautioned beforehand by the two high school faculties to exclude from the presentation materials that would be contrary to the teachings of the Catholic Church. The principals, administrators and teachers of Notre Dame and Presentation High Schools are solicitous in abiding by Church teachings in matters of faith and morals. The thrust of their teaching on sexuality outside of married life is definitely abstinence.

"It is my understanding that the text that was used in the two Catholic schools was modified from the original text used in non-church schools. The original version for the public schools, I believe, was the version of which appeared in the newspaper.

"But, apart from that, this matter has been given serious attention by the high schools and the Diocesan Education Department, and the Golden State Hospital presentation has not been made in any other Catholic schools in the diocese and will not be in the future. We are working with our School Office and the Diocesan Board of Education, made up principally of parents of school children, on all school matters such as sex education to make sure the curriculum is realistic and in keeping with the teachings of the Church."

. . .

Archbishop Canelo seemed to become even more serious, "The final question has to do with your personal acceptance of the magisterium, Bishop. We are concerned that you may have expressed some doubts about the official position of the Church on optional celibacy and the ordination of women."

This question surprised David. He tried to answer it forthrightly.

"I do have some personal questions about the way we should be dealing with these two subjects - topics very much on the mind of people in the United States. When anybody has asked me about these matters, I have said that, as a bishop, I support the official position of the Holy Father.

"On occasion, I have said that there have been times when I thought the Church was wrong on some topic or another; and then, six months later, I realized that the Church was right and I was wrong. I know, with its twenty centuries of wisdom and experience, that the Church is much smarter than I am.

"On the matter of optional celibacy for Catholic clergy in the Western Church, I have said privately, when asked, and in discussion with other bishops, that I thought the subject should continue to be studied by Church authorities. The increasing shortage of clergy in many parts of the world jeopardizes the availability of the Eucharist for the faithful.

"I realize that the Pope has foreclosed discussion on the ordination of women because he sees it as a position based on Scripture which cannot be tampered with. And I respect that teaching.

"Again, privately I have stated that if I could step aside from my role as bishop, humanly speaking apart from Faith, it seems that equality should extend to women even in ordination.

"Whatever is the eventual resolution of these delicate and, in some parts of the world, intensely heated issues, I know that the Holy Spirit will guide the Church.

"Sometimes I may bend human-made rules and regulations in particular situations for what I think is in the best interest of the Church or of an individual, but I have given my obedience to the Holy Father and I do not challenge the official teaching of the Church."

No one on the panel had further questions or observations. The Archbishop signaled that the interrogation was at an end.

The four members of the congregation expressed thanks to David, shook his hand as a lay staffer entered and escorted David from the conference room.

. . .

CHAPTER 64

Though David would meet face to face alone with the Pope later in the week, he had never attended a public papal audience at St. Peter's Square. For this reason, he made it a point to be at St. Peter's Piazza early Wednesday morning.

Dressed in the house cassock of a bishop, he was spotted by a Vatican attendant and escorted to the platform to join other bishops present in Rome that day.

Punctually, John Paul II appeared in the Campagnola beside the Basilica. His motorcade moved slowly toward the papal platform.

The Pope alighted from the popemobile, mounted the stairs of the raised dais facing out from the foot of the steps of St. Peter's Basilica. The tens of thousands gathered in the square roared their greeting as the Pope turned and waved with outstretched arms.

When the ovation subsided, John Paul II took his place at the gold and white papal chair.

Flanking the Pontiff were eleven bishops in their black house-cassocks with red piping - visiting bishops who were in Rome that week for their routine ad limina (to the threshold) reports to the Pope.

After a brief prayer, the Pope seated (literally, but not theologically "ex cathedra") addressed the throng; his voice amplified through speakers, bounced off Bernini's colonnade and echoed through the square.

At the end of his prepared text, the Pontiff acknowledged the presence of each national pilgrimage in its own tongue - some fifteen different languages in all. As the groups heard the welcoming words addressed to them, they waved their banners and sang or shouted back their appreciation.

The formal ceremony concluded when the Pope invited David and the bishops to join with him in a Latin blessing of the faithful, "Benedictio Dei omnipotentis . . ."

The Pontiff stepped from the platform to the waiting open popemobile which set out on its winding journey through the throng.

. . .

At his Masses that weekend, as he did every day, David said the formula prayer, "Free us from all anxiety." But that was not the way he felt personally; he was racked with anxiety awaiting the audience with the Pope on Monday morning.

He had no way of estimating how the Congregation for Doctrine reacted to his responses at the interrogation. He wondered what kind of report and recommendation had gone to the Supreme Pontiff. The inscrutable attitude of the investigating committee's priest-secretary did not bolster his confidence.

Monday morning came. Osservatore Romano would list the Pope's daily horarium, and Bishop David M. Carmichael's name would appear at 9:30 a.m.

Dressed in a "house cassock" with magenta piping, buttons and sash - magenta-colored because David had borrowed a newly purchased Monsignor's cassock for the occasion from one of the priests, and the color difference was not that noticeable -- he presented himself at the bronze doors just to the right of the embracing sweep of Bernini's columns, ascended the stairs to the courtyard of San Damaso. Crossing the wide square, he was ushered through five marbled corridors and rooms, and was directed up a further flight of stairs to an outer chamber of the papal quarters.

Promptly at nine-thirty, a secretary appeared at the door and summoned David into a small audience room.

On several occasions, David had asked veteran bishops how one was expected to greet the Pope. They had stated that it was no longer necessary to genuflect, suggesting out of courtesy that David simply briefly lift his zuchetta skull cap and kiss the papal ring. When the moment came, in his nervousness, David walked toward the Pope's desk, forgot all the advice and simply shook the Pontiff's hand.

The Pope invited David to sit next to him at the corner of his desk, as he opened a world atlas and turned to the map of the State of California.

As John Paul ran his finger down the length of the state, David pointed to a north central location on the map, the Diocese of Fairview. David's nervousness gradually drained away in the presence of the Pope's ease of manner and his down-to-earth approach. He began to feel as if he were at home and with a friend whom he had known most of his life.

To set his visitor at ease, John Paul began with some routine questions: "What is the total population of the diocese? What percentage is Catholic? What are the main occupations of the people?"

David was prepared with the figures and reported that agriculture, government and lumber were the main industries.

Throughout the conversation, the Pope mostly listened. He let his visitor do the talking. David noticed that the Holy Father seemed to be conversing in English without difficulty. He spoke slowly, but grammatically and with a natural idiom. This, even though David learned from one of the papal aides later, that English was only the Pope's seventh best language.

Despite the fact that he had recently returned from a stressful trip to Poland, the Pope seemed relaxed and vigorous. David observed that he had apparently lost some weight since the assassination attempt, but he appeared healthy, young for his years, with the complexion of a child.

John Paul was particularly interested in the state of Religious women, the Sisters. David reported that the nuns were the strong backbone of the diocese in educational, hospital and increasingly in pastoral ministry. He emphasized that a Sister was Chancellor of the diocese, and that women held other top administrative posts.

There was an awkward pause as David waited for the Pope to get to the subject of what the audience was about.

Finally, the Pope asked, "And how are ecumenical relations in your diocese?"

David could not discern whether this was prompted by one of the problematic interfaith episodes reported to the Vatican, or a routine question put to all "ad limina" bishops.

Since the Pontiff made no specific reference, David decided he would initiate a discussion of the interfaith controversies surfaced by the Congregation for the Doctrine three days earlier.

"In my judgment, Your Holiness, inter-church relations in our diocese are going well."

David was determined to meet the question head on.

"Holy Father, I think we should be reaching out to the other Faiths more. We can learn from them. Churches which are often termed 'mainline' in America, including the Catholic Church, seem to be struggling, according to statistics. The numbers attending services and Sunday Masses are down, the number of parishioners receiving the Sacraments, except Communion, has declined, applicants for the clergy and religious life are not as numerous as they were.

"Two reasons are given for this falling off: First, it is charged that the mainline churches, for example those who have followed the social spirit of the World Council of Churches, have abandoned their spiritual role and engaged in secular issues: war and peace, capital punishment, environment, the role of women, capitalism and socialism. Because of these current 'political' issues, many people claim they have become disenchanted with these religions.

"It is true, as Dean Inge has written, that one who is married to the spirit of the times will soon be a widow. However, should the churches refrain from addressing these pressing matters? If the Church teachers have seriously researched these issues and genuinely believe in their positions, they must preach them. These matters involve moral principles; they involve the Gospel. They may be painful messages. People may turn away. But some of Jesus' followers said, 'These are hard sayings,' and they no longer walked with Him.

"Your Holiness, the second reason alleged for the mainline churches' decline is that these faiths no longer speak with authority. They do not preach black and whites, but gray.

"I find myself not preaching with the certainty I had in my young priesthood. Some things do not seem to be as black and white as they once were. But clergy cannot preach on all topics with authority just for the sake of preaching with authority. They must preach honestly on what they see as the truth and admit the things of which they are not certain."

"Some of the denominations in America seem to be flourishing. Why are the evangelical churches and the fundamentalist churches successful?" the Pope asked.

"The evangelical churches apparently are touching a responsive nerve in many, including the young. I think it is because they are preaching a personal relationship with Jesus Christ. People are lonely today and they are yearning for an intimacy.

"Perhaps it's also because these churches are bringing people together in small prayer groups. People are lost and alienated in a technological world. They need to belong. 'Sometimes you want to go where everyone knows your name and they're always glad you came.'" David wondered if the Pope watched Cheers on T.V.

"We can learn also from the fundamentalist churches' emphasis on the Bible. People are hungering for the Sacred Scriptures. We can learn from the care fundamentalist preachers take to prepare their sermons. And we can learn from the topics they are emphasizing in their sermons, marriage stability and family life.

"And the Mormons. They seem to succeed. What example do they give us? They teach us the virtue of solidarity, community, and mutual support.

"The Jews. From these, our spiritual forebears, we learn fidelity -- faithfulness to the one true God. And the quality of perseverance under suffering.

"Islam can teach us a lesson in the effectiveness of missionary zeal.

"Buddhism and the Eastern religions model for us that pearl of great price -- interior personal peace.

"I believe we must accelerate inter-faith projects, Holy Father. We are brothers and sisters. We can share and learn from one another."

The Pope listened patiently. David knew he wasn't telling John Paul anything he didn't know already; but David's comments might soften whatever reprimand was coming.

"We, of course, want to keep the faithful in the Church, but at the same time, I do not think we should be overly alarmed when a Catholic in good faith joins another Christian religion. It may be that their faith in God is strengthened in some way by that change, and we must recall the Lord's words when His followers urged Him to rebuke those outside their group who were casting out devils in the Lord's name. He refused to chastise them, as much as saying he who is not against me is for me."

Still, David waited. At length, the pontiff spoke about the critical need for the bishops of the world to be in communion with Rome. He was, to be sure, specifically concerned about the conduct of Archbishop Lefevre, the arch-conservative prelate who had ordained his own bishops.

David was quite sure that the Pontiff was not drawing a parallel between David's episcopacy and Lefevre's. That was hardly the problem. But it may have been the indirect way to let David know that it was imperative for bishops to stay in union with the Vatican.

David expressed a conviction he had always fervently espoused. "I believe the centrality of the papacy is humanly speaking, after God's grace, the greatest strength of the Church. It gives the world-wide members of the Church an unmistakable point of self-identification. We would be a thousand separate factions if there were no Pope."

Again, there was an uncomfortable pause. When the Holy Father did not speak, David filled the silence, "Did you know, Your Holiness, that we are classmates?"

The Pope did not seem to comprehend, so David explained, "We were ordained to the priesthood in the same year."

John Paul smiled and nodded. David guessed that the word "classmates" was idiomatic American, a word that the pontiff would not have learned in an English vocabulary book.

Not understanding the reference, the Pope pressed a small ivory-covered button at his desk, which summoned the papal photographer into the room.

The Pope took from his desk a coffee table-sized volume about his travels in Latin America, handing this, three rosaries and a package of holy cards to David. The photographer's strobe light was flashing as David kissed the papal ring, expressed his gratitude and asked for the Pope's blessing.

As he left the audience room, he had a feeling of relief, but was wondering what the meeting was all about? There had been no incisive questions, no scolding.

When he recognized that the next visitor waiting to enter the audience room was Mary Robinson, President of Ireland, it occurred to David that it was very likely that the report on him from the Congregation for the Doctrine of the Faith had not yet come to the attention of the Pope. That would have to wait till sometime later. The pontiff was, no doubt, preoccupied with other matters, considering the caliber of visitors whom he was receiving in audience hour-by-hour, day-after-day.

He retraced his steps through San Damaso, exited the bronze doors and found himself again in the bright, sun-bathed St. Peter's Square.

. . .

David would recommend to every traveler to Rome to borrow a bishop's cassock, pectoral cross and skull-cap. These insignia were the key to Vatican City. As he passed, the Swiss Guard snapped to attention and stepped aside, permitting him to enter any door. Strangers smile at bishops. Catholic faithful reach out to kiss the episcopal ring. Tourists deferentially approach a bishop and ask if they can have their photographs taken with him. Observing the colorful house cassock, they are not sure just exactly who it is they have encountered - a bishop, a cardinal, a patriarch? In a city that must have a monument to the Unknown Pedestrian, even Honda motorbikes, Fiat automobiles and taxicab drivers sometimes stop at a red light to let a bishop cross the intersection.

In the days that followed, David said Mass at the Basilica of St. Paul Outside the Walls and returned to St. Peter's to visit the tombs of John XXIII, Pius XII, Paul VI and John Paul I.

He offered Mass at Peter's tomb in the crypt immediately under the basilica's primary altar with its twisting column baldachino by Bernini.

No matter how often David visited Rome, he experienced a great flood of pride and prayer. The antiquity of the Church and the impact of its history rushed through him.

. . .

On the day before he left Rome, David was invited to join the Pope for lunch in his private dining room, together with other bishops who were known to be visiting in Rome at the time.

The table conversation was necessarily bland, not touching on profound subjects because of the diversity of languages. But the noon meal was anything but bland; fish, assorted vegetables, fettuccini Alfredo, with an apricot cake, cheese and fruit for dessert. John Paul had the appetite expected of a young Polish mountain climber.

Toward the end of the meal, David made his contribution to the conversation, "Some of the teachings of the Church seem meaningless and even absurd to American people outside the Church. This is the case with the Church's seemingly inflexible position on contraception and the exclusion of women from the priesthood. Even the Catholic faithful need clear, patient catechesis and back-grounding on why the Church teaches what it does in these complex issues.

"Why Catholics would 'blindly' accept the Church's teachings is a mystery to those of other faiths or no faith. For them, it is necessary to put into place the preliminary pieces of the faith process before any of these particular beliefs make sense.

"Belief in the Church's teachings is not 'unenlightened' faith. The believer has, first of all, to become convinced of the existence of God, not mindlessly, but by a faith based on reasonable arguments. The believer then accepts that this God has been in touch with humans through the words of the Bible. Finally, the believer is persuaded from the Sacred Scriptures that an institution, a Church, has been founded by God to promulgate and preserve God's truths.

"Once these building blocks of foundation are in place, it is logical to accept what this God-established institution, the Church, teaches as true. When one understands these prior steps, acceptance of the Church's teaching can be seen as intelligent - not 'blind' faith."

David ventured to suggest that when pronouncements are made to the Church in America, it facilitates communication if it is done with a feeling of collaboration. The people of the United States have a tradition and background that is completely democratic. They seem to act negatively to ideas that are imposed from above. I suppose this is true of all nations that have a history of democratic government."

The Holy Father listened attentively and understood what David was saying. Smiling, he responded somewhat emphatically, "But we must remember that some things are objectively true."

The luncheon lasted over an hour. Though his schedule was backbreaking, John Paul was unhurried.

He offered his farewell individually, as each bishop left the dining room. David did not know whether he should be flattered or alarmed that the Pope remembered his name and his diocese.

With the other bishops, David left the papal quarters through hallways casually adorned with frescos by Donatello and Raphael, masterpieces of mosaics, paintings and sculptures everywhere.

. . .

Russia was in turmoil. David left Rome for an overnight stop in Berlin as the Soviet Union was collapsing. He took the time of the layover to tour the Brandenburg Gate, the gradually thawing Checkpoint Charlie, Unter den Linden, and the torn out tower and bombed nave of the Wilhelm Frederick Church, left standing as a memorial in the city shopping center.

The next day, as he left for the airport, he saw the jubilant throngs attacking from the East and West, dismantling the Berlin Wall slab by slab (graffitied on the West side, whitewashed on the East side), reuniting the old German capitol.

CHAPTER 65

From Berlin, David flew to Ireland to visit the seminaries which have, over the years, provided hundreds of priests in his diocese.

In Dublin David caught the bus to the suburb of Drumcondra, the site of All Hallows College. Father Kevin Raftery, the President of the seminary, led David on a tour of the seminary facilities, the chapel, the corridors lined with the medley photos of past-men, graduates of All Hallows. David delayed for over an hour picking out the photos of priests who serve Northern California as far back as Monsignor William Daly.

The following morning, David rented a car and, studying the traffic intently, drove on the left side of the street out of downtown Dublin to Naas and into Clane to Maynooth College. There, David met with the seminary president and faculty and, as he did at each stop, made a recruitment appeal for additional priests for his diocese.

Next, through Castle Dermot, he journeyed to Carlow, touring the liturgical center conducted by Father Sean Springey and meeting with St. Patrick's administration and teachers.

His recruitment trek took him to the southeast to St. Peter's in Wexford, a seminary located on the hills above the city, looking out into the bay and the Irish Sea.

From there, to New Ross and to Waterford. At St. John's, he celebrated Mass with President Father Martin Slattery and met with local Bishop Michael Russell.

David's circle of the south of Ireland led him toward Kilkenny, passing through the village of Stonyford, a name familiar to him in the hills west of Maxwell in California. St. Kieran's claims to be the oldest of Irish seminaries, the original foundation dating back to 1782. Here, David said a prayer in the students' chapel with its regular seating benches, rather than choir stalls.

Finally, passing through Urlingsford, David exited the turnpike turning right to Thurles. Another St. Patrick's -- where David enjoyed a lengthy visit with President Gus O'Donnell, whom he had met earlier in America.

Before leaving Ireland, David looked in on elderly priests from his diocese who had retired in Ireland, including Patrick O'Regan in Tralee and Cornelius O'Connor at Rose Cottage in Ballyheigue.

As David left Ballyheigue Bay, he turned his Ford Escort toward Ardfert, now a Kerry retreat center, which was once a house of formation for the Mercy Sisters of Auburn, California.

. . .

David was told the Faith was waning in Ireland now.

This was not the image he had of Ireland. As an altar boy familiar with Irish-born parish priests, he so identified the Mass with Ireland it was not until he was thirteen years old that he learned that Latin was not the language of Ireland.

From his earliest years, he had heard of the persecution in Ireland and of Masses said in hiding on "Mass rocks" in the fields. Those were the days when the price on the head of a priest was the same as the price on the head of a fox.

The opening words of the Irish Constitution were "In the name of the Holy Trinity . . .".

The airplanes on the Irish Airlines, Aer Lingus, bore the names St. Brigid, St. Patrick, St. Colmcille. As planes raced down the runway at Dublin or Shannon, passengers spontaneously made the Sign of the Cross.

In virtually every home in Ireland there was, on the wall, an image of the Sacred Heart and, very likely next to it, a picture of John F. Kennedy.

This was the land of Croagh Patrick; Knock and Lough Derg, the place of cobblestones and the austere penitential retreats; the family Rosary; the Angelus recited on the radio; the ritual tipping of the hat when passing the parish church; the everyday greeting, "Dia's Muire dhuit" ("God and Mary be with you"); and the response, "a's Padraig" ("And Patrick, too").

But times have changed. David, on this trip, found little success in recruiting seminarians for his diocese. Now there were barely enough religious vocations to fill Ireland's own needs.

Still, the Faith was not lacking in his own diocese.

He had often noticed back home in California as he visited the Irish-born priests' rectories that two things were predictable. Pasted in the lower corner of the bathroom mirror was the traditional Morning Offering prayer, "Jesus, through the Immaculate Heart of Mary, I offer you my prayers, works, joys and sufferings of this day . . ." Presumably, as he shaved each morning, the priest would read the words and put a frame of prayer around the coming day.

The second thing he invariably found in the rectories was that the soap in the shower was always Irish Spring.

CHAPTER 66

As he drove the loop of the southern counties of Ireland, David reflected on all the priests of his diocese.

David thought to himself, "One of the joys of being bishop is to see the dedication of the priests." He rarely came to a parish (and he often arrived unannounced) and not found the priest on the job diligently at work. Just the weekend before he left the States, he came across a rather elderly pastor waxing the floors of his parish hall, another young pastor nailing up a blackboard and some temporary walls for his religious education class.

Changes were taking place in the clergy's personal lives.

Priests after Vatican II and the reformation of the '60s, because of the constant ferment, seemed to talk incessantly about theology and Church matters at social get-togethers, rather than about the Kings, the 49ers and Giants.

Tentatively, some priests started praying together in the rectory.

Gradually, one after another, they gave up smoking.

Whereas before, pastors often looked on their parish as separate from, even in rivalry with, other parishes, now adjacent parishes began working together on projects such as Bible studies.

Individually, for physical exercise, the young clergy especially were inclined to hiking, working out, pick-up basketball games, racquetball and jogging.

The annual priests' retreats became more serious. In David's earlier years in the priesthood, the retreats had been social gatherings. Most likely they were correct for the times; perhaps the clergy needed to party, needed to find mutual support, and they found it in joyful, raucous get-togethers far into the night, playing cards, recounting stories about the eccentricities of their pastors. But the retreats became more serious. During the late '60s and '70s these sessions involved confrontational dialogues and then more subtle reflections on challenges and opportunities in the '80s and '90s.

As David drove, he composed in his mind what he wanted to say to his priests when he returned home.

"Older priests ordained before 1960 are sometimes shaken in various degrees of severity by the changing ideas, disciplines, and emphases today.

"Younger priests ordained since the middle sixties have not had the same background we older men have had. We have to remember the young are not rejecting something once held. Rather, they truly have a different kind of Faith, fundamentally different notions of what a priest is.

"The young do not have a lack of Faith. One approach to 'Church' is not right, and the other wrong. They are simply different. Each, I believe, is right for its time.

"We have an inclination to compare the Church today with the Church of the '50s in the United States. That earlier decade was an exceptional decade, not experienced before and not likely to be experienced again in our country.

"The Church in America now is settling into what the Church and, indeed, any institution experiences over an extended period of time. There is always a bell curve which goes through development, expansion, decline and renewal. It is part of the human condition.

"Nevertheless, (David continued to rehearse his remarks to the priests) I realize the shortage of vocations has some practical, painful consequences. The ministry that you are in today is a more demanding ministry. Most clergy are over-extended in their work because of shortages. This causes tension in the residence. An associate pastor may think he is being obliged to carry too much of the load.

"There is such a thing as burn-out. And there can be an exaggerated concern about rest and relaxation. One pastor told me in the East Bay that his associate came to him and said that he felt he needed some additional time off. He wanted to talk to the pastor about burn-out. And the pastor said, 'I'm not worried about your burn-out. I was about to have a talk with you about start-up.'

"We are all different in the pace we can keep.

"What is the future of the parishes? We must continue to work for religious vocations and we must study the signs of the time and make provisions now for preparing ministers among the Sisters and among laymen and laywomen, whatever the future holds.

"'A priest today,' researcher Robert Schmitz has observed, 'may be the only animal fully aware that he has been put on the endangered species list.'

"What will be the future for priests? If the decline in vocations continues and the population continues to grow, will priests of the future be circuit-riders, traveling each week hundreds of miles to serve widely scattered parishes and mission stations while laymen and women take over the non-sacramental functions of the Church?

"Some of you, I know, are by nature administrators - interested in buildings, maintenance, keeping books, seeing to repairs. You have become comfortable in this work as pastors and may not feel competent in conducting religious education, visiting the sick, and certain pastoral duties. When the temporalities, the management chores are taken away by lay ministers, you may feel you have nothing.

"Some priests may be shell-shocked; some may become passive/aggressive, and withdraw. They may seem lazy, but actually they are broken, afraid, feel useless, unable to cope.

"When the secretary has gone home after the day's work, some priests may turn off the rectory telephone, because they feel so besieged by parishioners and obligations. Then not answering the phone over a period of time, they begin to experience guilt feelings. And this becomes a vicious circle.

"When we are busiest, we are happiest. Many frustrations come from idleness, lack of sense of accomplishment.

"What has changed? In the earlier days, there was usually a younger man, a more resilient assistant pastor who would help. He was the one who would answer the phone during the night. Now, this is left completely to the one priest - the pastor.

"Another development: the young priests especially yearn for community. They can feel lost and unsupported, alone on assignment or in some cold, non-communicative rectory. On their first assignment, they are suddenly devastated in a residence without fraternity.

"Mealtimes are somber and, for the most part, silent. The rectory atmosphere is cold. There is no one to say, 'How was your day?' Separateness.

"It is an unexpected splash of cold water after years in the community environment of a seminary.

"There will be demanding times.

"The Catholic Church has been changing substantively. It is accepting the existing pluralist society in which it lives. It is no longer an institution independent of all other entities, closed in on itself. Though there may be a twinge of pain in being pried away from an unhealthy dominant clericalism, you and I will be more and more working in a warm, enlightened collaboration with the people of God.

"God maybe is reminding us that the people are the Church.

"This guidance, above all, I offer to you. Live your lives as you know you should. Not because there are Church rules and regulations governing you. But because of your convictions.

"Be inner-directed, self-starters. Not complying with laws just to avoid trouble or to impress authorities or in hopes for advancement.

"Be men of integrity."

David would stress these points at the next priests' retreat.

He was reluctant to leave the green fields of Ireland, but it was time to head for Shannon and make the journey home.

. . .

It would be sometime before David would learn the eventual outcome of his interrogation in Rome.

CHAPTER 67

In the meantime, reports were circulating about tensions between the United States bishops and the Vatican.

The reputed strain had to do with relationships between American theologians and Rome, the role of the National Conference of Bishops, a U.S. Bishops' statement on AIDS, considered by some to be misleading and dangerous, the question of female altar servers, the indult concerning the resumption of the Tridentine Mass, and inclusive gender language in liturgical texts.

Media stories suggested that there were forceful criticisms of the Vatican during the executive sessions of the National Bishops' meetings. Indeed, concerns were expressed in these closed sessions. But, for the most part, they were muted, perhaps due to a traditional reluctance to speak negatively of the See of St. Peter, perhaps partly because of fear, but also partly because bishops daily experience the sting of criticism themselves coming from clergy, Religious and laity.

Wherever they were inclined to criticize Rome, a least subconsciously, they understood the limitations of headquarter offices like the Vatican. In their better moments, they recognized the impossible task of the curial offices administering to one billion faithful throughout the world, with something over two thousand immediate salaried employees, and working with a budget smaller than the budgets of some American Catholic universities.

At certain times on certain issues, there are misunderstandings between Rome and local hierarchies. But these are usually not as severe as the public suspects. When John Paul II visited California, he had several public tender moments in the dialogue with teenagers, in the meeting with young armless guitar player, Tony Melendez, and in the embrace of five-year old AIDS victim, Brendan O'Rourke, at David's former parish, Mission Dolores Basilica in San Francisco.

The day after the Pope and the United States bishops emerged from their executive session in San Fernando Valley, media stories told of the pontiff's "scolding" of the bishops. The headline on one of the dailies read, "Pope Gentle with Children, Tough on Bishops."

Though it was a closed-door meeting, it should have been open to all, including the media. Nothing was said there that hadn't been said publicly.

Actually, in the session, John Paul challenged the bishops to high standards and to be brave proclaiming of truth. Both the Pope's formal address and the informal exchange which followed were honest, congenial and fraternal.

But there was one question plaguing the Church in the western world for which no one seemed to have the answer.

. . .

What was the Church to do to meet the problem of priest shortages? The population of the faithful was growing and the number of clergy declining precipitously.

The bishops of the United States gathered at a special convocation to seek solutions to the vocations crisis.

Bishop after bishop urged the clergy to redouble their efforts to recruit candidates for the priesthood. They urged the clergy and the Sisters and Brothers to reflect a genuine joy in their lives; they reminded the faithful that not just the bishops, the priests and the Religious superiors had to respond to this need; all parishioners should consider themselves religious vocation recruiters.

A panel of vocation directors spoke from the stage. Microphones were placed in the aisles of the bishops' assembly hall.

David approached a microphone and made his intervention:

"I most certainly do not disregard the Pope's position on these matters.

"I look for the clergy, the Religious and the people in my diocese to be loyal to and supportive of me. And I must be and want to be loyal to and supportive of the Holy Father.

"But the highest form of loyalty is to share one's honest convictions. I am confident this is what the Pope and the Apostolic Nuncio want.

"There is no more admirable expression of commitment to Our Lord than a life of celibacy. Speakers at this meeting have addressed very effectively many of the thoughts I have about celibacy.

"However, I believe that we should continue to study this topic. Not in any way to make life easier for the clergy (optional celibacy will not make their lives easier). We should continue to study the matter not primarily as a solution to the priest shortage, but as a matter of integrity.

"Celibacy is not the question. The question is mandatory celibacy for priesthood.

"I believe mandatory celibacy may be diminishing the beauty of celibacy. The de facto situation so often becomes not positive Christ-like celibacy, but an enforced bachelorhood.

"I know there are compelling arguments for mandatory celibacy. I accept the force of these arguments from scholar bishops here far more knowledgeable than I am.

"But when I get back in the diocese among the people, when I listen to the young, when I observe the lives of our priests, on balance I inevitably come back to the conviction that there is something not quite sound and stable in today's clerical arrangement.

"As regards vocation, I know the young admire the priest who is living a positive, joy-filled life of celibacy. But do many of the young people sense there is something unnatural and strained about a system of compulsory celibacy?

"The same recurring questions come to me about excluding women from ordained ministry.

"I believe these concerns have something to do with the liberation that characterized Christ's life and ministry.

"Christ was not inclined to law and regulation, unless absolutely necessary. Would Christ today be inclined to require celibacy of His ordained ministers, or rather to inspire them to this total commitment?

"In the spirit of freedom and equality which marked Christ's approach to ministry (neither slave nor free, Jew nor Gentile, male nor female), would He be likely today to exclude persons from full ordained ministry on the basis of gender?

"I recognize that there would be many practical problems involved, if changes ever were to be made. Any change would have to be carefully paced and with serious prior catechesis.

"What I believe to be important for the good of the Church, always within the magisterium, is that these subjects continue carefully and prayerfully to be studied."

The open forum discussion went on late into the evening.

Several months later, the Congregation for the Doctrine of the Faith issued a definitive pronouncement precluding discussion on the ordination of women.

. . .

At the same meeting of bishops in Collegeville, Minnesota, Ladd Franklin, representing the National Director, was assigned to give the CRS annual report.

He was also asked to be homilist at the Wednesday morning Mass. Ladd was reluctant but, at David's urging, agreed.

His homily may not have been what the planning committee had in mind.

"One of the most liberating experiences of a lifetime is the sudden discovery that out of our problems comes growth, out of suffering comes joy, out of dying comes life, out of Good Friday comes Easter Sunday. It is the Paschal mystery that surrounds our vocation as bishops.

"The Paschal Mystery amazingly means I will work out my salvation not despite my weaknesses and problems -- civic litigation and operating deficits--, but precisely because of them.

"'Unless the seed falls to the ground and dies, it remains just a seed.' 'Through the crevice in a broken heart, God is finally seen.'

"If we make this an operating principle in our life, it can give us personal hope.

"But what about the people's hope for the Church, hope and trust in the Church in these perplexing times?

"I think, because of the turbulence in the Church in recent years, there has been a Good Friday dying that has caused you bishops to re-examine the meaning of bishop, to hone your skills, to try harder, to live a leaner life, to serve rather than to be served.

454 Francis A. Quinn

"Although, at first blush, we might believe the opposite, I think we are in an age of special opportunities because of today's exceptional pressures, demands and challenges.

"Most Americans are convinced we are in a time of moral confusion. We are a society that has lost its ethical compass. It is a time that calls out for a new Bernard of Clairvaux, a new Anthony, a new John of the Cross.

"Do the people have hope for the Church? I believe they do have trust and hope to the extent that they see goodness in the clergy and Religious, in the leadership, in the bishops,

"Are you bishops deserving of that hope?

"It is true, growth comes from our failings. God is strongest in us when we are at our weakest. But God wants us to try to do something about our weaknesses, our shortcomings.

"Some publications, Catholic and secular, portray bishops in political cartoons as irrelevant, out of touch, power brokers, callous and insensitive.

"Rather than decry this criticism, might you not examine your consciences to see if there is anything you are doing or not doing that is contributing to the despondency which some people have about the direction of institutional religion today?

"God has been incredibly good to you, calling you to be a bishop, but have you become lax in the covenant you made on the day of episcopal ordination?

"With all respect, bishops, may I propose an examination of conscience, which I admit I need just as much as you?

Am I giving quality time to God in my prayer life - quality time? Not squeezed-in time?

Have I calculated and engineered my way to become a bishop?

Do I suffer from an addiction?

An addiction to control?

An addiction to power?

An inordinate desire to be loved, to be popular?

Do I fear confronting my addiction and getting help?

Have I found myself drifting away from the relatively simple message of Jesus of Nazareth?

Do people see in my conduct, in my remarks, in my mannerisms some of the very things that Christ condemned in the religious leaders of His time?

There is a perception, deserved or undeserved, that bishops fall victim to internal politics.

Am I contributing to that perception by maneuvering for advancement from auxiliary bishop to diocesan bishop, advancement from bishop to archbishop, from archbishop to cardinal?

Am I the first to criticize other dioceses yet not find any fault in my own.

Or, on the contrary, because of fear of failure or fear of rejection, do I exaggerate what I believe is the plank in my own eye, taking on a crippling sense of inadequacy? When I think back on the earlier bishops during my young priesthood, do I wonder: What am I doing in a position like this?

Do I go home from bishops' meetings feeling depressed because of a sense of inferiority to the other bishops, intimidated by their grasp of the agenda??

Do I look on some bishops as rivals?

Am I secretly pleased when some colleagues fail?

"In all this examination of conscience, are you simply admitting that you are human and have human limitations? Yes. But if you are giving in to these weaknesses, it can affect your leadership. And you can be giving the people a reason to lose hope in the Church.

"If each one of you can be a good human being, if all of you are really trying to be unselfish leaders, you will give the people hope, you can bring Easter Sunday out of these Good Friday times."

Ladd stepped down from the pulpit. His homily was accepted graciously by the bishops. David was glad his friend had been invited to speak. He was proud of their friendship.

CHAPTER 68

Moved by Ladd's homily to the bishops, David asked Ladd to dine with him that night.

"I've always wanted to be a bishop, but as I look back now, Ladd, I sometimes feel like the song, 'Dance, Ballerina, Dance.' You remember how the lyrics go: 'You wanted fame instead' and now you see 'the seat that's empty in the second row.' You neglect friends and relationships for the sake of your work, even for the sake of advancement. And then the loneliness sets in.

""You know, I am really happy to be a bishop and very grateful. And I know I can get a great deal accomplished in this position. But there are some things you give up.

"When you're ordained a bishop, you are given the prestigious title 'Successor of the Apostles'. But now that I think of it, when we were ordained priests, we were called 'Other Christs.' Maybe, as a bishop, I've been demoted."

"Don't sell yourself short, Dave. You have a hard time admitting you're human."

"But I seem always to be conducting my life in ways to advance myself," David continued. "I dislike myself for this, but I cannot escape it. It is more of an addiction to popularity -- the need to be well thought of.

"Is it because of low self-image? Was I put down as a child? I don't remember that being the case.

"Ladd, do you recall those psychological tests we took in 'The Ministry to Priests' program? In the Tennessee Self Concept Scale, I was above the line in being independent and self-supportive and in being sensitive to my own needs and feelings.

"But I was below average in self-worth, in warm interpersonal relations, fearful of expressing feelings.

"When he read my test profile, the counselor told me I had to learn to live in the present, not fretting about the past or anxious about the future. Also, I tend to be a workaholic."

Ladd laughed, "You don't need any test instrument to tell you that. You have to let other people do things for you. You want to give, but you are uncomfortable receiving. You are playing God. You are not the Messiah, Dave. There is only one Messiah. It is imperative for our physical and emotional health that we have enjoyable pastimes regularly included in our lives. Did you see that recent Harris Poll on favorite hobbies? It revealed the most frequent leisure time activity of Americans is Watching TV. In second place came Reading a book. Sex came in 11th place, right after Gardening. Do you keep up any hobby?

"Stress we will always have with us and some stress is positive or use-stress. Positive stress makes you sit down at the desk and write a homily. Positive stress prompts you to live up to obligations. Positive stress helps you get the most out of your talents, David. But I think you have too much negative stress. Don't press so hard."

"Each of us has different ways of relaxing," David replied. "There are times when I am more rested at the end of the day if I have spent it catching up on the backlog of work. That gives me a relaxed psychological state of mind. Clearing the obligations on my desk is more energizing and renewing than if I played a game of golf, because, during the golf game, I would probably be thinking of all the work I have to do."

"But you need a change of pace," Ladd insisted. "Everyone should have something enjoyable to look forward to each day; something enjoyable to look forward to each week; and something enjoyable to look forward to each month."

David said he would think about it.

. . .

As much as he tried, David knew Ladd was right. Still, he couldn't seem to change.

Ladd wanted some advice from David. "Our weaknesses also are our strengths. Though you and I don't always agree on what our priorities should be, I admire your approach to things. For a long time I've wanted to ask you your philosophy of life."

"I don't have a philosophy of life."

David thought for a moment. "Actually, about twenty years ago during a very low period, I tried to sum up what I judged were the most important attributes I should try to develop in my life. After much reflection, I finally distilled all the qualities down to four. I wrote them down on a piece of paper and, ever since then, I have carried this paper in my wallet.

"To make them easier to remember, I compressed the names of the qualities into four 4-letter words: Good, Guts, Wise and True.

Good: This simply means doing what my conscience tells me is the right thing to do. Several times a day, decisions have to be made. Often, a decision will involve a choice between what I know is right and what I know is wrong. I may be allured by an unfair personal gain or a prohibited pleasure. I may be tempted to deceit, vindictiveness or unkindness. It is at that moment that principles call me to make the choice to be good, no matter what the cost. When I do something seriously evil, it eventually comes back to haunt me - I don't mean in the next life - I mean in this life.

"The second 4-letter word is:

Guts: This is another word for courage. Courage to do what is right when my instincts of fear or self-indulgence entice me to do what is wrong. Courage to follow my conscience.

'Worry' is just another word for fear. So much of my life is strangled by worry. Most of the things I worry about in regard to the future actually never happen. Worry is such a waste. What was I worrying about last Thursday?

"The third word --

Wise: Many of my mistakes, many of my misdeeds are not because of malice. I frequently do wrong simply because I do not think carefully and clearly. And it is crucial for a life of integrity to think my choices through.

"And the fourth 4-letter word is:

True: Honesty: To be honest with others in small things as was crucial things. To have an abiding habit of speaking the truth.

Above all, I needed to be true to myself. Not to rationalize in order to justify wrongdoing.

Am I ready and willing at any time of the day to let my innermost thoughts be turned up to top volume for all the world to hear?

"Good, Guts, Wise and True.

"There is nothing profound in these remarks, Ladd. It is simply that these four words seem to be a summary of things I should have for a life of integrity.

"But these virtues are more on the slip of paper in my wallet than in my character."

. . .

David knew he had to get out of himself, to focus more on others. Intellectually, he knew that the key to happiness is to be absorbed in others and not in one's self.

Some of the smallest, seemingly least significant things in his life reminded him of this. When David left home to go to the minor seminary, he left his dog Bonzo. It had not even occurred to the young David how traumatic this must have been for the fox terrier, suddenly to lose his master, the center of his life.

Oznob, his second pet, a black cocker spaniel, had formed the same attachment to David, and suffered the same incomprehensible loss repeatedly at the end of brief vacations when David returned to school.

More recently, David knew he could not take his Shepherd/Labrador mix, Dolores, to what would be his bishop's residence in Fairview. There was no enclosed space where the large dog could exercise. David was the sole object of Dolores' life. She had waited for David to come home from work each night. He broke this attachment.

David gave Dolores to a friend in a neighboring rectory in San Francisco.

Suddenly again man's best friend had been torn away from the spiraling pole of its affection.

Surprisingly, David was relieved that he was able to be free of this obligation.

Sometime later, he would wonder if he broke human relationships that easily, if his human friendships were just as shallow.

. . .

The life of a modern day bishop is mostly crisis management. David's days as bishop were complicated, hectic days from morning to evening, seven days a week. But they were happy and fulfilling days. David felt the collaboration and support of the clergy, the Religious and the people. He would often say honestly, "These are the most satisfying years of my life."

David only half realized that these were happy days because his attention was totally focused on the needs of others and not himself.

PART VIII

CHAPTER 69

After learning of Willow's death, David and Ladd both made it a point to drop letters of condolence to the Caprice family. Subsequently, when Ladd returned to San Francisco, he and Dave frequently visited George and Emily Caprice at their Peninsula home to express their friendship and support.

Though the Soviet Union had collapsed and years had passed since the parents had learned the details of Willow's death and the sequence of Ladd's visit to Amsterdam, the duplication of the audio tape, and the abduction which followed, in gradual seething reflection, George Caprice grasped the realities of the tragic episode. He became more and more incensed that Ladd had endangered Willow by asking her surreptitiously to make a copy of the cassette.

No one could have anticipated that Ladd's request would put Willow in jeopardy. Muntplein, in the Amsterdam Centrum, should have been as safe as any place on earth.

Caprice did not see it that way. Though he said nothing at the time of their courtesy visits, George's hostility toward Ladd and David intensified. In the years that followed, Willow's father accelerated his campaign against what he believed these two stood for in the direction the Church was taking.

Caprice was privy to the details of the Curia's questioning of David in Rome. He contacted members of Guardians of Doctrine, urging them to have David removed from his position as Diocesan Bishop.

David did what he could to dialog with those who opposed his policies, but he could not dissuade them.

He would consult his staff and made it a point during parish visitations to question clergy and laity on whether they saw his ministry as being too "progressive." Recognizing that there can always be a measure of truth in complaints of this kind, David studied his administration and tried to moderate it where it could possibly be deemed extreme. Nevertheless, the letters of protest to the Apostolic Nuncio and to Rome continued. He knew it wouldn't be long before he would be called to Rome.

. . .

In early April, the axe fell. The Nuncio called from Washington to tell David he was to meet with the Pope the following week in Rome.

"I don't know how I can explain my ministry any differently than I did to the Congregation on Doctrine," David remarked to his Chancellor, Sister Elizabeth Marie.

"Just do what you did before," the nun replied. She worried for the bishop and was always supportive - and always candid. "When you go to Rome, say what you said before. You have nothing to hide. The diocese is in good shape and I know that all but a small percentage support the work you are doing."

Sister, as Chancellor, was one example of the positions of authority women were beginning to occupy.

The Church is part of society and it reflects the changes in society. Still, conditions were changing, but there was still a long way to go. Some women were expressing the frustration and rage they felt.

The Church still did not have a handle on this matter and there would be no easing of the tensions until the right course was found.

Actually, although they received none of the credit in many instances, women did most of the real work. David often admitted publicly that it was his secretary who took care of most of his duties. This was true of the women secretaries who worked with him throughout his priesthood. If necessary, they worked late; if asked, worked on weekends; were dedicated; forever on call; totally loyal.

David relied heavily on Sister Elizabeth and his secretary, Claudia, and sought their advice on every crucial subject.

. . .

David spent the next five days pondering what new questions might be asked at the Vatican and marshalling his responses. At the end of the week, he flew to Rome and, at the appointed time, was ushered to a small papal conference room. The Pope seemed graver than usual. At the direction of the pontiff, David seated himself at the desk, directly opposite John Paul.

"Bishop Carmichael, your work in the Diocese of Fairview has been brought to my attention. Because of this, I want to make a change."

David felt the blood in his face flush to the roots of the hair on his head.

"What I share with you now, I expect you to keep in complete confidence until such time as you are told it can be discussed."

"Yes, Your Holiness."

"As you know, Archbishop Paul Whelton of San Tomas, California will be retiring; he will have reached the mandatory retirement age. I am of a mind to appoint you to succeed him in this major archdiocese."

David felt like the tapestried walls had crashed down around him. David, in a whirl of confusion, accepted. In the following moment, the pontiff offered words of instruction and encouragement. David cleared his mind, expressed his gratitude, bowed to kiss the pontiff's ring and withdrew.

Quite a difference from the time he last walked out into the Courtyard of San Damaso.

The next morning he took the return flight to San Francisco and to Fairview. He could talk to no one about this development. He knew now the burdens would be much heavier, but he was ready for the challenge - heavy hangs the head that wears the miter."

The sensation was something more mature. He was relieved and grateful that the Church had confidence in him.

CHAPTER 70

On his last morning in Calcutta, Ladd met the ailing Mother Teresa.

At the Motherhouse of the Missionaries of Charity, he witnessed firsthand the lives of these world-famed women.

The nuns spend long periods in chapel in prayer each day. Tranquility and joy play on the faces of the Sisters as they mop the floors and scour the enormous cooking containers with ashes in the convent kitchen. After Mass, they scatter throughout the city to varied ministries.

. . .

As he vested for Mass in the sacristy, Ladd was visited by Mother Teresa, obviously failing and escorted by two of her Sisters. She looked no more than four feet tall, but she overwhelmed everyone in the sacristy by her presence. She was slightly stooped, smiling broadly. Teresa gave the genuine impression she was overjoyed to see Ladd.

During the Mass, Mother Teresa sat at the end of the first pew with her Sisters. The chapel was filled to capacity with visitors from around the world. As the faithful received Communion from Ladd's hand and returned to their pews, they edged over to where Mother Teresa was sitting. As they passed, several put a hand on her shoulder, on her head, on her side, or her back. Mother Teresa seemed to shrivel up even smaller as they did this. Some genuflected beside her. They reverenced her as a saint but she wanted no part of their gestures, and was trying to reflect on the Eucharist she had just received.

Before the last blessing, though she was critically ill, the nun mounted the pulpit, barely able to peer over the top of it. Without preface, she went straight to the point and began to condemn the world's evils, making no apologies about her words.

Ladd would meet with her two weeks later. But while he was in Bangalore, word came that the nun had suffered another cardiac arrest and was near death.

Returning to Calcutta, Ladd was surprised to learn that the fragile Sister insisted on going through with his promised meeting.

He was ushered into the bedroom by a young novice and found the striking countenance of Teresa ravaged even further by suffering. Ladd felt he had known this woman all his life.

To conserve her feeble energy, Ladd knew he must carry the conversation. "I joined CRS so that I could do the kind of work you are doing, Mother. When I was a parish priest, I began to question whether the rituals and the routine brick-and-mortar duties were really what God wanted me to do."

Ladd felt so much at home with Teresa that he recounted the problem he was having with the ceremonial part of his vocation. He took the opportunity to ask her a question related to his life-long puzzling indecisiveness about his priesthood.

"Mother Teresa, why do you have your Sisters spend two or three hours each day praying in chapel when they could spend this time on the streets helping more of the sick and dying?"

Teresa quietly responded, "If my Sisters were not in chapel two or three hours each day, they would not go out into the streets of Calcutta at all."

For the rest of that afternoon, Ladd reflected on that answer.

Ladd was being forced to renew his priorities.

Mother Teresa died that Saturday. Ladd remained in Calcutta to take part in the long cortege procession for the state funeral.

Two days later, back in California, he confided to David, the new archbishop, "You know, after all these years in this vocation, I realize more and more that the Mass sustains my priesthood.

"Each year, as time passes, I have come to realize that the rituals of the sacraments are a visible and tangible way of keeping me close to God. Through the centuries, it has been the liturgies of the Church that have actually generated the social energy and the humanitarian work of the Church.

"The mission of the Church is not just the corporal works of mercy and not just the rites and ceremonies. The message of the Gospels is both service and sanctuary."

. . .

In the first week of the New Year in St. Pius X Cathedral, David was installed as Archbishop of San Tomas, California.

He had taken over an archdiocese that had been exceptionally well tended by Archbishop Whelton and his predecessors. David would continue their policies. He remembered the words of Saint John Baptiste de LaSalle, ". . . try to do everything that has been left undone, or undo everything that has been done."

The retired Archbishop continued to work an hour or two each day at the Chancery and was supportive of his successor in every respect.

Now David would preside as metropolitan. As he sat in solemn ceremony in the archiepiscopal chair, wearing miter and with crozier in hand, looking out over the devout and attentive throng of the faithful, one thought ran through his mind: "I remember the giants - Archbishops McCauley and Costello - what am I doing here - a scared country kid from Napa?"

One of David's first acts as Archbishop was to request the transfer of Monsignor Gordon Caprice to San Tomas. "I need his talents in administration. He is an honest man."

. . .

David was obliged to fly to Rome again to receive the pallium, the circular band of lamb's wool which the Supreme Pontiff would place over his head and upon his shoulders to be worn around and just below the collar, as the symbol of a Metropolitan. David thought, "I trust this is the one and only time that Rome will pull the wool over my eyes."

David asked Ladd to accompany him to Rome for the investiture. Ladd agreed, especially since a mission to Yugoslavia coincided with the investiture date, June 29th, the feast of SS. Peter and Paul.

On a Saturday morning in the Sistine Chapel, against the backdrop of Michelangelo's refurbished Last Judgment, along with 15 other archbishops recently named worldwide, David received the pallium, the insignia of his new office, at the hands of the Pope.

Two hours later, in St. Peter's Square, Ladd took leave of David. "I just wish that Willow and Tyler could be with us today."

"What a waste of beautiful lives. Tyler is gone because of a lie. Human character is frail. It was the Cold War that took Willow away, and now that conflict is past and forgotten. The enmities between nations are fleeting, the alliances fragile.

"You're a good friend, Dave. We'll be back here together some day when you're made Pope."

David laughed, "I don't deserve any career advancement. And I don't want any. I am already higher than I should be."

"Whatever you say, Dave. Anyway, I'm off to Baghdad to negotiate the distribution of some wheat flour and vegetable oil.

"You do the sanctuary, Dave; I'll do the service. The world needs both."

CHAPTER 71

David was returning to San Tomas.

He opened his laptop. He would take advantage of the 9-hour flight to prepare his first address to the new archdiocesan family:

This is an age when institutional religions seem no longer to be in the ascendancy in the western world. Attendance at churches is down.

After Christianity's embrace by Emperors Constantine and Theodosius in the fourth century, one strain of the Church gradually developed through the centuries into a spirit of dominance, duress and triumphalism, politically, socially and theologically.

Alongside this trend, there was also the heroic effort of Pope Gregory VII to free the Church from the very destructive control of kings and wealthy nobles. In order to do this, he did use strong measures to assert papal power and despite good motives, the passing of time led to abuses.

However, some Christian leadership, in part knowingly but mostly unknowingly, separated diametrically from what Christ taught: non-coercion, the dignity of the individual, the priority of conscience, unconditional love and an identification with the poor and the suffering --- not as the world conceives success.

Many other leaders through the centuries tried to bring the Church back to the original charisma of Christ.

The Crusades, the Inquisition, political power and acquisitiveness, subjugation of "enemies", the religious wars among denominations – these un-Christ-like manifestations led a considerable part of the western hemisphere to forsake religion in favor of secularism.

Eventually came the age of Enlightenment, the reliance on reason. Those who could be educated began to recognize the contradiction implicit in power-Christianity as it had evolved. Many saw the churches as irrelevant.

Now we have a world that has trust in science – a world that more and more has turned away from institutional Faiths in the wake of Copernicus, Kepler, Bacon, Voltaire, Darwin, Marx, Freud, Einstein, Hawking.

Nevertheless, others in despair have come to the disturbing realization that reason and science alone do not ease one's personal crises or solve the world's problems. The twentieth century, with all of its technological progress, was the most brutal of centuries in warfare and destruction.

Science must have a moral ethical code. Science and religion are not in conflict.

We see them as respecting and supporting each other.

Society can rightfully use reason and science, freedom and the information age to provide a safer, healthier, better material world.

The last two young generations have turned away from the churches. Some of the young are atheists or agnostics, but most of them are "nones" belonging to no institutional church.

David remembered a church in his boyhood which was "enclosed, perfect in its circular inner logic, turned in on itself, but so vulnerable, so fragile, if one looked outward away from it . . . One touch of change could shatter it. No wonder Catholics protected the church's way of life as long as they could with a sense of its brittleness and some would leave it finally when it broke."

The Church today is, in the secular view, a Church in decline, but actually it is a community closer to the vulnerable Christ and it more nearly resembles the vulnerable first Christian communities. In today's church we will use the power of powerlessness.

It is as if the younger generations, having opportunities for higher education, no long accept the official Church's interpretation of life and morality.

They say they are spiritual but not religious.

I have some questions myself.

Perhaps it is time for a Vatican Council III. That council should unselfishly restudy the New Testament of the Bible to determine just what Jesus Christ actually said and really intended for His followers to be and to do.

And the council would examine the traditions of the Church honestly to decide on the appropriateness of those traditions today in the light of Sacred Scriptures and the current needs of the people.

We must distinguish between the Divine Tradition on the one hand and the policies of the Church which are often called "tradition" on the other.

I am not saying necessarily that we should change long-standing policies and practices of the Church, but that we should at least subject them to serious study.

Vatican Council III would be a regular ecumenical council of the world's bishops with the unifying guidance of Peter, but also including the voices of representative major theologians, scientists and other appropriate academicians, lay men and women, old and young, clergy and Religious, with representatives of other Faiths. These representatives in Vatican III perhaps would not have a vote, but they would have a voice.

The council and ensuing councils and synods would, among other things, study as priorities: the needs of the poor and the suffering, the involvement of the laity, the healthy exercise of authority in the Church, human sexuality, sexual molestations, the appropriateness of mandatory celibacy in the priesthood, the reasons for an institutional church, interfaith relations, world-wide inequality of wealth, climate change as a moral issue, role of women, role of men, faith and science war and peace, immigration, planning effective parishes, Sunday homilies addressing people's real needs, and a personal holiness in each one of us.

David said to himself "Personal holiness . . . in that I will have to being with myself."

He closed the laptop and began to reflect on the days ahead.

Now Willow is gone, Tyler is gone and Ladd is a thousand miles away.

David misses them. He feels alone and weak without them.

The human side of the church is also weak. That is why he is making the recommendations in his first talk to the people in his new archdiocese that in crisis times like these the human side of the Church may need self reflection and even structural changes.

But David will keep in mind the words of Carlo Caretto:

How much I must criticize my Church;
and yet how much I love you!
Never in this world have I seen anything more
compromised, more false.
Yet never have I touched anything more pure,
more generous or more beautiful.

Countless times I have felt like leaving you,
my Church.
And yet, every night I have prayed "that I might
die in your warm, loving arms".

CPSIA information can be obtained at www.ICGtesting.com
Printed in the USA
LVOW08s1018090115

422047LV00002B/15/P